MW00850227

Rethinking Cooperation with Evil

CATHOLIC MORAL THOUGHT

General Editor: Romanus Cessario, OP

Rethinking Cooperation with Evil

A Virtue-Based Approach

Ryan Connors

The Catholic University of America Press
Washington, D.C.

Copyright © 2023
The Catholic University of America Press
All rights reserved

Nihil obstat:
Rev. Christopher Mahar, STD, PhD
Censor deputatus

Approbatio:
Most Rev. Richard G. Henning, DD, STD
Bishop of Providence
October 10, 2023

The paper used in this publication meets the minimum
requirements of American National Standards for
Information Science—Permanence of Paper for Printed
Library Materials, ANSI Z39.48-1992.
∞

Cataloging-in-Publication Data is available
from the Library of Congress
ISBN: 978-0-8132-3725-1
eISBN: 978-0-8132-3726-8

To my parents, Joseph and Lisa Connors,
models of virtue—acquired and infused

Saints Justa and Rufina

The cover image of Saints Justa and Rufina presents a 1666 creation of the Baroque master Bartolomé Esteban Murillo (1617–82). In third-century Spain, these two martyr saints worked as pottery makers and marketers of earthenware. When asked to sell their wares for use in non-Christian festivals, they refused without compromise. Arrested by civil authorities and tortured, they demonstrated courage in their non-compliance with the request that they aid in the commission of the immoral act of idolatry. Invoked now as early martyrs for non-cooperation with evil, Justa and Rufina suffered violent death at the end of the third century. These saints reflect the Christian refusal to assist in wrongdoing despite the consequences.

In Murillo's painting now displayed in the Museum of Fine Arts of Seville, the two saints are portrayed holding the Giralda, the bell tower of the Seville Cathedral, and with smashed pottery at their feet. The destroyed pots recall their courageous refusal to cooperate with evil. The tower originally served as a minaret for the city's mosque during the Muslim occupation of that portion of Spain. The saints, as protectors of the tower, remind on-lookers that Christians need not retreat from the world but seek to convert and even utilize its resources for the worship of the true God.

Today, Justa and Rufina are invoked as patron saints of Seville as well as of potters. They fittingly serve also as models of the virtues necessary to refuse to cooperate immorally with any evil.

Contents

Acknowledgments

As a priest of the Diocese of Providence, I am indebted to Bishop Thomas Tobin, who ordained me a priest and assigned me to doctoral studies. My gratitude extends to Bishop Richard G. Henning, the ninth bishop of Providence, for his kindness and encouragement to me in this project. I have benefited also from the support of Bishop Robert Evans, Msgr. Albert Kenney, and the priests of the Diocese of Providence. I cannot fail to mention the kindness of the sixth Archbishop of Boston, Cardinal Seán Patrick O'Malley, OFM Cap., Msgr. James Moroney, Father Stephen Salocks, and the faculty of St. John's Seminary in Brighton, MA.

This book has its origins in a dissertation I completed at the Pontifical University of St. Thomas Aquinas in Rome. I owe a special debt of gratitude to my dissertation director Father Michael Sherwin, OP. I have been blessed that since the very start of my work he recognized the value of this project and has been a source of encouragement and wisdom along the way. I am grateful to the faculty of the Angelicum and, in particular, to Father Thomas Joseph White, OP, and Sister Catherine Joseph Droste, OP. I am grateful to The Catholic University of America Press for the professionalism and kindness their representatives have shown me during this process. The careful and generous work of two anonymous reviewers enriched this work significantly. Acquisitions editor John Martino renders a service to Catholic scholarship in the United States that merits special recognition.

I have been richly blessed by the communities in which I have lived and worked during this project. I am especially grateful for the warm hospitality and priestly fraternity I have received from Fathers Bernard Healey, Joshua Barrow, and Daniel Mahoney as well as the kindness and support of the people of Our Lady of Mercy Parish in East Greenwich, RI. I am grateful to the late Msgr. Ferdinando Berardi and the men with whom I lived at the Casa Santa Maria in Rome. Research for this project began during a semester of study in Fribourg, Switzerland. I remain in the debt of the Dominican Friars of the Albertinum who welcomed me into their life of prayer and study.

During my research in Rome, I was blessed by the assistance of the Dominican Sisters of Mary, Mother of Eucharist, who serve as librarians at the Pontifical North American College. Celebrating Mass for them, as well as for the Franciscan Sisters of the Eucharist and the Missionaries of Charity, was the most special blessing of my time in the eternal city.

This work has been enriched by conversations with Archbishop Anthony Fisher, OP, Msgr. Andrew McLean Cummings, Fathers Stephen Brock, Joseph Carola, SJ, Robert Gahl, Wojciech Giertych, OP, Aquinas Guilbeau, OP, Kevin Flannery, SJ, Christopher Seiler, and Professors Steven Long and Paul Gondreau. Father Cajetan Cuddy, OP, read the entire manuscript, and his edits improved this text considerably. Father Romanus Cessario, OP, has been most generous in helping to clarify my thinking about this topic. Years ago, he initiated in me a love of St. Thomas and the Thomist tradition for which I remain eternally grateful.

Finally, I recognize my parents, Joseph and Lisa Connors, who offer to me models of virtue and provide examples of connatural knowledge of virtuous cooperation in contemporary life. To them I dedicate this book.

Abbreviations

AAS	Acta Apostolicae Sedis
CCC	Catechism of the Catholic Church
CIC	Codex iuris canonici (1983)
DS	Heinrich Denzinger, Enchiridion symbolorum definitionem et declarationum de rebus fidei et morum, Latin-English. 43rd ed. Edited by Peter Hünermann. San Francisco: Ignatius Press, 2012.
ST	Thomas Aquinas, Summa theologiae
USCCB	United States Conference of Catholic Bishops

Rethinking Cooperation with Evil

Introduction

The central thesis of this book is two-fold. First, a proper analysis of the moral question of cooperation with evil represents an essential task for the Church today. Second, virtue-based moral reasoning offers the best method for such a project. No area of moral theology poses so many questions—and contains so many potential pitfalls—as this sphere of moral inquiry. The virtue-based moral reasoning of St. Thomas Aquinas—given papal approbation with the 1993 encyclical *Veritatis splendor*—offers the best grounding for such an analysis. Unfortunately, theologians have given only limited attention to this method of moral reasoning regarding questions of cooperation with evil. These twin propositions of the importance of this task and the need for virtue-based moral reasoning to address it will guide the course of our investigation.

The first conviction finds support in the pastoral activity of the Church. Those who pastor souls report frequently receiving questions from interested believers about whether some seemingly moral activity inadvertently contributes to some moral evil. Whether one may shop at a particular franchise known for its support of abortion, whether one may attend civil marriages outside the Church, or whether one may submit to government mandates that health insurance include payment for immoral practices provide just some of the manifold examples of possible cooperation with evil. Even the United States Supreme Court received an amicus brief of the kind usually reserved for scholarly journals of moral theology. A January 2016 *Amicus curiae* brief explained why the United States government Department of Health and Human Services health care mandate requiring health insurance providers to cover contraception, sterilization, and abortifacient drugs required an illicit moral cooperation with evil.[1]

---

1. In part, the brief argues that the "petitioners can reasonably conclude that complying with the [Obama administration] mandate ... would involve formal cooperation in wrongdoing, which is never permissible." See Brief of 50 Catholic Theologians and Ethicists as Amici Curiae in Support of Petitioners, *Zubik v. Burwell*, 578 U.S. ——, 136 S. Ct. 1557 (2016).

This mandate provides just one example of why sound analysis of moral cooperation is so timely.

The increase in the number of questions of moral cooperation with evil in the present day results from two principal factors. On the one hand, an increased awareness of human interconnectedness in a globalized world demands attention regarding how one's moral choices affect those of others. At the same time, the large-scale abandonment of traditional moral practice regarding the dignity of human life and the sanctity of marriage in the western world has created an enormous number of moral quandaries regarding virtuous participation in this largely secular social life. Advances in technology and increased industrialization and globalization have amplified the complexity of human interaction. One more easily evaluates how a medieval farmer would interact with those around him (given his relatively small number of daily collaborators) than one can analyze the nearly innumerable interactions a modern person faces. For this reason, the need for sound tools to analyze moral cooperation becomes apparent. Even a cursory reading of the daily newspaper reveals the many types of moral evil with which one comes into contact in contemporary economic, political, and social life. The present work will supply the means necessary to analyze cooperative acts, assist persons in identifying disordered cooperative acts, and ultimately aid them to avoid such actions. At the dawn of the modern era these issues took on new life. As the modern world became more complex with greater interactions in a capitalist economy and with the increased pluralism of religious and moral worldviews, moral theologians needed to address these issues extensively.[2] They did so largely from the standpoint of moral casuistry, the method of moral theology generally in use from roughly the seventeenth century until the Second Vatican Council.[3]

---

2. For an extensive treatment of how the complexities of modern living affected moral and spiritual outlooks, see Brad S. Gregory, *The Unintended Reformation: How a Religious Revolution Secularized Society* (London: The Belknap Press of Harvard University Press, 2012), and more generally, the magisterial contribution of Charles Taylor, *A Secular Age* (London: The Belknap Press of Harvard University Press, 2007).

3. For an extended history of this period, see John Mahoney, *The Making of Moral Theology: A Study of the Roman Catholic Tradition* (New York: Oxford University Press, 1990); and more critically, Servias Pinckaers, OP, *The Sources of Christian Ethics*, trans. Sr. Mary Thomas Noble, OP (Washington, DC: The Catholic University of America Press, 1995). For a brief yet insightful critique of this period, see Romanus Cessario, OP, *Introduction to Moral Theology*, Revised Edition (Washington, DC: The Catholic University of America Press, 2013), 219–32. For a more sympathetic treatment of the casuist period, see

The method of moral casuistry made ample use of the now familiar categories of moral discourse regarding cooperation: formal and material, remote and proximate, immediate and mediate. While the value of this method has been analyzed elsewhere, what is certain is that a level of disagreement remained even among the so-called approved authors. In addition, a person with a perplexed conscience was often left still wondering what to do in a given case. Often such a perplexus would be told that only a grave or sufficient reason would justify his cooperation in a given case. That is to say, his situation remained without definitive resolution. The complexity of the modern questions of cooperation and in particular the disparate answers given to them called for a renewed method of moral analysis.

Upon this scene entered the summons of the Second Vatican Council to renew moral theology.[4] The value of the rediscovery of virtue-based moral reasoning according to the mind of St. Thomas Aquinas forms the second fundamental conviction of the present study. The work of the renewal of moral theology was taken up in a particular way by the Dominican order, most especially by the Belgian friar Servais Pinckaers.[5] His work, especially the 1985 *The Sources of Christian Ethics,* as well as his contribution to the composition of 1992 *Catechism of the Catholic Church* and the papal encyclical of Pope John Paul II *Veritatis splendor,* has received significant attention.[6] Due in large part to his labors, the Church has experienced in

Albert R. Jonsen and Stephen Toulmin, *The Abuse of Casuistry: A History of Moral Reasoning* (Berkley and Los Angeles: University of California Press, 1988). For a similarly positive appraisal of the casuist period emphasizing particularly its Franciscan exponents, see James F. Keenan and Thomas A. Shannon, eds., *The Context of Casuistry* (Washington, DC: Georgetown University Press, 1995).

4. Second Vatican Council, Decree on Priestly Training, *Optatam totius,* no. 16. For a demonstration of the continuity of this document with the teaching of modern popes, especially Pope Leo XIII, see Romanus Cessario, OP, "Scripture as the Soul of Moral Theology: Reflections on Vatican II and Ressourcement Thomism," *The Thomist* 76 (2012): 165–88.

5. The works of Servais Pinckaers, OP, Romanus Cessario, OP, and Benedict Ashley, OP, stand out for their critical approach to the casuist period. The classic entry of Thomas Deman, OP, "Probabilisme," in the *Dictionnaire de theologie catholique,* 417–619 (Paris: Letouzey et Ane, 1936), also stands as a prophetic testament to the deeper Thomistic tradition in moral theology. For at least a partial defense of the Dominican approach to moral questions during the casuist period, see Benedict Ashley, OP, *The Dominicans* (Wilmington, DE: Michael Glazier Inc., 1991), 174–75.

6. See, for example, Romanus Cessario, OP, "On the Place of Servais Pinckaers (†7 April 2008) in the Renewal of Moral Theology," *The Thomist* 73 (2009): 1–27.

some respects a renewal in moral theology according to the vision of the Second Vatican Council. St. Thomas's method of virtue-based moral reasoning emphasizes the ultimate end of human activity, the habits or dispositions necessary for human flourishing, and the unique interaction of the natural and supernatural orders which gives Christian moral theology its specificity. The task that remains for contemporary moral theologians—in part already begun and which this present work attempts to chronicle—involves the application of virtue-based moral reasoning to questions of cooperation with evil. This vast and ever-increasing field of moral inquiry will benefit from robust engagement from virtue-based moral theology. On the basis of these efforts, one can establish criteria for making moral decisions regarding cooperation with evil.

Our project will have three areas of inquiry: a historical overview to glean resources for our study; an explanation of the virtue-based approach to this topic; and the application of this method to common and challenging cases. In the first three chapters we will gather resources available from the Thomist tradition and contrast them with the method of moral reasoning utilized by casuist authors. We will provide a general history—in very broad strokes—of the analysis of moral cooperation with evil since the time of St. Thomas Aquinas. This history records the story of the casuist turn away from the virtue-based moral reasoning of St. Thomas at the beginning of the modern period.[7] This casuistic turn occurred just when the issue of moral cooperation with evil took on new life. Precisely when virtue-based moral thought would have been useful for tackling an emerging question in the modern world, a variety of factors led to a casuist turn away from virtue-based moral reasoning.

Chapter one will examine the raw material, as it were, which will lay the foundation for our project. We will accomplish this task in three stages. First, we will gather the teachings of St. Thomas Aquinas related

---

7. For a reliable account of the venerable tradition of commenting on the texts of St. Thomas and the essential continuity between Aquinas and his commentators, see Romanus Cessario, OP, *A Short History of Thomism* (Washington, DC: The Catholic University of America Press, 2005); as well as Romanus Cessario, OP, and Cajetan Cuddy, OP, *Thomas and the Thomists: The Achievement of Thomas Aquinas and His Interpreters* (Minneapolis: Fortress Press, 2017). For further treatment on the history of Thomism, see Fergus Kerr, *After Aquinas: Versions of Thomism* (Oxford: Blackwell Publishing Company, 2002); Gerald McCool, *The Neo-Thomists* (Milwaukee: Marquette University Press, 1994); and, by the same author, *Nineteenth-Century Scholasticism: The Search for a Unitary Method* (New York: Fordham University Press, 1999).

to cooperation with evil. While he does not offer a full treatise on cooperation with evil, in several passages he offers instruction which will be relevant for this topic. Second, we will examine some examples of the reception of his teaching by his interpreters. Third, we will demonstrate the ways in which this Thomistic teaching has been at least partially jettisoned during the modern period. Attention to how St. Thomas treats the issues of borrowing from a usurer (*ST* IIa–IIae, q. 78, a. 4), the sin of scandal, (*ST* IIa–IIae, q. 43), when one is required to make restitution for an evil committed (*ST* IIa–IIae, q. 62, a. 7), enjoining oaths on those known to commit perjury (*ST* IIa–IIae, q. 98, a. 4), and the production of objects used for a sinful purpose (*ST* IIa–IIae, q. 169, a. 2, ad. 4) offers five helpful avenues for gathering Aquinas's position on how best to analyze moral cooperation with evil. A similar approach to the topic finds echoes within the Thomist tradition. We will look at three Thomist commentators, one from the fifteenth, sixteenth, and seventeenth centuries respectively. While Jean Capreolus (d. 1444), Thomas de Vio Cajetan (d. 1534), and John of St. Thomas (d. 1644), do not offer full treatments of moral cooperation with evil, each provides useful insights to establish a method grounded in the Thomist tradition.

The first chapter concludes with an account of the turn from virtue-based reasoning at the dawn of the casuist period. We will examine two authors, the sixteenth-century Jesuit Thomas Sanchez and the eighteenth-century Redemptorist St. Alphonsus Liguori. Sanchez's work lays the foundation for that of St. Alphonsus, upon which the remainder of the casuist account of moral cooperation is based. The shape of the initial casuist debates regarding cooperation with evil dealt with a number of cases of possibly immoral cooperation. In one important instance, controversy erupted surrounding Pope Innocent XI's 1679 condemned proposition of the servant and the ladder.[8] This case revolved around whether a servant could hold a ladder for his master to climb into a woman's residence for the purpose of engaging in sexual intercourse. The work of Sanchez and Liguori play a special role in this debate over what sort of cooperation the servant provides.

In chapter two, we will demonstrate that the work of the casuist au-

---

8. For a more complete history of this question, interested readers should consult the work of Andrew McLean Cummings. His *The Servant and the Ladder: Cooperation with Evil in the Twenty-First Century* (Leominster: Gracewing, 2014) offers a comprehensive account of the modern attempts to analyze questions of cooperation with evil.

thors of the pre-conciliar period was marked by two unfortunate flaws hampering their ability to provide sufficient answers to questions of moral cooperation. These flaws include the disparity of conclusions reached and the ultimate lack of resolution given to particular situations. Such conflict among trusted authors and lack of resolution even within the work of a given author leaves the perplexed moral actor without adequate guidance. The disparity of conclusions these authors advance despite their shared premises will reveal that any consensus reached in the casuist period did not widely extend to particular topics in the area of moral cooperation with evil.

In this chapter, we will examine the work of some of the most significant theologians writing in the late nineteenth and early twentieth centuries. We will consider the work of the Dominicans Benoît-Henri Merkelbach and Dominicus Prümmer, as well as John McHugh and Charles Callan, the Capuchin Franciscans Heribert Jone and Urban Adelman, the Jesuit manuals of Aloysius Sabetti, Noldin-Schmitt, Thomas Slater, and Henry Davis, and finally the work of the German Redemptorist Bernhard Häring. While the scope of this work does not allow for a complete history of these authors, we will provide a broad outline of the casuist approach to issues of cooperation through the immediate pre-conciliar period.

Chapter three will highlight the renewal of moral theology from the virtue tradition as it has been applied to questions of cooperation with evil. We will consider the documents of the Magisterium, most especially the 1993 encyclical of now Saint John Paul II *Veritatis splendor*. We will also analyze other documents of the Holy See, especially the 1995 encyclical of Pope John Paul II, *Evangelium vitae*, attending to their role in renewed thought on moral cooperation with evil. We will also examine the *Ethical and Religious Directives for Catholic Health Care Services* of the United States Conference of Catholic Bishops regarding their approach to questions of moral cooperation.

The third chapter will conclude with an outline of the contributions of three contemporary authors: Steven A. Long of Ave Maria University, the Dominican Archbishop Anthony Fisher, presently Archbishop of Sydney, Australia, and the American theologian Andrew McLean Cummings. From these three authors we can glean a broadly Thomistic foundation for a method of moral analysis regarding moral cooperation with evil. We will make particular reference to the way in which their approach differs from that of the authors of the casuist period as well as the extent to which their thought relies on natural teleology and the *per se* effects of a human act. Each author varies in the extent to which he treats directly the issue of moral cooperation with evil, but their approach to moral questions more generally is what will ultimately serve our present inquiry. It is our hope that this analysis will provide a method faithful to the Church's teaching and at the same time eminently practical for the challenging debates in our day.

Chapter four, then, will outline this method of virtue-based reasoning for matters of moral cooperation. We will demonstrate that an approach to moral cooperation grounded in virtue-ethics will avoid the pitfalls to which the casuist method is prone. This method will attend to the natural teleology of human action and focus on the *per se* effects of human acts. We will pay particular attention to the virtue of prudence which will play an indispensable role in this approach. Since prudence can obtain essentially practical knowledge of moral action in a particular instance, it will not remain at the general or theoretical level but actually will ensure that one engages in a sound moral action. The effort of this chapter will be to show precisely how a virtue-based approach to moral cooperation can both reach a greater consensus than did the casuist authors as well as actually aid in the accomplishment of virtuous cooperation. That is to say, the goal of this method is not to provide merely theoretical guidance but to aid inquirers to accomplish virtuous actions in concrete instances.

Finally, in Chapter five we will apply the virtue-based method to five disputed areas of moral cooperation. We will analyze questions surrounding voting in political elections for candidates who espouse immoral positions, the payment of taxes when they will be used to support immoral practices, issues of moral cooperation surrounding the celebration of weddings between those of the same sex, contraceptive mandates in health care, and issues in the education of children related to gender ideology and sexual education. While each of these areas has been subject to one degree or another to a casuist analysis, little, or in some cases nothing, has been written from a virtue-based perspective. If this work is successful, some basic moral principles regarding each of these challenging areas can be identified for the work of the Church in navigating these waters.

CHAPTER ONE

The Teaching of St. Thomas Aquinas

Received and Jettisoned

The achievement of St. Thomas Aquinas

In recognition of his near universal treatment of the themes of Catholic theology, St. Thomas Aquinas has merited the title "Common Doctor" of the Church.[1] Despite the suggestion in some quarters that Aquinas enjoys diminished influence in Catholic theology, the Magisterium continues to employ this universalizing title even in the present day.[2] Due both to his impressive theological and philosophical corpus and his consistently rational method of doing theology, few areas escape his influence. While no thinker can be expected to treat every topic that ever might arise in a given field, through the centuries the teachings of St. Thomas have remained at the forefront of theological debates. We will examine five particular areas in the teaching of St. Thomas where his influence on the question of moral cooperation with evil proves helpful.[3] His permission to borrow from known usurers, his treatment of the sin of scandal, his extended text examining which malefactors are required to make restitution for sins to which they were a party, the challenge of enjoining oaths on known perjurers, and examining the moral goodness of producing objects utilized for a sinful purpose prove helpful in our inquiry.

1. For an impressive chronicling of the magisterial interventions ascribing authority to the teaching of St. Thomas, see Santiago Ramirez, OP, "The Authority of St. Thomas Aquinas," *The Thomist* 15 (1952): 1–109.

2. Pope Benedict XVI, General Audience, June 2, 2010. See also Pope John Paul II, *Fides et ratio*, no. 43. The Second Vatican Council recommended the thought of only one theologian, St. Thomas Aquinas, see *Optatum totius*, no. 16. The 1983 Code of Canon Law requires that students of theology be grounded in the thought of St. Thomas, see *CIC* 252 §2.

3. The phrases "cooperation with evil" and "cooperation in evil" are used interchangeably in this book. No distinction exists in the relevant literature between the phrases.

Borrowing from usurers

In St. Thomas Aquinas's treatise on justice in the *secunda-secundae* of the *Summa theologiae*, the Church's Common Doctor asks whether it is lawful to borrow money under the condition of a usurious loan. Since lending money at interest is understood to be sinful, St. Thomas asks whether one might borrow from someone known habitually to practice usury.[4] Perhaps surprisingly St. Thomas answers that one may borrow money under such conditions. Aquinas teaches: "He who borrows for usury gives the usurer an occasion, not for taking usury, but for lending; it is the usurer who finds an occasion of sin in the malice of his heart."[5] Despite the nearly certain knowledge that the lender will use the very funds provided to him for the sin of usury, Aquinas holds that borrowing money from a usurer is morally permitted.[6] According to St. Thomas, borrowing money from a known usurer does not represent an illicit cooperation in the evil act of usury.

According to the now commonly used categories of moral analysis, one could be inclined to argue that St. Thomas employs the distinction between material and formal cooperation. One might conclude that Aquinas does not invoke the precise terms material and formal cooperation since theologians did not utilize these expressions until the time of St. Al-

---

4. For a brief history of the moral implications of the practice of usury, see Albert R. Jonsen and Stephen Toulmin, *The Abuse of Casuistry: A History of Moral Reasoning* (Berkley and Los Angeles: University of California Press, 1988), 181–94. For the argument that Catholic magisterial teaching has reversed itself in this area, see John T. Noonan Jr., *A Church That Can and Cannot Change: The Development of Catholic Moral Teaching* (Notre Dame, IN: University of Notre Dame Press, 2005). Noonan's view, however, has received a convincing rebuttal. See Brian M. McCall, *The Church and the Usurers: Unprofitable Lending for the Modern Economy* (Washington, DC: The Catholic University of America Press, 2013).

5. *Summa theologiae* IIa–IIae, q. 78, a. 4, ad. 2. English translations of the *Summa theologiae* follow those of the Fathers of the English Dominican Province, *The Summa Theologiae of St. Thomas Aquinas*, Second and Revised Edition (New York: Benziger Brothers, 1920). Unless otherwise noted, all translations of other texts are my own.

6. Aquinas makes essentially the same point in the *De Malo*, q. 13, a. 4, ad. 19: "A man ought not to consent to the sin of another to avoid any bodily harm. But nevertheless a man can lawfully use the wickedness of another or not withhold from him but offer him the matter of sin for the sake of avoiding bodily harm to himself; for example, if a thief were about to cut a person's throat and to avoid the danger of death the person were to reveal to the thief the location of his treasure that could be stolen, he would not sin, according to the example of those ten men who said to Ishmael, 'Kill us not, for we have stores in the field,' as related in Jeremiah 41:8." *De Malo*, trans. Jean Oesterle (Notre Dame: University of Notre Dame Press, 1995).

phonsus Liguori in the eighteenth century. One might then assume that Aquinas allows the borrowing of money because it represents an instance of merely material cooperation *ante litteram*. Likewise, one could argue that since the borrower does not want to be party to a usurious loan he does not cooperate formally with the usurer. At the same time, even in the most lax moral analysis, the very fact that cooperation is material (and not formal) does not by that very fact justify cooperating with the evil.[7] In the now standard moral analysis, in order to justify the material cooperation, one must consider both the proximity of the cooperation to the evil committed and the extent to which the cooperation might be required for the accomplishment of the evil act.

However, in the example of borrowing from known usurers, moralists who utilize the standard casuist categories of material and formal cooperation will struggle to explain fully the method of reasoning found in St. Thomas's text. In the case of borrowing money from one known to practice usury, the cooperation—that is, the borrowing of money—stands in extremely close proximity to the evil act. Indeed, the borrowing of money represents the sole material cause of the usury committed. For this reason, it becomes difficult to understand how St. Thomas could justify borrowing from a usurer under the now commonly utilized categories of material and formal cooperation. In the present work I will argue that St. Thomas employs an older and more commonsensical method of moral analysis: namely, he investigates the kind of act in which the borrower is engaged. He analyzes the teleology of the act of borrowing, including the act's *per se* effects. When examining human action, one can discover a *per se* ordering of the act, which includes what necessarily follows from a given kind of act.[8] In the case of borrowing money from a known usurer,

7. See, for example, the manual of Jone-Adelman, Heribert Jone, OFM Cap., and Urban Adelman, OFM Cap., *Moral Theology* (Westminster, MD: The Newman Bookshop, 1951), §147: "Material cooperation, i.e. concurrence in an action which is only a preparation to a sinful deed, is also wrong as a rule." The authors go on to explain, "[Material cooperation] may be permitted if the preparatory action is good or at least indifferent and a correspondingly good reason is had." See also, the manual of Henry Davis who teaches that material cooperation is "in general sinful." Henry Davis, *Moral and Pastoral Theology*, vol. 1 (London: Sheed and Ward, 1958), Tr. V, Ch. VIII, Sec. 2.

8. The language of natural teleology and *per se* ordering to an end utilized in this volume draws heavily from the work of Steven A. Long. We will examine his *The Teleological Grammar of the Moral Act* in the third chapter of the present work. While aspects of his analysis have come under criticism by Steven J. Jensen and Kevin L. Flannery, SJ, it is my contention that their concerns remain at a technical level without rising to the point

the one seeking the loan simply borrows money, an act from which no *per se* effect of usury follows. The issue at hand is not so much the proximity of the cooperation to the sin of usury (for in this case it is very proximate indeed). Instead, the issue under consideration remains whether the act of borrowing money is the kind of act from which an evil thing—namely usury—necessarily follows. As St. Thomas explains, usury does not necessarily follow the borrowing of money. Thus, borrowing money from a known usurer is morally permissible.

The above manner of reading St. Thomas is not innovative but rather stands as part of a venerable tradition. The eminent Thomas de Vio Cardinal Cajetan himself explains the text in a similar fashion. His commentary of St. Thomas's *Summa theologiae*, published first in 1521, appears now in the Leonine edition of the *Summa* by order of Pope Leo XIII. The sixteenth-century Dominican cardinal explains that Thomas's permission to borrow from a usurer results from the fact that nothing about the act of borrowing necessarily implies usury. Instead of examining the proximity of the borrowing to the usury, Cajetan evaluates whether what the borrower asks for can be granted without sin. Cajetan explains: "Always therefore attend in these cases to whether an act can be done by another without sin: this is the root of whether it is licit or illicit."[9] The question at hand remains whether the request of the borrower implies usury. Indeed, it does not. The usurer could easily comply with the request to borrow money without resorting to the sin of usury. Understanding why one can borrow from a usurer without sin requires attention to the nature of the act of borrowing.

When examining this passage of Cajetan's commentary, one author puts the issue succinctly: "[T]the rule for determining whether or not I can lawfully ask something of another is «Can that which I request be carried out by the other without the sin on his part». If so, then my request is lawful."[10] Simply put, nothing about asking for a loan necessi-

---

of questioning the basic premises of his work. That is to say, the language of natural teleology and *per se* order of human action remains a helpful paradigm for understanding human action. It extends beyond the scope of this work to consider—and still less to pronounce—on this debate.

9. The commentary of Thomas de Vio Cardinal Cajetan can be found in the Leonine edition of the *Summa theologiae*, Tome 9, 166: "Adverte ergo semper in casibus ut discernas si actus petitus potest ab eo a quo petitur sino peccato fieri: quia haec radix est liciti vel illiciti."

10. E. T. Hannigan, SJ, "Is it ever lawful to advise the lesser of two evils?" *Gregorianum* 30 (1949): 105.

tates usury. As St. Thomas explains, the sin of usury on the other hand, flows from the malice in the usurer's heart.[11] Nothing in either the text of St. Thomas or in Cajetan's commentary suggests the appropriate line of inquiry to be an evaluation of the *proximity* of the borrowing of money from a usurer to the sin of usury.[12] Rather, the relevant and necessary question for evaluating the act of the cooperator (in this case, the borrower) attends to the nature of the act of borrowing money and what *per se* follows from it. Attention to the nature of the act itself and its *per se* effects provides a clearer method of analysis in cases of moral cooperation with evil than does the category of proximity utilized by casuist authors.

The sin of scandal

St. Thomas Aquinas does not offer an extended treatise regarding moral cooperation with evil. The well-known distinction of material and formal cooperation does not appear in the works of Aquinas or those of any author of the medieval period. St. Alphonsus Liguori first invoked this principle in the eighteenth century to analyze cases of moral cooperation.[13] The moral complexity of the early modern period—due both to technical advance and to a collapse of certain elements of a Christian culture—only partially accounts for this change in moral reasoning. In addition to these cultural shifts, the decision of modern moralists to treat cooperation as a subset of scandal led to unfortunate consequences. Manualist theologians by and large treated cooperation with evil as a sin against charity. In so doing, they elected to place their analysis of sins of cooperation with evil immediately following their treatise on scandal. That decision hindered the ability of manualist authors to evaluate properly this moral topic.

11. See *Summa theologiae* IIa–IIae, q. 78, a. 4, ad. 2.

12. For a more complete treatment of Cajetan's commentary on this text, see Kevin L. Flannery, SJ, "Counseling the Lesser Evil," *The Thomist* 75 (2011): 245–89. Specifically, on page 256 Flannery explains that for Cajetan, "what is decisive in establishing the difference between inducing and not inducing to sin is not any talk about providing merely the matter for the sin but the fact that in certain cases the malefactors are determined to perform an evil no matter what the other person might say. When these objectively determinable circumstances are in place, it can be assumed (on at least a prima facie basis) that the will of the person who attempts to draw the malefactors towards the lesser evil is not bound up in whatever evil is performed."

13. See Roger Roy, CSsR, "La coopération selon Saint Alphonse de Liguori," *Studia Moralia* 6 (1968): 411.

The custom of the casuist period to treat cooperation as a subset of the sin of scandal set the stage for the type of analysis which followed. However, no warrant can be found for examining cooperation with evil merely as a subset of the sin of scandal. When questions about what we would now call cooperation with evil arose at the time of Aquinas, the method he chose involved rigorous analysis of human acts in the context of a virtue-based approach to moral theology. The method of St. Thomas provides a salutary lesson for how to approach questions of moral cooperation. While this seeming lacuna in Aquinas's thought may be frustrating, it offers a point of instruction for those who seek a method of analyzing cooperation with evil according to the mind of the Common Doctor.

According to Aquinas, one need not rely on a distinct method for analyzing questions of moral cooperation apart from how one should analyze the morality of human action in general. One would need an entirely new schema for analyzing moral cooperation with evil only if one were able to apply ready-made categories to instances or cases of cooperation. If, on the other hand, cooperation does not present a new category of moral acts then one does not require a separate treatise on cooperation. Here one perceives a certain parallel to the principle of double-effect and its overutilization in the casuist authors. Steven Long, for example, argues that for Aquinas there is no principle of double effect *per se* as much as it is the application of his overall moral theory to a very limited number of cases.[14]

In much the same way, Aquinas does not present a separate treatise on ecclesiology and yet theologians can glean a Thomist ecclesiology from his works.[15] In fact, the lack of a separate ecclesiological treatise provides an

---

14. Long explains: "One would do better to fathom the natural teleological grammar governing the constitution of object and species of the moral act than to dwell upon the standard conditions of the 'principle of double-effect.' For the latter is merely a special case of the application of the former, and a special case has been overextended to cases to which it does not apply, and which has been wrongly interpreted with respect even to the cases to which it *does* [emphasis in original] apply." See Steven A. Long, *The Teleological Grammar of the Moral Act*, 2nd ed. (Washington, DC: The Catholic University of America Press, 2015), 148. While he disagrees with Long's analysis of Aquinas on self-defense, Stephen Brock holds essentially the same point about the possibly exaggerated place of double-effect reasoning. Brock prefers to speak of the "indirect voluntary" or "indirectly intended" aspects of human action. Like Long, Brock does not find warrant in the texts of Aquinas for widespread use of the schema of double-effect. See Stephen L. Brock, *Action and Conduct: Thomas Aquinas and the Theory of Action* (Edinburgh: T&T Clark, 1998), 216–25.

15. Despite the absence of an explicit ecclesiological treatise in work of St. Thomas,

essential starting point for understanding Thomas's ecclesiology. Namely, no one should seek to understand the nature of the Church correctly apart from a robust Christology, Sacramental theology, and a theology of grace. Thus, it is precisely the lack of a separate ecclesiological treatise that signals the proper starting point for a sound ecclesiology. In the same fashion, the lack of a separate account of moral cooperation with evil in the work of St. Thomas helps us to understand that cooperation with evil does not present a new and separate set of moral questions to which extrinsic rules or new categories of explanation need apply. Instead, a sound analysis of moral cooperation with evil requires only an application of Aquinas's general moral thought. Aquinas offers a full account of his moral theology principally in the *secunda pars* of the *Summa theologiae.*

Only if the relevant moral question for understanding cooperation with evil involves recognizing how good or neutral acts relate to bad acts, then a whole new schema on cooperation would become necessary. The authors of the casuist period used this approach—applying ready-made categories to acts considered morally neutral before their relation to some positively bad act. However, if the better method of moral analysis relies instead on analyzing the act of the cooperator itself with its teleological ordering and *per se* effects, the general method of analyzing moral acts remains unchanged.

From as early as the seventeenth century, manualist authors treat cooperation as closely related to the sin of scandal, a topic which Aquinas did treat directly.[16] Most moral manuals treat cooperation after a treatise on scandal, without acknowledging that this represents an important extension from Aquinas's treatment.[17] Placing the treatise on cooperation after the treatment of scandal is not in itself illegitimate. Certain complexities arise, however, in the attempt to address moral cooperation with evil under the framework of the sin of scandal. Aquinas provides the first fully systematic treatment of the sin of scandal in the Middle Ages. In distinction thirty-eight in the fourth book of the *Sentences*, Peter Lombard of-

---

both Benoît-Dominique de La Soujeole, *Introduction au mystère de l'Église,* (Toulouse: Parole et Silence, 2006) and Charles Journet, *L'Église du Verbe incarné,* 3 vols. (Paris: Desclée de Brouwer, 1943, 1951, 1969) provide a robust ecclesiology grounded in the Thomist tradition.

16. See *Summa theologiae* IIa–IIae, q. 43.

17. For example, Roger Roy holds that the sixteenth-century Jesuit Thomas Sanchez considered the issue of cooperation with evil to be a particular case of scandal. See Roy, "La coopération selon Saint Alphonse de Liguori," 398: "Sanchez a considéré ce problème comme un cas particulier de scandale."

fers a passing reference to scandal regarding religious vows.[18] In Aquinas's commentary on the *Sentences*, the Angelic Doctor offers limited treatment of the sin of scandal. Not until the *Summa theologiae* does he offer a comprehensive examination of the topic.

In the treatise on charity in the *secunda-secundae* of the *Summa*, Aquinas examines vices opposed to charity in questions thirty-four through forty-three. He treats hatred, sloth, envy, discord, contention, schism, war, strife, and sedition before examining scandal in question forty-three which unfolds in eight articles.[19] In the prelude to the first article, Aquinas explains that some "vices which are opposed to beneficence ... come under the head of injustice, those to wit, whereby one harms one's neighbor unjustly."[20] He distinguishes those vices opposed to justice from those he will treat immediately, namely scandal, which he says "seems especially opposed to charity."[21] Here Aquinas does not assert that sins of scandal do not also oppose justice, which of course they do. Rather, he recognizes that for those seeking to live in the divine friendship, the sin of scandal poses a particular opposition to the charity that should characterize Christian behavior.

This connection between sins against justice and those opposed to charity finds warrant in the treatment of scandal in the *Catechism of the Catholic Church*. The *Catechism* treats scandal under sins against the fifth commandment, namely "Respect for the Dignity of Persons—Respect for the Souls of Others". The *Catechism* teaches: "Scandal is an attitude or behavior which leads another to do evil. The person who gives scandal becomes his neighbor's tempter.... Scandal is a grave offense if by deed or omission another is deliberately led into a grave offense."[22] While not placing scandal precisely as a sin against charity as Aquinas does, the teaching of the *Catechism* nonetheless corresponds with Aquinas's thought. This relationship between sins opposed to justice and those opposed to charity will

18. See Stephen L. Vileo, *A Theological Analysis of Scandal in the Summa Theologiae of St. Thomas Aquinas* (Rome: Pontifical Lateran University Academia Alphonsiana, 1993), 11–12.

19. For an extended commentary on these articles, see Vileo, *A Theological Analysis of Scandal*. Particularly important is the section dealing with how the Thomist commentatorial tradition has approached the question on scandal in Aquinas. For translations and appreciations of the commentaries of Cajetan, Suarez, John of St. Thomas, Billuart, and Garrigou-Lagrange, see 271–334.

20. *Summa theologiae* IIa–IIae, q. 43.

21. *Summa theologiae* IIa–IIae, q. 43.

22. *CCC*, no. 2284.

prove important as we will see that the treatment of the sin of cooperation under the virtue of justice will offer greater clarity for our investigation.

In article one, Aquinas defines scandal as "something less rightly done that occasions spiritual downfall."[23] Such a definition embraces both evil acts in themselves and those things which, while not wrong in themselves, occasion the sin of another. Aquinas offers the example of eating meat in an idol's temple.[24] While such an act is not evil in itself, since it could induce other good-willed persons to sin it should be avoided. In Article two, Aquinas explains that scandal always lacks rectitude in some way and therefore "scandal is always with sin."[25] Here one recalls the Lord's unequivocal condemnation of scandal: "Occasions for stumbling are bound to come, but woe to anyone by whom they come! It would be better for you if a millstone were hung around your neck and you were thrown into the sea than for you to cause one of these little ones to stumble."[26] St. Thomas explains that scandal can be passive, as in the one who is scandalized or active as in the one who gives scandal.[27] Scandal is a special sin in that it is "directly opposed to fraternal correction," as one intends a "special harm" to his neighbor.[28] Scandal need not always be a mortal sin as when one scandalizes someone to commit merely venial sin.[29] Aquinas explains that perfect men cannot fall into passive scandal as "no man can be unsettled, who adheres firmly to something immovable."[30] In a similar fashion, active scandal cannot be found in the perfect, as it only occurs "when a man says or does a thing which in itself is of a nature to occasion

23. *Summa theologiae* IIa–IIae, q. 43, a. 1.

24. *Summa theologiae* IIa–IIae, q. 43, a. 1, ad. 2. The scriptural warrant for such a view is clear. See, for example, Romans 14:20–21: "Do not for the sake of food, destroy the work of God. Everything is indeed clean, it is wrong to cause anyone to stumble by what you eat; it is good not to eat meat, drink wine, or do anything that makes your brother or sister stumble." This and all Biblical quotations are from the *New Revised Standard Version*. Similarly, 1 Corinthians 8:10: "For if others see you, who possess knowledge, eating in the temple of an idol, might they not, since their conscience is weak, be encouraged to the point of eating food sacrificed to idols?"

25. *Summa theologiae* IIa–IIae, q. 43, a. 2.

26. Luke 17:1–2.

27. *Summa theologiae* IIa–IIae, q. 43, a. 2. For further reflection on Aquinas's treatment of active and passive scandal, see Kevin L. Flannery, SJ, "Aquinas and the NNLT on the Object of the Human Act," *The National Catholic Bioethics Quarterly* 13 (Spring 2013): 79–104, especially 91–92.

28. *Summa theologiae* IIa–IIae, q. 43, a. 3.

29. *Summa theologiae* IIa–IIae, q. 43, a. 4.

30. *Summa theologiae* IIa–IIae, q. 43, a. 5.

another's spiritual downfall, and that is only when what he says or does is inordinate."[31] Finally, Aquinas explains that one need not always forgo either material or spiritual goods to avoid giving scandal.[32]

Most authors of the casuist period utilized Aquinas's account of scandal as the framework for their discussion of cooperation. The manual of the Austrian Jesuit Jerome Noldin (1838–1922) for example, treats cooperation immediately after scandal in the sins against charity. The manual provides another treatment of specific issues of cooperation relating to restitution in the section "De septimo decalogi praecepto."[33] This manual is representative of thinking in the United States as it was the most popular seminary text of moral theology in the immediate pre-conciliar period, with over half of the American seminaries teaching from it.[34]

There were some exceptions to the heavy reliance on treating cooperation so closely with the sin of scandal. The Dominican theologian Benoît-Henri Merkelbach (1871–1942), for example, offers no discussion of cooperation related to his treatment of scandal. Instead, he treats cooperation in the chapter "De Peccatis", specifically the "exterior causes of sin."[35] Merkelbach provides citations from Aquinas under the heading of each section of his moral manual. In his treatment of cooperation, interestingly, he offers no citation to the question on scandal. Instead, he offers two citations, both to passages where Aquinas treats the question of restitution, namely, *Summa theologiae* IIa–IIae, q. 62, a. 7 and *De Malo*, q. 13, a. 4, ad. 19.[36] In the section on commutative justice, specifically on the need to make restitution, Merkelbach treats what he calls "unjust cooperation." This, however, does not represent a full treatise on the subject. In his treatment of scandal, he

31. *Summa theologiae* IIa–IIae, q. 43, a. 6.

32. See *Summa theologiae* IIa–IIae, q. 43, a. 7–8.

33. See H. Noldin, SJ, and A. Schmitt, SJ, *Summa Theologiae Moralis*, vol. 2 (Innsbruck: Feliciani Rauch, 1957), §116–29, for cooperation treated under sins against charity; and §498–500, for the principles of restitution in cases of cooperation with evil treated under the seventh commandment.

34. See Charles E. Curran, *Catholic Moral Theology in the United States: A History* (Washington, DC: Georgetown University Press, 2008), 38. Curran explains that when first assigned to teach moral theology at St. Bernard's Seminary in Rochester, NY in 1961 he used the thirty-third edition of the Noldin moral manual. It had first been published in 1887. We will treat the Noldin manual's analysis of cooperation with evil in the second chapter of this work.

35. Benoît-Henri Merkelbach *Summa Theologiae Moralis ad mentem D. Thomae et ad normam juris novi*, vol. 1 (Bruges: Desclée de Brouwer, 1954), §487–92.

36. Merkelbach *Summa Theologiae Moralis*, §487.

does make reference to three of the passages of Aquinas treated in the present chapter: borrowing from a usurer (*ST* IIa–IIae, q. 78, a. 4), enjoining oaths on a perjurer (*ST* IIa–IIae, q. 98, a. 4), and the production of items for sinful use (*ST* IIa–IIae, q. 169, a. 2).[37] By separating his examination of cooperation with evil from his treatment of scandal Merkelbach represents a clear minority position among both casuist authors and even those who followed Aquinas more closely in commenting upon the *secunda pars*.[38]

When moralists place discussions of cooperation in the framework of scandal they tend to draw a less than helpful parallel between scandal and material cooperation. Casuist authors who treat material cooperation as a subset of scandal wind up conceiving of material cooperation as wrong in principle. According to these theologians, one should avoid material cooperation unless one can establish a proportionately grave justifying reason. For example, the manual of Jone-Adelman argues that material cooperation is "wrong as a rule."[39] In a similar way, the manual of Henry Davis argues that material cooperation is "in general sinful."[40] According to Davis, this possibility of sin can be avoided only if two conditions can be met, namely: "(a) That the act by which we co-operate is in itself not sinful. This act has two effects; we need not necessarily wish or intend the bad effect. (b) That there should be sufficient cause for permitting the sin of another."[41] While St. Thomas teaches that scandal is something "less rightly done," at the same time, the manualists' treatment of cooperation with evil under the same framework does not elucidate the matter so as to avoid confusion.

In principle, we should avoid acts that would scandalize others. Acts that can be understood to materially cooperate with evil, on the other hand, are not necessarily actions that should never be chosen. In the example given by Aquinas of borrowing from a known usurer, we recall that St. Thomas allows such an action. He does not speak of a proportionately grave reason to borrow from the usurer but instead addresses directly

37. Merkelbach, §968.

38. See, for example, Michel Labourdette, OP, *La Charité: Grand cours de théologie morale/10* (Paris: Parole et Silence, 2016), 389–95. In this otherwise outstanding (and posthumously published) text, Labourdette adopts the usual practice of his day to treat cooperation immediately following his treatment of scandal.

39. Heribert Jone, OFM Cap., and Urban Adelman, OFM Cap, *Moral Theology*, §147.

40. Henry Davis, *Moral and Pastoral Theology*, vol. 1 (London: Sheed and Ward, 1958), Tr. V, Ch. VIII, Sec. 2.

41. Davis, *Moral and Pastoral Theology*, Tr. V, Ch. VIII, Sec. 2.

the nature of the act of borrowing. In the casuist period, moralists tended to treat questions of cooperation with evil as a sub-species of scandal. For that reason, from the outset, these cooperative acts were considered evil and therefore necessarily acts that should be avoided. A more fruitful approach to these matters will be to distinguish more clearly cooperation from scandal. It is true, as Kevin Flannery observes: "[P]ractically any situation in which immoral cooperation is an issue is also a situation in which scandal is an issue."[42] Moralists do well to ask whether a given type of cooperation is the kind of act one can pursue virtuously. If it is, the action itself is not evil. It may be the case that one should still not pursue the act to avoid giving scandal, but these are distinguishable questions. As we will discover, issues of cooperation will be treated more fruitfully as sins against justice, that is, what is owed to one's neighbor.[43]

On the necessity of making restitution

In the treatise on justice, question sixty-two of the *secunda pars* of the *Summa theologiae*, Aquinas treats the challenging issue of making restitution for sins committed against justice. The virtue of justice, for Aquinas, indicates "a habit whereby a man renders to each one his due by a constant and perpetual will."[44] The *Catechism of the Catholic Church* offers a similar definition of justice: "Justice is the moral virtue that consists in the constant and firm will to give their due to God and neighbor."[45]

When one commits an evil against another, the virtue of justice requires that one make adequate restitution for the sin committed. Theft provides the most obvious example. If one steals one hundred dollars from another person, an essential sign of genuine contrition and necessary for reconciliation between the parties would be, in principle, the return of the one hun-

42. Kevin L. Flannery, SJ, *Cooperation with Evil: Thomistic Tools of Analysis* (Washington, DC: The Catholic University of America Press, 2019), 99.

43. Kevin Flannery maintains that instead of "attempting to identify and parse such interior acts of the mind ... a more promising approach would be to consider the ways in which acts of cooperation are situated within the reality of justice itself." See his *Cooperation with Evil: Thomistic Tools of Analysis*, 204.

44. *Summa theologiae* IIa–IIae, q. 58, a. 1. For an extended reflection on the virtue of justice, see Jean Porter, "The Virtue of Justice (IIa–IIae, qq. 58–122)" in *The Ethics of Aquinas*, ed. Stephen J. Pope (Washington, DC: Georgetown University Press, 2002), 272–86. In the same volume, see Martin Rhonheimer, "Sins Against Justice (IIa, IIae, qq. 59–78)," trans. Frederick G. Lawrence, 287–303.

45. *CCC*, no. 1807.

dred dollars. Confessors would be familiar with this principle as, at minimum, the desire to make restitution and the intention to do so insofar as one is able would be necessary for the valid celebration of the Sacrament of Penance.[46]

The Catholic tradition recognizes two species of particular justice: distributive justice and commutative justice. Aquinas explains that distributive justice concerns "the order of the whole to the parts, to which corresponds the order of that which belongs to the community in relation to each single person" and "distributes common goods proportionately."[47] Commutative justice is "concerned about the mutual dealing between two persons."[48] The *Catechism* again employs the distinction following the treatment of Aquinas.[49] The act of restitution falls under the virtue of commutative justice, as it involves one individual rendering a due to another.[50]

In a matter particularly useful for examining his position on how to evaluate moral cooperation with evil, Aquinas asks whether restitution is binding on those who have not actually stolen goods. He asks if those who cooperate in the stealing but have not actually stolen must make restitution for the pilfered goods. St. Thomas answers in the affirmative. The sinful cooperators are bound to make restitution. He then precisely delineates those who must make restitution depending on the type of involvement in the theft. Aquinas explains:

[A] person is bound to restitution not only on account of someone else's property which he has taken, but also on account of the injurious taking. Hence whoever is cause of an unjust taking is bound to restitution. This happens in two ways, directly and indirectly. Directly, when a man induces another to take, and this in three ways. First, on the part of the taking, by moving a man to take, either by express command, counsel, or consent, or by praising a man for his courage in thieving. Secondly, on the part of the taker, by giving him

46. See, for example, Thomas Slater, SJ, *A Manual of Moral Theology for English Speaking Countries* (New York: Benziger Brothers, 1925), Bk. VI, Part VII, Div. III, Ch. II on the roots of restitution. For the obligations of confessors to ensure that penitents are aware of the need to make restitution, see Watkin W. Williams, *The Moral Theology of the Sacrament of Penance* (Milwaukee: The Morehouse Publishing Co., 1919), 128–29 and Augustino Lehmkuhl, *Theologia Moralis* (Friburg: Herder, 1890), §472.

47. *Summa theologiae* IIa–IIae, q. 61, a. 1.

48. *Summa theologiae* IIa–IIae, q. 61, a. 1.

49. See *CCC*, no. 2412.

50. *Summa theologiae* IIa–IIae, q. 62, a. 1.

shelter or any other kind of assistance. Thirdly, on the part of the thing taken, by taking part in the theft or robbery, as a fellow evil-doer. Indirectly, when a man does not prevent another from evil-doing (provided he be able and bound to prevent him), either by omitting the command or counsel which would hinder him from thieving or robbing, or by omitting to do what would have hindered him, or by sheltering him after the deed.[51]

For Aquinas, the nature of the "injurious taking," that is, the nature of the act of the thief and the nature of the act of his cooperators, determines whether these wrongdoers must make restitution. St. Thomas poses the question: in what sort of activity did the cooperator engage? What precisely was he doing?

For this evaluation, Aquinas offers nine categories of activity which cooperate with evil.[52] In so doing Aquinas does not impose ready-made categories extrinsic to human acting, but rather, each category he lists—command, counsel, flattery, etc.—represents a real genus of human activity.[53] In any action which is a possible cooperation with evil, one can ask if this action represents an example of command, counsel, flattery, etc. This categorization differs from situating actions within the framework of material, formal, remote, and proximate cooperation. In that classically casuist categorization one cannot intuitively know how to categorize one's action. Thus, the perplexed moral agent must refer frequently to the so-called approved authors.[54] The distinction of material and formal cooperation, even if useful for making sound moral judgments, represents an imposed category upon human activity. One doesn't stumble upon an act of formal cooperation. Traditionally, moralists consider the act of instructing someone to steal a bag of money a formal cooperation in the theft. However, instructing one to steal a bag of money is more basically

51. *Summa theologiae* IIa–IIae, q. 62, a. 7.

52. For the origin of this list, see Albert the Great, *In Sent.* IV, 15, 42, as referenced in the commentary of Thomas Gilby, OP, on this article in *Justice*, vol. 37 of the Blackfriars *Summa Theologiae* (New York: McGraw-Hill Book Company, 1975), 123.

53. For an extended treatment of the nine types of cooperative acts, see Gregory Mellema, *Complicity and Moral Accountability* (Notre Dame, IN: University of Notre Dame Press, 2016), 18–30.

54. For a critique of this method of moral reasoning, specifically the weighing of various opinions, see Servais Pinckaers, *The Sources of Christian Ethics*, trans. Sr. Mary Thomas Noble, OP (Washington, DC: The Catholic University of America Press, 1995), 273–77. For a further critique of the casuist systems, see Romanus Cessario, OP, *Introduction to Moral Theology*, Revised Edition (Washington, DC: The Catholic University of America Press, 2013), 219–32.

an example of command. We recognize immediately such an action as an example of commanding. For Aquinas, the categories of command, counsel, etc. are natural types of human action.[55]

Aquinas explains that a cooperator is not bound to make restitution in every case. Instead, only in those cases where his cooperation is a true cause of the evil must he make restitution. Aquinas explains:

> All these are expressed as follows: 'By command, by counsel, by consent, by flattery, by receiving, by participation, by silence, by not preventing, by not denouncing.' It must be observed, however, that in five of these cases the cooperator is always bound to restitution.
>
> First, in the case of command: because he that commands is the chief mover, wherefore he is bound to restitution principally. Secondly, in the case of consent; namely of one without whose consent the robbery cannot take place. Thirdly, in the case of receiving; when, to wit, a man is a receiver of thieves, and gives them assistance. Fourthly, in the case of participation; when a man takes part in the theft and in the booty. Fifthly, he who does not prevent the theft, whereas he is bound to do so; for instance, persons in authority who are bound to safeguard justice on earth, are bound to restitution, if by their neglect thieves prosper, because their salary is given to them in payment of their preserving justice here below.[56]

In these five cases, the cooperator is bound to make restitution. St. Thomas explains that in these cases the cooperator's action represents a true cause of the evil committed. The evil flows *per se* from the cooperator's action. The cooperator has not done a good act that the malefactor has subsequently misused. Instead, in these five cases cooperators must make restitution because they truly committed unjust acts.

Aquinas asserts that five types of behavior—command, consent, receiving or giving assistance, participation, and not preventing the evil action—represent unjust participation in the evil committed. He distinguishes these types of activity from flattery or counsel which do not necessarily cause another to commit an evil. St. Thomas observes:

> In the other cases mentioned above, a man is not always bound to restitution: because counsel and flattery are not always the efficacious cause of robbery.

---

55. For further reflection on the nine categories of actions or omissions that could represent cooperation with evil, see Anthony Fisher, OP, "Co-operation in Evil," *Catholic Medical Quarterly* 44 (1994): 15–22.

56. *Summa theologiae* IIa–IIae, q. 62, a. 7.

Hence the counsellor or flatterer is bound to restitution, only when it may be judged with probability that the unjust taking resulted from such causes.[57]

The issue of when one is required to make restitution stands as an important topic in moral theology in its own right.[58] For our present purposes, however, the crucial matter remains the method St. Thomas employs when determining whether an act of cooperation requires restitution. Aquinas does not consider the act's "proximity to evil" but instead examines the nature of the action itself.

The question of oaths

In the treatise on justice in the *secunda-secundae* of the *Summa theologiae*, St. Thomas treats the virtue of religion (*ST* IIa-IIae, q. 81) and its proper acts (*ST* IIa-IIae, qq. 82–89). He follows with an examination of the vices of superstition and idolatry and their related acts (*ST* IIa-IIae, qq. 92–100). In question ninety-eight, Aquinas discusses the sin of perjury.[59] Here Aquinas adopts the definition of perjury offered by Hugh of St. Victor: "Perjury is defined as a falsehood confirmed by oath."[60] In the fourth article of the same question, St. Thomas asks if one sins by demanding an oath of a perjurer.[61] In many respects, this question mirrors St. Thomas's treatment of the sin of usury. In that case, St. Thomas allowed borrowing from a known usurer. Despite the close proximity of the borrowing to the sin of usury, Aquinas explained that the sin arises not from the borrowing but from the evil will of the usurer. Nothing about borrowing money implies—or is *per se* ordered to—the sin of usury. In the same way, nothing about asking one to swear an oath demands perjury. As in the case of usury, Aquinas attends to the nature of the act in question, not its proximity to the subsequent bad act.

---

57. *Summa theologiae* IIa–IIae, q. 62, a. 7.

58. For an interesting treatment of the principles of just restitution, see Benedict M. Ashley, OP, *Living the Truth in Love: A Biblical Introduction to Moral Theology* (Staten Island: Alba House, 1996), 337–38. In this text Ashley relies extensively on the work of Benoît-Henri Merkelbach, OP. For his treatment of restitution, as cited in Ashley, see Merkelbach's *Theologia Moralis*, vol. 2, §277–343.

59. For a history of the early modern treatments of perjury, see Albert R. Jonsen and Stephen Toulmin, *The Abuse of Casuistry: A History of Moral Reasoning* (Berkley and Los Angeles: University of California Press, 1988), 195–215.

60. *Summa theologiae* IIa–IIae, q. 98, a. 1.

61. *Summa theologiae* IIa–IIae, q. 98, a. 4.

The Church's Magisterium condemns perjury as a serious sin.[62] In fact, moral theologians traditionally consider swearing a false oath to be a sin of grave matter.[63] Recalling the holiness of God and the worship His creatures owe Him in justice serves to illuminate the particular disorder of sins which fail to honor God. In an age in which the worship of God has been relegated to an optional add-on instead of the natural law requirement of any intelligent creature, one understands why sins against God's name are not well understood. The gravity of the sin of perjury, however, does not cause Aquinas to abandon his general theory of moral action. He allows one to demand an oath from a perjurer if done out of some public duty. He holds that such an action does not represent an immoral cooperation in the evil of perjury.

The myth at work in much of the analysis of cases of cooperation with evil revolves around a misunderstanding of the importance of proximity to evil acts. St. Thomas offers an alternative way of proceeding. He explains:

If, on the other hand, a man demands an oath as a public person, in accordance with the requirements of the law, on the requisition of a third person: he does not seem to be at fault, if he demands an oath of a person, whether he knows that he will swear falsely or truly, because seemingly it is not he that exacts the oath but the person at whose instance he demands it.[64]

One might opine that when a malefactor is set on committing some bad act it is best not to get too close to it. The closer one gets to the bad act, the argument goes, the more one would be cooperating with it. According to this view, one would need a more and more grave reason to cooperate more and more closely with this other bad act. In such a scenario the sole malefactor is the other person who possesses the bad will to commit a bad act. Yet, this analysis remains entirely in the head, as it were. It attends solely to the cooperator's intention, asking if he wishes such and such bad act to take place.[65] This is not the method of moral analysis of St. Thomas. Instead,

62. See *CCC*, no. 2152.

63. See, for example, the statement of the bishops of the United States regarding the worthy reception of Holy Communion, "'Happy are Those who are Called to His Supper': On Preparing to Receive Christ Worthily in the Eucharist," USCCB, November 14, 2006, 9. The bishops include "swearing a false oath while invoking God as a witness" in the listed sins of grave matter.

64. *Summa theologiae* IIa–IIae, q. 98, a. 4.

65. For a sound demonstration of the errors associated with overemphasizing the

Aquinas asks what the so-called cooperator is doing. In essence, Aquinas does not treat him as a secondary actor at all. Rather, for St. Thomas, the person in question is not merely a cooperator. His analysis revolves around what sort of act this person—the would-be cooperator—is doing. In the case of perjury, according to St. Thomas both the known perjurer and one who demands the oath of his own accord act badly. However, the one who out of public duty demands an oath of a perjurer—despite such close proximity to the perjury—does not sin.

Producing items of sinful use

In questions 155–69 of the *secunda-secundae*, St. Thomas treats the potential parts of temperance. He describes continence (although not fully a virtue) and incontinence in questions 155–56, clemency, meekness and their contrary vices anger and cruelty in questions 157–159.[66] In questions 160–65 he treats modesty and humility and then the vice of pride and related issues. St. Thomas addresses the virtue of studiousness in question 166 and the vice of curiosity or *curiositas* in 167. Finally, at the conclusion of the treatise on justice, Aquinas deals with special issues of modesty in speech, deeds, and attire. *Summa theologiae* IIa–IIae, q. 169, a. 2 offers an additional locus for how Aquinas might treat cooperation with evil.

In question 169, article 2 of the *secunda-secundae* Aquinas asks whether women sin mortally by wearing excessive jewelry or other adornments. This matter forms part of a broader argument about whether inducing another to lust is mortally sinful. In one objection to the claim that one sins by such adornment, St. Thomas asks what about those who manufacture these adornments. Do they also sin in making these objects? St. Thomas explains:

In the case of an art directed to the production of goods which men cannot use without sin, it follows that the workmen sin in making such things, as directly affording others an occasion of sin; for instance, if a man were to make

<hr />

role of intention in examining moral cooperation with evil, see Andrew McLean Cummings, *The Servant and the Ladder: Cooperation with Evil in the Twenty-First Century* (Leominster: Gracewing, 2014).

66. For a Thomist account of the virtue of chastity including treatment of the sins of incontinence, see John S. Grabowski, *Sex and Virtue: An Introduction to Sexual Ethics* (Washington, DC: The Catholic University of America Press, 2003); and Thomas Petri, OP, *Aquinas and the Theology of the Body: The Thomistic Foundations of John Paul II's Anthropology* (Washington, DC: The Catholic University of America Press, 2016).

idols or anything pertaining to idolatrous worship. But in the case of an art the products of which may be employed by man either for a good or for an evil use, such as swords, arrows, and the like, the practice of such an art is not sinful.[67]

While this passage receives limited attention in contemporary analysis of cooperation with evil, here St. Thomas offers salutary guidance concerning cooperation.

St. Thomas explains that workmen sin in making products which have only a sinful purpose. The manufacturers of instruments used exclusively for procured abortion, for example, sin in their production. An instrument that could be used for a good or evil purpose, such as a gun, could be produced without sin on the part of the manufacturers. One observes that unlike many writers of the casuist period, Aquinas does not refer to the proximity of the production to its sinful use. He does not argue that because an instrument may be used in committing some sin, therefore the producer participates or cooperates in the sin of the principal malefactor. Aquinas does not enter the mind of the producer of the instrument, parsing whether or not he approves of the subsequent sin.

Instead, St. Thomas addresses the act of production of the instrument on his own terms. What is one doing in the production? Isolating the act of the producer—without further reference to additional parties—allows one to analyze clearly what the producer of the object is actually doing. St. Thomas's analysis does not require recourse to a separate method of analyzing proximity to the principal bad act nor a weighing of the effects of the production.[68] Rather, he analyzes the nature of the production of the evil instrument on its own terms. Producing something that can have only a sinful purpose—as in the case of an idol for example—is always evil.[69] The absence of any excursus on the reason for the production proves most noteworthy for Aquinas's analysis. While future moral theologians will ascribe a heightened significance to the role of intention in the quality of moral choice, no warrant for such an emphasis can be found in the texts of St. Thomas. Here—as in many passages from the Angelic Doctor—the act itself, without reference to one's reason for acting, provides the principal locus for a moral analysis.

---

67. *Summa theologiae* IIa–IIae, q. 169, a. 2, ad. 4.

68. For a critical assessment of moral theories which emphasize the weighing of good and evil effects of acts, see *VS*, nos. 74–75.

69. See *CCC*, nos. 2113–14.

Aquinas's condemnation of the production of objects that have only a sinful purpose also proves useful for our analysis. The question that we will raise repeatedly in this area is whether an action has an intelligibility apart from the evil which may follow it. Can the production of a certain product be understood apart from the sinful purpose for which it may be used? Aquinas answers in the affirmative if the product serves multiple purposes, even if at times it may be used for a sinful end. However, the production of an item which can be used exclusively for sin is always evil.

Echoes in the Thomist tradition

Until the early modern period no Catholic theologian composed a full treatise on cooperation with evil. Neither St. Thomas nor his commentators offered a comprehensive study of the topic. For that reason, later theologians have tended to neglect the resources which are available in the Thomist tradition that are useful for dealing with this question. The present work contends that the virtue-based approach to moral matters utilized by Aquinas and his authentic interpreters will provide a sound method for analyzing moral cooperation with evil. Unfortunately, because neither Aquinas nor any author employing his virtue-based approach has provided a comprehensive treatment of cooperation with evil, until now, examinations of the topic have largely neglected their contributions.[70] Jean Capreolus, Thomas de Vio Cajetan, and John of St. Thomas stand as three crucial figures of the Thomist tradition. While none offers a treatise on how to analyze questions of cooperation with evil specifically, each offers important contributions to the topic. In the section that follows we identify useful resources from the Thomist tradition which can be employed to establish a virtue-based method for analyzing questions of moral cooperation.

Capreolus (d. 1444)

Historians could hardly exaggerate the theological contribution of the fifteenth-century Dominican Jean Capreolus. The extent to which his

---

70. For example, even the outstanding work of Andrew McLean Cummings, *The Servant and the Ladder: Cooperation with Evil in the Twenty-First Century*, does not offer an examination of how Aquinas or his commentators would approach the topic. See also my review of Cummings's work in *Studia Moralia* 55 (2017): 211–14.

name has fallen into obscurity in large sectors of the theological world hints at a certain deficiency in contemporary theological discourse. For those in the Thomist tradition, however, the name Jean Capreolus recalls the beginnings of the venerable commentatorial tradition. Held on the 550th anniversary of his death, a September 1994 conference at Rodez in the south of France presented one effort to recall the influence of this fifteenth-century Thomist commentator.[71] The ensuing years have witnessed an increase of interest in scholarship on Capreolus. The English-speaking world has benefited from the first English translation of a limited portion of his corpus.[72]

Born in the Diocese of Rodez in the second half of the fourteenth century, Capreolus entered the Dominican order at the convent of Rodez. The general chapter held in Poitiers in 1407 assigned him to serve as professor at the University of Paris where he began teaching the following year.[73] As was the custom of the period, he lectured on the *Sentences* of Peter Lombard. He lectured and wrote with a view toward defending the teaching of St. Thomas Aquinas from the objections of his adversaries. Capreolus lived in tumultuous times for both Church and state. He worked during both the Hundred Years War and the Great Western Schism in the Church.[74] Through this turmoil, he gave himself assiduously to the defense of the thought of St. Thomas. His masterwork, *Defensiones Theologiae Divi Thomae Aquinatis*, comprised four volumes. The method of Capreolus involved recording the disputed passages from the works of St. Thomas and the arguments of his opponents. He answered the objecting positions of John Duns Scotus, Durandus of Saint-Pourcaon, Peter

---

71. The papers of the conference were collected and published as *Jean Capreolus en son temps, 1380–1444: Colloque de Rodez*, ed. Guy Bedouelle, OP, Romanus Cessario, OP, and Kevin White (Paris: Editions du Cerf, 1997). For a positive appraisal of this effort, see Edward P. Mahoney, "The Accomplishment of Jean Capreolus, OP", *The Thomist* 68 (2004): 601–32.

72. See John Capreolus, *On the Virtues*, translated with an Introduction and Notes by Kevin White and Romanus Cessario, OP (Washington, DC: The Catholic University of America Press, 2001).

73. P. Mandonnet, *Dictionnaire de théologie catholique* (Paris: Letouzey et Ane, 1936), 1694. For a more complete biography, see Thomas-M. Pègues, OP, "La Biographie de Jean Capréolus," *Revue thomiste* VII (1899): 317–34. For an extended treatment of the role of Capreolus in what is often called renaissance Thomism, see Denis R. Janz, *Luther and Late Medieval Thomism: A Study in Theological Anthropology* (Waterloo, ON: Wilfrid Laurier University Press, 2009), 60–91.

74. See Pègues, OP, "La Biographie de Jean Capréolus," 325.

Aureolus, Henry of Ghent, and others. Through a judicious citation of passages of St. Thomas, Capreolus demonstrated the veracity of Aquinas's conclusions.

Capreolus died at Rodez on April 7, 1444. The noted Dominican historian Pierre Mandonnet explained that Capreolus merited the designation "Prince of the Thomists" as he was "incontestably the most authoritative commentator and defender of Thomist doctrine at the end of the middle ages."[75] Because he initiated a new method of theological reflection— using the words of St. Thomas himself to respond to objections—he is often referred to as "the first Thomist."[76] In an insightful essay exhibiting the basic continuity between the teaching of St. Thomas and the work of Capreolus, Servais Pinckaers explains that Capreolus "is a good representative of the Thomist school at war."[77] Capreolus established the basic method of Thomistic commentary with fierce fidelity to the teaching of St. Thomas as a model for future Thomistic commentators.[78]

The present work seeks to demonstrate that the Thomist virtue-based tradition offers a more robust method of moral reasoning than that of modern casuistry. In particular, the moral system of St. Thomas and his commentators presents hitherto unearthed resources for a theological approach to questions of moral cooperation. The continuation of the teaching of St. Thomas—especially regarding the virtues—in Capreolus and later Thomists presents an apt resource for this project. One area which required Capreolus to defend the teaching of St. Thomas was against those who objected to his virtue-centered approach to moral matters. Even in the fifteenth century Capreolus saw how destructive a departure from virtue would be for moral inquiry. Specifically relevant for the question of moral cooperation, Capreolus argued in favor of the role of prudence and rectified appetite in the moral life. In book three of his *Defen-*

---

75. Mandonnet, *Dictionnaire*, 1694: "il est incontestablement le commentateur et le défenseur le plus autorisé des doctrines thomistes vers la fin du moyen âge."

76. See the White and Cessario introductory essay to John Capreolus', *On the Virtues*, xxviii.

77. Servais Pinckaers, OP, "Capreolus's Defense of Aquinas: A Medieval Dispute about Virtues and Gifts," in *The Pinckaers Reader: Renewing Thomistic Moral Theology*, ed. John Berkman and Craig Steven Titus, trans. Sr. Mary Thomas Noble, OP, Craig Steven Titus, Michael Sherwin, OP, and Hugh Connolly (Washington, DC: The Catholic University of America Press, 2005), 305.

78. For an extended reflection on the role of Capreolus in the history of Thomistic commentary, see Thomas-M. Pègues, OP, "Du Rôle de Capréolus dans la Défense de Saint Thomas," *Revue thomiste* VII (1899): 507–29.

siones, Capreolus argues for the position of St. Thomas that the exercise of prudence requires the presence of the moral virtues. John Duns Scotus had objected to this teaching of Aquinas, asserting that prudence could coexist with a poor moral choice. In Scotus's view, prudence could then exist without moral virtue.[79] Through a careful citation of the texts of Aquinas, Capreolus demonstrates that Scotus's position relies on a misunderstanding of prudence, portraying it as a merely theoretical knowing. Instead, prudence can both know what is to be done in a particular case and actually enact a sound moral decision.[80] Because prudence possesses the capacity to command, this virtue occupies a foremost place in the moral life.

At the 1994 Rodez conference, Servais Pinckaers took up this question of Capreolus's defense of Aquinas on the role of prudence. Pinckaers explains: "Capreolus rightly replies that a capital point in this matter is to understand that prudence is not limited to judging and counseling well, but finds its completion in the 'command' or imperium which forms the choice; we could call this the decision to act joined to the impetus to act."[81] In describing the balance the moral virtues require of one another, one author has called prudence "the fulcrum for this lever."[82] Prudence commands that the good action be done. In eschewing this role of prudence, the moral manuals of the casuist period instead rely excessively on conscience or resort to forms of voluntarism to describe the moral life.[83] Misunderstanding prudence as a kind of purely speculative knowing re-

79. See Capreolus, *On the Virtues*, 325–35.

80. For a more complete treatment of the diminished role of prudence in the writing of John Duns Scotus, see Thomas M. Osborne, Jr., *Human Action in Thomas Aquinas, John Duns Scotus, and William of Ockham* (Washington, DC: The Catholic University of America Press, 2014), 83–88.

81. Servais Pinckaers, OP, "Capreolus's Defense of Aquinas: A Medieval Dispute about Virtues and Gifts," in *The Pinckaers Reader: Renewing Thomistic Moral Theology*, 318.

82. See Reginald Garrigou-Lagrange, OP, *The Theological Virtues*, vol. 1, *On Faith*, trans. Thomas a Kempis Reilly, OP (St. Louis: B. Herder Book Co., 1965), 32. He explains: "[T[here is a balance in the moral virtues in which they all share. Prudence is the fulcrum for this lever. As directive causes, the other moral virtues are steadied by it in a general way."

83. For an insightful description of the dangers of what Michel Labourdette calls 'moralities of conscience', see John R. T. Lamont, "Conscience, Freedom, Rights: Idols of the Enlightenment Religion," *The Thomist* 73 (2009): 169–239, particularly 177–98. For an alternative perspective on the place of conscience in the moral life, see two essays by James F. Keenan, SJ, "Redeeming Conscience," *Theological Studies* 76 (2015): 129–47; and "Receiving *Amoris Laetitia*," *Theological Studies* 78 (2017): 193–212.

quires many casuist authors to exalt the place of the will in human action. Since they jettison the capacity of prudence to command, manualist authors tend to rely too heavily on the role of the will for their account of moral action. These authors' failure to grasp prudence's capacity to enact sound moral action leads them to diminish the role of prudence in the moral life.[84]

Pinckaers continues his explanation of Capreolus's defense of St. Thomas by recalling the need for rectified appetites to perform sound moral actions. Pinckaers explains:

We should note that, in the analysis of the prudential act, the command is not external but interior to the acting subject, and proceeds from his "willing reason." In order to form this command to act, and to act in this particular way, prudence has need of the appetite's rectitude, which is produced by temperance, courage, and justice.[85]

A virtue-based approach to cooperation with evil requires this robust account of prudence. While the modern classification of moral cooperation—formal, material, remote, proximate, etc.—may provide a certain insight into what types of cooperation should be avoided, knowledge of these categories does not of itself ensure that one actually will make a sound moral choice. While those of the nominalist school assign to the will the principal mechanism of the moral life, according to St. Thomas, only prudence, relying on rectified appetite, actually can instantiate virtuous moral action.[86] The importance of rectified sense appetites becomes clear in a virtue-based approach to moral cooperation. If some form of cooperation is deemed illicit—for example complying with a government mandate to provide contraception—only one who possesses a well-developed fortitude will be willing to endure whatever difficulties come from refusing such cooperation. In the case of government mandates this could involve fines, loss of business, or even imprisonment.[87] While it can be difficult to see clear-

84. For the influence of the nominalists of the Franciscan school, particularly William of Ockham, on the tendency to replace prudence with conscience, see Servais Pinckaers, OP, *The Sources of Christian Ethics*, 240–53.

85. Servais Pinckaers, OP, "Capreolus's Defense of Aquinas: A Medieval Dispute about Virtues and Gifts," in *The Pinckaers Reader: Renewing Thomistic Moral Theology*, 318.

86. For a more complete treatment of the work of Capreolus against the nominalists of the fourteenth and fifteenth centuries, see Sigrid Müller, "The Ethics of John Capreolus and the 'Nominales'," *Verbum: Analecta Neolatina* 6 (2004): 301–14, especially 307–12.

87. See *VS*, nos. 90–94 on the place of martyrdom in the moral life. For an extended reflection on the place of martyrdom in the Christian life, see Servais Pinckaers, OP,

ly if a certain form of cooperation is immoral, a well-ordered appetite that truly loved the good would be prepared to grasp by means of a connaturality to the good the virtuous moral action to be accomplished.

Related to his account of sound moral acting, Capreolus offers another avenue to glean a Thomist approach to dealing with cooperation with evil. Throughout the Middle Ages, theologians debated the question of whether one may commit or counsel a lesser evil. The principle at work concerned whether, when confronted with a challenging moral choice, it could be possible without sin to choose to commit—or to counsel another to commit—the lesser of two evils.[88] For example, throughout the medieval period theologians asked if one could counsel a thief to steal from the rich instead of the poor to limit the damage done by his thievery. In a similar vein, theologians asked if one could instruct a sexual philanderer to limit his acts of fornication to only a single partner. These moral quandaries have particular application to the analysis of questions of moral cooperation with evil. Often moralists will claim that counseling or cooperating in a lesser evil can be done without fault precisely because it is the lesser evil than might otherwise be done. The teaching of Capreolus suggests that the Thomist tradition again has something to offer which other accounts of the matter have neglected.

In his *Moral Dilemmas in Medieval Thought: From Gratian to Aquinas*, M. V. Dougherty explains that Capreolus resolved this dilemma by refusing to accept its premises.[89] Dougherty opines: "Capreolus considers the principle of the lesser of two evils to be unnecessary for resolving moral dilemmas, at least insofar as he appears to endorse Aquinas's view that there are no situations of absolute perplexity."[90] He identifies the key moment of Capreolus's teaching: "concerning two such evils neither is to be chosen; because each of them is evil, and as a consequence neither the more evil nor the less evil

---

The Spirituality of Martyrdom: to the Limits of Love, trans. Patrick M. Clark and Annie Hounsokou (Washington, DC: The Catholic University of America Press, 2016).

88. For an extended treatment on the related issue of the principle of the lesser of evils, see Kevin L. Flannery, SJ, "Counseling the Lesser Evil," *The Thomist* 75 (2011): 245–89. For a more in-depth treatment, especially with reference to the views of twentieth-century proponents of proportionalism, see Robert C. Morlino, *The Principle of the Lesser of Evils in Today's Conflict Situations: New Challenges to Moral Theology from a Pluralistic Society* (Rome: Pontifical Gregorian University, 1990).

89. M. V. Dougherty, *Moral Dilemmas in Medieval Thought: From Gratian to Aquinas* (Cambridge: Cambridge University Press, 2011), 190.

90. Dougherty, *Moral Dilemmas in Medieval Thought*, 109.

is to be chosen."[91] Many moralists, especially of the proportionalist school, resort to calculations of costs and benefits in moral quandaries where obvious solutions may not be apparent. Capreolus helps us to understand, however, that there do not exist situations in which one is left no choice but to sin. One does not get stuck in the moral life unable to do anything but sin. Instead, no one should ever elect to sin. There are some actions which are never worthy of moral choice. In the manifold questions surrounding cooperation with evil, it will become necessary to recall frequently this salutary reminder of the Prince of the Thomists, Jean Capreolus.

Cajetan (d. 1534)

Giacomo de Vio was born in February 1468 in the coastal town of Gaeta halfway between Rome and Naples.[92] At the age of fifteen, he entered the Dominican order, taking the name Thomas in religion. Thomas de Vio Cajetan completed his studies in both Naples and Bologna before entering the theology faculty at the University of Padua in 1493. He produced commentaries on both the *Sentences* of Peter Lombard and the *Summa theologiae* of St. Thomas Aquinas. His *The Analogy of Names* composed in 1498 remains to the present day a standard—even if highly controversial—point of reference for discussions about analogy.[93] Cajetan's writ-

---

91. Jean Capreolus, *Defensiones* IV, 437, trans. M. V. Dougherty, in his *Moral Dilemmas in Medieval Thought*, 186: "De talibus duobus malis neutrum est eligendum; qui utrumque est malum, et per consequens nec plus nec minus eligendum." For an excellent treatment of why no situation exists when one must sin, see Serge-Thomas Bonino, OP, "St. Thomas Aquinas in the Apostolic Exhortation *Amoris Laetitia*," *The Thomist* 80 (2016): 499–519, especially 509–13.

92. For an extended biography, see the volume edited and translated by Jared Wicks, SJ, *Cajetan Responds: A Reader in Reformation Controversy* (Washington, DC: The Catholic University of America Press, 1978), 3–46.

93. Cajetan's teaching on the central place of the analogy of proper proportionality in the works of St. Thomas Aquinas remains much disputed. For an alternative view, see Ralph M. McInerny, *Aquinas and Analogy* (Washington, DC: The Catholic University of America Press, 1996). In another book McInerny returned to his treatment of Cajetan, but this time defended him on the question of the distinction between nature and grace. See McInerny's *Praeambula Fidei: Thomism and the God of the Philosophers* (Washington, DC: The Catholic University of America Press, 2006). For at least a partial defense of Cajetan on analogy, see Joshua P. Hochshield, *The Semantics of Analogy: Rereading Cajetan's De Nominum Analogia*, (Notre Dame: University of Notre Dame Press, 2010); and Steven A. Long, *Analogia Entis: On the Analogy of Being, Metaphysics, and the Act of Faith* (Notre Dame, IN: University of Notre Dame Press, 2011).

ings are likewise recalled for his clear distinction between the natural and supernatural orders. Theological discourse regarding his teaching on the topic remains highly controverted today.[94] In each of his works, Cajetan defended and expounded upon the teaching of his great Dominican master St. Thomas Aquinas.

Cajetan's labors included both service to his Dominican order and to the universal Church. In 1508, Thomas de Vio was elected the thirty-ninth Master of the Order of Friars Preachers. In this role, he is remembered as a reformer of Dominican life stabilizing the order after a period of internal challenge in the late fifteenth century. Cajetan provided clarity during the upheavals following the disputed Council of Pisa (1409) which had advanced the position of conciliarism elevating the authority of an ecumenical council over that of the Roman Pontiff. This issue received definite resolution at the Fifth Lateran Council with the decree *Pastor Aeternus* (1516).[95] This conciliar decree affirmed Cajetan's teaching regarding the unique role of the Roman Pontiff. In recognition of his service to the universal Church, Thomas de Vio was created Cardinal of the holy Roman Church by Pope Leo X in 1517. During this period, Cajetan completed his extensive commentary on the *secunda pars* of the *Summa theologiae*. Passages from this section of the *Summa* prove useful to establish a virtue-based approach to addressing moral cooperation with evil.

In the twenty-first century Cardinal Cajetan is often recalled for his famous confrontation with Martin Luther. In 1518, as delegate of Pope Leo X, Cardinal Cajetan answered the claims of Luther regarding indulgences and other matters about which the German monk had departed from Catholic doctrine.[96] In October of 1517 Luther had proposed his ninety-five theses objecting both to aspects of Catholic doctrine and pastoral practice. Throughout his active labors for the good of the universal Church, Cajetan continued work on his commentary on the *Summa* of

94. For a defense of Cajetan's position regarding the relationship between the natural and supernatural orders, see Lawrence Feingold, *The Natural Desire to See God in St. Thomas Aquinas and His Interpreters* (Naples, FL: Sapientia Press, 2010). For an impressive collection of essays about this lively debate, see *Surnaturel: A Controversy at the Heart of Twentieth-Century Thomistic Thought*, ed. Serge-Thomas Bonino, OP, trans. Robert Williams, trans. revised by Matthew Levering (Naples, FL: Sapientia Press, 2009).

95. See DS 1445, from the Bull *Pastor Aeternus gregem*, Lateran Council V, (Session XI), December 19, 1516.

96. For a more complete account of this meeting, see Jared Wicks, SJ, ed. and trans., *Cajetan Responds: A Reader in Reformation Controversy*, 14–29; and Mandonnet, *Dictionnaire*, 1316–18.

St. Thomas. These commentaries received papal approbation during the Leonine revival of the study of Aquinas. In light of his 1879 encyclical *Aeterni Patris*, which initiated a renewal of the study of St. Thomas, Pope Leo XIII ordered the commentaries of Cajetan to be published alongside the texts of the *Summa*.

Two areas of Cajetan's commentary on the *Summa theologiae* offer salutary guidance to develop a virtue-based method of analysis for questions of cooperation with evil. Cajetan's commentary on question fifty-eight, article five of the *prima-secundae* regarding the relationship of prudence to the moral virtues, as well as his commentary on question seventy-eight, article four of the *secunda-secundae* dealing with usury are relevant for our project. In question fifty-eight of the *prima-secundae*, St. Thomas discusses the difference between the intellectual and moral virtues. After his explanation that there exist virtues that are rightly called intellectual virtues (article one) and then that they differ from moral virtues (article two), Aquinas teaches that virtue can be divided adequately between the two (article three).[97] In article four of question fifty-eight he explains that no one can possess moral virtue without also possessing intellectual virtue. In article five, St. Thomas expounds upon the true nature of prudence when he asks whether there can be intellectual without moral virtue. Aquinas asks if one can truly possess prudence without at the same time possessing the moral virtues of justice, fortitude, and temperance.

In his commentary on this article, Cardinal Cajetan sheds light on the matter. He explains: "Aristotle, St. Thomas, and their followers, understand by the name prudence right reason about action accomplished and sustained through rectified appetite of a particular end.... Therefore prudence is not a *habitus* in reason alone.... therefore prudence depends on appetite."[98] A properly functioning prudence requires rightly ordered appetites. Many believe that theoretical knowledge about a subject will ensure sound moral judgment. On the contrary, Cajetan teaches: "The act proper to prudence is to make a good command about things to be done. Therefore, prudence depends on rectified appetite."[99]

Much like Capreolus's defense of Aquinas in the fifteenth century, here

---

97. For discussion of the distinction between intellectual and moral virtue, see Gregory M. Reichberg, "The Intellectual Virtues (Ia IIae, qq. 57–58)," in *The Ethics of Aquinas*, ed. Stephen J. Pope, 131–50 (Washington, DC: Georgetown University Press, 2002).

98. *Sancti Thomae de Aquino Opera omnia*, vol. 6, Leonine edition (Rome, 1882), 377.

99. *Sancti Thomae de Aquino Opera omnia*, 6:377.

Cajetan argues for the position of St. Thomas. Unlike John Duns Scotus, Aquinas held that prudence depends upon rectified appetite. As will become clear in the second chapter of the present work, authors of the casuist period often adopted a Scotist view of prudence and its diminished place in the moral life. When the intellect and will are separated such that they are understood to act independently, one can imagine a functioning prudence without rectified appetite.[100] As Thomas Osborne observes, "For Scotus, the intellect functions well even if the agent chooses poorly."[101] For Aquinas, on the other hand, prudence can be corrupted by vicious habits. As Cajetan explains, "therefore an inclination of appetite [can] corrupt the judgment of prudence."[102] When analyzing questions of cooperation, many are tempted to create ready-made categories into which various forms of activity will fit neatly. Moralists should give increased attention to appetite formation to ensure that human agents will enact a sound moral choice. That is to say, the emphasis on theoretical categorization of instances of cooperation so common in the casuist period, relies upon an insufficient view of the place of human appetite in the moral life. The Scotist error underappreciating the role of rectified appetite fails to provide the counsel necessary for sound judgments in this area. A Thomistic virtue-based approach to these questions, on the other hand, will rely heavily on how appetites and desires can be properly shaped according to Christian teaching and the truth about the human person.[103]

The second passage from Cajetan's commentary useful for determining a Thomist approach to evaluating moral cooperation with evil comes from his treatment of usury. As we saw above, both St. Thomas and Cajetan permit borrowing from one known to practice usury. Aquinas dis-

100. For a more complete treatment of the deep interconnection between intellect and will, see Michael S. Sherwin, OP, *By Knowledge and by Love: Charity and Knowledge in the Moral Theology of St. Thomas Aquinas* (Washington, DC: The Catholic University of America Press, 2011). Against those who argue for a dramatic shift in the thought of Aquinas on this relationship between intellect and will, see Daniel Westberg, "Did Aquinas Change His Mind about the Will?" *The Thomist* 58 (1994): 41–60.

101. For a more complete treatment of the Scotus's understanding of prudence, see Thomas M. Osborne, Jr., *Human Action in Thomas Aquinas, John Duns Scotus, and William of Ockham*, 80–90.

102. *Sancti Thomae de Aquino Opera omnia*, 6:379. "Ideo appetitus affectio corrumpit aestimationem prudentiae." Unpublished translation by William E. May.

103. For a sound treatment of how the natural inclinations to the good shape the moral life, see Servais Pinckaers, OP, *The Sources of Christian Ethics*, 400–56.

tinguishes between inducing another to sin, which remains unlawful, and making use of the sin of another. Aquinas teaches:

It is by no means lawful to induce a man to lend under a condition of usury: yet it is lawful to borrow for usury from a man who is ready to do so and is a usurer by profession; provided the borrower have a good end in view, such as the relief of his own or another's need. Thus too it is lawful for a man who has fallen among thieves to point out his property to them (which they sin in taking) in order to save his life, after the example of the ten men who said to Ishmael (Jeremiah 41:8): 'Kill us not: for we have stores in the field.'[104]

Cajetan follows Aquinas by observing a relation between borrowing from a usurer and the story recounted in the book of the prophet Jeremiah. There we learn of ten men who point out their hidden treasures to avoid being killed. The commonsense conclusion that one may identify his property to a thief in order that he not be killed finds scriptural warrant here.

Both Aquinas and Cajetan recognize that one need not describe this action as material cooperation in the sin of theft. Instead, it is rightly identified as the act of pointing out one's property. Only the thief bears guilt for using that action for his evil end of thievery. Cajetan explains: "to use the sin of another for one's own good or that of another is not a sin."[105] Making use of the sin of another—in this case, utilizing the malefactor's commitment to theft—for the purpose of avoiding being killed should not be considered sinful.[106] The person who points out his own property does not, strictly speaking, induce another to sin. Rather, such a person acts in a way that has its own intelligibility apart from sin. Saying "those are my treasures in the field" to one already committed to stealing them does not induce the sin. Instead, it utilizes the sin for a noble purpose, namely, saving one's life.

In his 1949 *Gregorianum* article regarding counseling the lesser of two evils, Edward Hannigan observes that for Cajetan one may provide the material for a sin but cannot induce a sin, even to avoid a greater sin.[107]

104. *Summa theologiae* IIa–IIae, q. 78, a. 4.

105. The commentary of Thomas de Vio Cardinal Cajetan can be found in the Leonine edition of the *Summa theologiae*, Tome 9, 166: "Quod quia uti peccato alterius bonum suum vel alterius non est peccatum."

106. For one treatment of the distinction between cooperation in an evil act and making use of the effects of an already committed evil, see M. Cathleen Kaveny, "Appropriation of Evil: Cooperation's Mirror Image" *Theological Studies* 61 (2000): 280–313.

107. E. T. Hannigan, SJ, "Is it ever lawful to advise the lesser of two evils?" *Gregorianum* 30 (1949): 106.

Likewise, Kevin Flannery explains that Cajetan utilizes the distinction between "offering the material of sin as opposed to inducing to sin."[108] Cajetan's concern, like others in the Thomist tradition, remains the precise nature of the act to be accomplished. He eschews both consequentialist and intentionalist explanations of human action. Rather, the eminent Cardinal rightly attends to the particular action at hand. A retrieval of such a rigorous analysis of the moral object—such as pursued by Cardinal Cajetan—will play a crucial role in a virtue-based approach to moral cooperation with evil.

John of St. Thomas (d. 1644)

Acclaimed in his day as a "second Thomas," Jean Poinsot is widely considered the greatest Thomistic commentator of the modern period.[109] The son of pious and noble parents, Poinsot was born in Lisbon in July 1589. His father from Vienna and mother from Portugal ensured their son received a sound education in the humanities. While pursuing further studies at Louvain, Poinsot encountered the famed Dominican master Thomas de Torres, who would later become bishop of Tucuman in northern Argentina. Through de Torres, Poinsot met the order of St. Dominic and at the age of twenty-three, entered the Dominican convent of Our Lady of Atocha at Madrid in 1612. His name in religion was John of St. Thomas.[110]

John of St. Thomas worked for several decades as professor of theology at the University of Alcalá in Spain. His duties extended beyond university teaching as he served as confessor for Philip IV during the tumultuous times for the Spanish empire of the Thirty Years War. His two principal works include his *Cursus philosophicus* covering logic and natural theology and his *Cursus theologicus*, an extended commentary on the *Summa theologiae* of St. Thomas Aquinas. In many respects he is most remembered today for his shorter tract on the gifts of the Holy Spirit. In his classic account of the gifts in the *Dictionnaire de Spiritualité*, the Toulouse Dominican

---

108. Kevin L. Flannery, SJ, "Counseling the Lesser Evil," *The Thomist* 75 (2011): 255.

109. See Dominic Hughes, OP, and Mark Egan, OP, from their Introduction to John of St. Thomas's, *The Gifts of the Holy Ghost*, trans. Dominic Hughes, OP, (New York: Sheed & Ward, 1951), 5.

110. For a full biography and list of publications, see J.M. Ramirez, "Jean de Saint-Thomas," *Dictionnaire de théologie catholique* (Paris: Letouzey et Ane, 1947), 803–8. See also the introduction of Dominic Hughes, OP, and Mark Egan, OP, to John of St. Thomas, *The Gifts of the Holy Ghost*, 3–13.

Michel Labourdette explains that the doctrine of the gifts became more or less fixed with the writings of John of St. Thomas.[111]

By remaining faithful to the doctrine of Aquinas, John of St. Thomas was able to elucidate the teaching of the Angelic Doctor on the gifts of the Holy Spirit. Aquinas attempted to situate the gifts alongside his instruction on the virtues in his commentary on the *Sentences* of Peter Lombard, as well as in both the *prima-secundae* and *secunda-secundae* of the *Summa theologiae*.[112] Aquinas did not offer a definite resolution, however, to the challenging question of precisely what role each of the gifts plays in the life of the believer. This issue receives a full treatment in the work of John of St. Thomas. Attention to the role of the gifts of the Holy Spirit will prove indispensable for formulating an approach to questions of cooperation with evil. No textbook could account for the multifarious forms of questionable collaboration that confront contemporary believers. Only those open to the grace of the Holy Spirit—the genuine *instinctus* for Christian living offered in the gifts—will be moved to act in accord with the Gospel. Only the gifts of the Holy Spirit can account for the diversity of authentically Christian approaches to challenging issues of moral cooperation. Put simply, only the gifts of the Holy Spirit account for the actions of the saints.

Pinckaers explains that those who eschew the role of the gifts, whether aspects of the Franciscan tradition in the Middle Ages or others in the modern period, fall quickly into a morality of commandments and obligations.[113] Authors who remove the gifts from their moral paradigm tend

---

111. See M.-Michel Labourdette, *Dictionnaire de Spiritualité Ascétique et Mystique* (Paris: Beauchesne, 1957), 1603–35.

112. For a rich treatment of the gifts of the Holy Spirit, especially on the evolution of the teaching of Aquinas, see Edwin D. O'Connor, C.S.C., *The Gifts of the Holy Spirit*, vol. 24 of the Blackfriars *Summa* (New York: McGraw-Hill Book Company, 1974), especially appendix 4, 110–30. For a helpful resource on how each gift functions, see Marie-Eugene, O.C.D., *I Want to See God: A Practical Synthesis of Carmelite Spirituality*, trans. Sister M. Verda Clare, C.S.C. (Westminster, MD: Christian Classics, Inc. 1978), especially 345–50. For a general treatment on the role of the gifts, see Steven A. Long, "The Gifts of the Holy Spirit and Their Indispensibility for the Christian Life: Grace as Motus," *Nova et Vetera*, English edition, 11 (2013): 357–73.

113. Servais Pinckaers, OP, "Capreolus's Defense of Aquinas: A Medieval Dispute about Virtues and Gifts," in *The Pinckaers Reader: Renewing Thomistic Moral Theology*, 317. Pinckaers maintains: "In the thought of Duns Scotus, there is no need to consider the gifts, any more than the beatitudes or the fruits of the Holy Spirit, as *habitus* distinct from the virtues.... These suffice, if brought to perfection. It is not necessary to add other *habitus*."

to focus predominantly on charity. Pinckaers observes: "For Scotus everything leads to charity, since virtue is centered in the will."[114] In such an outlook, virtue must be situated entirely in the will due to the absence of the related *habitus* of infused moral virtue and the gifts of the Holy Spirit. Without attention to the place of the gifts in the moral life, believers struggle to analyze and execute sound moral action when dealing with situations of possible cooperation with evil.

In the *secunda-secundae* on the *Summa theologiae*, Aquinas offered only four articles on the gift of counsel (*ST* IIa-IIae, q. 52). While St. Thomas provides the foundation for understanding the place of this gift in the sanctified believer, questions, nonetheless, remain regarding the intricacies of its activity. St. Thomas teaches: "The gift of counsel is befitting the children of God in so far as the reason is instructed by the Holy Ghost about what we have to do."[115] In article two of the same question, Aquinas teaches that counsel corresponds to the virtue of prudence. He does not offer a full account, however, of the precise way in which acquired and infused prudence and the gift of counsel relate to one another. To address that challenging matter, the work of John of St. Thomas will prove useful.

Christians in seventeenth-century Europe experienced new and complex moral quandaries. One recalls the magisterial instructions of Popes Alexander VII (1665–1666) and Innocent XI (1679) against the laxism taught in moral matters at that time.[116] For instruction on dealing with difficult moral issues, the Dominican commentator John of St. Thomas turned instead to the gifts of the Holy Spirit. Specifically, he offers instruction on the gift of counsel, especially useful for our inquiry into moral cooperation with evil.[117] John of St. Thomas explains: "For counsel directs actions not precisely as known by reason or by faith or prophecy (such direction can be found in sinners), but from love and an internal experience of divine things."[118] Unlike the obligation-based moral systems of the casuist period, the teaching of John of St. Thomas emphasizes the

---

114. Pinckaers, OP, "Capreolus's Defense of Aquinas," 317.

115. *Summa theologiae* IIa–IIae, q. 52, a. 1, ad. 3.

116. See DS 2021–65 for the condemnations of Alexander VII; and DS 2101–67 for the condemnations of Innocent XI.

117. For an extensive treatment of John of St. Thomas's teaching on the gift of counsel, see Romanus Cessario, "John Poinsot: On the Gift of Counsel," in *The Common Things: Essays on Thomism and Education*, ed. Daniel McInerny, 163–78, (Mishawaka: American Maritain Association, 1999).

118. See John of St. Thomas, *The Gifts of the Holy Ghost*, 159.

place of the sensible appetites. He stresses knowledge by connaturality—an affection for the good—which proves decisive in sound moral acting in difficult matters. John of St. Thomas clarifies that the gift of counsel "is not subject to the virtue of prudence, inferior to it, or to be resolved by it." Instead, counsel moves believers "toward a determination of whether a given impulse is from God."[119]

This excursus on the gift of counsel confirms the typical advice those who pastor souls proffer when perplexed believers seek specific answers to what types of cooperation are possible in today's world. Attention to the gifts of the Holy Spirit confirms the exhortation to pray always. The admonition to pray and draw near to the Lord does not mean that God will necessarily reveal a precise roadmap of what concretely must be done. Instead, in especially difficult moments, Christians must rely on knowledge by connaturality of the goods of Christian life.[120] The gift of counsel both confirms in them the knowledge of what must be done and strengthens them to do it. Romanus Cessario explains:

Moreover, since even virtuous counsel naturally follows the measure of human reasoning, the soul's journey to God requires a special guidance from the Holy Spirit. This guidance, however, does not amount to the bestowal of new information, as if a gift of the Holy Spirit supplies the believer with personal revelations. Rather, counsel works by connaturality; that is, it develops out of a familiarity with divine things that grace gives to the human person.[121]

The work of John of St. Thomas offers clarity to challenging questions of how the virtues relate to the gifts of the Holy Spirit. His attention to these matters provides a salutary reminder of the place of the gifts in the moral life. Analyzing cooperation with evil from a virtue-based perspective will require similar attention to these unique helps offered in the Christian life.

The casuist turn amidst modern complexities

The history of theological analysis of moral cooperation with evil suffers from an unfortunate irony. While moralists did not offer a compre-

---

119. John of St. Thomas, 168.

120. See *VS*, no. 64.

121. Romanus Cessario, OP, *The Virtues, or the Examined Life* (New York: The Continuum International Publishing Group Inc., 2002), 124.

hensive treatment of cooperation until the modern period, the resources useful for a proper analysis are present in Aquinas's works composed in the medieval era. Just as the question of moral cooperation took on new life in the seventeenth century, the moral theologians of the period eschewed the method of St. Thomas and his authentic commentators. Cooperation with evil took on prominence as a subject of moral discourse just as the casuist system began to flourish. For that reason, moral theologians have given limited attention to the method of St. Thomas as applied to these disputed questions. In the section which follows we treat the work of two thinkers who addressed issues of cooperation in the early modern period. Both the Jesuit Thomas Sanchez and the Redemptorist founder St. Alphonsus Liguori made decisive contributions to the topic. The manner in which they address cooperation, however, represents something of a departure from the moral reasoning of Aquinas.

Thomas Sanchez

Historians mark a watershed moment in the history of the analysis of moral cooperation with the condemnations of Pope Innocent XI in 1679.[122] In that year the Pope condemned sixty-five propositions in large part for their moral laxity. Among them one finds a proposition concerning the possibility of cooperation with evil. The condemned proposition reads:

A servant who knowingly by offering his shoulders assists his master to ascend through windows to ravage a virgin, and many times serves the same by carrying a ladder, by opening a door, or by cooperating in something similar, does not commit a mortal sin, if he does this through fear of considerable damage, for example, lest he be treated wickedly by his master, lest he be looked upon with savage eyes, or, lest he be expelled from the house.[123]

The condemnation of this proposition began a series of studies of moral cooperation, among which the most notable remains that of St. Alphonsus

122. See, for example, Andrew McLean Cummings, *The Servant and the Ladder*, 3–6.
123. "Famulus, qui submissis humeris scienter adiuvat herum suum ascendere ad fenestras ad stuprandam virginem, et multoties eidem subservit deferendo scalam, aperiendo ianum aut quid simile cooperando, non peccat mortaliter, si id faciat metu notabilis detrimenti, puta ne a domino male tractetur, ne torvis oculis aspiciatur, ne domo expellatur." (Denzinger, Latin 2151 no. 51/English 1201, no. 51).

Liguori (1696–1787).[124] St. Alphonsus's work became the standard point of reference for these questions, and twentieth-century moralists largely based their own treatments upon his conclusions.[125] Analysis of this case of the servant's would-be cooperation with his master's sin formed the basis for much discussion regarding cooperation more generally. Debate ensued about precisely why the Pope had condemned the servant's action. Some argued it was because this type of cooperation could never be justified, while others maintained that the servant did not have a sufficient reason for offering his assistance. The view of St. Alphonsus held the fundamental position in these debates.

St. Alphonsus Liguori, whose *Theologia moralis* was first published in 1753, relied heavily on the work of the Spanish Jesuit Thomas Sanchez (1550–1610). Understanding Liguori's position on the matter requires attention to the work of Sanchez who preceded him. After entering the Society of Jesus in 1567, Sanchez taught moral theology and canon law. He became well-known for his three-volume treatise on the Sacrament of Marriage. That work remains a standard reference for moralists and canon lawyers to the present day.[126] Sanchez himself did not escape papal condemnation when Pope Innocent XI rejected his teaching on mental reservation regarding the sin of lying. For our purposes, Sanchez authored an important moral treatise which included attention to moral cooperation with evil. His *Opus morale in Praecepta Decalogi* was not published until 1613, three years after his death. In his treatise on moral theology Sanchez expounds on cooperation, treating it in relation to the sin of scandal, about which St. Thomas speaks directly (*ST* IIa-IIae, q. 43). Sanchez does not

124. The classic account of this history is given by Roger Roy, CSsR, "La coopération selon Saint Alphonse de Liguori," *Studia Moralia* 6 (1968). For a more in-depth treatment, see P. Mandonnet, OP, *Le Decret D'Innocent XI Contre Le Probabilisme* (Paris: Bureaux de la *Revue Thomiste*, 1903). For a more recent treatment of the controversy, see Fabrice Bouthillon, "Le diable, probablement: Le P. Mandonnet, les Jésuites et le probabilisme (1901–1903)" in *Saint Thomas au XXᵉ siècle: Actes du colloque du Centenaire de la "Revue thomiste*, ed. Serge-Thomas Bonino, 53–76 (Toulouse: Éditions Saint-Paul, 1994).

125. For this history I am indebted to the work of Andrew McLean Cummings. His *The Servant and the Ladder: Cooperation with Evil in the Twenty-First Century* provides both comprehensive historical treatment as well as careful exposition of the theological underpinnings of this history.

126. For a more complete treatment of the place of Thomas Sanchez in the history of Catholic theology—and especially his treatise on the Sacrament of Marriage—see R. Brouillard, "Sanchez," in the *Dictionnaire de théologie catholique* (Paris: Letouzey et Ane, 1932), 1075–85.

utilize the distinction of formal and material cooperation. Only in the eighteenth century will St. Alphonsus Liguori introduce this distinction as the central category of inquiry into moral cooperation with evil.[127]

In the Redemptorist Roger Roy's classic treatment of the origins of the position of St. Alphonsus on moral cooperation with evil, he highlights the role of Sanchez in Liguori's development. Roy explains that Sanchez affirms that "all cooperation is culpable participation in the fault of another."[128] For Sanchez, there really is no cooperation at all unless the cooperator participates (in a culpable way) in the act of the evil agent.[129] Roy summarizes Sanchez's description of direct cooperation. It requires: "[M]oral participation in the fault of another, participation through an intrinsically evil act, or by the form of the same act of sin, finally by participation through an indifferent act with the will favoring the sin of the other."[130] Already in this early modern discussion of cooperation the difficulty emerged of reliance on the category of indifferent acts. Reliance on the category of indifferent acts places one outside the moral teaching of St. Thomas. Aquinas held that all free and knowing acts were human acts and therefore moral acts.[131] St. Thomas teaches: "Consequently every human action that proceeds from deliberate reason, if it be considered in the individual, must be good or bad."[132] These acts may also be subject to some other analysis, i.e., a given act could be more or less skillful or more or less beautiful. For St. Thomas, while the generic species of an act may be morally indifferent, in an individual instance, there exist no morally

127. See Roy, CSsR, "La coopération selon Saint Alphonse de Liguori," 411. He explains: "ce qui l'amène à bâtir une définition de la coopération matérielle et formelle et à préciser ce qu'il entend, en matiére de coopération, par un acte de soi indifférent et par un acte intrinsèquement mauvais."

128. Roy, CSsR, 390: "tout coopération est une participation coupable à la faute du prochain."

129. For a more in-depth treatment of this history, see Joseph Parkinson's *Material Cooperation and Catholic Institutions* (doctoral dissertation, College of Theology, University of Notre Dame Australia, 2001), 13–17.

130. Roy, CSsR, "La coopération selon Saint Alphonse de Liguori," 390: "la participation morale à la faulte d'autrui, la participation par un office intrinsèquement mauvais, ou bien par la position de l'acte même du péché, enfin la participation par un acte indifférent avec la volonté de favoriser le péché du prochain."

131. See *Summa theologiae* Ia–IIae, q. 1, a. 1. See also Ralph McInery, *Aquinas on Human Action: A Theory of Practice* (Washington, DC: The Catholic University of America Press, 1992), 3–9; and, by the same author, *Ethica Thomistica: The Moral Philosophy of Thomas Aquinas*, rev. ed. (Washington, DC: The Catholic University of America Press, 1997), 60–69.

132. See *Summa theologiae* Ia–IIae, q. 18, a. 9.

indifferent acts.[133] In both Sanchez and St. Alphonsus, however, we encounter a description of individual indifferent acts.[134]

In examining species of acts, Sanchez refers to some acts as "intrinsically evil." An intrinsically evil act is one which can never become good by means of a good intention. Sanchez does offer a caveat, however. There may be an excusing reason which would allow one to perform an intrinsically evil act, or, more precisely, a situation which would alter the object of an otherwise intrinsically evil act. Andrew McLean Cummings identifies the passage most difficult to reconcile with future magisterial pronouncements: "And the reason is that such acts are so proximately connected to sin and are ordered to it as that they are worthy to be called evil *ex se*, unless they are excused for some urgent reason."[135] Here, Sanchez outlines what would become known as "virtually intrinsically evil," since almost no circumstance could justify such an act. Still, the strength of the argument for the existence of intrinsically evil acts is seriously undermined when theologians assert that proportionate reason—even if rarely invoked—can justify an evil action. Today, no Catholic theologian can hold that this position might be reconciled with the instructions presented by the Church's Magisterium.[136] Regarding the case of the servant and

133. See St. Thomas Aquinas, *De Malo*, q. 2, a. 5: "But if we speak about the moral act as an individual act, in this way every particular moral act is necessarily good or bad by reason of some circumstance. For no singular act can be performed without circumstances which make it right or wrong."

134. For a useful primer on St. Thomas's teaching that no act is indifferent in an individual instance, see McInerny, *Ethica Thomistica*, 83–84. For a helpful discussion of Aquinas's teaching that human acts are "susceptible" to being either good or bad (and therefore not indifferent in any given case), see Kevin L. Flannery, SJ, *Cooperation with Evil: Thomistic Tools of Analysis*, 83–90, and, in particular, on page 88 where he explains: "Because a human act is a human act only in as much as it exists within this context of particular circumstances (relations within the larger context of justice and charity), every particular human act is susceptible—as Thomas says in *Sent*. 2.40.I.5.—of moral goodness and badness. There are no indifferent acts."

135. Sanchez, *Opus morale in praecepta decalogi* (Paris: Apud Michaelem Sonnium, 1615), lib. I, VII, n. 16: "Et ratio est, quia tales actiones ita proxime peccato accedunt, ad illudque ordinantur ut ex se malae dici merito quaeant, nisi causa aliqua urgenti excusentur," trans. Andrew McLean Cummings, *The Servant and the Ladder*, 37. Roger Roy makes the same point. Sanchez argues that an excusing reason must be proportionate to the gravity of the fault and the proximity of the participation. See Roy, CSsR, "La coopération selon Saint Alphonse de Liguori," 391: "La raison excusante doit être proportionnée à la gravité de la faute, proportionée aussi à la proximité de la participation."

136. See, for example, *VS*, no. 81: "Consequently, circumstances or intentions can never

the ladder, Sanchez's position on excusing reasons which justify other-wise intrinsically evil acts proved influential. Reference to proportion-ate reason or justifying reasons which excuse from the moral law repre-sents another moral universe from that of St. Thomas. St. Alphonsus will rely heavily on the work of Sanchez when he begins his moral treatise on cooperation with evil.[137] While he can be credited with an advancement from the teaching of Sanchez, the starting point would be within the modern framework. The world of Aquinas and his authentic commenta-tors would unfortunately not be the place of departure for modern evalu-ations of moral cooperation with evil.

St. Alphonsus Liguori

Born to a noble Neapolitan family in 1696, Alphonsus Liguori stud-ied both civil and canon law before discovering the grace of a priestly vocation.[138] After his ordination in 1726, Liguori grew concerned that many persons, especially the poor and those in rural communities, lacked sound pastoral care. In response to this challenge, he founded the Con-gregation of the Most Holy Redeemer, commonly known as the Redemp-torists. These Redemptorist fathers became known for preaching mis-sions and offering pastoral care to those, especially in rural communities, who would otherwise labor without it. Committed as they were to the practice of the Sacrament of Penance, the training of adequate confes-sors would stand as a high priority for the Congregation and its founder. Thus, St. Alphonsus set to work on a moral manual for confessors.[139]

---

transform an act intrinsically evil by virtue of its object into an act 'subjectively' good or defensible as a choice."

137. Roy, CSsR, "La coopération selon Saint Alphonse de Liguori," 378. Roy ex-plains: "Il est le plus ancient des moralists casuists que s. Alphonse dexploite dans le traité de la coopération et c'est par une référence à Sanchez que le Saint commence son proper commentaire."

138. For an extended biography of St. Alphonsus, see Frederick M. Jones, CSsR, *Alphonsus de Liguori: The Saint of Bourbon Naples 1696–1787* (Dublin: Gill and MacMillan, 1992).

139. For further treatment on the theology of St. Alphonsus, see Guiseppe Angeli-ni and Ambrogio Valsecchi, *Disegno storico della teologia morale* (Bologna: Dehoniane, 1972), 120–23. For a near exhaustive bibliography of recent secondary literature on the theolo-gy of St. Alphonsus, see Kent Lasnoski, "Alphonsus Liguori's Moral Theology of Mar-riage: Refreshing Realism, Continued Relevance," *Nova et Vetera*, English edition, 9 (2011): 1003–4.

In 1748 Alphonsus Liguori published the first edition of his moral manual. This text served as a commentary on the moral theology of Hermann Busenbaum (1600–1668).[140] Busenbaum, a German Jesuit, served as confessor to the prince-bishop of Munster, Bernard-Christophe de Galen.[141] He also authored one of the most significant and commented upon moral manuals in the casuist period. His *Medulla theologiae moralis* was first published in 1645. Due to its relative brevity and practical scope, the Busenbaum manual had broad appeal for confessors and seminary instructors. The volume was not without its critics, however. The condemnations of both Pope Alexander VII and Pope Innocent XI were widely considered to include certain views of Busenbaum, specifically regarding his treatment of the morality of tyrannicide.[142]

In his commentary on Busenbaum's moral manual, St. Alphonsus followed the more rigorous reading of the famed case of the servant and the ladder. At this time, Alphonsus held that the servant's action was intrinsically evil. He believed that the Pope condemned the servant's action because his offer of assistance to his master in this fashion was the type of act that could never be justified. In later editions of his moral manual, however, St. Alphonsus abandoned this interpretation and instead held that the servant's action could not be justified because he lacked a sufficient motive for acting in such a manner.[143] St. Alphonsus's later work, and the tradition following him, held that the servant's action was best classified as unjustified material cooperation. While the servant's action

140. See Lucius I. Ugorji, *The Principle of Double Effect: A Critical Appraisal of its Traditional Understanding and its Modern Reinterpretation* (Frankfurt: Peter Lang, 1993), 96. For more information on the influence of Busenbaum on later moral manuals, see Paul E. McKeever, "Seventy-Five Years of Moral Theology in America," *The Historical Development of Fundamental Moral Theology in the United States*, ed. Charles E. Curran and Richard A. McCormick, SJ, (Mahwah, NJ: Paulist Press, 1999), 7.

141. For a more complete biography, see Jos. Brucker, "Busenbaum," in the *Dictionnaire de théologie catholique*, (Paris: Letouzey et Ane, 1932), 1265–68. Brucker's article is noteworthy for his defense of Busenbaum against the charge of his moral laxism on the question of tyrannicide.

142. For a further treatment of St. Alphonsus's decision to use the Busenbaum manual, see Jones, CSsR, *Alphonsus de Liguori*, 207–8.

143. For an extended treatment of the change in the thought of St. Alphonsus, see Andrew McLean Cummings, *The Servant and the Ladder*, 66; Ugorji, *The Principle of Double Effect*, 96; and Roy, CSsR, "La coopération selon Saint Alphonse de Liguori," 420–23. For Alphonsus's teaching on conscience and its reliance on the work of Busembaum, see Louis Vereecke, CSsR, "La Conscience selon Saint Alphonse de Liguori," *Studia Moralia* 21 (1983): 259–73.

was not intrinsically evil, Liguori argued, his holding the ladder could not be justified since he lacked a sufficient reason for acting in the manner he did.

St. Alphonsus altered his position on the case of the servant and the ladder in part to make clear the difference between cooperation and the related sin of scandal. As explained above, St. Thomas had treated scandal directly in the *secunda-secundae* in his treatise on charity. Aquinas defined scandal as "something less rightly done or said that occasions another's spiritual downfall."[144] It was clear for Aquinas that an act of scandal was lacking in rectitude in some way. Scandal truly causes, at least in some manner, the sin of another.[145] It induces one to sin who is not already inclined to sin. Scandal, properly speaking, is a sin against the charity—and specifically the beneficence—owed to one's neighbor.

While often treated alongside scandal, cooperation represents a different species of moral act than scandal. When one cooperates in the sin of another person, he does not cause the other to sin but rather aids one already committed to sinning. According to the traditional analysis, in an act of cooperation in the sin of another, a good act of the cooperator is misused by the primary agent of evil. In this context, both to distinguish clearly the sin of scandal from that of cooperation and to avoid the apparent rigor of his earlier treatment of the servant and the ladder, St. Alphonsus established the distinction between formal and material cooperation.[146] His use of this distinction became the classic definition for subsequent moral manuals, in use even to the present day. St. Alphonsus explains: "Cooperation is formal when it concurs in the bad will of another and cannot be without sin; it is material when it concurs only with the bad action of the other, beside the intention of the cooperator."[147] An examina-

144. *Summa theologiae* IIa–IIae, q. 43, a. 1.

145. See *CCC*, no. 2284.

146. While previous authors including Herman Busenbaum, Thomas Sanchez, and Pio Tommaso Milante referred to the terms formal and/or material cooperation, it is only with St. Alphonsus that the distinction between the two becomes clear. For this history, see Andrew McLean Cummings, *The Servant and the Ladder*, 33–82. For reference to this history and an outstanding treatment of this matter more generally, see Charles F. Capps, "Formal and Material Cooperation with Evil," *American Catholic Philosophical Quarterly* 89 (2015): 681–98.

147. "Illam esse *formalem*, quae concurrit ad malam voluntatem alterius, et nequit esse sine peccato; *materialem* vero illam, quae concurrit tantum ad malam actionem alterius, praeter intentionem cooperantis." Alphonsus Liguori, *Theologia Moralis*, vol. 1 (Rome: Vatican, 1905), Lib. II, Tract. III, Cap. II, §63.

tion of the casuist authors of the late nineteenth and early twentieth centuries will demonstrate that moralists have offered diverse interpretations of the distinction between material and formal cooperation. The exact nature of what it means to share the evil will or evil intention of another has been the subject of considerable dispute, including in contemporary discussions surrounding the specification of moral objects.[148]

For St. Alphonsus and the tradition that followed him, formal cooperation with evil can never be justified. An act of material cooperation, on the other hand, can be without sin only if certain conditions are met.[149] Theologians disagree on precisely what forms of material cooperation can be pursued without moral fault. St. Alphonsus offers two conditions to determine whether such material cooperation is licit. First, he explains that the action of the cooperator is just "when the action in itself is good or indifferent."[150] Second, St. Alphonsus explains that only "when there is a just cause proportionate to the gravity of the sin of the other and to the proximity of that which concurs in the execution of the sin" is the act licit.[151] These two conditions set the stage for centuries of discussion regarding cooperation with evil. However, Alphonsus's reliance on the ethical categories of indifferent acts, proximity to sin, and a just cause proportionate to sin are all absent in St. Thomas or his commentators. Instead, these elements represent new conditions specific to the modern period. As shown above, for Aquinas no human action in the concrete is an indifferent act. It takes on a moral species in its execution.[152] A weighing of consequences—for example, whether the inconvenience of failing to cooperate would be proportionate to the evil in which one was cooperating—is also absent in the writings of St. Thomas.[153] If one avoids rig-

---

148. For a careful explanation of the meaning of the terms formal and material cooperation in the thought of St. Alphonsus Liguori, see Kevin L. Flannery, SJ, "Two Factors in the Analysis of Cooperation in Evil," *The National Catholic Bioethics Quarterly* 13 (2013): 79–104.

149. For a careful reading of St. Alphonsus's use of the distinction between formal and material cooperation, see Flannery, SJ, *Cooperation with Evil: Thomistic Tools of Analysis*, 23–39.

150. Alphonsus Liguori, *Theologia Moralis*, vol. 1, Lib. II, Tract. III, Cap. II, §63: "quando per se action est bona vel indifferens."

151. Alphonsus Liguori, *Theologia Moralis*, Lib. II, Tract. III, Cap. II, §63: "quando adest justa causa et proportionata ad gravitatem peccati alterius, et ad proximitatem concursus, qui praestatur ad peccati exsecutionem."

152. See *Summa theologiae* Ia–IIae, q. 18, a. 9.

153. For a convincing critique of the use of so-called proportionate reason in moral

orous analysis of moral objects and the natural teleology of human action and its *per se* effects, one is forced to rely on the category of proximity to evil in order to determine the moral quality of an action.

The contribution of St. Alphonsus to the question of cooperation with evil remains considerable.[154] He established in a clear way the difference between inducing another to sin, as in the case of scandal, and the situation of aiding another person already committed to sinning. The distinction between formal and material cooperation—despite the confusions surrounding the classification of particular acts as either formal or material—promoted a humanization of moral theology. In so doing, St. Alphonsus helped distance Catholic moral thought from overly rigorist positions.[155] Since many actions appear to cooperate with evil at least in some fashion, Alphonsus's account of material cooperation helps one avoid unnecessarily limiting one's collaboration with the world. St. Alphonsus labored during a period known for its rigor in moral matters. His invoca-

---

theology, especially insofar as it represents a departure from the method of moral reasoning utilized by St. Thomas Aquinas, see Christopher Kaczor, *Proportionalism and the Natural Law Tradition* (Washington, DC: The Catholic University of America Press, 2002). For a similar critique of proportionalism, see William E. May, "John Paul II, Moral Theology, and Moral Theologians," in *Veritatis Splendor and the Renewal of Moral Theology*, ed. J. A. DiNoia, OP, and Romanus Cessario, OP, (Chicago: Midwest Theological Forum, 1999), 211–39.

154. One notes that recent magisterial teaching has emphasized the enduring value of the spiritual theology of St. Alphonsus while refraining from necessarily endorsing the method of moral casuistry. For example, see Pope John Paul II, *Spiritus Domini*, Apostolic Letter for the Bicentenary of the death of St. Alphonsus de' Liguori, August 1, 1987; and Pope Benedict XVI, General Audience, August 1, 2012; and General Audience, March 30, 2011. The enduring legacy of St. Alphonsus remains in the field of spiritual theology. One recalls his long list of spiritual works, including *The Glories of Mary*, *The Practice of the Love of Jesus Christ*, and *Visits to the Blessed Sacrament*. The complete ascetical works can be found in the volume, *Opere Ascetiche di S. Alfonso Maria de Liguori*, 4 vols. (Turin: Marietti, 1867–1873).

155. Recognizing the achievement of St. Alphonsus does not require that one endorse the prevailing system of moral reasoning in use during his lifetime. Instead, his particular moral judgments—judgments of pastoral prudence—might most often be correct. That fact does not, however, mean the prevailing system in use in the eighteenth century needs to be followed today. See the judgment of Servais Pinckaers, OP, *The Sources of Christian Ethics*, 277: "Without going so far as to assert explicitly that his 'theory of equal probability' was the best system for moral theology, the Church declared him a Doctor in 1871. Thus Alphonsus became the patron of moralists. The patronage of St. Alphonsus, which merits our respect and esteem for his achievements, still leaves ethicists free in regard to following his reasoning."

tion of the category of material cooperation prudently allowed his readers to participate without scruple in some disputed—but morally licit—affairs. For many succeeding casuist authors, the tendency to treat cases of cooperation as material—and therefore possibly justified—became very strong. In part this predilection toward the classification of acts as material cooperation was due to the emphasis of the casuist authors on the need to make restitution for sins committed.[156] Since material cooperation is at least in principle justifiable, a merely material cooperator may not need to make restitution. However, the casuist treatment of issues of cooperation under the framework of restitution had the unfortunate result of moving many actions—including, for example, the case of the servant and the ladder—into the realm of material and not formal cooperation.

Restitution for wrongdoing represents an important ethical category useful for moral theologians.[157] However, one wonders about the effect the casuist emphasis on restitution had on treatises dealing with cooperation with evil. In the casuist period authors treated cooperation in reference to the obligation of charity. Failures in fulfilling this obligation require restitution in justice. In this framework, the question inevitably becomes, when does the obligation cease? When does the law cease to apply and therefore mitigate the need for restitution? While St. Alphonsus can be credited with popularizing the category of material cooperation with evil, the effects of this categorization are not universally beneficial. I maintain that perplexed readers will find a more fruitful method for examining questions of moral cooperation in a careful examination of the would-be cooperator's act itself. What precisely is the cooperator doing in a given set of circumstances? This type of examination, relying on an evaluation of an act's natural teleology, places a limit on the manifold distinctions between various types of cooperation. In the following chapter we will demonstrate how casuist authors tried to force actions into ready-made categories of permissible or objectionable forms of cooperation, often based on the extrinsic category of proximity to evil. Moralists will be better served by asking what kind of act the cooperator is engaged in and whether that action can be a good act or not.

---

156. For one extensive treatment of restitution, see John A. McHugh, OP, and Charles J. Callan, OP, *Moral Theology: A Complete Course*, vol. 2 (New York: Joseph F. Wagner, Inc., 1958), §1751–1803.

157. See *CCC*, no. 2412.

Conclusion

In our effort to establish a historical overview of the analysis of cooperation with evil, one can immediately note that Aquinas and his authentic interpreters approach the topic differently than the sixteenth-century Jesuit Thomas Sanchez and later St. Alphonsus Liguori. These authors pivot from the virtue-based reasoning of Aquinas. This casuistic turn occurred just when the issue of cooperation with evil took on new prominence. And so here we observe a paradox. When virtue-based moral reasoning would have been useful for tackling a new question in moral theology, a variety of factors led moral theologians to relegate virtue-based moral thought.

In the chapter that follows we examine several prominent moral manuals composed in the late nineteenth and early twentieth centuries. While it extends beyond the scope of the present work to provide a full summary of each manual, or even the treatment of each manual on the multifarious issues regarding cooperation with evil, we will offer a flavor of the type of analysis utilized during the period. Specifically, we will demonstrate that contrary to popular conception, the manuals achieved only limited consensus regarding precisely what forms of cooperation must be avoided. Of considerable difficulty for both a perplexed moral agent and priest confessor or spiritual counselor, most often the difficult questions of moral cooperation were left without sufficient resolution. Inquirers were left to consider whether they possessed a truly grave or proportionate reason to justify their cooperation. This admittedly broad-strokes history of the casuist treatment of cooperation will demonstrate the necessity of finding a more fruitful method of moral analysis for these pressing questions of cooperation with evil.

CHAPTER TWO

A Broad Sampling of Nineteenth- and Twentieth-Century Casuist Authors

Authors examined: Sabetti; Slater; Prümmer; Merkelbach; Noldin-Schmitt; Jone Adelman; McHugh-Callan; Davis; Häring

To demonstrate the need for a virtue-based approach to moral cooperation with evil one does well to focus attention on the limitations present in alternative methods of analyzing the topic. The authors of the late nineteenth and early twentieth centuries took up the issue of cooperation with evil with great fervor. Typical questions involved the obligations of servants, merchants, and innkeepers in fulfilling the requests of their employers and patrons. Questions surrounding collaboration with non-Catholics occupied a significant place in the moral manuals of the casuist period.[1] Roughly from the sixteenth-century Council of Trent until the reforms initiated at the Second Vatican Council, moral casuistry dominated Catholic moral thought.[2] During this time, Catholics were especially concerned to avoid immoral collaboration with non-Catholic worship.[3] Questions of whether Catholic bookmakers could print Prot-

---

1. For a fruitful exchange on the continuity of Catholic teaching on religious liberty, see Martin Rhonheimer, "Benedict XVI's 'Hermeneutic of Reform' and Religious Freedom," *Nova et Vetera*, English edition, 9 (2011): 1029–54; Thomas Pink, "The Interpretation of *Dignitatis Humanae*: A Reply to Martin Rhonheimer," *Nova et Vetera*, English edition, 11 (2013): 77–121; and Martin Rhonheimer, "*Dignitatis Humanae*—Not a Mere Question of Church Policy: A Response to Thomas Pink," *Nova et Vetera*, English edition, 12 (2014): 445–70.

2. For an overview of this period, see Servais Pinckaers, OP, *The Sources of Christian Ethics*, trans. Sr. Mary Thomas Noble, OP (Washington, DC: The Catholic University of America Press, 1995), 254–79.

3. See, for example, the 1928 encyclical letter of Pope Pius XI, *Mortalium animos*, expressing the Church's hesitation about the emerging ecumenical movement. Already in

estant hymnals or whether laborers could construct non-Catholic sanctu-
aries occupied their attention. The moral manuals of the late nineteenth
and early twentieth centuries observe the relative rigor of the casuist period. Few book sellers in the twenty-first century, for example, worry
that their patrons may be scandalized by the books they sell. Not many
twenty-first-century hotel proprietors fret over the marital status of those
renting rooms. All that is to say, believers of the nineteenth and early
twentieth centuries took sin seriously. They knew the consequences of
sin, and their efforts to avoid sin merit admiration.

This chapter unfolds in three parts. First, we offer a summary of the
treatment of cooperation with evil according to several prominent late
nineteenth- and early twentieth-century authors. We identify nine moral
manuals of particular relevance during this period. We will examine the
texts of (1) Aloysius Sabetti, author of what is widely regarded as the most
influential nineteenth-century manual in the United States; (2) Thomas
Slater, who composed the first moral manual in English; (3) Dominicus
Prümmer and (4) Benoît-Henri Merkelbach, Dominican authors of two
significant moral manuals; (5) Noldin-Schmitt, the most utilized manual in American seminaries during the pre-conciliar period; (6) McHugh-
Callan, authors of the first English moral manual specifically for an American audience; (7) Jone-Adelman, whose work provides one of the longest
lists of specific cases of moral cooperation with evil; (8) Henry Davis,
whose long-standing influence was demonstrated by a citation in the 2014
US Supreme Court *Hobby Lobby* decision regarding moral cooperation;[4]
and finally, (9) Bernhard Häring, who represents a clear bridge between

---

July 1919, the Sacred Congregation of the Holy Office responded to a *dubium* asking
whether Catholics could attend ecumenical gatherings. The Holy Office responded that
they could not attend such events. See Sacra Congregatio S. Officii, *"De Participatione Catholicorum"* AAS 11 (1919): 312–16. Despite an alteration in tone, one observes an essential
continuity with recent magisterial teaching. See Second Vatican Council, Decree on Ecumenism, *Unitatis Redintegratio*; and Pope John Paul II, *Ut Unum Sint*, May 25, 1995, AAS 87
(1995): 921–82.

4. See footnote 34 of the majority opinion of Associate Justice Samuel Alito in the
decision *Sylvia Burwell, Secretary of Health and Human Services, et al., Petitioners v. Hobby Lobby
Stores, Inc., Mardel, Inc., David Green, Barbara Green, Steve Green, Mart Green, and Darsee Lett; Con-
estoga Wood Specialties Corporation, et al., Petitioners v. Sylvia Burwell, Secretary of Health and Human
Services, et al.* Alito cites Davis's *Moral and Pastoral Theology*, 341 (1935): "Cooperation occurs
'when A helps B to accomplish an external act by an act that is not sinful, and without
approving of what B does.'"

moral casuistry and the proportionalism advanced during the latter third of the twentieth century.

In the second portion of this chapter, we identify several areas of disagreement between authors of the period. This section refutes the common myth of near unanimity among casuist authors.[5] Finally, this chapter closes with a discussion of the challenges faced by the perplexed moral actor when left without definitive resolution to moral quandaries. Despite the relative rigor of the casuist period, challenging moral questions often remained unresolved. Readers were left to wonder what constituted a sufficient, proportionate, serious, or grave reason for them to engage in an act of material cooperation with evil. Taken together, these sections demonstrate the need for an alternative approach to analyzing moral cooperation with evil.

Aloysius Sabetti

The moral manual of the Jesuit Aloysius Sabetti (1839–1898) occupies an important place in the history of moral theology in the United States. First published in 1884, Sabetti's *Compendium Theologiae Moralis* has been called the "most influential and long-lasting of the nineteenth-century moral manuals written in the United States."[6] Only outpaced by the manual of his fellow Jesuits Jerome Noldin and Albert Schmitt, Sabetti's text was used in ten diocesan seminarians in the United States in the first half of the twentieth century.[7]

Sabetti was born in the town of Roseto in the Puglia region of Italy.

---

5. Recent decades have seen efforts to revive the system of moral casuistry. See, for example, Albert R. Jonsen and Stephen Toulmin, *The Abuse of Casuistry: A History of Moral Reasoning* (Berkley and Los Angeles: University of California Press, 1990). Jonsen and Toulmin argue that casuistry gives greater certainty to moral judgments than methods of moral analysis that cling too firmly to principles applicable in every case. For an alternative perspective, see the review of the book by Romanus Cessario, OP, "Review: Albert R. Jonsen & Stephen Toulmin, *The Abuse of Casuistry: A History of Moral Reasoning*," *The Thomist* 54 (1990): 151–54.

6. Charles E. Curran, "The Manual and Casuistry of Aloysius Sabetti," in *The Context of Casuistry*, ed. James F. Kennan, SJ, and Thomas A. Shannon (Washington, DC: Georgetown University Press, 1995): 161.

7. Curran, "The Manual and Casuistry of Aloysius Sabetti," 161. Curran relies on the research of the American Benedictine Theodore H. Heck. See Heck's *The Curriculum of the Major Seminary in Relation to Contemporary Conditions* (Washington, DC: National Catholic Welfare Conference, 1935).

He entered the Society of Jesus in 1855 and after studies in France and Rome was sent to teach at the Jesuit seminary in Woodstock, Maryland.[8] In Rome, he studied morals with the Italian Jesuit Antonio Ballerini (1805–1881) and dogma with the legendary Austrian Cardinal Johann Baptist Franzelin (1816–1886).[9] While the work bears his name, Sabetti likely borrowed some ninety percent of the text from the influential moral manual of his fellow Jesuit Jean Pierre Gury.[10] Gury (1801–1866) has been called the "leading Jesuit casuist of the nineteenth century."[11] Born at Mailleroncourt in northeastern France, Gury entered the Society of Jesus in 1824. Gury completed his studies at the Roman College where he was made chair of moral theology in 1847. A disciple of both the seventeenth-century Jesuit Hermann Busenbaum and the eighteenth-century Redemptorist St. Alphonsus, Gury is credited with contributing to the final defeat of Jansenism in the later part of the nineteenth century.[12]

8. For both an autobiographical essay and the reflections of his fellow Jesuits, see "Father Aloysius Sabetti: A Fellow Professor's Reminiscences," *Woodstock Letters* 29 (1900): 208–33. For a review of Sabetti's contribution to moral theology in the nineteenth century, see Charles E. Curran, *Catholic Moral Theology in the United States: A History* (Washington, DC: Georgetown University Press, 2008), 17–22.

9. See Aloysius Sabetti et al., "Father Aloysius Sabetti: A Fellow Professor's Reminiscences," 212. For an insightful look at the theology of the Roman College in the nineteenth century, see Joseph Carola, SJ, "La metodologia patristica nella teologia preconciliare dell'Ottocento," *Gregorianum* 97 (2016): 605–17. For an excellent overview of the theology of the Roman School, see C. Michael Shea, "*Ressourcement* in the Age of Migne: The Jesuit Theologians of the *Collegio Romano* and the Shape of Modern Catholic Thought," *Nova et Vetera*, English edition, 15 (2017): 579–613; as well as Joseph Carola, SJ, *Engaging the Church Fathers in Nineteenth-Century Catholicism: The Patristic Legacy of the Scuola Romana* (Steubenville, OH: Emmaus Academic, 2023). For a broad history of Catholic theology in the nineteenth century, see Gerald A. McCool, *Nineteenth Century Scholasticism: The Search for a Unitary Method* (New York: Fordham University Press, 1999).

10. For an evaluation of the state of moral theology at the beginning of the twentieth century, see the 1899 essay by Thomas J. Bouquillon which first appeared in the *Catholic University Bulletin* 5, and was then reproduced at the end of the twentieth century as, "Moral Theology at the End of the Nineteenth Century," in *The Historical Development of Fundamental Moral Theology in the United States, Readings in Moral Theology, No. 11*, ed. Charles E. Curran and Richard A. McCormick, SJ (New York: Paulist Press, 1999), 91–114.

11. See Albert R. Jonsen and Stephen Toulmin, *The Abuse of Casuistry*, 155. For a similar evaluation, see Christopher Kaczor, *Proportionalism and the Natural Law Tradition* (Washington, DC: The Catholic University of America Press, 2002), 27. Gury is recalled especially for his formulation of the so-called "principle of double-effect." See Kaczor, 27–34.

12. See *Dictionnaire de théologie catholique*, 1993–95 (Paris: Letouzey et Ane, 1947): "Disciple fidèle de Busembaum et de saint Alphonse de Liguori, le P. Gury a contribué pour une large part à comprimer les dernières tendances jansénistes."

Following the custom of the period, moral manuals often were not exclusively the work of a single author. They were routinely updated, edited, and revised according to local customs or more recently promulgated ecclesiastical directives. The Gury manual, in particular, became the basis of the future texts, including those of Sabetti, Ballerini, and Noldin.[13] After its initial publication in 1884, the Sabetti manual underwent some thirty-four editions. The American Jesuit Timothy Barrett (1862–1935) oversaw its most significant reediting.[14] The significance of the Sabetti-Barrett manual looms large in the history of Catholic theology in the United States. Like most moral manuals of the period, Sabetti treats cooperation with evil in two places. First, he considers cooperation as a sin against charity.[15] His treatise regarding cooperation with evil immediately follows his treatment of the sin of scandal. In the second place, Sabetti reviews the circumstances that make restitution necessary for some injustice committed.[16] Here he considers the restitution warranted for the commission of a variety of cooperative acts. Following St. Alphonsus, Sabetti distinguishes formal and material cooperation. He maintains that "formal cooperation is never licit."[17] "Material cooperation," however, "can be licit with the presence of a just cause, proportionate to the gravity of the other's sin, and depending on how proximate it is to the execution of the sin."[18]

Regarding specific matters of cooperation with evil, Sabetti treats cases dealing with servants, merchants, and laborers. He asks if it is licit for a Catholic to confer a masonic sign. The response is negative, he explains: "unless there is present a truly grave cause."[19] Sabetti allows the sale of

---

13. See John A. Gallagher, *Time Past, Time Future: An Historical Study of Catholic Moral Theology* (New York: Paulist Press, 1990), 51. Gallagher explains: "The authority of these writings was not the product of the talents or insights of a particular author, but rather the authority of a self-authenticating tradition. The manuals retain a medieval notion of authority residing in the text and the tradition, rather than in the authority of the author."

14. Paul E. McKeever, "Seventy-Five Years of Moral Theology in America," in *The Historical Development of Fundamental Moral Theology in the United States*, ed. Charles E. Curran and Richard A. McCormick, SJ (Mahwah, NJ: Paulist Press, 1999), 7.

15. See Aloysius Sabetti, SJ, *Compendium Theologiae Moralis* (New York: Frederick Pustet Co., 1931), §194–99.

16. Sabetti, SJ, *Compendium Theologiae Moralis*, §426–41.

17. Sabetti, SJ, §195: "Cooperatio formalis nunquam licita est."

18. Sabetti, SJ, §195: "materialis vero potest evadere licita, si adsit causa justa et proportionata gravitati peccati alterius, et proximitati concursus ad peccati executionem."

19. Sabetti, SJ, §197: "Nisi adsit causa vere gravis."

items that could have a sinful purpose, so long as they also could be utilized for a good or "indifferent" purpose.[20] While in principle Sabetti
does not allow Catholic nurses to call non-Catholic ministers to assist dying non-Catholics, he does permit a nurse to notify the minister that such
a patient wishes to see him.[21] In utilizing these distinctions, one observes
the extent to which authors of the period were concerned to avoid what
they considered unjust collaboration with non-Catholic worship.

Sabetti treats the obligation of servants to fulfill the unjust wishes of
their masters. Specifically, he takes up the celebrated question of whether
a servant may assist his master to enter the home of one with whom the
master intends to sin against the sixth commandment. Sabetti asks if the
servant "may open the door to the house of a prostitute."[22] Interestingly, after citing the decree from Pope Innocent XI which declared that a
servant may not provide such assistance, Sabetti explains that the words
"opening the door" refer *specifically* to the door of someone else's home, in
this case, the prostitute.[23] Sabetti implies that servants could licitly open
the door to the master's own house even with knowledge that he would
commit these sins. With this qualification, Sabetti introduces an important distinction in analyzing cases of moral cooperation. Can we consider
a particular cooperative act as an ordinary part of one's duties? Could one
accomplish the act without specific reference to the evil which the principal malefactor intends to commit? These questions will arise continually
in the debate surrounding cooperation with evil.

Aloysius Sabetti's treatment of moral cooperation with evil reflects the
standard treatment of the topic in the late nineteenth century.[24] It occu-

20. Sabetti, SJ, §198: "An licet mercatoribus vendere aleas, gladius, fucos, mulierum
ornamenta, etc., cum futurus abusus praevidetur? Resp. Affirm., quia hujusmodi vendi-
to per se mala non est, cum res illae indifferentes sint, et possint ad bonum usum con-
verti."

21. Sabetti, SJ, §199: "Quod si nullus adsit acatholicus, catholicus illcicum est vocare
ministrum, ut ritus suos haereticos peragat. Dicere autum ministro: infirmus iste vult
ut ipsum convenias, ob gravissimam rationem." For further reflection on Sabetti's treatment of Catholic participation in non-Catholic worship, see Charles E. Curran, *The Origins of Moral Theology in the United States: Three Different Approaches* (Washington, DC: Georgetown University Press, 1997), 155–58.

22. Sabetti, SJ, §196: "An possit ancilla ostium domus meretrici aperire?"

23. Sabetti, SJ, §196: "Sec haec verba aperiendo januam intelligi manifesto debent de
aperienda per vim aliena domo, ut ex contextu patet."

24. For a fuller appreciation of the place of Sabetti in the history of moral theology in the United States, see Aloysius Sabetti et al., "Father Aloysius Sabetti: A Fellow

pied an important place in American seminary instruction from the turn of the century until the Second Vatican Council.[25] Relying on the now well-known distinctions of formal, material, remote and proximate cooperation, Sabetti supplies American readers with a useful point of reference for questions of cooperation with evil. His suggestion that the intelligibility of an action—apart from a malefactor using it for evil ends—will prove useful in establishing a virtue-based approach to these questions. Recognizing whether an action possesses an intelligibility apart from its contribution to an evil act will offer a helpful path in identifying truly unjust cooperative acts.

Thomas Slater

In 1906, the English Jesuit Thomas Slater (1855–1928) composed the first moral manual originally published in English. After the period of exclusively Latin manuals, the turn of the twentieth century saw the publication of those in German, French, Italian, and Spanish.[26] Reissued after the promulgation of the universal Code of Canon Law in 1917, the Irish Jesuit Michael Martin adapted the text for an American audience.[27]

Professor's Reminiscences," 208–33; in particular, 216, where we learn that his moral work had "given him more than a national reputation."

25. Many authors have observed that since the 1960s casuistry has seen a marked decline. For example, Romanus Cessario, OP, writes: "After the Second Vatican Council, casuistry suffered a serious reverse. The eclipse of the casuist model is one of the most remarkable signs of renewal effected by the Second Vatican Council." See his *Introduction to Moral Theology*, rev. ed. (Washington, DC: The Catholic University of America Press, 2013), 232.

26. Slater explains: "In German we have Pruner, Probst, Linsenmann, and many others; in French, the well-known works of Gousset and Gaume; in Italian, Frassinetti; in Spanish, Villafuertes, Moran and others. It may then confidently be expected that especially the ecclesiastical students and Catholic clergy of English-speaking countries will welcome a book intended chiefly for their benefit." See Thomas Slater, SJ, *A Manual of Moral Theology for English-Speaking Countries*, vol. 1 (New York: Benziger Brothers, 1925). For an evaluation of Slater's thought, see James F. Keenan, SJ, *A History of Catholic Moral Theology in the Twentieth Century: From Confessing Sins to Liberating Consciences* (New York: Continuum International Publishing Group, 2010), 10–18.

27. For an engaging essay on the importance of the promulgation of the 1917 Code of Canon Law, see both the curator's introduction (xxiii–xxxiv) by Edward N. Peters and the preface to the 1917 promulgation by Pietro Cardinal Gasparri (1–19). Both can be found in Edward N. Peters's translation and commentary of *The 1917 Pio-Benedictine Code of Canon Law* (San Francisco: Ignatius Press, 2001). For the influence of the 1917 Code on

A year later it was published for use in the United States.[28] Slater's decision to reissue his text after the promulgation of the Code of Canon
Law demonstrates the influence of the 1917 Code on moral theology.[29]
Throughout the early part of the twentieth century moralists like Slater would become increasingly attentive to how canonical directives im-
pacted their work. While clerics remained the primary audience of his
moral manual, Slater's choice of an English language text made his work
accessible to interested lay readers. The German Dominican Dominicus
Prümmer called Slater's work "succinct and clear."[30] Slater's moral treatise guided confessors and seminary professors for the first third of the
twentieth century. It represents an important moment in the history of
analyzing moral cooperation with evil.

Like most of the manuals produced by Jesuit authors, Slater organized
his text around the commandments rather than around the virtues. Utilizing a more legalistic approach to moral theology even than other works
of the casuist period, Slater's understanding of his discipline proves instructive. Slater explains:

> Manuals of moral theology are technical works intended to help the confessor
> and the parish priest in the discharge of their duties. They are as technical as
> the text-books of the lawyer and the doctor. They are not intended for edifica-
> tion, nor do they hold up a high ideal of Christian perfection for the imitation
> of the faithful. They deal with what is of obligation under pain of sin; they are
> books of moral pathology.... Ascetical and mystical literature which treats of
> the higher spiritual life is very abundant in the Catholic Church, and it should
> be consulted by those who desire to know the lofty ideals of life which the
> Catholic Church places before her children and encourages them to practice.
> Moral theology proposes to itself the humbler but still necessary task of de-
> fining what is right and wrong.[31]

---

moral theology in the United States, see also Charles E. Curran, *Catholic Moral Theology in
the United States*, 38–39.

28. For a more extensive treatment of this period, see Paul E. McKeever, "Seventy-
Five Years of Moral Theology in America," especially 8–9.

29. For more information on the relationship between Canon Law and moral theology during this period, see James F. Keenan, SJ, *A History of Catholic Moral Theology in the
Twentieth Century*, 18–19.

30. Dominicus M. Prümmer, OP, *Manuale Theologiae Moralis: Secundum Principia S. Thomae
Aquinatis*, vol. 1 (Fribourg: Herder & Co., 1923), xxxiii: "opera succincta et clara."

31. Slater, SJ, *A Manual of Moral Theology for English Speaking Countries*, v–vi.

As the most widely used manual for several decades in the early twentieth century, Slater's text represents a highpoint of the obligation-oriented approach of moral casuistry. With many future moral manuals relying on his text, Slater's description of moral theology is not an exceptional view. Rather, it is representative of the pre-conciliar casuist period.[32] The relegation of Christian perfection to ascetical and mystical theology posed a challenge to the full flourishing of the Christian moral life. Even some theologians who acknowledge the usefulness of certain types of moral casuistry have noted this deficiency.[33]

In the context of his short treatise on the theological virtues, Slater addresses the question of cooperation with another's sin. This treatise precedes his much longer treatment of the Ten Commandments. Distinguished from both scandal and the obligation of fraternal correction, cooperation, properly speaking, is "participation in the sin of another."[34] Slater holds that formal cooperation is the "concurrence in the bad action of another and in the bad intention with which it is performed."[35] Material cooperation, on the other hand, is "the concurrence in the ex-

32. In similar fashion, John C. Ford and Gerald Kelly identify one view of moral theology common in the early part of the twentieth century. See John C. Ford, SJ, and Gerald Kelly, SJ, *Contemporary Moral Theology*, vol. 1 (Westminster, MD: The Newman Press, 1964), 65: "Abbe Hogan, Sulpician Rector of St. John's Seminary in Boston [writes]: 'As found in St. Liguori, and as taught in the schools, the main object of Moral Theology is in no wise to establish an ideal, but simply to determine a minimum of duty.... The moral theologian, or the casuist, as he is often called, considers only to what a man is strictly bound.' This comment is noteworthy because it comes from one fairly critical of the moral manuals at the time." For a more complete assessment of Hogan's views on moral theology, see Charles E. Curran, *Catholic Moral Theology in the United States*, 27–29. For a more extended treatment, see also Charles E. Curran, *The Origins of Moral Theology in the United States: Three Different Approaches*, 257–95. For more information on Hogan and his role as seminary rector, see the standard history of the Archdiocese of Boston, Robert H. Lord, John E. Sexton, and Edward T. Harrington, *History of the Archdiocese of Boston*, vol. 3 (New York: Sheed & Ward 1944), 61–62.

33. See especially Reginald Garrigou-Lagrange, OP, *Beatitude: A Commentary on St. Thomas' Theological Summa, ia iiae, qq. 1–54* (London: B. Herder Book Co., 1956); and by the same author, *Christian Perfection and Contemplation* (London: B. Herder Book Co., 1937). The sharp division described by Slater between moral and ascetical theology is difficult to reconcile with the teaching of St. Thomas Aquinas. See *Summa theologiae* IIa–IIae q. 184, a. 3. For a further treatment of this issue, see Thomas Gilby, OP, *Principles of Morality*, vol. 18 of the Blackfriars *Summa Theologiae* (New York: McGraw-Hill Book Company, 1966), 130.

34. Slater, SJ, *A Manual of Moral Theology for English Speaking Countries*, Bk. V, Part III, Ch. VII, §1.

35. Slater, SJ, Bk. V, Part III, Ch. VII, §1.

ternal action of another but not in the evil intention with which it is done."[36] He further distinguishes between proximate and remote cooperation depending on how "closely connected with the action of the principal agent" is the act of the cooperator. While one is never permitted to cooperate formally with evil, material cooperation may be permitted when three conditions are met. For material cooperation to be licit, Slater requires: (1) the action of the secondary agent must not be evil in itself; (2) there can be no evil intention; and (3) there is a just cause. The secondary agent, Slater maintains, is bound only to prevent the sin of another out of charity, "which does not bind with relatively serious inconvenience."[37]

Slater takes up several specific cases of cooperation with evil, although he does so far less extensively than some of the moral manuals that would follow him.[38] Slater holds that a dealer may sell to anyone things which are "in themselves indifferent" even if they will be put to bad use. Even if one is certain they will be put to bad use, a "correspondingly serious inconvenience or loss will excuse his selling."[39] Tavern proprietors cannot sell intoxicating drink to those who have already consumed too much, even though, he explains, some authors allow this if quarreling is sure to result. Booksellers may not sell immoral books, nor may producers sell instruments that have only an immoral purpose. Although he acknowledges its dangers, those who organize social gatherings may permit dancing. Those who sin frequently at dances, however, should refrain from attending. He argues, on the other hand, those who only sin occasionally may attend when they take precautions.[40]

As the first moral manual composed in English, historians cannot fail to note its influence. For several decades Slater's work was the most widely consulted manual, with ensuing authors relying extensively upon his text. As regards cooperation with evil, Slater makes an able attempt to isolate the act of the cooperator (from that of the principal malefactor) and analyze the action according to its nature. He appears to classify an

---

36. Slater, SJ, Bk. V, Part III, Ch. VII, §1.

37. Slater, SJ, Bk. V, Part III, Ch. VII, §2.

38. Consider, for example, the manual of McHugh-Callan. These Dominican authors devote twenty-seven pages to the topic of cooperation, compared to Slater who offers only three pages (with another four regarding restitution in cases of moral cooperation with evil).

39. Slater, SJ, *A Manual of Moral Theology for English Speaking Countries*, Bk. V, Part III, Ch. VII, §2, b.

40. Slater, SJ, Bk. V, Part III, Ch. VII, §2.

intrinsically evil act of a cooperator who does not share the evil intention of the principal agent as unjustifiable material cooperation.[41] This differs from those manuals that utilize the category of implicitly formal cooperation.[42] To his credit, Slater is still able to determine that there are certain kinds of cooperation which can never be justified regardless of whether one shares the evil intention of the principal agent or not. Like the majority of the manuals of the time, Slater provides generally sound counsel for concrete situations; the examination of which remains useful today.

Critical readers might raise two specific questions about Slater's approach to moral cooperation with evil. First, he identifies the reason why one may never cooperate formally with evil in less than felicitous terms. He explains that formal cooperation "is obviously to wish evil."[43] This description fails to allow the possibility of implicitly formal cooperation—which exists regardless of the good intentions (or wishes) of the cooperator. By identifying formal cooperation only with an agent who "wishes evil," Slater affords too great a place to intention in this aspect of the moral life.[44]

The second area where readers may express hesitations concerns his description of an obligation of charity. Charity does not bind, he explains, in "relatively serious inconvenience."[45] This represents a slightly laxer view

41. See Slater, SJ, Bk. V, Part III, Ch. VII, §2, where he explains: "Nor is it lawful to cooperate materially with the sin of another when the action of the secondary agent is itself wrong."

42. See, for example, John A. McHugh, OP, and Charles J. Callan, OP, *Moral Theology: A Complete Course*, vol. 1 (New York: Joseph F. Wagner, Inc., 1958), §1511. They explain, "Formal cooperation is implicit, when the cooperator does not directly intend to associate himself with the sin of the principal agent, but the end of the external act (*finis operis*), which for the sake of some advantage or interest the cooperator does intend, includes from its nature or from circumstances the guilt of the sin of the principal agent."

43. Slater, SJ, *A Manual of Moral Theology for English Speaking Countries*, Bk. V, Part III, Ch. VII, §2.

44. For an examination of the dangers of placing too great an emphasis on intention when analyzing moral objects, see Steven J. Jensen, *Good and Evil Actions: A Journey through St. Thomas Aquinas* (Washington, DC: The Catholic University of America Press, 2010); 44–72. For a related perspective, see Andrew McLean Cummings, *The Servant and the Ladder*; and Steven A. Long, *The Teleological Grammar of the Moral Act*, 2nd ed. (Naples, FL: Sapientia Press, 2015). For a careful exposition on the role of intention in the specification of moral objects, see Stephen L. Brock, *Action and Conduct: Thomas Aquinas and the Theory of Action* (Edinburgh: T&T Clark, 1998), especially 87–93.

45. See Slater, SJ, *A Manual of Moral Theology for English Speaking Countries*, Bk. V, Part III, Ch. VII, §2.

than that of the Dominican manual McHugh-Callan. McHugh-Callan affirm the stronger obligation, "charity does not oblige under serious inconvenience to self."[46] In any case, either view fails to address the important question of whether cooperation with evil is best understood as part of the obligation of charity. While it may be true that in charity one ought to attempt to prevent the sin of another, one must address other aspects of the topic of cooperation with evil to analyze properly the quality of a given action. From the perspective of virtue ethics, the primary question in analyzing an act of cooperation remains what kind of act the cooperator is doing and whether it is the kind of act that conforms to the truth about the good of the human person. The obligation to act in a manner conforming to the truth about the good does not cease under any inconvenience. There exists no space of liberty of indifference where the laws of charity cease to obtain.[47]

Slater contends that some acts of material cooperation ordinarily forbidden under the obligation of charity can be allowed under relatively serious inconvenience. He explains that cooperative acts are permitted when "the secondary agent does nothing that is wrong in itself" but merely allows another party to "take advantage of his action in order to commit sin."[48] Slater, like most authors of the period, views the principal question involved in cooperation with evil to concern the sin of the principal malefactor. While Slater forbids formal cooperation, he treats material cooperation as a question of when the virtue of charity requires one to prevent the sin of another. He leaves unaddressed the question of whether a materially cooperative act may itself fall short of a sound moral action. While Slater recognizes that a cooperator must not do something "wrong in itself" he does not address acts that may be wrong specifically *as acts of cooperation*.

46. John A. McHugh, OP, and Charles J. Callan, OP, *Moral Theology: A Complete Course*, vol. 1, §1514.

47. For a more extensive treatment of the liberty of difference, see Servais Pinckaers, OP, *The Sources of Christian Ethics*, especially 330–53. See also Servais Pinckaers, OP, *Morality: The Catholic View*, trans. Michael Sherwin, OP (South Bend, IN: St. Augustine's Press, 2001), 65–81; and, by the same author, "Conscience and the Virtue of Prudence," in *The Pinckaers Reader: Renewing Thomistic Moral Theology*, ed. John Berkman and Craig Steven Titus, trans. Sr. Mary Thomas Noble, OP, Craig Steven Titus, Michael Sherwin, OP, and Hugh Connolly (Washington, DC: The Catholic University of America Press, 2005), specifically 342–47.

48. Slater, SJ, *A Manual of Moral Theology for English Speaking Countries*, Bk. V, Part III, Ch. VII, §2.

One thinks, for example, of handing instruments to an abortionist. The act of "handing instruments" is not wrong in itself. This is a physical description of an act that has not yet been placed in its moral species. The act of handing instruments to one performing an abortion, however, constitutes immoral cooperation in the taking of innocent human life. Such an act fails to conform to the truth about the good of the human person, and, as such, no inconvenience can justify such a bad act. One wonders how Slater could reconcile his view permitting certain acts due to serious inconvenience with the Church's consistent teaching regarding martyrdom.[49] While God may not call every person to this heroic sacrifice, certain occasions exist where one must die a martyr before committing a grave evil.[50] Treating cooperation solely as an obligation of charity which ceases under "inconvenience"—and the corresponding failure to address how this might apply to martyrdom—demonstrates a gap in casuist thinking. This example shows the danger of the casuist approach where imposed obligation, or extrinsic law, can cease under certain circumstances. An example like this demonstrates how a different approach to analyzing cases of moral cooperation with evil serves an important purpose. A virtue-based approach to moral cooperation, with reference to analyzing the act of the cooperator by means of the act's natural teleology, provides such an alternative. Such an analysis attends to the nature of human acting and does not cease to apply under difficult circumstances.

As Slater admits in his introduction, his view of moral theology principally involves efforts to avoid sin. Moral theology, for Slater, does not directly treat the pursuit of Christian perfection. Slater did not anticipate the appeal of the Second Vatican Council to renew moral theology with reference to Christians' lofty calling. *Optatum totius*, the Decree on Priestly Training, teaches:

Special care must be given to the perfecting of moral theology. Its scientific exposition, nourished more on the teaching of the Bible, should shed light on

---

49. See, for example, the teaching of Pope John Paul II in *VS*, no. 91 regarding those who bear witness as martyrs to the unchangeable truth of the moral law.

50. For an alternative perspective, see Martin Rhonheimer, *Vital Conflicts in Medical Ethics: A Virtue Approach to Craniotomy and Tubal Pregnancies*, ed. William F. Murphy, Jr. (Washington, DC: The Catholic University of America Press, 2009), xv. In reference to a so-called vital conflict in which the mother's life is at risk in a difficult pregnancy, Rhonheimer writes: "[I]t is offensive to demand of the mother that she sacrifice herself not for the survival of her child (who will die anyway), but, it seems, simply to safeguard the moral principle that 'an innocent should not be killed directly.'"

the loftiness of the calling of the faithful in Christ and the obligation that is theirs of bearing fruit in charity for the life of the world.[51]

A decade later, the Vatican Congregation for Catholic Education echoed this teaching. The Congregation elaborated on this desired renewal in the teaching of moral theology. In the 1976 instruction regarding priests' theological training, the Congregation explained:

> Moral theology has at times in the past exhibited a certain narrowness of focus and contained lacunae in its perspective. This was in part due to a certain legalism and individualism, as well as to a separation from the sources of Revelation. To overcome all of this it becomes necessary to clarify the epistemological status of moral theology.... With regard to this, we would do well to return to the perspective of St. Thomas Aquinas, who, like other great masters, never separated moral from dogmatic theology.[52]

Proponents of the casuist method of moral reasoning surely would respond that sound moral theologians always understood the importance of the pursuit of Christian perfection and the life of virtue animated by the Holy Spirit. They may contend, however, that moralists considered these aspects of Christian life as the purview of ascetical and mystical theology. This truncated view, however, impedes one's capacity to understand the discipline of moral theology in its proper light.[53] Moral theol-

---

51. Second Vatican Council, Decree on Priestly Training, *Optatam totius*, 16. For an insightful analysis of how the judgment of the Council can be understood as an extension of the Thomistic commentatorial tradition, see Romanus Cessario, OP, "Scripture as the Soul of Moral Theology," *The Thomist* 76 (2012):165–88. For an excellent reflection on the use of Sacred Scripture in moral theology, see Servais Pinckaers, OP, "The Use of Scripture and the Renewal of Moral Theology: The *Catechism* and *Veritatis Splendor*," *The Thomist* 59 (1995): 1–19. For a more extended reflection on the Decree on Priestly Training and its continuity with the teaching of the Council of Trent, see Anthony A. Akinwale, OP, "The Decree on Priestly Formation, *Optatam Totius*," in *Vatican II: Renewal within Tradition*, ed. Matthew L. Lamb & Matthew Levering (Oxford: Oxford University Press, 2008), 229–50.

52. Congregation for Catholic Education, *Document on the Theological Formation of Future Priests*, February 22, 1976, 3.2.4. For more information on the importance of the Second Vatican Council and the instruction of the Congregation for Catholic Education on the renewal of moral theology, see Servais Pinckaers, OP, *Morality: The Catholic View*, 42–62.

53. For an excellent treatment of the debate surrounding the distinction between moral and ascetical/mystical theology, see Jordan Aumann, OP, "Spiritual Theology in the Thomistic Tradition," *Angelicum* 51 (1974): 571–98. For the influence of the Spanish Jesuit Juan Azor on this division, see also Servais Pinckaers, OP, *The Sources of Christian Ethics*, 260–66.

ogy itself—the study of how to live the Christian life—necessarily in-cludes a full treatment of the acquired and infused virtues, the gifts of the Holy Spirit, and man's vocation in beatitude.[54]

Specifically, regarding cooperation with evil, a more restricted approach to moral theology fails to assist one who seeks to inculcate the specif-ic virtues necessary for virtuous cooperation. On the other hand, a vir-tue-based approach to moral cooperation offers an indispensable aid for the development of a connaturality for virtuous—and against vicious—forms of cooperation. This connaturality depends on properly shaped ap-petites as true sources of moral knowledge.[55] This kind of knowledge by connaturality will prove necessary for virtuous participation in an increas-ingly complex and often secular world.[56] No system of cases can account for the complexities present in the twenty-first century. Pope John Paul II hinted at the inadequacy of case-based systems of moral theology when he explained that knowledge of what is required in a given situation is "neces-sary, but it is not sufficient" to act well. Rather, the Pope continues, "what is essential is a sort of 'connaturality' between man and the true good."[57] The mere application of cases of conscience, on the other hand, fails to instill the virtues necessary for sound participation in the moral complexities pres-ent in the world today. This lacuna becomes apparent in Slater's treatise with its restricted account of moral theology. With its lack of reference to

54. For an alternative perspective defending the replacement of the treatise on beati-tude with one on conscience, see Bernhard Häring, CSsR, "Reciprocity of Conscience: A Key Concept in Moral Theology," in *History and Conscience: Studies in Honor of Sean O'Riordan, CSsR*, ed. Raphael Gallagher, CSsR, and Brendan McConvery, CSsR (Dublin: Gill and MacMillan, 1989), 60–84.

55. For an outstanding treatment of Aquinas's teaching on human emotion, see both Nicholas E. Lombardo, *The Logic of Desire* (Washington, DC: The Catholic University of America Press, 2011); and Robert Miner, *Thomas Aquinas on the Passions: A Study of Summa Theologiae, 1a2ae 22–48* (Cambridge: Cambridge University Press, 2009). For an excellent treatment of the role of the passions in the development of virtue, see Servais Pinckaers, OP, *Passions & Virtue*, trans. Benedict M. Guevin, OSB (Washington, DC: The Catho-lic University of America Press, 2015). For the Thomistic teaching on the passions of Christ—and its implications for Aquinas's understanding of the passions more gener-ally, see Paul Gondreau, *The Passions of Christ's Soul in the Theology of Thomas Aquinas* (Provi-dence, RI: Cluny Media, 2018).

56. See *Summa theologiae* IIa–IIae, q. 45, a. 2. For an extended treatment of connatural-ity, see Antonio Moreno, OP, "The Nature of St. Thomas' Knowledge 'Per Connatural-itatem,'" *Angelicum* 47 (1970): 44–62; as well as Craig Steven Titus, *The Development of Vir-tue and "Connaturality" in Thomas Aquinas' Works* (STL thesis, University of Fribourg, 1990).

57. See *VS*, no. 64.

Christian perfection, infused virtues, or the gifts of the Holy Spirit, Slater's system fails to provide a comprehensive framework to induce sound moral acting.

Dominicus Prümmer

The German Dominican Dominicus M. Prümmer (1866–1931) taught theology at the University of Fribourg in the early part of the twentieth century. Born outside of Aachen, he entered the Order of Friars Preachers in 1884. After theology studies in Louvain, he completed a doctorate in canon law in Rome in 1908. In addition to his duties teaching moral theology in Fribourg, he also founded the Institute of Canon Law at the prestigious Swiss university.[58] Today Prümmer is remembered principally for his three-volume *Manuale Theologiae Moralis*. In light of the Thomistic revival initiated by Pope Leo XIII, some authors were inspired to organize their moral manuals more closely with the structure of St. Thomas's *Summa theologiae*. The Belgian Dominican Benoît-Henri Merkelbach and the German Dominicus Prümmer were among them.[59] First published in 1914, Prümmer's work represented the Dominican approach to a more virtue-based moral theology than found in other casuist authors.[60] Servais Pinckaers, known for his critical approach to the casuist period, still called Prümmer "a fine, solid representative of the manuals of the period." In fact, Pinckaers continues, "actually Father Prümmer, in an effort to return to St. Thomas, had undertaken a renewed presentation of this classic morality, centering on the virtues rather than the commandments."[61] Prümmer's shorter one volume *Vademecum* was translated into English as the *Handbook of Moral Theology*.[62] The work, first pub-

---

58. See "Cloister Chronicle," *Dominicana Journal* 16, no. 3 (September 1931): 255.

59. Servais Pinckaers, OP, *The Sources of Christian Ethics*, 299.

60. See Dominicus M. Prümmer, OP, *Manuale Theologiae Moralis: Secundum Principia S. Thomae Aquinatis* (Fribourg: Herder, 1955).

61. Servais Pinckaers, OP, *The Pinckaers Reader: Renewing Thomistic Moral Theology*, ed. John Berkman and Craig Steven Titus, trans. Sr. Mary Thomas Noble, OP, Craig Steven Titus, Michael Sherwin, OP, and Hugh Connolly (Washington, DC: The Catholic University of America Press, 2005), 76.

62. Dominicus M. Prümmer, OP, *Handbook of Moral Theology*, trans. Gerald W. Shelton (Cork: The Mercier Press, 1956). More recently, the text was republished. See Dominic M.Prümmer, OP, *Handbook of Moral Theology*, trans. Gerald W. Shelton (Manchester, NH: Benedictus Books, 2022. For a general review of Prümmer's one volume *Handbook*, see

lished in 1921, has experienced a resurgence of popularity among seminarians into the early part of the twenty-first century. In 2005 the Pontifical Academy of Life utilized the work of Father Prümmer when it addressed the challenging topic of vaccines created from cells taken from aborted fetuses.[63] The Pontifical Academy turned to the Dominican author to provide the "principles assumed in classical moral doctrine with regard to the problem of cooperation in evil."[64]

Prümmer's one-volume English work offers limited instruction on the matter of cooperation with evil. Interested readers must consult the three-volume Latin manual to find Prümmer's extended treatment of the question. Prümmer's work treats the issue of cooperation with evil in two places. First, the general treatise on cooperation comes under the sins against charity towards one's neighbor. It immediately follows the treatment of scandal.[65] Later, in the treatise on justice, Prümmer examines the obligations for restitution for those who unjustly cooperate with evil.[66] A sin of cooperation with evil, he maintains, represents a failure of the virtue of charity to be exercised towards one's neighbor. Prümmer explains: "therefore cooperation with evil is concurrence in another's evil act."[67] Cooper-

---

Matthew Levering, *The Abuse of Conscience: A Century of Catholic Moral Theology* (Grand Rapids, MI: Eerdmans, 2021), 78–81.

63. See the Pontifical Academy for Life, "Moral Reflections on Vaccines Prepared from Cells Derived from Aborted Human Fetuses," June 9, 2005. For more information on the use of vaccines obtained from fetal cells, see two documents from the Congregation for the Doctrine of the Faith, the 'Note on the morality of using some anti-Covid-19 vaccines' December 21, 2020; and the Instruction *Dignitas personae*, nos. 34–35: *AAS* 100 (2008): 882–84; and from the Pontifical Council for the Pastoral Care of Health Care Workers, *Nuova Carta degli Operatori Sanitari* (Rome: Libreria Editrice Vaticana, 2017), nos. 69–70. For a thoughtful reflection on the use of cell-lines derived from aborted fetuses, see Alexander R. Pruss, "Cooperation with past evil and use of cell-lines derived from aborted fetuses," in *Cooperation, Complicity & Conscience: Problems in healthcare, science, law and public policy*, ed. Helen Watt (London: The Linacre Centre, 2005), 89–104.

64. Pontifical Academy for Life, "Moral Reflections on Vaccines Prepared from Cells Derived from Aborted Human Fetuses." See footnote 10: "D. M. Prümmer O. Pr., *De cooperatione ad malum*, in *Manuale Theologiae Moralis secundum Principia S. Thomae Aquinatis*, Tomus I, Friburgi Brisgoviae, Herder & Co., 1923, Pars I, Trat. IX, Caput III, no. 2, 429–434."

65. See Prümmer, OP, *Manuale Theologiae Moralis*, vol. 1, §617.

66. Prümmer, OP, *Manuale Theologiae Moralis*, vol. 2, §100–110.

67. Prümmer, OP, *Manuale Theologiae Moralis*, vol. 1, §617: "cooperari igitur ad malum est concursus praestitus actioni pravae alterius." See also Prümmer, OP, *Handbook of Moral Theology*, §233.

ation differs from scandal which actually causes the evil will in another. A malfeasant cooperator aids in bringing the preexisting evil will present in another person to completion in an immoral act. Prümmer distinguishes between immediate and mediate cooperation, proximate and remote co-operation, and formal and material cooperation. Immediate cooperation participates precisely in the bad act or sin of another while mediate coop-eration provides another with objects or assistance of some kind not tied up in the very act of sinning.[68]

Proximate cooperation refers to those acts intimately connected to the sin of another. Prümmer gives the example of selling poison to a mur-derer. This differs from remote cooperation which is less immediately related to the bad act of another. Finally, cooperation should be consid-ered formal if it is given precisely in order that another may sin. Coop-eration is material, Prümmer explains, if it "cooperates in the physical action only." Prümmer's conclusion follows that of St. Alphonsus and corresponds with the authors of this period. He explains: "Formal coop-eration in the sin of another is intrinsically evil and never licit."[69] "Ma-terial cooperation in the sin of another," on the other hand, he explains as "sometimes licit provided there is present sufficient reason and right intention."[70]

While not contained in the shorter *Vademecum*, in the longer three-vol-ume manual Prümmer provides several examples of licit and illicit types of cooperation. For example, while often illicit, in principle one may sell alcohol to those who will become inebriated.[71] On a matter of particu-lar interest to American Catholics in the twenty-first century, Prümmer does not permit the sale of contraceptives, at least those that of their na-ture could serve no other end than the sterilization of the conjugal act. He asserts: "It is not licit to sell these instruments which serve the abuse of marriage."[72] Prümmer explains that while "the principle of material cooperation is clear and certain, in application, however, singular cases

---

68. See Prümmer, OP, *Manuale Theologiae Moralis*, vol. 1, §617.

69. See Prümmer, OP, vol. 1, §618: "Cooperatio formalis ad peccatum alterius est in-trinsecus mala ideoque numquam licita est."

70. See Prümmer, OP, vol. 1, §619: "Cooperatio materialis ad peccatum alterius ali-quando licita est, dummodo adsit sufficiens causa et recta intention."

71. Prümmer, OP, vol. 1, §622.

72. Prümmer, OP, vol. 1, §623: "Hinc, e.g. non licet vendere illa instrumenta, quae in-serviunt ad abusum matrimonii."

often are difficult."[73] Basing himself on the work of both Hermann Busenbaum and St. Alphonsus, Prümmer attempts to establish rules to determine whether a sufficient reason exists to engage in material cooperation
with evil. The Fribourg Dominican explains:

A more serious reason is required 1. When the sin that results from it is more
serious; 2. When it is more probable that the other would not sin without your
cooperation or when the sinful result is more certain; 3. When your cooperation
is more closely in contact with the sin; 4. When you have less right to such an
act; 5. And finally, when the sin greatly offends justice by injuring a third party.[74]

While one may admire the rigor these criteria present, in truth they leave
the moral agent uncertain of the proper course of action in a perplexed
state. How can one determine precisely if a reason for cooperation is sufficiently just? Prümmer's norms provide a scale to determine if one sin
should be considered more serious than another. However, his rules fail
to establish the first step in the scale. While Prümmer's norms can determine the gravity of sins of cooperation, readers are left wondering how to
characterize (as permissible or not) any particular act of cooperation with
evil. According to his system, only once one can know with certainty the
justification for a particular cooperative act, can one utilize his norms to
examine other—more or less serious—reasons offered to justify other
cooperative acts.[75] Prümmer's work does not offer definitive resolution to
the challenging issue of "sufficient reason" for material cooperation.

During his examination of issues surrounding cooperation with evil,
Prümmer cites Pope Innocent XI's condemnation of laxist moral propositions. Specifically, Prümmer refers to the condemned proposition:
"Whoever moves or induces another to bring a serious loss upon a third
party is not bound to restitution of that loss incurred."[76] The proposi-

73. See Prümmer, OP, vol. 1, §619: "Principium de cooperation materiali est clarum
et certum; *applicatio* autem illius in singulis casibus occurrentibus saepe est difficillima."
74. Prümmer, OP, vol. 1, §619: "Tanto gravior requiritur causa, 1. quanto gravius est
peccatum, cuius occasio datur; 2. quanto probabilius est, te non cooperante, alterum
non peccaturum, aut quanto certior est effectus peccati; 3. quanto propinquius tua cooperatio peccatum attingit; 4. quanto minus iuris habes ad tale opus; 5. denique, quanto
magis peccatum cum iustitia pugnat, idque propter damnum tertii."
75. The American Dominicans John A. McHugh and Charles J. Callan offer a similar
approach to determining justifications for material cooperation. While their system provides greater detail, it does not entirely escape the same shortcomings. See McHugh, OP,
and Callan, OP, *Moral Theology*, vol. 1, §1519–25.
76. DS 2139: "Qui alium movet aut inducit ad inferendum grave damnum tertio, non

tion phrase "moves or induces" indicates a certain kind of action which would be necessary for the completion of another's bad act. By condemning this proposition, Pope Innocent teaches that one is bound to restitution if one's action has induced the sin of another. Here we do not have a case of cooperation with evil as much as an action which brings about the evil done. The condemned proposition limits itself to those actions which *"movet aut inducit"* that is, truly bring about the loss of goods. Prümmer rightly identifies the place of movement as essential for determining the quality of a cooperative act. This description will prove useful for a teleological account of human action which this study proposes.

One common example of the moral manuals of the period concerned the moral quality of selling inebriating drinks to those who would become intoxicated.[77] On this question, Prümmer argues that while such acts entail material (and not formal) cooperation, they often remain illicit.[78] According to Prümmer, however, this qualification does not follow from the teleology of the act of selling drinks. Instead, he gave principal attention to the reasons for one's acting. Prümmer explained that often such a proprietor possessed an "insufficient excusing reason."[79] Like the other authors of this period, Prümmer categorizes cooperation with evil as a vice contrary to the charity owed one's neighbor. While many authors categorized cooperation in this way, for Prümmer it is crucial, as he organizes his manual around the virtues without a further treatise on the commandments. Still, Servais Pinckaers's insight remains entirely valid. Like other Dominicans of the period, Prümmer tried to return to the method of St. Thomas by organizing his moral treatise around the virtues instead of the commandments. However, it is difficult not to wonder if this structure provided only a different manner of organizing what remained in large part an obligation-based treatment of moral questions.[80]

One observes this truncated view of the moral theology in Prümmer's

---

tenetur ad restitutionem istius damni illati." A decree of the Holy Office, dated March 2, 1679, condemned this view among sixty-five propositions cited for their moral laxity.

77. For a further reflection on the sin of drunkenness, see *Summa theologiae* IIa–IIae, q. 150. For an insightful presentation of the context of Aquinas's teaching, see Thomas Gilby, OP, "Thirteenth-Century Food and Drink (2a2ae. 146–150)," in vol. 43 of the Blackfriars *Summa Theologiae* (New York: McGraw-Hill Book Company, 1968), 251.

78. See Prümmer, OP, *Manuale Theologiae Moralis*, vol. 1, §622: "Est cooperatio materialis quidem, sed saepe illicita, si caupo ministrat potum inebriantem alicui, qui iam ebrius est aut sub brevi ebrius erit si ampliorem potum sumpserit."

79. Prümmer, OP, vol. 1, §622: "insufficiens causa excusans."

80. See Servais Pinckaers, OP, "Dominican Moral Theology in the 20th Century," 76.

failure to provide a robust account of the good act. While Prümmer attempts to ground his work in the texts of St. Thomas, he ultimately fails to provide a full presentation of the place of a good act in the moral life. Prümmer maintains that a good act is a licit one, one that does not violate a law.[81] Instead of describing a good act as one which leads man to his end in beatitude, by moving the human actor according to his natural inclinations to his full flourishing, Prümmer reduces the good act to merely the law-abiding act.[82] A restricted view of the good act relates also to Prümmer's treatment of the issue of cooperation. Prümmer places cooperation as a topic under the virtue of charity. Yet, it remains largely a question of obligation in which he pays less than sufficient attention to the teleological nature of the act. It is the contention of this study that only when the acts of the cooperator are rigorously analyzed in their teleological structures with attention to the *per se* effects of the action that one can develop a moral theology that can be internalized or connaturalized. As opposed to the obligation-based and ultimately extrinsic system in use during the casuist period, a virtue-based approach to questions of cooperation will allow for a habituated, connatural knowledge of the distinction between virtuous and vicious types of cooperation.

Benoît-Henri Merkelbach

A privileged place in twentieth-century moral theology belongs to the Belgian-born Dominican Benoît-Henri Merkelbach (1871–1942).[83] Born in

---

81. See Prümmer, OP, *Manuale Theologiae Moralis*, vol. 1, §99: "Actus, qui est conformis huic regulae (normae moralitatis) est rectus seu licitus seu bonus; qui vero est difformis est illicitus seu malus," as cited in Servais Pinckaers, OP, *Les Actes Humains*. Ia-IIae, Questions 18–21, *Somme Théologique*, Notes et Appendices (Paris: Desclée & Cie, 1966), 163.

82. For a more robust view of the quality of the good act, especially its relation to man's beatitude, see *Summa theologiae* Ia–IIae, q. 5, a. 7. In the same vein, see Servais Pinckaers, OP, *The Sources of Christian Ethics*, 269–71; and Romanus Cessario, OP, *Introduction to Moral Theology*, especially 29–49. For a similar explanation of the place of beatitude in the moral life, see *CCC*, nos. 1716–29. For a helpful primer on the nature of the human act, see Daniel Westberg, "Good and Evil in Human Acts (Ia IIae, qq. 18–21)," in *The Ethics of Aquinas*, ed. Stephen J. Pope (Washington, DC: Georgetown University Press, 2002), 90–102. For an outstanding examination of Aquinas's teaching on human action more generally, see Ralph McInerny, *Aquinas on Human Action: A Theory of Practice* (Washington, DC: The Catholic University of America Press, 1992).

83. Unfortunately, recognition of Merkelbach's influence has varied. While some authors like Servais Pinckaers, OP, and Benedict M. Ashley, OP, have acknowledged the great debt owed to Merkelbach, others have neglected his influence. For example, he

Tongres, he was ordained a priest for the Diocese of Liège in 1894. After some years of pastoral work, he entered the Dominican order in 1917. With teaching assignments in both Rome and Louvain, he authored a treatise on Mariology hailed as the standard in the field.[84] His most prominent work remains his three-volume study of moral theology, the *Summa theologiae moralis*. Merkelbach's moral theology represented a departure from the strictly casuist approach utilized by many of his predecessors. While still influenced by the obligation-based moral theology of the period, with his work readers can discover the beginnings of a return to the place of virtue in moral reasoning. Indeed, the emphasis on virtue in Merkelbach's work influenced future moral theologians. Servais Pinckaers called the volumes "a work centered on the virtues from the perspective of St. Thomas."[85] The American Dominican Benedict Ashley turned to Merkelbach when composing his own textbook of moral theology.[86] Ashley explains that he "shamelessly began with the outline of … Merkelbach's old manual of moral theology." Why did he choose the Belgian Dominican's Latin volumes composed nearly seventy years previous? Ashley explains: "From among the manualists I used Merkelbach, because by following Aquinas he had already largely escaped deontological voluntarism."[87] One finds the same judgment in the *New Catholic Encyclopedia*. There we learn that Merkel-

---

essentially escapes notice (except for a single footnote) in two essays regarding Thomistic moral thought in the twentieth century. See Thomas F. O'Meara, OP, "Interpreting Thomas Aquinas: Aspects of the Dominican School of Moral Theology in the Twentieth Century"; and Clifford G. Kossel, SJ, "Thomistic Moral Philosophy in the Twentieth Century." Both can be found in *The Ethics of Aquinas*, ed. Stephen J. Pope, 355–73 and 385–411.

84. See Benedictus Henricus Merkelbach, OP, *Mariologia* (Paris: Desclée de Brouwer, 1939). For more information, see Mark Heath, OP, "War-Time Analecta," *Dominicana Journal* 32, no. 1 (March 1947): 31. Reginald Garrigou-Lagrange, OP, relied heavily on Merkelbach's *Mariologia* when composing his treatise on the Blessed Virgin Mary. See Reginald Garrigou-Lagrange, OP, *The Mother of the Saviour and Our Interior Life*, trans. Bernard J. Kelly, C.S.Sp. (Dublin: Standard House, 1949), especially the preface where he expresses his debt to his Dominican confrere.

85. See Servais Pinckaers, OP, *Morality: The Catholic View*, 39.

86. See Benedict M. Ashley, OP, *Living the Truth in Love. A Biblical Introduction to Moral Theology*, (Staten Island: Alba House, 1996), especially 34–38, for his defense of the virtue-based approach to moral inquiry and its Biblical basis.

87. Benedict M. Ashley, OP, *Barefoot Journeying: The Autobiography of a Begging Friar* (Chicago: New Priory Press, 2013), 532–33. In his moral textbook Ashley specifically cites Merkelbach when treating the gravity of theft (320), the validity of contracts (325–26), and restitution (337–38). See Ashley, OP, *Living the Truth in Love*.

bach's work "not only embodied Thomistic principles but also marked a departure from the casuistic method in moral theology and a return to that of St. Thomas."[88]

Merkelbach treats cooperation with evil in two places. First, in the chapter "De Peccatis," he expounds on the topic of cooperation under the heading the "exterior causes of sin."[89] Second, Merkelbach deals with co-operation in his treatment of commutative justice. He explains when one is required to make restitution after committing acts of "unjust coopera-tion." His treatment unfolds as a commentary on St. Thomas's text re-garding restitution.[90] Several species of acts, such as counsel and flattery, represent approval for unjust behavior. Merkelbach offers scriptural war-rant for his concern with those who would approve or counsel wrongdo-ing. In his Letter to the Romans, St. Paul teaches that those who prac-tice or approve of various evil acts deserve death. St. Paul exhorts the Romans: "They know God's decree, that those who practice such things deserve to die—yet they not only do them but even applaud others who practice them."[91]

Merkelbach provides a delineation of the various categories of coop-eration. He condemns formal cooperation as always illicit.[92] Purely im-mediate material cooperation is also illicit.[93] Even mediate cooperation can ordinarily be considered illicit.[94] Mediate material cooperation is lic-it only if a proportionate grave reason is present.[95] According to Merkel-bach, a most grave proportionate reason excuses the sale of things which

---

88. C. Lozier, "Benoît Henri Merklebach," in *The New Catholic Encyclopedia*, 2nd ed. (Washington, DC: The Gale Group, 2003), 514.

89. Benoît-Henri Merkelbach, *Summa Theologiae Moralis ad mentem D. Thomae et ad normam juris novi*, vol. 1 (Bruges: Desclée de Brouwer, 1956), §487–92.

90. Merkelbach, *Summa Theologiae Moralis*, vol. 2, §309–19. Aquinas lists nine collabora-tive actions that may or may not require one to make restitution, namely, "by command, by counsel, by consent, by flattery, by receiving, by participation, by silence, by not pre-venting, by not denouncing." See *Summa theologiae* IIa–IIae q. 62, a. 7.

91. Romans 1:32. For an excellent treatment of St. Thomas's use of the writings of St. Paul in the *Summa theologiae*, see Matthew Levering, *Paul in the Summa Theologiae* (Washing-ton, DC: The Catholic University of America Press, 2014).

92. Merkelbach, *Summa Theologiae Moralis*, vol. 1, §489: "Cooperatio formalis semper est illicita."

93. Merkelbach, vol. 1, §489: "Cooperatio immediate etiam mere materialis est illicita."

94. Merkelbach, vol. 1, §489: "Cooperatio mediate mere materialis, licet non semper et necessario, tamen per se et ordinario est illicita."

95. Merkelbach, vol. 1, §489: "Cooperatio mediate mere materialis per accidens est licita, si adsit ratio proportionate gravis."

are not evil in themselves. Readers may be surprised to learn that he offers the example of obscene images or instruments used in abortion.[96]
One presumes this refers to instruments which could also have another
use but would not by utilized solely for direct and intentional killing.

With his volumes of moral theology, Merkelbach parts ways with
many moralists of the casuist period. With his work we reenter, at least in
part, the Thomist commentatorial tradition. Attentive readers will note
his departure from other manualists in his treatment of cooperation with
evil. While he organized his text around the theological and moral virtues instead of the commandments, unlike the majority who treat cooperation as a sin against the virtue of charity, Merkelbach does not offer commentary on cooperation with evil there. Instead, adhering to the
method of St. Thomas, Merkelbach acknowledges that the sin of scandal
is a sin against charity.[97] Cooperation is distinct from scandal and thus
is treated elsewhere. With this alteration, Merkelbach points at an important element of a Thomistic approach to analyzing questions of cooperation with evil. The choice against treating cooperation as a sin against
charity has been noted by other Thomist authors. The Toulouse Dominican Michel Labourdette identified Merkelbach as an exception to the
custom of treating cooperation as a sin against charity.[98]

The importance of removing the treatise on cooperation from the schema on charity does not escape attentive readers. When moralists consider
cooperation with evil principally as a sin against charity, they understand a
cooperative act as failing to prevent the sin of another.[99] Instead of exam-

---

96. See Merkelbach, vol. 1, §492: "Res non indifferentes sed ad malum usum, ex se
vel ex institutione, destinatas et vix alium usum habentes, sicut venenum, imagines vere
obscenas, medium abortivum, non est licitum vendere nisi constet abesse periculum
abusus, vel nisi gravissima causa proportionata excuset."

97. See *Summa theologiae* IIa–IIae, q. 43.

98. See Michel Labourdette, OP, *La Charité: Grand cours de théologiae morale/10* (Paris:
Parole et Silence, 2016), 389–90: "Vous trouverez cette question traitée, dans les Manu-
els de Morale, généralement en ce lieu-ci. Merkelbach la rattache au traité de péchés en
général; cela peut se justifier; il est néanmoins difficile de l'analyser sans avoir précisé la
nature du scandale et le devoir de la correction fraternelle."

99. See, for example, the remark of Thomas Slater, SJ. He holds that charity does
not oblige in "relatively serious inconvenience." See Slater, SJ, *A Manual of Moral Theology for English Speaking Countries*, Bk. V, Part III, Ch. VII, §2. The Dominican authors
McHugh-Callan affirm a similar, although slightly stronger, obligation: "charity does
not oblige under serious inconvenience to self." See McHugh, OP, and Callan, OP, *Moral
Theology*, vol. 1, §1514.

ining the act of cooperation directly, these moralists consider cooperative acts in relation to charity and thus analyze them only in relation to the sin of the principal malefactor. Merkelbach effectively escapes this conundrum by examining cooperative acts more rigorously in their own right.

Noldin-Schmitt

The Austrian Jesuit Jerome Noldin (1838–1922) taught theology at Innsbruck during the latter part of the nineteenth century. Ordained a priest at the age of twenty-three, Noldin entered Jesuit formation four years later in 1865. He served as editor of *Zeitschrift für katholische Theologie* and authored several important works, including a study of marriage and the sixth commandment (1898) and another on ecclesiastical penalties (1899).[100] His principal moral manual, first published in 1897, became the most popular moral manual used in the United States prior to the Second Vatican Council.[101] In fact, according to a study conducted in the early twentieth century, more than half of US seminaries made use of the Noldin manual.[102] Like several important manuals of the period, the Noldin volumes were guided heavily by the work of his fellow Jesuit Jean Pierre Gury.[103] Father Noldin's successors at Innsbruck took up the task of editing new editions of his work. The contribution of the Jesuit Albert Schmitt (1871–1948) remains most noteworthy in this regard. Unlike some other moral manuals, the Noldin manuals never saw either an English translation or an edition specifically for use in the United States.[104]

The Noldin-Schmitt manual treats cooperation with evil in two places: first regarding "the precepts of charity towards others" and, second, in reference to which cooperative acts require restitution.[105] The manual divides cooperation into formal and material, immediate and mediate, and proximate and remote. The division of formal and material cooperation follows the pattern of the period.[106] Noldin-Schmitt hold that an act is

100. For additional biographical information, see Celestino Testore, "Noldin, Hieronymus" in *Enciclopedia Cattolica*, vol. 8 (Città del Vaticano: 1952), 1916.

101. Curran, *Catholic Moral Theology in the United States: A History*, 38.

102. Curran, 38.

103. See Gallagher, *Time Past, Time Future*, 51.

104. Curran, *Catholic Moral Theology in the United States: A History*, 38.

105. See H. Noldin, SJ, and A. Schmitt, SJ, *Summa Theologiae Moralis*, vol 2 (Rome: Feliciani Rauch, 1941), §116–29 and §477–501.

106. For an exposition of the distinction between formal and material cooperation in

formal cooperation when "one shares in the intention of an evil action"[107] whereas the cooperation is merely material when "it shares only in the evil action."[108] As Kevin Flannery observes: "For Noldin, the only thing that can bring an act into the category of formal cooperation is the cooperator's intention."[109] While formal cooperation is never licit, the Noldin manual offers criteria for the liceity of material cooperation. Licit material cooperation must involve an action that is good or at least indifferent. Licit material cooperative acts must also demonstrate a proportionately grave reason to permit the sin of another.[110] Among the types of cooperative acts which occupy the attention of the Noldin volume, a large number deal with collaboration with non-Catholics.[111] Noldin-Schmitt hold that it is illicit to offer prohibited food on fast days, at least in Catholic places. Serving to minors makes this sin especially grave.[112]

In order to deal with difficult issues of cooperation with evil, the Noldin-Schmitt manual relies on the so-called principle of double effect. Under the heading of the principles of licit cooperation, Noldin offers an extended commentary on this matter. He explained this principle in the first volume of his moral manual, the *De Principis*. There Noldin explains that nothing prevents an action from having both a good and bad effect. In order for such an act to be morally licit, four conditions must be present: The act can be permitted only if: (1) the act is good or indifferent or at least not prohibited;[113] (2) the good effect does not follow from the bad effect;[114] (3) the bad effect must not be intended or approved but

---

the Noldin manual, see Kevin L. Flannery, SJ, *Cooperation with Evil: Thomistic Tools of Analysis* (Washington, DC: The Catholic University of America Press, 2019), 39–52.

107. Noldin, SJ, and Schmitt, SJ, *Summa Theologiae Moralis*, vol. 2, §117: "In formalem, si cooperans tum ad intentionem tum ad actionem pravam concurrit."

108. Noldin, SJ, and Schmitt, SJ, vol. 2, §117: "et in materialem, si solum ad actionem pravam concurrit."

109. Flannery, SJ, *Cooperation with Evil*, 44.

110. Noldin, SJ, and Schmitt, SJ, vol. 2, §118: "Condiciones sub quibus cooperation materialis licita evadat, duae sunt: ut action sit bona aut saltem indifferens, ut adsit causa proportionate gravis permittendi alterius peccatum."

111. Noldin, SJ, and Schmitt, SJ, vol. 2, §122.

112. Noldin, SJ, and Schmitt, SJ, vol. 2, §125: "Non licit ultro hospitibus offerre cibos prohibitos saltem in locis catholicis, praesertim minoribus, hoc enim esset illos invitare ad peccatum."

113. Noldin, SJ, and Schmitt, SJ, vol. 1, §83: "Si actio ipsa est bona vel indifferens vel saltem non praecise ideo prohibita."

114. Noldin, SJ, and Schmitt, SJ, vol. 1, §83: "Si effectus bonus non sequitur per effectum malum."

merely permitted;[115] and (4) there is a proportionately grave reason to permit the bad effect.[116] Since both authors followed the work of Jean Pierre Gury, readers will not be surprised to discover that Noldin's analysis mirrors that of Aloysius Sabetti.[117] Heavy reliance on double-effect reasoning does not ensure total clarity in one's conclusions.[118] As some authors have shown, extensive use of double-effect reasoning cannot find warrant in the texts of St. Thomas Aquinas.[119] Instead, reliance on the principle of double effect, especially its fourth premise regarding proportionate reason, can easily lead to consequentialism in moral thought. One could argue that a certain form of cooperation could be justified since failing to cooperate could bring about all manner of other evils. This analysis, however, fails to examine rigorously the nature of the cooperator's act on its own terms.[120]

Father Prümmer observed that the Noldin manual "merits consideration as among the best at the time for its clarity, solid doctrine, and skillful way of treating practical questions."[121] Much like the moral theology of St. Alphonsus himself, the Noldin manual is among the best avail-

---

115. Noldin, SJ, and Schmitt, SJ, vol. 1, §83: "Si effectus malus, qui praevidetur secuturus, non intenditur neque approbatur sed *mere permittitur.*"

116. Noldin, SJ, and Schmitt, SJ, vol. 1, §83: "Si adest *ratio proportionate gravis* ponendi causam et permittendi effectum malum."

117. See Sabetti, SJ, *Compendium Theologiae Moralis*, §7–8. For a description of changes to double-effect reasoning from Jean Pierre Gury through the nineteenth-century casuists, specifically with reference to the increasingly greater reliance on the principle of proportionate reason, see Christopher Kaczor, *Proportionalism and the Natural Law Tradition*, 27–29.

118. The literature regarding the so-called principle of double effect is vast. Interested readers should consult the classic article of James T. Mangan, "An Historical Analysis of the Principle of Double Effect," *Theological Studies* 10 (1949): 41–61. More recently, the most significant book-length study is Thomas Cavanagh, *Double-Effect Reasoning: Doing Good and Avoiding Evil* (Oxford: Clarendon Press, 2006).

119. While many authors point to St. Thomas's treatment of killing in self-defense in *Summa theologiae* IIa–IIae, q. 64, a. 7, others have demonstrated that heavy reliance on double-effect reasoning cannot claim St. Thomas as its origin. See Steven A. Long, *The Teleological Grammar of the Moral Act*, 131–48. For a critique of Long's view, see Lawrence Dewan, OP, "St. Thomas, Steven Long, and Private Defense," *Nova et Vetera*, English edition, 8 (2010): 191–205.

120. Eschewing an overreliance on double-effect reasoning, Stephen L. Brock has developed a robust account of the importance of "side-effects" or "indirect intention." See his *Action and Conduct: Thomas Aquinas and the Theory of Action*, especially 200–42.

121. Prümmer, OP, *Manuale Theologiae Moralis*, vol. 1, xxix: "quod merito recensetur inter optima huius temporis propter claritatem, solidam doctrinam et modum concinnum tractandi omnes quastiones practicas."

able in a less than ideal system. The manual offers sound counsel about particular questions from within the casuist system. Unlike other manuals, principally those authored by Dominicans, Noldin feels no need to escape the legalism of late nineteenth- and early twentieth-century casuistry. While his conclusions remain valuable for examination today, his commitment to a deeply casuist method points to the need for a more robustly virtue-based approach to moral cooperation with evil.

Jone-Adelman

In his 1982 novel *Monsignor Quixote* Graham Greene recounts a conversation between the main characters Father Quixote and his traveling companion Sancho.[122] The married layman Sancho recounts his difficulties living Catholic teaching regarding sexual morality. Greene portrays Sancho reading the work of a particular moralist who eases his conscience to engage in marital acts closed to their procreative possibility. "Last night before I slept I was reading your Jone and his *Moral Theology.*"[123] The moralist, so well-known that he required no introduction in this fictitious tale, was the German Capuchin Heribert Jone (1885–1967).

Jone entered the Capuchin order in 1904. After missionary work in the Caroline Islands, he earned a doctorate in canon law from the Gregorian University in 1922. Jone produced a celebrated commentary on the 1917 Code of Canon Law as well as a popular and readable moral manual in the first part of the twentieth century.[124] First published by Jone in 1929 and later translated and adapted for use in the United States by a fellow Capuchin Urban Adelman, Jone-Adelman's *Moral Theology* provides an extensive treatment of issues of cooperation with evil. Its specific advice and straightforward approach made the work especially useful for those charged with care of souls.[125] Unlike the Dominican manuals outlined ac-

---

122. See Graham Greene, *Monsignor Quixote* (New York: Simon and Schuster, 1982), 74–77. Romanus Cessario, OP, recalls this amusing anecdote in his *Introduction to Moral Theology*, 221.

123. Greene, *Monsignor Quixote*, 74.

124. See Heribert Jone, OFM Cap., *Commentarium in Codem iuris canonici* (Paderborn: F. Schoningh, 1950); and Heribert Jone, OFM Cap., *Moral Theology*, trans. Urban Adelman, OFM Cap. (Westminster, MD: The Newman Bookshop, 1951). For a commentary on the work of Heribert Jone, see Keenan, SJ, *A History of Catholic Moral Theology in the Twentieth Century*, 25–29.

125. See Paul E. McKeever, "Seventy-Five Years of Moral Theology in America," in *The Historical Development of Fundamental Moral Theology in the United States*, 10.

cording to the virtues, Jone-Adelman follows the Jesuit and Redemptorist structure of the moral manual by ordering the material according to the commandments.[126] Theologian Servais Pinckaers referred to the volume as "much employed and very juridical."[127] Dominicus Prümmer called Jone's volume "a brief work with great clarity that is doctrinally solid and practically useful."[128] Another writer remarks: "If [the English moralist Henry] Davis was clear and thorough, Jone was quick and convenient."[129]

Jone-Adelman's treatment of cooperation with evil follows an explanation of the principles of moral theology generally, including a section on the three theological virtues and the obligations which flow from them. Like the other manuals of the casuist period, Jone-Adelman treats the issue of cooperation under the sins against fraternal charity. Instead of utilizing the more traditional formal/material, immediate/mediate, and proximate/remote distinctions among types of cooperation, Jone-Adelman employ three distinctions followed by the treatment of particular cases.[130] First, Jone-Adelman condemn formal cooperation as the "concurrence in which one takes part in the external sinful deed of another and at the same time consents to his evil intention."[131] Second, they condemn immediate cooperation. They explain that immediate cooperation should be understood as: "a concurrence in positing an action, which, according to its nature (*ex fine operis*) apart from the intention of one's accomplice (*finis operantis*) directly tends to produce the evil effect intended by the principal agent ... even when done under grave moral duress."[132] Third, they treat material cooperation as the "concurrence in an action which is only a preparation to a sinful deed" and is "wrong as a rule." They explain that it may be permitted

126. For an examination of the differing moral manuals of the various schools, see Raphael Gallagher, CSsR, "The Manual System of Moral Theology," *Irish Theological Quarterly* 51 (1985): 8.

127. See Pinckaers, OP, *Morality: The Catholic View*, 39.

128. Prümmer, OP, *Manuale Theologiae Moralis*, vol. 1, xxv: "opus breve quidem, sed excellens claritate, et solida doctrina, utilitate practica."

129. Keenan, SJ, *A History of Catholic Moral Theology in the Twentieth Century*, 25.

130. While casuist authors most often utilize the distinctions formal/material, immediate/mediate, and proximate/remote, other authors provide still further categories of cooperation. For example, "necessary/contingent" provides yet another possible manner of distinguishing types of cooperative acts. See Russell E. Smith, "The Principles of Cooperation in Catholic Thought," in *The Fetal Tissue Issue: Medical and Ethical Aspects*, ed. Peter J. Cataldo and Albert S. Moraczewski, OP (Braintree, MA: The Pope John Center, 1994), 81–92.

131. Jone-Adelman, *Moral Theology*, §147.

132. Jone-Adelman, §147.

"if the preparatory action is good or at least indifferent, and a corresponding good reason is had."[133]

Through their examination of eight examples of cooperation with evil, Jone-Adelman offer solutions to questions regarding the most common forms of moral cooperation. They include (a) cooperation in non-Catholic worship, (b) donations for the buildings and maintenance of non-Catholic schools and orphanages, (c) contributions to socialistic or liberalistic societies, (d) cooperation in the publication of books, papers, or magazines inimical to faith or morals, (e) cooperation in immoral shows and dances, (f) cooperation of employees in the sins of their employers, (g) cooperation of laborers and tradesmen, and (h) cooperation of the judge in executing an unjust law by passing sentence in accordance with the law.[134]

In treating cases of cooperation, Jone-Adelman provide specific counsel. They allow servants to accompany their employers to Protestant services although they must refrain from singing or praying along. Catholic religious sisters serving in a hospital may not summon a non-Catholic minister for a dying person. Only a "very weighty reason" justifies informing the minister that a patient desires to see him.[135] The ringing of bells in non-Catholic churches or advertisements in newspapers may be permitted as these acts only make known the times of the services and do not encourage attendance. One may contribute money to non-Catholic schools or orphanages since their principal purpose is charity and not proselytization. The Jone manual instructs readers that they may make similar contributions to socialist organizations, but only if the reason is charitable and not to support the socialist agenda. A Catholic vendor may sell publications known for advancing positions contrary to the Catholic faith but may not display them as if to encourage their sale. If proprietors display these publications, they should be done so alongside better publications to further discourage the sale of the erroneous works. The authors will only permit writing a good article for a bad newspaper for a just cause and with

133. Jone-Adelman, §147.

134. Jone-Adelman, §148–54.

135. Jone does not offer an explanation of how a "weighty" or "very weighty" reason compares with a "serious," "grave," or "proportionate" reason. The manual of McHugh-Callan, while not resolving the question, does provide an explanation of much greater depth as to what constitutes sufficient reasons for cooperation. See McHugh, OP, and Callan, OP, *Moral Theology*, vol. 1, §1519–25. For an extended reflection on the calculation of proportion, see Bernard Hoose, *Proportionalism: The American Debate and its European Roots* (Washington, DC: Georgetown University Press, 1987), 81–91.

the bishop's permission.[136] One can presume the bishop's permission, they argue, in an urgent case.

Musicians who play for immoral dances sin gravely, Jone-Adelman maintain, "unless excused by some weighty reason." Policeman and watchmen who are required to be present are excused. Servants may serve meat on a day of abstinence or distribute alcohol even if they know intoxication will follow. Of particular interest for debates surrounding twenty-first-century contraceptive mandates, Jone-Adelman allow druggists to sell contraceptives in order to retain their jobs. A druggist may not, however, direct customers to purchase contraceptives.[137] The question goes unanswered if those in positions with greater responsibility, e.g. the manufacturer of the contraceptives or the clerk who sells exclusively contraceptives as opposed to one who stocks the shelves, may continue to do so under the guise that they have a grave or proportionate reason to do so.[138] Merchants may sell things that will be misused, e.g. cards, dice, etc., but a grave reason is necessary if it is certain that the items will be misused. A judge can never sentence anyone to do anything intrinsically wrong such as making an offering to an idol. He may, however, convict someone of a violation of an unjust law if "the common good demands that a good judge remain in office."[139]

The Jone-Adelman manual provides a comprehensive treatment of the most common issues of cooperation during the early to middle part of the twentieth century. No one can reasonably fault them for failing to anticipate the great many new forms of cooperation experienced in the twenty-first century, most especially in medicine and biotechnology. Who could have envisioned the complexities of contemporary issues in bioeth-

---

136. In this case, Jone simply repeats a regulation found in the 1917 Code of Canon Law. See the 1917 *CIC* 1386, §2: "In diariis vero, foliis vel libellis periodicis qui religionem catholicam aut bonos mores impetere solent, nec laici catholici quidpiam conscribant, nisi iusta ac rationabili causa suadente, ab Ordinario loci probata." See *The 1917 or Pio-Benedictine Code of Canon Law in English Translation*, Edward N. Peters (curator) (San Francisco: Ignatius Press, 2001).

137. Jone-Adelman, *Moral Theology*, §152.

138. For a critique of the use of proportionate reason in the casuist system, see Servais Pinckaers, OP, "Revisionist Understanding of Actions in the Wake of Vatican II," in *The Pinckaers Reader: Renewing Thomistic Moral Theology*, 236–70.

139. Jone-Adelman, *Moral Theology*, §154. This accords with the teaching of St. Thomas. See *Summa theologiae* IIa–IIae, q. 64, a. 6, ad. 3: "[The judge] does not sin if he pronounce sentence in accordance with the evidence, for it is not he that puts the innocent man to death, but they who stated him to be guilty."

ics? Likewise, no one could predict completely the technological advances making the financial industry more interconnected and complex. Given its pocket size and straightforward language, this manual suits seminarians and others in need of quick answers to disputed moral questions. However, with Jone-Adelman, as with many of the manuals of the period, the perplexed conscience is often left with as many questions as answers.[140]

One wonders what ultimately constituted a grave reason to play music for immoral dances. How often need customers ask for anti-Catholic publications before a shop owner may display them in advance? These are not easy questions to answer, then or now. More troubling though is the extent to which Jone-Adelman utilizes proportionate reason. In reference to the liceity of material cooperation, they explain "the reason must be greater, in proportion to the gravity of the other's sin."[141] This stress on the weighing of consequences offers a recipe for great disparity of opinion. Reliance on the category of proportionate or sufficient reason also renders the category of intrinsically evil acts difficult to uphold. In a system in which proportionate reason is used to justify what would be otherwise immoral activity, a situation is created which, in principle, allows for the justification of any act so long as one can claim a sufficiently proportionate reason.[142]

In their account analyzing cooperation with evil, Jone-Adelman stress the subjective teasing out of which effects the cooperator subjectively intends. This focus is insufficiently attentive to the nature of the moral act in which the cooperator is engaged.[143] While distinct from the revisionist theologians of the proportionalist school in their conclusions regarding which acts they would permit, in Jone-Adelman one perceives a certain continuity between the conscience-based theories of the casuist

140. For a harsher criticism of Jone-Adelman, see Raphael Gallagher, CSsR, "The Fate of the Moral Manual Since Saint Alphonsus," in *History and Conscience: Studies in Honor of Sean O'Riordan, CSsR*, 212–39. Gallagher argues: "[Jone-Adelman] shows the poverty of the theological vision and moral prudence to which the manual had descended by the middle of the twentieth century" (238).

141. Jone-Adelman, *Moral Theology*, §147.

142. For a negative evaluation of the reliance on proportionate reason utilized by the proportionalist school, see Pope John Paul II, *VS*, no. 75. For a more positive examination of the proportionalist view, see Bernard Hoose, *Proportionalism: The American Debate and Its European Roots*. For a similar defense of the use of proportionate reason, see Richard A. McCormick, SJ, "Proportionalism: Clarification Through Dialogue," in *The Historical Development of Fundamental Moral Theology in the United States*, 181–99.

143. For an elaboration on this point and how it differs from Aquinas's view of the voluntary, see Romanus Cessario, OP, *Introduction to Moral Theology*, 104–110.

period and the proportionalist school which followed in the second half of the twentieth century.[144] The continuity between certain forms of moral casuistry and the thinking of the proportionalist school has been noted elsewhere. The Dominican Benedict Ashley, for example, argues for a continuity between these moral schools based in a shared philosophical framework. Ashley maintains:

> As someone who thinks in the Dominican tradition, I cannot help but see in proportionalism, proposed under the very nose of the Pope at a Roman university noted for its orthodoxy, a revival of the great controversy that raged in the Catholic Church from the sixteenth through the eighteenth centuries over the competing theories of conscience: "rigorism," "probabiliorism," "probabilism," and "laxism." This controversy, never definitively settled by the popes, is intelligible only in the context of the deontological, voluntaristic type of late medieval theology.[145]

While the conclusions of the casuist and proportionalist schools often differ, the framework from which they approach moral topics remains largely the same.[146] The philosophical framework underlying moral casuistry with nominalist, voluntarist, and legalistic leanings emerged in the modern period. It contrasts with the virtue-based, metaphysically rich approach of Aquinas and his authentic commentators. Among the casuist authors, the Jone-Adelman manual, in particular, suffers from this deficiency.

McHugh-Callan

Longtime editors of the American journal *Homiletic and Pastoral Review*, John A. McHugh and Charles J. Callan, both of the Order of Friars Preachers, co-authored a popular moral manual entitled *Moral Theology: A Complete Course*.[147] First published in 1929, the text combines both the

144. For a critique of the manuals of the immediate pre-conciliar period, in particular Jone-Adelman, especially for the ways in which they neglected the insights of St. Alphonsus Liguori, see Raphael Gallagher, CSsR, "The systematization of Alphonsus' Moral Theology through the Manuals," *Studia Moralia* 25 (1987): 247–77. For a broader treatment of the similarities between casuistry and proportionalism, see Romanus Cessario, OP, "Casuistry and Revisionism: Structural Similarities in Method and Content," in *"Humanae Vitae": 20 Anni Dopo. Atti del II Congresso Internazionale di Theologia Morale*, vol. 3 (Milano: Edizioni Ares, 1990): 385–409.

145. Benedict M. Ashley, OP, *Barefoot Journeying*, 407.

146. In his *Proportionalism and the Natural Law Tradition*, Christopher Kaczor also identified the essential continuity between casuistry and proportionalism.

147. For a thoughtful recognition of their contribution, see Norbert Reynolds, OP,

scholarly and pastoral, as the authors did in their own priestly work. Both served for many years at Holy Rosary Church in Hawthorne, New York giving their text a certain real-world feel that can be absent from other manuals of the time. First-rate scholars as well, in 1940 Callan received the distinction of being the first American appointed to the Pontifical Biblical Commission.[148] In a joint ceremony in March 1931, McHugh and Callan each received the designation ""Master of Sacred Theology," the highest honor in the Dominican order.

McHugh-Callan treat cooperation with evil as a sin against charity, specifically against the virtue of beneficence. In this sense, they treat co-operation closely with the sin of scandal. Readers will recall that while St. Thomas does not address directly the issue of cooperation, he does treat scandal as a vice specifically opposed to beneficence.[149] One may distinguish cooperation from scandal, McHugh-Callan maintain, as the co-operator does not induce another to sin but participates in, or aids in some way, the sin of another. The authors divide cooperation into formal and material cooperation "according as one does or does not intend the sin whose external commission one is aiding."[150] Cooperation can like-wise be positive or negative depending on whether one positively aids the evildoer or does not do something to stop his evil action. Cooperation can also be immediate or mediate depending on whether one shares in the sinful act of the agent or rather in an act that leads up to the princi-pal evil action. The act of cooperation can be indispensable or not indis-pensable depending on whether the agent would be able to act without it. It also can be unjust or merely unlawful depending on whether it involves an injury done to a third party.[151]

"Very Reverend John A. McHugh, OP, Very Reverend Charles J. Callan, OP, Masters of Sacred Theology," *Dominicana* 16, no. 2 (1931): 148–49.

148. For the history of the Pontifical Biblical Institute, including the work of the Pontifical Biblical Commission, see Maurice Gilbert, SJ, *Pontifical Biblical Institute: A Cen-tury of History (1909–2009)* (Rome: Gregorian and Biblical Press, 2014). Historians of theology also recall McHugh as the author of an important book in the field of Mari-ology. See John McHugh, *The Mother of Jesus in the New Testament* (London: Darton, Long-man & Todd, 1975).

149. See the preface to question 43, *Summa theologiae* IIa–IIae, q. 43, on scandal. St. Tho-mas explains, "Next we must consider the vices which stand against beneficence."

150. John A. McHugh, OP, and Charles J. Callan, OP, *Moral Theology: A Complete Course*, vol. 1, §1508.

151. For an equivalent division of the types of cooperation, see E. Dublanchy, "Co-opération," in the *Dictionnaire de théologie catholique*, 1762–70 (Paris: Letouzey et Ane, 1936).

If the commission of a cooperative act does result in an injury to a third party, McHugh-Callan require that the cooperator assume the responsibility of making restitution for the injustice to the third party. On the other hand, merely unlawful cooperation indicates cooperation where a third party has suffered no obvious injustice. Whereas in the case of stolen goods because an injustice has been done to a third party, restitution—and not only repentance—becomes necessary after this unjust cooperation.[152] The authors divide acts of formal cooperation into explicit and implicit formal cooperation. This division depends on whether the cooperator intends the end of the primary agent (*finis operantis*), making the cooperation explicit, or the end of the external act (*finis operis*), making the cooperation implicit.[153] In yet a final division, mediate cooperation can be either proximate or remote "by reason of nearness" to the evil act.[154] McHugh-Callan invoke explicitly this category of proximity to evil, to which authors often appealed during the casuist period.

McHugh-Callan take up an extensive treatment of various types of cooperation that they believe can or cannot be justified. They offer twenty-six dense pages of cases and analysis, making their moral manual the most exhaustive treatment available in English.[155] McHugh-Callan make frequent use of the category of a sufficient or grave reason necessary to justify an action, especially if it involves immediate cooperation with evil. Likewise, they invoke the so-called principle of double effect to analyze the good and evil effects which result from one's cooperation. The gravity of the reason for cooperating, McHugh-Callan maintain, must correspond to the gravity of the evil committed. For example, they hold:

The greater the dependence of the evil act on one's cooperation, the greater the reason required for cooperation. Thus, a more serious reason is needed to justify giving intoxicants to a person who abused liquors, if he is unable to procure them elsewhere, than if he can easily get them from others. But the

---

152. McHugh-Callan, *Moral Theology*, §1510.

153. For an extended reflection on how the Thomist tradition has distinguished the *finis operis* from the *finis operantis*, see Servais Pinckaers, OP, "A Historical Perspective on Intrinsically Evil Acts," in *The Pinckaers Reader: Renewing Thomistic Moral Theology*, 185–235. For a similar perspective on the relationship of the *finis operis* to the *finis operantis*, see Steven J. Jensen, *Good and Evil Actions: A Journey through Saint Thomas Aquinas* (Washington, DC: The Catholic University of America Press, 2010), 28–34.

154. McHugh-Callan, *Moral Theology*, §1512.

155. See McHugh-Callan, §1508–46.

fact that, if you deny intoxicants or other cooperation, another person will grant what you deny, is not of itself a sufficient reason for cooperation.[156]

As one can imagine, this approach can become extraordinarily complex. For example, McHugh-Callan explain, "Graver reasons for cooperation are those that surpass the very grave without being supreme."[157] One wonders how much aid these varying levels of reasons for cooperating actually provide in a concrete circumstance. Moral realists remain concerned with how these categories might actually lead to virtuous cooperation as opposed to merely providing ready-made solutions to theoretical cases.

One wonders if the method of analyzing moral cooperation with heavy reliance on purported reasons for acting can be reconciled with the teaching of *Veritatis splendor*. In this regard, Pope John Paul II explained:

The weighing of the goods and evils foreseeable as the consequence of an action is not an adequate method for determining whether the choice of that concrete kind of behavior is "according to its species", or "in itself", morally good or bad, licit or illicit. The foreseeable consequences are part of those circumstances of the act, which, while capable of lessening the gravity of an evil act, nonetheless cannot alter its moral species.[158]

In *Veritatis splendor* the Holy Father reminds the Church that in any adequate moral analysis purported reasons for acting cannot take priority over the kind of act committed. No one can blame McHugh-Callan for failing to account for an encyclical issued sixty years after the publication of their manual. The issue though offers a cautionary tale for how challenging it can be to reconcile the underlying premises of a virtue-based moral world view with the categories of the casuist system.

Among the situations they analyze, McHugh-Callan take up the noted case of the servant and the ladder. They hold that the servant's cooperation is "not intrinsically evil" but rather "proximate and positive and habitual, and the wrong done so serious that only a most grave reason ... could justify" the servant's action.[159] This view, following that of St. Al-

---

156. McHugh-Callan, §1519. For a similar view, relying specifically on the text of McHugh-Callan, see Peter Cataldo, "Compliance with contraceptive insurances mandates: licit or illicit cooperation in evil?," *The National Catholic Bioethics Quarterly* 1 (2004): 103–30. Here, Cataldo argues that an otherwise immoral act—employer payment for contraception—can be justified if there is sufficient reason for doing so.

157. McHugh-Callan, *Moral Theology*, §1520.

158. *VS*, no. 77

159. McHugh-Callan, *Moral Theology*, §1542.

phonsus, holds that the Pope condemned the view that the servant's action was permissible not because his action was intrinsically evil but rather because he lacked a sufficient reason for acting in the manner he did.[160]

Succeeding in their attempt to give a Thomistic exposition of moral theology, Dominican Fathers McHugh and Callan provide one of the strongest moral manuals of the period. Not only is their text organized around the virtues, but specifically the theological virtues form the basis for their text. While differences abound between their treatment and the theologians of the school of virtue ethics that has flourished since the latter portion of the twentieth century, one can perceive a certain parallel (especially in structure) between McHugh-Callan and the work of some virtue-based theologians.[161] McHugh-Callan anticipate some portion of the criticism lodged by Servais Pinckaers and others who insisted that moral theology needed renewal. Far from the mere cataloging of sins, McHugh-Callan offer a moral theology that encompasses the full truth about human flourishing. They explain:

It would be a mistake to think that, while Moral Theology is a technical and scientific treatise on human conduct, it deals exclusively or primarily with vice and sin, and that it is intended only to enable the priest rightly to administer the Sacrament of Penance, distinguishing between the various classes of sins and their consequences. Of course, it does all this but it should do much more.... The subject is indeed more positive than negative.[162]

The extent to which they accomplish fully this task remains an open question. McHugh-Callan seem able to ground their moral theology in the tradition of St. Thomas more thoroughly than other authors of the period. Still, much in their treatise remains grounded heavily in the system of imposed obligation. Like other authors of the period, they present human freedom in opposition to moral law.[163] The question therefore re-

---

160. For an alternative perspective on this question, see Andrew McLean Cummings, *The Servant and the Ladder*, 65–72.

161. See, for example, Benedict M. Ashley, OP, *Living the Truth in Love*.

162. McHugh-Callan, *Moral Theology*, iv.

163. For an example of an argument relying on the opposition of liberty and law, see John F. O'Malley, "Sale of Contraceptives," *The Homiletic and Pastoral Review* 40 (Dec. 1939): 282–90, specifically, 290: "We have two opinions, one in favor of the law of binding [one] not to sell these instruments [contraceptive devices], and the other opinion in favor of the liberty of [one] in this case. The second opinion, like the first, is regarded a very probable opinion, subscribed to by learned moralists. In a conflict of two equally probable opinions, one in favor of liberty and the other in favor of the law, we are at liberty to follow either opinion."

mains as to the possibility of reconciling the moral system of St. Thomas with that of the casuist authors.[164] While both approaches—Thomist and casuist—often result in similar conclusions for sound moral action, no one can ignore the disparity of their moral methods.[165]

Another area of concern presented by the McHugh-Callan manual is the importance laid upon an action's proximity to evil. At the very center of their argument regarding norms for cooperation with evil, McHugh-Callan appeal to the category of proximity to evil. They explain: "The nearer the cooperation is to the act of sin, the greater the reason required for cooperation. Thus, he who sells paper to the publisher of obscene books cooperates remotely; he who sets the type or reads the proofs of such books cooperates proximately."[166] While there may be something commonsensical to this moral analysis, the inadequacy of a proximity-based approach to moral judgments readily becomes clear. How close an act gets to another evil act cannot ultimately be the judge of the moral quality of the act. What would one make of an act that, while geographically distant from the evil action, remained indispensable to its execution? In the example given, the proper question remains what the cooperator is doing. Can a book publisher accurately describe his work apart from the assistance given to the dissemination of obscene books? Does the typesetter provide a valuable service to authors generally but cannot be held responsible for the quality of the works produced? These questions form a teleological-based moral inquiry that refrains from proximity-driven moral analysis. In chapter four below, we provide a more extensive critique of proximity-based arguments regarding moral cooperation with evil.

Finally, McHugh-Callan's treatment of theft, similar to other manu-

---

164. Thomas Gilby, OP, expresses the inability to reconcile the method of St. Thomas with that of the casuist system. See his *Principles of Morality*, vol. 18 of the Blackfriars *Summa Theologiae* (New York: McGraw-Hill Book Company, 1966), 186: "The preoccupation was not shared by St. Thomas. Nor is it congenial to a moral science which has revived his temper, biological rather than legal, and works with the internal finalities in nature and grace rather than with the extrinsicism, and sometimes the pharisaism of the codes."

165. Michel Labourdette, OP, expresses the view that the two systems cannot be reconciled. For example, see his "Théologie morale," *Revue Thomiste* 50 (1950): 190–230, particularly, 230: "Plusieurs fois loué et recommandé par les Souverains Pontifes, et tout récemment encore par Sa Sainteté Pie XII, saint Alphonse reste un Maître «*omni exceptione major*». Certes, on reste libre de préférer à sa conception de la morale comme science, celle de saint Thomas; nous croyons pour notre part qu'entre les deux il faut choisir et qu'on ne peut les amalgamer à ce plan-là."

166. McHugh-Callan, *Moral Theology*, §1519.

als of the time, could induce confusion. They hold that one who assists a thief who puts him at gunpoint during an act of robbery can be classified as a justified material cooperator with evil.[167] While few would quibble with the description of this act as morally justified, it seems better to say that under the circumstances, one held at gunpoint is not doing the stealing.[168] Theft involves the taking of goods against the reasonable will of another. It is not that theft can be justified under certain conditions as much as the moral object itself can be changed by certain object-specifying circumstances.[169] In this case, from the perspective of the cooperator, it is not an act of cooperation in theft in which he is engaged. This becomes crucial for understanding that certain circumstances cannot justify a bad act. Since theft involves only the taking of goods against the reasonable will of another, one who is forced at gunpoint to assist a thief acts appropriately in not risking his life to save material goods. The reasonable will of the owner of those goods could not claim that one ought to die rather than allow the goods to be taken.[170] In this case, the circumstances do not justify acting badly. Rather, they create a new moral object where the reasonable will of the owner—the essential criterion for specifying an act of theft—does not extend to risking one's life to protect material goods. While there are certain object-specifying circumstances that may change the object of an act, there are no circumstances that can transform a bad act into a good one. Turning over one's goods to a thief who threatens one's life does not describe just reasons for acting badly. Rather, such a scenario introduces a new moral object, i.e., acting prudently with material goods for self-preservation. On the other hand, no circumstance can justify an intrinsically evil act. For example, a consensus of sound moral theologians recognizes that the sterilization of the conjugal act when one

167. McHugh-Callan, §1518.

168. St. Thomas Aquinas holds that one acts appropriately in providing assistance to a thief when one's life is threatened, such as in the case described above. See *De Malo*, q. 13, a. 4, ad. 19.

169. See the definition of theft in the *Catechism of the Catholic Church*, no. 2408, This view relies on the position of St. Thomas expressed in *Summa theologiae* Ia–IIae, q. 18, a. 10. For further elaboration on the role of circumstance in the specification of moral objects, see Romanus Cessario, OP, *Introduction to Moral Theology*, 171–75.

170. Archbishop Anthony Fisher holds a similar view. He argues that examples of destruction of property do not provide a parallel to a duress exception for objective moral evil. Rather, understanding the true nature of property rights provides a sound framework for examining these questions. See his *Catholic Bioethics for a New Millennium* (Cambridge: Cambridge University Press, 2012), 89–90.

spouse is HIV positive does not present a changed moral object from the sin of contraception.[171] Rather, it presents only a new reason one may give for the act of sterilization. Reasons for acting cannot transform bad acts into good ones. Clear thinking about cooperation with evil is only possible when moralists examine critically the nature of cooperative acts. They can engage in this type of analysis when they commit to a rigorous examination of moral objects.

Henry Davis

One of the most popular moral manuals used in the United States during the immediate pre-conciliar period was that of the English Jesuit Henry Davis (1866–1952).[172] Born in Liverpool, he began studies for the Society of Jesus in 1883. Davis served as professor of moral theology at St. Beuno's College, the Jesuit theologate in North Wales, until the school relocated to become part of Heythrop College in 1926. All told, for forty years Davis instructed Jesuit clerics in moral matters. He produced an important edition of the work of the Spanish Jesuit Francisco Suárez as well an acclaimed translation of St. Gregory the Great's *Pastoral Care*.[173] Historians of theology principally remember Davis for his four volume *Moral and Pastoral Theology*. First published in 1935, this moral manual boasts both a comprehensive treatment of moral questions as well as an extensive study of the Sacraments. Organized around the commandments and the duties of Christian life, Davis's treatise represents the classic Jesuit manual utilized in the casuist period. Published in English, it could boast a wide readership both in English-speaking seminaries and among learned laymen. One author remarks: "[Davis] was certainly one of the outstanding Catholic moral theologians in the English-speaking world in the second quarter of the 20th century."[174]

171. See, for example, Pope Paul VI, *Humanae vitae*, no. 14; and Pope Pius XI, *Casti connubii*, no. 54.

172. For a more extensive review of the work of Henry Davis, see James F. Keenan, SJ, *A History of Catholic Moral Theology in the Twentieth Century: From Confessing Sins to Liberating Consciences*, 18–25.

173. See St. Gregory the Great, *Pastoral Care*, trans. and annotated by Henry Davis, SJ (Westminster, MD: The Newman Press, 1950); and, in particular, Davis's excellent introduction to the work, 3–15.

174. See T. Corbishley, "Henry Davis," in the *New Catholic Encyclopedia*, vol. 4 (Washington, DC: The Catholic University of America Press, 1967), 663. John Mahoney

Henry Davis treats cooperation with evil in the first volume of his moral manual under the heading "Charity and Cooperation." After he treats the sins against fraternal charity, namely, hatred, cursing, and scandal, Davis examines the obligations of Christians in the area of moral cooperation with evil. Distinguishing between formal and material cooperation, Davis defines formal cooperation as that "which helps in [the] external sinful act and intends the sinfulness of it."[175] Davis further distinguishes between mediate and immediate cooperation where immediate cooperation participates in another's sinful act itself. Finally, he utilizes the distinction between remote and proximate cooperation according to the extent to which the act of cooperation is "intimately connected with the act of another."[176]

While condemning formal cooperation in absolute terms, like other authors of the period Davis allows material cooperation under certain conditions. Famously, he describes the challenge of determining the conditions under which we may consider material cooperation to be licit. Davis opines: "[T]here is no more difficult question than this in the whole range of Moral Theology."[177] In order to tackle this demanding issue, Davis makes expansive use of the category of sufficient or grave reason. He condemns immediate cooperation in another's sinful act as "always wrong, though there are many apparent exceptions."[178] The sale of certain objects which have only a sinful use is condemned ordinarily but

---

echoes that view when he calls Davis, "one of the most influential of English-speaking moral theologians." See John Mahoney, *The Making of Moral Theology: A Study of the Roman Catholic Tradition* (Oxford: Clarendon Press, 1987), 27. For a noted summary of moral theology beginning in this period and extending through the latter part of the twentieth century, see Richard A. McCormick, SJ, "Moral Theology 1940–1989: An Overview," *Theological Studies* 50 (1989): 3–24.

175. Henry Davis, SJ, *Moral and Pastoral Theology*, vol. 1 (London: Sheed and Ward, 1958), Tr. V, Ch. VIII, Sec. 1.

176. Davis, SJ, *Moral and Pastoral Theology*, Tr. V, Ch. VIII, Sec. 1.

177. Davis, SJ, Tr. V, Ch. VIII, Sec. 2: "In estimating the sufficiency of the excuse for material co-operation, we must consider the spiritual character and needs of another, our relations to him, what and how great is his offense against God, the harm that may accrue to a third person, the public harm likely to ensue, how close the co-operation, how indispensable it may be. So many factors enter into all questions of material co-operation, that only the most general principles can be laid down. Great varieties of opinion, therefore, on any given case except the most obvious, are inevitable, and there is no more difficult question than this in the whole range of Moral Theology."

178. Davis, SJ, Tr. V, Ch. VIII, Sec. 2.

"a very serious reason would justify the seller in not preventing the sin of another."[179] One notes that Davis examines cooperation exclusively under the lens of a failure to prevent the sin of another. While this is certainly one aspect of the question of cooperation with evil, Davis offers markedly less instruction on the question of the nature of the cooperative act itself.

Davis permits material cooperation with a surgeon about to perform a sinful operation "for a very serious reason, and provided there is no scandal."[180] This classification begs the question of whether there are certain types of assistance given at an operation that could be nothing other than an act of formal cooperation. However, according to Davis, one must "intend the sinfulness" of an act for it to be classified as formal cooperation with evil. For that reason, he struggles to explain why even egregious forms of cooperation—such as direct assistance at a sinful operation—can never be justified. According to Davis, a register may witness a civil marriage of those who have been divorced "for a very grave reason." While ordinarily a servant may not seek a prostitute for his employer, Davis explains, "[a] very grave cause would excuse."[181] In principle, the Davis manual permits a certain level of participation in the selling of books or articles which oppose the Catholic faith.[182] At the same time, he acknowledges that positive ecclesiastical law often rejects such participation.[183] In those circumstances, therefore, such distribution could not be justified. Davis forbids absolutely the participation of one spouse in a conjugal act with a spouse who uses a contraceptive device. One can distinguish this act from the spouse who is known to interrupt routinely conjugal acts in a way that is effectively contraceptive.[184] The former actions by their very nature must be condemned while the later are made immoral by the premature cessation of the act by an individual spouse.[185]

---

179. Davis, SJ, Tr. V, Ch. VIII, Sec. 3.

180. Davis, SJ, Tr. V, Ch. VIII, Sec. 3.

181. Davis, SJ, Tr. V, Ch. VIII, Sec. 3.

182. Davis, SJ, Tr. V, Ch. VIII, Sec. 3. Davis writes: "To sell papers that are contrary to faith or morals is proximate co-operation in sin and on the grounds of charity is not permissible, except for the very gravest reason and for a short time."

183. See the 1917 *CIC* 1386, §2.

184. Davis, SJ, *Moral and Pastoral Theology*, vol. 1, Tr. V, Ch. VIII, Sec. 3.

185. For a similar view of this topic, see the Pontifical Council for the Family, *Vademecum for Confessors, Concerning Some Aspects of the Morality of Conjugal Life*, no. 13. For a further elaboration on this point see Joseph M. Arias and Basil Cole, OP, "The *Vademecum* and Cooperation in Condomistic Intercourse," *The National Catholic Bioethics Quarterly* 11 (2011):

Despite its limitations, Davis's manual provides largely sound counsel and generally balanced conclusions.[186] He offers a readable text which addresses the most common issues that would face those concerned about moral cooperation in his day. Davis tends towards the more laxist position than some other authors, allowing participation in certain acts so long as a sufficiently grave reason is present. It is this aspect of his thought—specifically his use of the category of sufficient reason—that requires some examination. Heavy reliance on the category of grave or sufficient reason presents a two-fold difficulty. First, untold disagreement exists about what constitutes a grave or sufficient reason necessary to cooperate morally. The use of grave or sufficient reason ends up reinforcing individual, personal judgments of cases of conscience—the very thing casuist manuals attempt to avoid. Grave reason for one reader may not be sufficiently grave for another. Second and more troubling, sufficient reason can be used to justify all manner of sins on the basis that a grave or proportionate reason justifies such participation.[187] One experiences a certain surprise when reading early twentieth-century moral manuals. While the texts are remembered for their rigor, instead, often these manuals permit a number of unjust cooperative acts, for example, direct participation in an objectively sinful medical procedure. Rather than invoking the category of sufficient reason, moralists would do better to analyze acts of cooperation if they consider the nature of the act itself. We can describe rightly some acts of cooperation as objectively sinful behavior—for example, assisting in the procurement of an abortion. In this case, one

---

301–28. For a concise review of the history of magisterial interventions on this matter, see Andrew McLean Cummings, *The Servant and the Ladder*, 355–56.

186. For example, James Keenan considers Davis's work on cooperation particularly lucid. Keenan explains: "Davis's treatment of charity mostly concerned co-operation in the wrong-doing of another. The lucidity of his expression prompted these passages to be quoted with some frequency. Not only were the rules clear, so were the examples.... He tended to illuminate exactly where the traditional lines had been drawn so as to let priests and laity comfortably negotiate what appeared to be ambivalent issues by following his probable, clear opinion." See James F. Keenan, SJ, *A History of Catholic Moral Theology in the Twentieth Century*, 22.

187. For an outstanding critique of the use of proportional or sufficient reason, see Benedict M. Ashley, OP, *Living the Truth in Love*, 134–38. Ashley argues, in part, that proportionalism is self-contradictory. He explains: "Proportionalists therefore contradict themselves by claiming first to weigh pre-moral values to determine their proportionate weight when in fact they are either already weighing them as moral values, or they are weighing them with respect to characteristics which are morally irrelevant" (136).

need not have recourse to sufficient reason or possible consequences. The nature of the activity itself makes it the kind of action that cannot be made a virtuous act.

In the 1993 encyclical *Veritatis splendor* Pope John Paul II responded primarily to revisionist moral theologians of the post-conciliar period. At the same time, his words have bearing when we examine aspects of older manuals as well. The Pope explains: "The morality of the human act depends primarily and fundamentally on the 'object' rationally chosen.... The object of the act of willing is in fact a freely chosen kind of behavior."[188] According to the Pope, one can address effectively moral questions with reference to the type of activity one is performing without reference to the proportionally grave or less grave reasons one has for undertaking such activity. Regardless of circumstance, certain objects are not conformable with the truth about human flourishing. There is no doubt Henry Davis would be mortified to see revisionist theologians utilize these categories of thought to reach conclusions he rejects explicitly. At the same time, one can find the same categories of moral inquiry, such as heavy reliance on sufficiently grave reasons for cooperating, both in Davis's work and in that of the revisionist authors.[189]

Bernhard Häring

The German Redemptorist Bernhard Häring (1912–1998) remains among the most controversial and prolific moral theologians of the twentieth century. Born into a pious family, he was the eleventh of twelve children. Häring entered the Redemptorist order, taking his first vows in 1934. After studies in Tübingen, he served as professor of moral theology at the Alphonsianum in Rome. His only interlude from forty years of

---

188. *VS*, no. 78.

189. On the continuity between the moral casuistry of the pre-conciliar period and proportionalism, see Christopher Kaczor, *Proportionalism and the Natural Law Tradition*, 205–9. Kaczor explains: "proportionalism can be understood in part, as an extension of the scholasticism of the manuals rather than as a recovery of Thomas." Livio Melina holds a similar view. See his *Sharing in Christ's Virtues: For a Renewal of Moral Theology in Light of Veritatis Splendor*, trans. William E. May (Washington, DC: The Catholic University of America Press, 2001), 4. For a similar perspective, demonstrating the common features of casuistry and the revisionist approach to moral theology, see Romanus Cessario, OP, "Casuistry and Revisionism: Structural Similarities in Method and Content," in *"Humanae Vitae": 20 Anni Dopo, Atti del II Congresso Internazionale di Teologia Morale* (Milan: Edizioni Ares, 1989), 385–409.

moral instruction came when he was drafted as a medic during the Second World War.[190] The experience of war would shape his view of moral matters throughout his life. His 1954 publication of *The Law of Christ* represented a certain break with the classical moral manual. With this work Häring integrated more properly spiritual topics by placing the entire treatise more clearly in the realm of Christian discipleship.[191] One author refers to its publication as a "watershed moment in the history of moral theology."[192] During the 1960s, when older moral manuals were thought to be too rigid, seminaries utilized Häring's work as a textbook. Charles Curran notes that until the 1978 publication of Timothy O'Connell's *Principles for a Catholic Morality*, Häring's *The Law of Christ* was the only available English text of fundamental moral theology from the revisionist perspective.[193] Häring served as a *peritus* at the Second Vatican Council and later received the privilege of preaching the annual retreat to Pope Paul VI and members of the Roman Curia.[194] While he claimed the support of Pope John XXIII for his moral manual,[195] Häring ultimately came under suspicion for rejecting certain aspects of the Church's moral teaching, most especially in the area of sexual morality.[196] Still, his influence has been widely felt. His three-volume manual has been translated into a

190. For a more complete treatment of his life, see Bernard Häring, *Free and Faithful: My Life in the Catholic Church: An Autobiography* (Liguori, MO: Liguori/Triumph, 1998).

191. Gallagher, *Time Past, Time Future*, 204–5. For one perspective, emphasizing the discontinuity between Häring and the manuals that preceded him, see Keenan, SJ, *A History of Catholic Moral Theology in the Twentieth Century*, 88–98.

192. Gallagher, *Time Past, Time Future*, 169. Gallagher writes: "The publication of *The Law of Christ* was a watershed moment in the history of moral theology. From the date of its publication (1954) a process was set in motion that would result in the gradual removal of the neo-Thomist manuals of moral theology from the seminaries of Europe and the United States."

193. Curran, *Catholic Moral Theology in the United States: A History*, 176.

194. Curran, 157–59.

195. Häring, *Free and Faithful: My Life in the Catholic Church: An Autobiography*, 157–58: "Though neither he nor I had asked for it, the superior general of my order got a letter in which the pope expressed his recognition, in the warmest terms, for my work *The Law of Christ*. Meanwhile, this same work was under investigation by the Holy Office because letters of complaint that were being sent to that body [*sic*]. I was glad to think and feel that somehow this kindly pope and I were on the same wavelength."

196. Charles E. Curran, Häring's student and priest of the Diocese of Rochester, New York, popularized Häring's method of moral theology in the United States. Curran recounts Häring's influence upon him in his own autobiography. See Charles E. Curran, *Loyal Dissent: Memoir of a Catholic Theologian* (Washington, DC: Georgetown University Press, 2006), especially 13–14 and 120–26.

dozen languages as he remains a crucial figure into the twenty-first century.[197]

The Law of Christ treats the issue of cooperation with evil under the general theme of sins against the love of neighbor. Häring defines cooperation as "any and every physical or moral assistance in the commission of a sinful action in union with others."[198] In dividing formal and material cooperation, he condemns the former absolutely and makes divisions in the latter to determine when material cooperation may be justified. Häring outlines norms that require consideration to justify material cooperation. They include the following basic principles: (1) the love of self and neighbor oblige us to prevent our action from being perverted to evil ends; (2) the reasons justifying material cooperation must be more valid and weighty the greater extent to which our actions are perverted and the more proximate our contribution to the sinful action; and (3) material gain may not be our motive for justifying cooperation.[199] More clearly than some other authors of the period, Häring scrutinizes the act of the cooperator itself. He maintains the morally upright cooperator must be able to say: "What I am doing is in itself good. I am doing it sincerely and with worthy motives. The perversion of my act is entirely due to human malice."[200] In a lengthy treatment of the types of cooperation which may or may not be justified, Häring offers his judgments about several common cases. He permits a servant to perform his or her ordinary duties, even if these are perverted to bad ends. He allows a cashier to ring up contraceptives but thinks the pharmacist who assists in their sale more deeply participates in this evil. A taxi driver is permitted to take a customer where he or she wishes to go even if he knows it is a place of ill-repute. He may not, however, counsel a customer or provide any assistance that suggests approval of the customer's actions.[201]

---

197. For a positive evaluation of Häring's influence on the field of moral theology, see Brian V. Johnstone, CSsR, "Bernhard Häring: An Appreciation," *Studia Moralia* 36 (1998): 587–95. For a similarly positive portrayal of Häring's work, see James F. Keenan, SJ, *A History of Catholic Moral Theology in the Twentieth Century*, 83–110.

198. Häring, CSsR, *The Law of Christ*, 495.

199. Häring, CSsR, 499.

200. Häring, CSsR, 498.

201. Häring does not, however, require the taxi driver to positively discourage the immoral activity. Germain Grisez, on the other hand, offers a rigorous treatment of the taxi driver ushering clients to locations known for immoral activities. In this case, to discourage sinful behavior, Grisez counsels that drivers carry cards with them to distribute with "carefully prepared exhortations suitable for various situations." See

While he offers sensible counsel on many subjects, Häring's arguments also present deficiencies. Häring allows a nurse to assist in a medical procedure by the "handing of instruments during the operation ... (perhaps even an abortion)."[202] While he offers various qualifications that may aggravate the nurse's complicity, Häring fails to provide a close examination of how best to describe the nurse's action. A nurse, in this case, provides positive assistance to an actual abortion. One gets the impression reading Häring's work—which overall contains a genuine rigor—that there always remains an effort to demonstrate when an obligation does not apply or when laws cease to be in force. Insofar as his manual prepared priests to hear confessions, specifically regarding the need to make proper restitution for sins of cooperation, one can understand why he would undertake this approach. Still, readers will find something wanting in his method. Why would a Christian moral theologian hesitate to instruct a nurse handing instruments for an abortion to summon the courage to object and provide positive assistance to the unborn child instead of the abortionist?[203] Despite sound pieces of counsel offered elsewhere in his text, the inability to understand the gravity of cooperating directly in abortion presents a serious lacuna in Häring's work.

Despite his offering sensible conclusions to many of the cases he addresses, questions remain about Häring's moral method. For example, Häring claims that a soldier who follows orders to kill an innocent person is "guilty of formal cooperation in the sin of murder."[204] It would

Germain Grisez, *Difficult Moral Questions: The Way of the Lord Jesus*, vol. 3 (Quincy, IL: Franciscan Press, 1997), 609.

202. Häring, CSsR, *The Law of Christ*, 505. He advances a similar view in his later work, *Free and Faithful in Christ: Moral Theology for Priests and Laity*, vol. 2. (Middlegreen: St. Paul Publications, 1979), 486. There, in addition to allowing a certain assistance in abortion, Häring explicitly allows cooperation in a direct sterilization: "A good reason for allowing doctors who, in conscience, are convinced that this is a positive health service in the particular case, and are ready to offer it only to those patients requesting it in good conscience, can be taken from a broad understanding of tolerance and respect for a sincere conscience, especially in questions and situations where the givenness of an objective moral evil is doubtful."

203. For a view differing from Häring, urging prophetic resistance to cooperation with abortion, see Pope John Paul II, *EV*, no. 74: "To refuse to take part in committing an injustice is not only a moral duty; it is also a basic human right."

204. Häring, CSsR, *The Law of Christ*, 515. One cannot but wonder about the extent to which Häring's own experience serving as a chaplain and medical orderly in World War II influenced his views on these matters. See Häring, *Free and Faithful: My Life in the Catholic Church: An Autobiography*, 23–44.

strike most authors as more accurate to say that the solider has committed the sin of murder, albeit in unique circumstances.[205] While in either case the direct and intentional killing of the innocent can never be justified, it is instructive to note how pervasive the category of cooperation can become. When the category of cooperation extends beyond its proper place as a category of moral thinking, a lack of clarity develops. When moralists incorrectly consider certain actions as acts of cooperation with evil instead of individual acts in their own right, they can no longer examine these actions with sufficient precision. Instead, the acts find themselves inappropriately subject to the principles of moral cooperation.

In a more general way, one discovers that Häring, like many of those in the casuist period, operates under the category of extrinsic obligation and imposed law. Despite his later sympathies for the school of proportionalism, Häring remained deeply imbued with the spirit of casuistry.[206] The very title *The Law of Christ* shows under what framework he will examine Christian morality. Very little in Häring's treatise on cooperation affirms that moral laws arise from the very nature of man's activity. Moral norms are not laws imposed from the outside but rather spring from the nature of human action. In this way, freedom should not be understood in opposition to law, but, rather, as a precondition for keeping the law as the path to human flourishing.[207]

One example makes clear Häring's tendency to oppose liberty to law. In his instruction given to a confessor, Häring explains, the confessor need not burden a conscience by pointing out that one cooperates in an unjust way in a particular action so long as he has a sufficiently grave rea-

205. For confirmation of the doctrine regarding the immorality of the direct taking of innocent human life, see *EV*, no. 57.

206. In an essay in honor of Richard A. McCormick, Häring's student Charles E. Curran explains his view that the proportionalism he advocated was in continuity with the method of moral casuistry in which he was trained. See Charles E. Curran, *The Living Tradition of Catholic Moral Theology* (Notre Dame: University of Notre Dame Press, 1992), 100: "Richard McCormick continues the best of the casuist tradition. Deeply schooled and trained in the pre-Vatican II casuistry of Jesuit education, our American Jesuit has brought the skilled use of this approach to the problems facing the Church and the world in the post-Vatican II era."

207. For an alternative view on the relationship between liberty and law, see Pope John Paul II, *VS*, no. 35: "God's law does not reduce, much less do away with human freedom; rather, it protects and promotes that freedom. In contrast, however, some present-day cultural tendencies have given rise to several currents of thought in ethics which center upon *an alleged conflict between freedom and law.*"

son for withholding this information from the penitent.[208] While sound confessors recognize that times exist for discreet silence during the celebration of the sacrament of Penance, as a general rule, the confessional should be a place where moral truth is expounded, not withheld. To cooperate unjustly is a bad act, which carries its own consequence. A penitent's ignorance of this truth provides little consolation. One searches in vain for this type of instruction in Häring's treatise.[209]

Conflicting opinions

One can detect a certain myth present among contemporary students of moral theology. Some appear to believe that if twenty-first-century moralists would submit to the casuist framework, moral disagreements would disappear. Students of St. Thomas, on the other hand, intuit that casuistry does not lead necessarily to consensus. For example, the age of the manuals experienced disagreements about the moral liceity of cooperative acts. When proportionate or sufficient reason occupies a significant role in moral judgements, sizeable disagreement cannot be avoided, as one author may wish to draw a line a bit further than another. A brief survey of the disagreements among authors of the casuist period about the liceity of cooperative acts reveals considerable disparity even among those who share similar first principles. This level of disagreement suggests that another method of moral analysis may place issues of moral cooperation on firmer ground.[210]

The celebrated case of the servant and the ladder offers just one example where authors held conflicting views. While Pope Innocent XI tried to settle this moral quandary with a 1679 intervention, one author explains that the period following the decree "lacks unanimity, confidence, and perfect coherence."[211] Moralists disagreed about whether a servant's aid to his master's sin represented formal, material, or implicitly formal cooperation. For centuries moral theologians argued about the moral quality

---

208. Bernhard Häring, CSsR, *The Law of Christ*, 504.

209. For a further critique of Häring's theological progress from his early to later writings, see Germain Grisez, *The Way of the Lord Jesus: Christian Moral Principles*, vol. 1 (Chicago: Franciscan Herald Press, 1983), 37n25.

210. For a vivid portrayal of the drama of the casuist debates concerning the schools of moral theology, see the noted article of Thomas Deman, OP, "Probabilisme," in the *Dictionnaire de théologie catholique*, 417–619 (Paris: Letouzey et Ane, 1936).

211. Cummings, *The Servant and the Ladder*, 65.

of the servant's act. Even papal intervention could not produce consensus on this matter. Indeed, theologians of the casuist period held conflicting views on a variety of topics. The Dominican Dominicus Prümmer maintained that a Catholic architect requires "grave reason" in order to build a Protestant church.[212] The manual of the Capuchin Franciscans Jone-Adelman, on the other hand, teaches that for such an architect to design buildings for non-Catholic worship he requires only "some very good reason."[213] On the important issue of the sale of contraceptives, Dominicus Prümmer held that, in principle, one could not make such a sale. According to Prümmer, vendors were equally forbidden to sell obscene images.[214] Not all manuals in use at the time took the same position. In fact, some explicitly permit such a sale.[215] Prümmer's Dominican confrere Benoît-Henri Merkelbach allows the sale of objects which are not indifferent but evil in themselves. While only a most grave proportionate reason excuses the sale of such things, Merkelbach does allow such a sale. He offers the example of obscene images or instruments used in abortion.[216]

More serious than even the disagreements about particular moral topics, disparity of opinion in the casuist period extended to the principles by which moral decisions should be made. The presentation of the conditions necessary to justify one's material cooperation with evil differed among the authors of the period. While acknowledged to be among the most difficult issues moral theologians face, the determination of the conditions needed to justify material cooperation with evil produced great disparity.[217] Authors reached no agreement regarding the precise distinc-

212. See Prümmer, OP, *Manuale Theologiae Moralis*, vol. 1, §620: "si architechtus catholicus aedificat templum protestanticum, *exsistente gravi ratione*, potest permitti."

213. See Jone-Adelman, *Moral Theology*, §148.

214. See Prümmer, OP, *Manuale Theologiae Moralis*, vol. 1, §623: "Numquam licet vendere res, quae ex ipsa natura sua non habent nisi usum malum. Hinc, e.g. non licet vendere illa instrumenta, quae inserviunt ad abusum matrimonii; pariter non licet vendere imagines obscoenas."

215. For example, see Jone-Adelman, *Moral Theology*, §152: "Clerks in a drug store may never advise customers in the purchase of contraceptives, but to keep their positions they may sell these things to those that ask for them."

216. See Merkelbach *Summa Theologiae Moralis*, vol. 1, §492: "Res non indifferentes sed ad malum usum, ex se vel ex institutione, destinatas et vix alium usum habentes, sicut venenum, imagines vere obscenas, medium abortivum, non est licitum vendere nisi constet abesse periculum abusus, vel nisi gravissima causa proportionata excuset."

217. One recalls the remark of Henry Davis, SJ: "There is no more difficult question than this in the whole range of Moral Theology." See Davis, SJ, *Moral and Pastoral Theology*, vol. 1, Tr. V, Ch. VIII, Sec. 2.

tion between grave, still more grave, most grave, sufficient, and proportionate reason.[218] Some authors of the casuist period even disagreed about how to define formal cooperation. While manualist authors opposed formal cooperation with evil in principle, how formal cooperation should be defined was the subject of dispute. The English Jesuit Thomas Slater holds that formal cooperation is the "concurrence in the bad action of another and in the bad intention with which it is performed."[219] In a similar fashion, the Jesuits Noldin-Schmitt hold that formal cooperation occurs when "one shares in the intention of an evil action"[220] On the other hand, the German manual Koch-Preuss defined formal cooperation as "that in which the sin itself is willed."[221] This insistence that one actually needs to will the sin in order to cooperate formally requires more than mere participation in the commission of the evil act. To hold that one actually must will the sin requires that the cooperative act be directed to the conscious violation of the moral law. This view easily becomes the equivalent of a kind of intentionalism. To maintain that so long as one does not will the actual sin of another, one has not formally cooperated presents too narrow a definition of formal cooperation with evil.

The question of how to treat difficult pregnancies occupied the attention of moralists during the late nineteenth and early twentieth centuries. These thinkers disagreed even regarding an issue as fundamental as the protection of innocent human life. Specifically, the use of craniotomy resulting in the death of a partially born child led to serious disputes at the turn of the twentieth century.[222] At one point, an editor of the official records of the Church, the Italian professor Joseph Pennacchi, hoped to publish his support for craniotomy in the *Acta Sanctae Sedis* (which would become the *Acta Apostolicae Sedis* in 1909). Only an intervention by the Master of the Sacred Palace prevented the publication.[223] On an issue closely related to craniotomy, the Jesuit fathers Aloysius Sabetti and Augus-

---

218. For one effort to elaborate on these conditions for material cooperation, see McHugh-Callan, *Moral Theology*, vol. 1, §1520.

219. Slater, SJ, *A Manual of Moral Theology for English Speaking Countries*, Bk. V, Part III, Ch. VII, §1.

220. Noldin, SJ, and Schmitt, SJ, *Summa Theologiae Moralis*, vol. 2, §117: "In formalem, si cooperans tum ad intentionem tum ad actionem pravem concurrit."

221. Antony Koch, *A Handbook of Moral Theology*, vol. 5, adopted and edited by Arthur Preuss (New York: Vail-Ballou Press, 1924), 41.

222. See John Connery, SJ, *Abortion: The Development of the Roman Catholic Perspective* (Chicago: Loyola University Press, 1977), 226.

223. Connery, SJ, *Abortion*, 256.

tine Lehmkuhl and the Redemptorist Joseph Aertnys each held differing views about what could be done regarding an ectopic pregnancy.[224] Aertnys held the removal of the embryo to be a direct killing and thus opposed its removal.[225] Sabetti and Lehmkuhl allowed the removal of the embryo although for markedly different reasons. Lehmkuhl held that a physician could remove the child based on the claim that this action represented a mere acceleration of the child's birth. Sabetti, on the other hand, rejected this view and proposed that the child could rightly be considered an unjust aggressor against his mother.[226] Historians of moral theology remain grateful to the Jesuit Timothy Bouscaren who authored an important study of the turn of the century debate around this topic.[227]

Even on such an important topic as the absolute immorality of taking innocent human life conflict arose. The disparity of available biological science only partially accounts for the divergence of opinion. The debate surrounding the ethics of treating mothers with challenging pregnancies continues today.[228] In truth, casuist authors—both at the turn of the cen-

224. See Curran, *The Origins of Moral Theology in the United States*, 114. For a more complete history of the controversy surrounding the morality of craniotomy and the treatment of ectopic pregnancy, see Connery, SJ, *Abortion*, 225–303.

225. See Connery, SJ, *Abortion*, 301.

226. See Curran, *The Origins of Moral Theology in the United States*, 114. Curran explains: "The *American Ecclesiastical Review* carried on a long discussion about this case beginning in 1893 including comments from many medical doctors and solutions proposed by three moral theologians—Joseph Aertnys, a Dutch Redemptorist; August Lehmkuhl; and Aloysius Sabetti. Aertnys judged that the removal of the nonviable ectopic pregnancy was wrong. Lehmkuhl justified it on the basis of his theory of accelerated birth (this debate was before the 1895 condemnation). Sabetti strongly disagreed with Lehmkuhl's reasoning but came to somewhat the same conclusion on the basis that the ectopic pregnancy, precisely because it was where it should not be, was a materially unjust aggressor against the mother's life and could therefore be directly removed or killed."

227. See Timothy L. Bouscaren, SJ, *The Ethics of Ectopic Pregnancy: Catholic Ethics Regarding Ectopic and Pathological Pregnancies* (Rouchas Sud, France: Tradibooks, 1933).

228. For a summary of the arguments, see William E. May, *Catholic Bioethics and the Gift of Human Life* (Huntington, IN: Our Sunday Visitor, 2000), 182–86. May later changed his view, accepting the morality of salpingostomy. See the third edition of his *Catholic Bioethics and the Gift of Human Life* (Huntington, IN: Our Sunday Visitor, 2013), 196. Greater clarity is afforded to those who adopt a Thomist analysis of moral objects. See Long, *The Teleological Grammar of the Moral Act*, 161–68; and Nicanor Pier Giorgio Austriaco, OP, *Biomedicine and Beatitude: An Introduction to Catholic Bioethics*, 2nd. ed. (Washington, DC: The Catholic University of America Press, 2021), 81–83. For an alternative perspective on these topics, see Martin Rhonheimer, *Vital Conflicts in Medical Ethics: A Virtue Approach to Craniotomy and Tubal Pregnancies*, ed. William F. Murphy, Jr. (Washington, DC:

tury and today—hold opposing views regarding intention, the specification of moral objects, and whether an unborn child should be classified as an aggressor in a problem pregnancy. All that is to say, unanimity alludes those committed to casuist moral theology.

Unresolved questions

The conflicting opinions proffered by casuist authors in the modern period demonstrate that the method of moral casuistry failed to achieve a complete consensus about disputed moral questions. The various casuist schools, i.e., laxist, probabilist, equiprobabilist, probabiliorist, and tutiorist were separated precisely by how they evaluated this disparity of opinion among approved authors.[229] The casuist system, in fact, presumed and relied upon difference of opinion regarding uncertain moral topics.[230] This disparity of opinion, however, should by no means be considered the only lacuna present in the manualist authors. Rather, the regularity with which a perplexed believer was left without sufficient resolution to a moral quandary reveals an even more serious shortcoming.

One author provides several different levels of reason which could excuse, to one degree or another, unjust cooperation. Readers cannot be blamed for remaining perplexed after receiving the following counsel:

He sins mortally who takes part in, arranges, conducts, finances or invites others to mortally sinful shows and dances. If the same are only slightly inde-

---

The Catholic University of America Press, 2009). For a critical review of Rhonheimer's work, see Basil Cole, OP, "Review: *Vital Conflicts in Medical Ethics: A Virtue Approach to Craniotomy and Tubal Pregnancies*," *The Thomist* 74 (2010): 160–64. Interested readers may also consult William B. Smith, "Questions Answered: Management of Ectopic Pregnancy," *Homiletic and Pastoral Review* 99, no. 10 (July 1999): 66–68; William E. May, "The Management of Ectopic Pregnancies: A Moral Analysis," in *The Fetal Tissue Issue: Medical and Ethical Aspects*, ed. Peter J. Cataldo and Albert S. Moraczewski, OP, 121–47 (Braintree, MA: The Pope John Center, 1994); John E. Foran, "Ectopic Pregnancy: Current Treatment Options déjà vu Humanae Vitae," *The Linacre Quarterly* 66 (February 1999): 21–28; and Kevin L. Flannery, SJ, "What is Included in a Means to an End?" *Gregorianum* 74 (1993): 499–513.

229. For a critical evaluation of the casuist system, see Pinckaers, OP, *The Sources of Christian Ethics*, 273–79.

230. For a brief description of the varying casuist schools, see Sabetti, *Compendium Theologiae Moralis*, §48–55; Noldin, SJ, and Schmitt, SJ, *Summa Theologiae Moralis*, vol. 1, §228–56; Merkelbach, *Summa Theologiae Moralis*, vol. 2, §77 and appendix I; McHugh-Callan, *Moral Theology*, vol. 1, §672–742; and Cessario, OP, *Introduction to Moral Theology*, 224–26.

cent there would only be a venial sin in so doing. Musicians who play for immoral dances sin gravely unless excused by some weighty reason.—Policemen or watchmen who must be present on duty are excused. Those that keep the theater or hall in repair, etc. co-operate only remotely and are, therefore, excused for a less weighty reason. A very serious reason is necessary to rent one's place for such purposes, when his refusal to do so would prevent their taking place. Less reason suffices if other locations are easily available.[231]

The passage delineates why some moral agents might licitly choose what would otherwise be unjust acts of material cooperation. The justifications vary: some weighty reason, less weighty reason, very serious reason, less serious reason, or no stated reason at all in the case of the police. While the counsel given may be generally sound, it is by no means completely clear. It is no wonder great disparity of opinion followed this sort of moral analysis.

Another example proves helpful. The question of when a Catholic could legitimately contribute to anti-Catholic publications does not offer easy resolution. In principle, the Christian faithful would not seek to contribute to publications known to attack openly the Catholic faith. For both reasons of scandal and unjust collaboration with the sins of calumny and blasphemy, believers should avoid giving aid to such publications. Some might argue that the evangelical mission of the Church requires them to be present in media known for their hostility to the Catholic religion. Individual Catholics who reach opposing conclusions on this question could lead to confusion about Christian teaching. For that reason, bishops and those responsible for pastoral care should provide clear guidance to perplexed believers. The 1917 Code of Canon Law gave concrete expression to this moral principle. The Pio-Benedictine Code, which regulated the life of the Church for the most part of the twentieth century, offered sound instruction on this matter:

Neither shall laity, unless persuaded by just and reasonable cause approved by the local Ordinary, write for newspapers, pamphlets, or periodical literature that is accustomed to attacking the Catholic religion or good morals.[232]

---

231. See Jone-Adelman, *Moral Theology*, §151.

232. 1917 *CIC* 1386, §2: "In diariis vero, foliis vel libellis periodicis qui religionem catholicam aut bonos mores impetere solent, nec laici catholici quidpiam conscribant, nisi iusta ac rationabili causa suadente, ab Ordinario loci probata." See *The 1917 or Pio-Benedictine Code of Canon Law in English Translation*, Edward N. Peters (curator) (San Francisco: Ignatius Press, 2001).

The 1983 Code of Canon Law promulgated by Pope John Paul II repeats this instruction:

Except for a just and reasonable cause, the Christian faithful are not to write anything for newspapers, magazines, or periodicals which are accustomed to attack openly the Catholic religion or good morals; clerics and members of religious institutes, however, are to do so only with the permission of the local ordinary.[233]

The slightly altered formulation of the 1983 Code raises the question: who should decide what constitutes a just and reasonable cause? The 1917 Code of Canon Law left these judgements to local ecclesial officials entrusted with the care of a particular church. The 1983 Code requires that priests and members of religious institutues, but not laity, receive the explicit permission of the local ordinary for such publication. The principle remains that all the faithful should refrain from contributing to publications which routinely undermine the Church unless persuaded by some clear benefit from this collaboration. Still, the wisdom of the 1917 formulation should not be lost on those interested in establishing sound principles for dealing with questions of cooperation with evil. In the Catholic religion, bishops occupy an indispensable place. No Catholic life exists apart from episcopal oversight. In fact, only with and under the bishop can Catholic life flourish. The wisdom of ensuring that questions of scandal are resolved by legitimate ecclesiastical authorities represents a wisdom required for dealing with cooperation with evil. In order for the Church to address challenging matters of cooperation with evil she depends upon such clear episcopal guidance.

The Dominican authors John McHugh and Charles Callan provide specification to the degree of reasons necessary for licit material cooperation. They provide principles to understand what sort of reasons are required to render licit otherwise forbidden material cooperation with evil.[234] McHugh-Callan offer five principles by which to judge the suf-

---

233. *CIC* 831, §1: "In diariis, libellis aut foliis periodicis quae religionem catholicam aut bonos mores manifesto impetere solent, ne quidpiam conscribant christifideles, nisi iusta et rationabili de causa; clerici autem et institutorum religiosorum sodales, tantummodo de licentia loci Ordinarii." The 1975 Holy Office Decree *Ecclesiam pastorum* provides the background for this canon. The document proves helpful in recalling how the Church has attempted to dissuade believers from thoughtless collaboration with those who undermine Christian faith.

234. McHugh-Callan, *Moral Theology*, vol. 1, §1520.

ficiency of the reason for engaging in a cooperative act. The principles include: (1) the graver the sin the graver the reason needed to cooperate; (2) the nearer the cooperation to the sin the greater the reason needed to cooperate; (3) the greater the dependence upon the cooperation for the commission of the sin the greater the reason needed; (4) the more certain the commission of the sin the greater the reason needed; (5) the more obligation one is under to avoid this cooperation the greater the reason needed for cooperating.[235] McHugh-Callan offer the example of eating meat on a day of abstinence. The cook who prepares the meal requires a greater reason to cooperate materially in the sin of violating a fast day than the butcher who provides the meat.

The gradation of grave to graver to still more grave reason offers a certain sensible approach for one to determine when disputed forms of cooperation could licitly be chosen. Such terminology represents a more useful schema than alternatives in use during the casuist period. For example, some moral manuals referred not to grave reason but instead to serious inconvenience.[236] The category of mere inconvenience does not correspond to a robust account of the Christian moral life. How serious an inconvenience, readers may ask, would justify contributing to evil? Readers will search in vain for sustained exposition of the virtue of fortitude in these moral treatises. Here one observes the wisdom of the Second Vatican Council which called for a renewal in moral theology.[237] The Council recognized the dangers of minimalism in the moral life. *Optatam totius*, the Decree on Priestly Formation, encouraged students of moral theology to embrace the "loftiness" of their Christian vocation.[238] Rather than teach people to observe the most minimal standards of Christian living, the Council called believers to fulfill their true mission in Christ. Simple inconvenience in living out the Christian vocation hardly constitutes the most helpful moral category for believers seeking to embrace their lofty calling.

Many casuist authors maintain that questions of possible cooperation

235. McHugh-Callan, vol. 1, §1520.
236. See, for example, Slater, SJ, *A Manual of Moral Theology for English Speaking Countries*, vol. 1, Bk. V, Part III, Ch. VII, §2. Regarding a merchant selling products that he is certain will be used for a bad purpose, Slater remarks that "a correspondingly serious inconvenience or loss will excuse his selling."
237. See Second Vatican Council, Decree on Priestly Formation, *Optatum totius*, no. 16.
238. Second Vatican Council, Decree on Priestly Formation, *Optatum totius*, no. 16: The Latin text refers to the "celsitudinem vocationis" of the faithful in Christ.

with evil should be examined exclusively under the framework of the charity owed by the cooperator to the primary agent engaged in a bad act.
Charity ordinarily obliges one to help this person refrain from sinning,
but, under this framework, inconvenience removes the obligation. As representative of the period, McHugh-Callan explain: "Material cooperation,
in case of great necessity, is not sinful; for charity does not oblige under
serious inconvenience to self."[239] One finds something missing from this
analysis. The question of cooperation with evil cannot be considered exclusively from the perspective of whether one is obliged in charity to prevent another from sinning.[240] Rather, one must account for whether what
the cooperator is doing can be understood as a good act in itself. What
about the cooperator's obligations in justice to the one against whom the
sin is being committed? Similarly, what about the question—first in the
mind of the virtue ethicist—of how an act of cooperation affects the cooperator himself? Does it make him more just, courageous, and temperate? Or rather does his avoidance of unjust cooperative acts—even if not
strictly "obliged" in charity to avoid this cooperation— make the cooperator more virtuous?[241] What are the ill effects of repeated acts of material cooperation on the material cooperator? These are the questions that
go unanswered—and in most cases even unasked—in the casuist moral
manual. One wonders if treating cooperation so closely with the issue of
scandal did not cause as many difficulties as it solved. By treating cooperation akin to scandal, the casuist authors found themselves required to
locate the question of cooperation exclusively in relation to the primary
agent. A third party who would be affected by any act of cooperation received significantly less attention.

An alternative approach for examining questions of moral cooperation

239. McHugh-Callan, *Moral Theology*, vol. 1, §1514.

240. The confusion surrounding the obligation of charity pervades the discussion of
cooperation with evil. Andrew McLean Cummings makes this point regarding the position of St. Alphonsus about the case of the servant and the ladder. He maintains that
St. Alphonsus fails to address the obligations of the servant to the woman the master
intends to violate. The holy doctor (like others at the time) erroneously connects the
obligation of charity to the principal malefactor (the master) and not as an obligation of
charity to any third party (the woman about to be violated). See Cummings, *The Servant
and the Ladder*, 69: "The concern ignored by the holy doctor is that a servant, by helping
his master commit this crime, risks violating not a positive commandment to 'help thy
neighbor' but the negative commandment, 'do not rape.'"

241. See *VS*, no. 72: "Activity is morally good when it attests to and expresses the voluntary ordering of the person to his ultimate end."

would attend to the moral quality of the cooperator's action itself. St. Thomas provides a clue to how certain acts of cooperation might be better addressed outside the treatise on charity. In his preface to his examination of the sins against charity, St. Thomas explains: "Next we must consider the vices which stand against beneficence. Among them some come under the study of justice, those, namely, which do an injustice to our neighbor. But scandal seems to go especially against charity."[242] While one may agree with St. Thomas that scandal—acting to cause another to sin—should be classified as a sin against charity, treating cooperation in the same way does not necessarily follow. A sin of cooperation with evil should itself be understood as a bad act in its own right. It represents an injustice to the one harmed. It may very likely involve the sin of scandal as well, but the act of cooperation can be examined most fruitfully on its own. For example, traditionally, moralists have examined the cooperation exercised in the case of the servant and the ladder exclusively with reference to the charity the servant owes to the master. In charity, the servant should attempt to prevent the master from sinning. In this case, the cooperation can be understood as a failure of the virtue of fraternal correction.[243] One wonders if a more helpful method of examination would be analyzing the act of the cooperator in relation to the woman injured by the master's action. Removing the question of cooperation from its exclusive treatment under the virtue of charity may offer the ground for a more robust analysis of all the elements involved in a cooperator's action.

Conclusion

The search for a new method of moral analysis for cases of cooperation with evil does not mean eschewing entirely the work of the manuals. Rather, many of the conclusions of casuist authors for disputed cases of cooperation with evil remain sound. Even one as critical of the casuist period as Servais Pinckaers recognized that one must "distinguish between the container and the contents."[244] By no means do all the conclusions of

---

242. *Summa theologiae*, IIa–IIae, q. 43.

243. See *Summa theologiae*, IIa–IIae, q. 33, on fraternal correction.

244. See Pinckaers, OP, *The Sources of Christian Ethics*, 293: "This is not to say that the teaching of the manuals should be discarded as old-fashioned or outmoded. We need to distinguish here between the container and the contents, between a systematization of moral theology that is a period piece and its contents, which include positions and concrete moral laws belonging to revelation and the tradition of the Church. These latter have permanent value."

the manualists need to be jettisoned, but their method of moral analysis could be improved. In certain quarters, authors esteem what they consider to be the rigor and clarity of the casuist method. The evidence this chapter uncovered suggests that considerable disagreement divides even the so-called approved authors. More troubling, in the casuist system the case of a perplexed conscience was often left unresolved. The virtue-based approach to analyzing cooperation with evil will seek to analyze rigorously cooperative acts and propose the virtues necessary to avoid unjust cooperation. For that task, the Thomist renewal of moral theology initiated in the mid-twentieth century will prove most helpful.

CHAPTER THREE

The Renewal of Moral Theology

A Return to Virtue

In the first chapter, we examined five passages from St. Thomas Aquinas's *Summa theologiae* that prove useful to establish a virtue-based approach to analyzing moral cooperation with evil. We likewise found resources from three of his commentators who remained faithful to his moral method.[1] Next, we identified a flight from virtue-based moral reasoning initiated in the seventeenth century. In the second chapter, we reviewed the work of nine moralists working in the late nineteenth and early twentieth centuries. These thinkers utilized the categories of moral casuistry to analyze questions of moral cooperation with evil. These theologians were unable to reach complete consensus about many disputed moral topics. In addition, they often left perplexed moral actors without sufficient resolution to their moral quandaries. These deficiencies point to the need for an alternative approach to address the challenging matter of cooperation with evil.

The next step in our analysis brings us to examine the twentieth-century resources for establishing a virtue-based approach to moral cooperation. Specifically, we will chronicle the Thomist renewal in moral theology as present in the work of both theologians and the documents of the Church's Magisterium. This third chapter unfolds in three parts. First, we examine the work of the Belgian Dominican Servais Pinckaers, a pivotal figure for the renewal of moral theology in the Thomist tradition.[2]

---

1. We examined the contributions of Jean Capreolus, Thomas de Vio Cajetan, and John of St. Thomas. The thought of these three figures hardly exhausts the resources present in the Thomist commentatorial tradition on the matter of cooperation with evil. For a positive assessment of the contributions of many Thomist commentators, see Romanus Cessario, OP, and Cajetan Cuddy, OP, *Thomas and the Thomists: The Achievement of Thomas Aquinas and His Interpreters* (Minneapolis: Fortress Press, 2017).

2. For an excellent treatment of the importance of Servais Pinckaers for the renewal of

He played a significant role in the recovery of the place of virtue in Catholic moral theology in the twentieth century. Second, we present documents of the Magisterium since the Second Vatican Council which offer salutary guidance to establish a virtue-based approach to moral cooperation. By and large, these magisterial texts avoid the categories of technical casuistry and instead utilize rigorous moral analysis of the moral objects which specify human acts. A virtue-based approach to moral cooperation will follow the lead of the Magisterium by emphasizing the role of moral objects more than intentions or consequences in moral inquiry. The Thomist approach also shares a strong caution regarding scandal, which also finds resonance in the texts of the Magisterium.[3] Finally, three thinkers at work in the early twenty-first century offer insights on a renewed attention to moral cooperation with evil. We will examine the thought of Steven Long, Australian Archbishop Anthony Fisher, and Andrew McLean Cummings. While none offers a complete theoretical account of a virtue-based approach to moral cooperation with evil, each provides an essential element necessary to realize such a method. Taken together, we discover the resources necessary to establish and utilize a Thomist account of moral cooperation with evil.

---

moral theology, see Romanus Cessario, OP, "On the Place of Servais Pinckaers (†7 April 2008) in the Renewal of Moral Theology," *The Thomist* 73 (2009): 1–27. For a moving and insightful reflection upon Pinckaers's death, see Michael Sherwin, OP, "Eulogie pour le P. Servais Pinckaers, OP," *Nova et Vetera*, English edition, 84 (2009): 133–36.

3. See, for example, *Donum vitae*, I. 4: "*The corpses of human embryos and foetuses, whether they have been deliberately aborted or not, must be respected just as the remains of other human beings.* In particular, they cannot be subjected to mutilation or to autopsies if their death has not yet been verified and without the consent of the parents or of the mother. Furthermore, the moral requirements must be safeguarded that there be no complicity in deliberate abortion and that the risk of scandal be avoided." See also *Dignitas personae*, no. 32: "The use of embryonic stem cells or differentiated cells derived from them—even when these are provided by other researchers through the destruction of embryos or when such cells are commercially available—presents serious problems from the standpoint of cooperation in evil and scandal." For several principles that elucidate this matter, see the Congregation for the Doctrine of the Faith, *Some Principles for Collaboration with Non-Catholic Entities in the Provision of Health Care Services*, as published in *The National Catholic Bioethics Quarterly* 14 (2014): 337–40, for example, no. 10: "'Scandal is an attitude or behavior which leads another to do evil' (*Catechism of the Catholic Church*, §2284). 'Anyone who uses the power at his disposal in such a way that it leads others to do wrong becomes guilty of scandal and responsible for the evil that he has directly or indirectly encouraged' (*CCC*, §2287). When a board member or administrator of a Catholic healthcare entity 'uses the power at his disposal' to approve or administer immoral procedures, this diminishes the entity's—and the Church's—prophetic witness to the Faith."

The *ressourcement* launched by Servais Pinckaers

The 1985 publication of Servais Pinckaers's *Les sources de la morale chré-tienne: Sa méthode, son contenu, son histoire* marked a watershed moment in the history of moral theology. Published in English as *The Sources of Christian Ethics* in 1995, Pinckaers's work has attracted a wide readership and exerted considerable influence in restoring virtue-based moral theology to prominence in the Catholic world—and beyond.[4] While one can find a deeper stress on virtue in Dominican authors in the early part of the twentieth century, for the most part the obligation-based moral theology of the casuist period remained firmly in place until the time of the Second Vatican Council.[5] Put simply, Pinckaers played a crucial role in the recovery of the truth about human action. He eschewed both the legalism of extrinsic moral theories and the laxism of the proportionalist and consequentialist thinking of the mid-twentieth century. In sum, he offers a robust description of the nature of the moral act according to the principles of St. Thomas.[6]

Longtime professor at the University of Fribourg, Servais Pinckaers, OP (1925–2008) occupied the chair of moral theology that once belonged to distinguished Dominican moralists Norbert Del Prado and Santiago Ramirez. From this Swiss university post, Pinckaers initiated a revival of St. Thomas's moral theory that continues to the present day. No doubt

4. The particular importance of *The Sources of Christian Ethics*, trans. Sr. Mary Thomas Noble, OP (Washington, DC: The Catholic University of America Press, 1995) should not overshadow Pinckaers's extensive list of publications. Beginning with scholarly articles in the 1950s, and especially his 1964 *Le renouveau de la morale*, Pinckaers compiled an extensive list of publications. For a complete bibliography, see *The Pinckaers Reader: Renewing Thomistic Moral Theology*, ed. John Berkman and Craig Steven Titus, trans. Sr. Mary Thomas Noble, OP, Craig Steven Titus, Michael Sherwin, OP, and Hugh Connolly (Washington, DC: The Catholic University of America Press, 2005), 397–411.

5. For a more extended treatment of the Dominican contributions to moral theology in the early part of the twentieth century, see Servais Pinckaers, OP, "Dominican Moral Theology in the Twentieth Century," in *The Pinckaers Reader*, 73–89. Interested readers may also consult Thomas F. O'Meara, OP, "Interpreting Thomas Aquinas: Aspects of the Dominican School of Moral Theology in the Twentieth Century," in *The Ethics of Aquinas*, ed. Stephen J. Pope (Washington, DC: Georgetown University Press, 2002), 355–73.

6. For a summary of his teaching on human action, and particularly how St. Thomas's teaching avoids the errors of both casuistry and proportionalism, see his "Revisionist Understandings of Actions in the Wake of Vatican II," in *The Pinckaers* Reader, 236–70.

the seeds of renewal could be found in the early part of the century. Another one of Pinckaers's predecessors at Fribourg, Thomas Deman, OP,
(1899–1954) authored a 1921 entry on "Probabilism" in the *Dictionnaire de
théologiae catholique* that stands out for its prophetic treatment of these topics. Deman anticipated the renewal that Pinckaers would initiate later in
the century.[7] As early as his 1921 article in the *Dictionnaire*, Deman argued
for the clear distinction between the virtue-based ethics of Aquinas and
the casuist system of moral theology that emerged in the modern period. Deman explains: "Between St. Alphonsus and St. Thomas there remains the lack of harmony of two irreconcilable systems. Every attempt
at reconciliation is doomed to concordism, that is to say, to artifice, that
is to say, to failure. The historical reality of their misunderstanding cannot be denied."[8] Without neglecting the value of St. Alphonsus's work,

7. See Thomas Deman, OP, "Probabilisme," in the *Dictionnaire de théologie catholique*,
417–619 (Paris: Letouzey et Ane, 1936). For another example of Deman's treatment of
these questions, see his *Aux origines de la théologie morale* (Paris: Librairie J. Vrin, 1951). For
yet another example of early twentieth-century attempts to ground moral theology
more deeply in the Thomistic tradition, see Reginald Garrigou-Lagrange, OP, "Du caractère métaphysique de la théologie morale de saint Thomas, en particulier dans les rapports de la prudence et de la conscience," *Revue Thomiste* 30 (1925): 341–55. The recently
published editions of the course notes of Michel Labourdette, OP, also bear witness to
the virtue-based moral theology he taught in Toulouse during his tenure (1940–1990).
His frequent contributions to the journal he edited, *Revue Thomiste*, also chronicle his
Thomistic approach to moral theology. See especially Michel Labourdette, OP, *Cours
de théologie morale: Tome 1, Morale fondamentale* (Paris: Parole et Silence, 2010); and *Cours de
théologie morale: Tome 2, Morale spécial* (Paris: Parole et Silence, 2012). For a positive appraisal
of Labourdette's place in the restoration of Thomist moral theology, see Matthew Levering, *The Abuse of Conscience: A Century of Catholic Moral Theology* (Grand Rapids, MI: Eerdmans, 2021), 92–101. The work of the French Dominican Jean Tonneau represents a
similar standpoint from his work at La Saulchoir. For an outstanding reflection on his
contribution, see S.H. De Franceschi, "La rénovation de la théologie morale catholique
à l'époque préconciliaire," *Revue thomiste* 116 (2016): 383–419. The work of Wojciech Giertych, OP, at the Pontifical University of St. Thomas Aquinas in Rome, in addition to
his role as Theologian to the Papal Household or "Master of the Sacred Palace," stands
as a continuation of the work of Labourdette, Tonneau, and Pinckaers.

8. Deman, "Probabilisme," col. 590: "Entre saint Alphonse et saint Thomas, subsiste
le désaccord de deux systèmes inconciliables. Tout essai de conciliation, nous l'avons dit,
est ici voué au concordisme, c'est-à-dire à l'artifice, c'est-à-dire à l'échec. On n'évincera
pas la réalité historique de leur malentendu;" as cited in Pinckaers, OP, "Dominican
Moral Theology in the 20th Century," 77. For an alternative perspective suggesting a
greater continuity between the system of St. Alphonsus and that of St. Thomas, see Raphael Gallagher, CSsR, "Interpreting Thomas Aquinas: Aspects of the Redemptorist
and Jesuit Schools in the Twentieth Century," in *The Ethics of Aquinas*, 374–84.

the Thomistic view maintains that the enduring legacy of St. Alphonsus can be found in his particular prudential judgments about moral topics, not the prevailing moral system in use in the eighteenth century.[9] Indeed, the distinction between the Thomist and Liguorian systems of moral reasoning becomes apparent when one examines carefully their two approaches.[10]

The Belgian Benedictine Odon Lottin stands as another notable precursor to the work of Father Pinckaers.[11] This monk of Mont César offered a critique of the reductions of the casuist authors. One author maintains that no one was more critical of the moral manuals than Lottin.[12] Lottin's critique of the casuists, however, did not cause him to embrace the fullness of St. Thomas's moral teaching. For example, Lottin rejected the place of the infused moral virtues, siding instead with the Franciscan tradition which denies the presence of these virtues in the moral life.[13] Unlike Pinckaers, however, the eclecticism of Lottin has not attracted successor generations of moralists in his line.

9. For a similarly critical appraisal of the system of moral casuistry, but, at the same time, an appreciative assessment of the contribution of St. Alphonsus, see Louis Vereecke, CSsR, "Moral Theology, History of (700 to Vatican Council I)," *New Catholic Encyclopedia* (New York: McGraw-Hill, 1967), 9, 1119–22. Citing Michel Labourdette, OP, Vereecke writes: "But the greatness of St. Alphonsus did not lie in his system. It consisted in his finding in the 'swarm of probable opinions, more probable, less probable, certain, more certain, or less certain, some manifestly rigorist, others evidently lax, a collection of moral opinions truly certain, equally removed from extremes, scrupulously weighed in the conscience of a saint.'"

10. For example, see Kevin L. Flannery, SJ, *Cooperation with Evil: Thomistic Tools of Analysis*, 98–124 for an examination of the distinctions between St. Thomas's and St. Alphonsus's teaching on scandal.

11. For a positive appraisal of the work of Odon Lottin, see Fernand Van Steenberghen, "In Memomiam. Don Odon Lottin, OSB," *Revue Philosophique de Louvain* 63 (1965): 181–84. Interested readers may also consult James F. Keenan, SJ, *A History of Catholic Moral Theology in the Twentieth Century: From Confessing Sins to Liberating Consciences* (New York: Continuum International Publishing Group, 2010), 35–58; and Clifford G. Kossel, SJ, "Thomistic Moral Philosophy in the Twentieth Century," in *The Ethics of Aquinas*, 385–411.

12. See James F. Keenan, SJ, "Raising Expectations on Sin," *Theological Studies* 77 (2016): 165–80.

13. For a critique of Lottin in this regard, see Michael Sherwin, OP, "Infused Virtue and the Effects of Acquired Vice: A Test Case for the Thomistic Theory of Infused Cardinal Virtues," *The Thomist* 73 (2009): 29–52, and, in particular, for Pinckaers's critical assessment of Lottin, see note 10 on page 31. For further discussion on Lottin as an interpreter of St. Thomas, see Kevin L. Flannery, SJ, *Acts Amid Precepts: The Aristotelian Structure of Thomas Aquinas's Moral Theory* (Washington, DC: The Catholic University of America Press, 2001), 111–16.

In the second half of the twentieth century virtue-based moral theology saw increased attention, initially in philosophical ethics. Elizabeth Anscombe's 1958 essay "Modern Moral Philosophy" recalled the value of virtue-based moral thinking found in Aristotle. Anscombe highlighted the extent to which moral thinking had lost its way since adopting the categories of David Hume and Immanuel Kant in the eighteenth century.[14] Alasdair MacIntyre's 1981 *After Virtue: A Study in Moral Theory* brought the contrast between Aristotle's virtue-based approach to moral thinking and Nietzsche's nihilist ethics into sharp focus.[15] The work of Servais Pinckaers, however, provided both the historical and theological treatment of moral inquiry that render his contribution so important to the renewal of moral theology in the twentieth century. While this is not the place to treat exhaustively Pinckaers's contribution to the renewal of moral theology, it remains important to understand how his approach—and that of St. Thomas Aquinas—differed from the system of moral casuistry. The method of moral casuistry flourished in the time roughly between the conclusion of the Council of Trent (1563) and the Second Vatican Council (1962–65). This distinction of approaches to moral theology remains important to demonstrate the need for a virtue-based method to address questions of cooperation with evil. The method of moral inquiry utilized by St. Thomas—and by Pinckaers and virtue-based moral theologians—proves more effective in analyzing questions of cooperation than the system of casuistry. Specifically, if virtue-based moral thinking is a more reliable method of moral inquiry, the work that remains for moral theologians is to apply this approach to particular areas of moral theology, in this case, to questions of cooperation with evil.[16]

14. See G.E.M. Anscombe, "Modern Moral Philosophy," *Philosophy* 33 (1958). Reprinted in *Ethics, Religion, and Politics* (Minneapolis: University of Minnesota Press, 1982). For an overview of Anscombe's moral theory, see the collection of essays *The Moral Philosophy of Elizabeth Anscombe*, ed. Luke Gormally, David Albert Jones, and Roger Teichmann (Exeter: Imprint Academic, 2016). For an insightful review of the literature leading to the renewal of virtue ethics, see Michael S. Sherwin, OP, "The Return to Virtue: Challenges and Opportunities," in *Dominicans and the Challenge of Thomism*, ed. Michał Paluch and Piotr Lichacz (Warsaw: Instiytut Tomistyczny, 2012), 183–202.

15. For an appreciative essay of MacIntyre's place in the renewal of virtue-based moral thinking, see Romanus Cessario, OP, "*After Virtue*, Thirty Years After: Laudatio for Alasdair MacIntyre," *Nova et Vetera*, English edition, 10 (2012): 895–900.

16. For an alternate view defending the casuist tradition against the criticisms of Fathers Pinckaers and Cessario, see Brian Besong, "Reappraising the Manual Tradition," *American Catholic Philosophical Quarterly* 89 (2015): 557–84.

In continuity with the work of his Dominican predecessors, Pinckaers describes the contrast between the moral systems. He explains: "In
St. Thomas we are dealing with a morality of beatitude and the virtues,
centering around charity and prudence, and with our modern moralists,
with commandments and legal obligations, focusing on conscience and
sins."[17] For Pinckaers, the starting point for addressing moral matters
must be human beatitude and the virtues that lead to human flourishing. The casuist manuals offer a fundamentally different paradigm for examining moral questions.[18] Pinckaers rarely expresses disagreement with
a particular conclusion found in the manuals. Instead, he believes they
provide generally sound counsel for particular questions in the Christian
moral life. By and large, however, they do not offer a sufficient framework
for understanding the moral life. Specifically troubling to Pinckaers are
those manuals which lack an extensive treatment of the infused virtues
and the gifts of the Holy Spirit.[19]

One aspect of the renewal Servais Pinckaers initiated is the stress on
the intrinsic nature of moral theology. As opposed to an obligation-based
moral system where external laws are imposed on human conduct in the
form of obligations, the virtue-based approach sees moral laws as deriving from the nature of human action itself. For Pinckaers, acts have na-
tures.[20] Human acts contribute—or diminish—man's capacity to reach

17. Pinckaers, OP, "Dominican Moral Theology in the 20th Century," 78. For a
further description of the contrast between moral systems, see Servais Pinckaers, OP,
"Aquinas and Agency: Beyond Autonomy and Heteronomy?," in *The Pinckaers Reader*, 167–
84, especially 183–84.

18. See, for example, Pinckaers, OP, *The Sources of Christian Ethics*, 279: "I believe one
good method of succeeding at this [task of the contemporary ethicist] is to compare different systems of moral theology operative through the course of history, notably those
of St. Augustine, St. Thomas, and casuistry. A penetrating glance soon observes that a
system built on obligation, such as we observe today, is not the only possibility, and that
there have been other models of moral theology in the Church. The fact that they are
ancient does not prevent them from corresponding better to the profound aspirations
of moderns."

19. Some commentators remained more faithful to St. Thomas's presentation and
laid adequate emphasis on the virtues and the gifts, for example St. Antoninus of Florence (1389–1459). See Pinckaers, OP, *The Sources of Christian Ethics*, 257. The moral thought
of St. Antoninus represents another important step in the Thomist commentatorial
tradition. In Renaissance Florence, he perceived the need for sound moral analysis at the
beginnings of modern economic and social life. For a terrific exposition of his thought
on economic matters, see Bede Jarrett, OP, *S. Antonino and Medieval Economics* (London:
The Manresa Press, 1914).

20. See, for example, Pinckaers's description of the proportionalist inattention to

his ultimate finality in beatitude. A virtuous person can develop a con-naturality for good acts only if his acts are of a certain quality which conform to the truth about the good of the human person. As Pinckaers explains, beatitude occupies the primary place in Aquinas's explanation of the moral life.[21] The first five questions of the *secunda pars* of the *Summa theologiae* deal with the question of beatitude and set the framework for the exposition of the moral life which follows.[22] For that reason, the question in virtue-based moral theology cannot be which external rule an action may violate but rather the extent to which this kind of action helps or hinders one to reach his final end.[23] For Aquinas, man always acts in view of an end which gives shape to the nature of his actions.[24] We will exposit the specific application of these theses to the question of cooperation with evil in chapter four below. For the time being it suffices to recognize the distinction between a system of moral analysis that sees moral laws primarily as external rules, extrinsic to human goods, and one that recognizes them to be the very means of human flourishing.[25]

Even casual observers will notice the prominent place virtue occupies in

---

true finality in human acting. He writes: "Thus proportionalism, which is a crisis of casuist morality, many of whose perspectives of thought it inherits, strikes us as insufficient, not only from the viewpoint of the moral objectivity defended by the manuals, but also from that of finality, which it makes its strongest point. Remaining fixed on the question of obligation, it is unable to handle competently the principal 'final' questions, which have been practically banished from morality for four centuries and to which the Gospel brings the best and sometimes the only answers in a very direct manner." See Pinckaers, "Revisionist Understandings of Actions in the Wake of Vatican II," in *The Pinckaers Reader*, 270.

21. Pinckaers, OP, *The Sources of Christian Ethics*, 222.

22. For a helpful treatment of the place of the first five questions of the *prima-secundae* in the structure of the *Summa theologiae*, see Giovanni Kostko, *Beatitudine e vita cristiana nella Summa Theologiae di S. Tommaso d'Aquino* (Bologna: Edizioni Studio Domenicano, 2005), 32–39.

23. See *Summa theologiae* Ia–IIae, q. 5, a. 1. For an elaboration on this point, see Michel Labourdette, OP, *Cours de théologie morale: Tome 1, Morale fondamentale*, 78–81.

24. For further treatment of the important role of beatitude in the moral life, see two essays by Servais Pinckaers, OP, "Aquinas's Pursuit of Beatitude: From the *Commentary on the Sentences* to the *Summa Theologiae*," in *The Pinckaers Reader*, 93–114; and "Beatitude and the Beatitudes in Aquinas's *Summa Theologiae*," in *The Pinckaers Reader*, 115–29.

25. For a similar judgment regarding the history of moral theology, see Louis Vereecke, *Da Guglielmo d'Ockham a sant'Alfonso de Liguori: Saggi di storia della teologia morale moderna 1300–1787* (Milan: Edizioni Paoline, 1990); as well as Livio Melina, *Sharing in Christ's Virtues: For the Renewal of Moral Theology in Light of Veritatis Splendor*, trans. William E. May (Washington, DC: The Catholic University of America Press, 2001), 167–68.

St. Thomas's exposition of the moral life. While virtues develop by means of concrete actions, the most significant concern for the Thomist moral theologian remains the particular virtue exercised in a given action. Individual choices result from the presence (or absence) of particular virtues. For Aquinas, attention to the acquisition of virtuous habits proves more helpful than analyzing a particular choice without reference to the emotions or habits which make such a choice possible. Pinckaers wisely adopts Aquinas's understanding of *habitus* and puts it at the service of his moral framework.[26] A virtue-based approach to moral cooperation with evil requires precisely such *habitus* formation according to the vision of St. Thomas.[27] Unlike casuist methods of analysis, a Thomist approach remains especially interested in how to develop the necessary habits to actually engage in concrete moral action. A *habitus* of shunning vicious engagement with the world produces a genuine source of moral knowledge.

One of the most important contributions of Pinckaers's work in moral theology remains his reflections on human freedom. Human freedom, properly understood, is freedom for excellence. Not merely the choice between opposites of a freedom of indifference, genuine freedom leads to the excellence of human flourishing.[28] Pinckaers provides the examples of learning a foreign language or playing a musical instrument.[29] While the freedom of these activities is subject to grammatical rules or the truth about the form of music, one skilled at the piano or speaking a foreign language exercises a freedom more fundamental than choice between contraries. This freedom, Pinckaers maintains, is "not to be confused with the freedom to make mistakes, which is implied by the choice of contraries, but lies rather in the ability to avoid them, without conscious

26. See, for example, his *The Sources of Christian Ethics*, 335–36. The inadequacy of the English translation habit for *habitus* has been widely noted. See, for example, Servais Pinckaers, OP, "Virtue Is Not a Habit," trans. Bernard Gilligan, *Cross Currents* (1962): 65–81. The subtleties involved in understanding *habitus* correctly have eluded many thinkers. For a sound explanation of the Thomistic understanding of *habitus*, see Mark K. Spencer, "The Category of *habitus*: Accidents, Artifacts, and Human Nature," *The Thomist* 79 (2015): 113–54.

27. For a helpful exposition of Aquinas's teaching on habit, see Robert Edward Brennan, OP, *Thomistic Psychology: A Philosophic Analysis of the Nature of Man* (Tacoma, WA: Cluny Media, 2016), 201–16.

28. See Pinckaers, OP, *The Sources of Christian Ethics*, 375. For further treatment on the truth about freedom, see Servais Pinckaers, OP, "Ethics and the Image of God," and "Aquinas and Agency," both in *The Pinckaers Reader*, 130–43 and 167–84.

29. Pinckaers, OP, *The Sources of Christian Ethics*, 354–56.

effort."[30] This freedom for excellence finds its source in the natural inclinations of man to truth and goodness. Pinckaers explains: "Freedom is no longer characterized by indifference, but rather by the spontaneous attraction and interest experienced in regard to all that is true and good, or at least to whatever seems so to us. The morality issuing from this freedom is a morality of attraction, not obligation."[31] For Pinckaers, the continuity of Scriptural, patristic, and early medieval thought on the issue of freedom suffered a rupture in the fourteenth century. Pinckaers lays a large portion of the blame at the feet of the Franciscan William of Ockham (1288–1348).[32] Ockham offered a critique of Aquinas's view of freedom. He rejected St. Thomas's teaching that freedom is "a faculty proceeding from reason and will, which unite to make an act of choice." Ockham, instead, claimed that "free will preceded reason and will in such a way to move them in their acts."[33] When freedom is seen principally as a faculty of choice between contraries—to will this or that—the entire schema of St. Thomas, with freedom uniting reason and will in view of the natural inclinations to various goods, breaks down.

In this effort to distinguish virtue-based ethics from moral casuistry, one profitably attends to Pinckaers's recovery of the place the infused virtues and the gifts of the Holy Spirit occupy in the Christian moral life. The infused virtues and gifts of the Holy Spirit will prove significant in the virtue-based approach to moral cooperation and too often were absent in the casuist manuals. One searches in vain for any extended treatment of the gifts of the Holy Spirit in manuals of moral theology in the

---

30. Pinckaers, 356.

31. Pinckaers, 359

32. For a careful exposition of Ockham's thought on human action, see Thomas M. Osborne, Jr., *Human Action in Thomas Aquinas, John Duns Scotus, and William of Ockham* (Washington, DC: The Catholic University of America Press, 2014).

33. See Pinckaers, OP, *The Sources of Christian Ethics*, 331. For a further critique of Ockham's view, see Romanus Cessario, OP, *Introduction to Moral Theology*, rev. ed. (Washington, DC: The Catholic University of America Press, 2013), 220: "The historical roots of this conception of human freedom as a liberty of indifference lie in the *via moderna* and, especially, as has been said, in the work of William of Ockham. Much of Ockham's theological thinking is determined by his resolute attempt to eliminate anything that would limit the divine omnipotence and God's freedom. Significantly, Ockham considered the doctrine of the eternal law, that is, how God knows the world to be, as an overly restrictive one, for it appeared to place constraints on God's freedom to do as he pleases in the world. The casuist conception of freedom as unfettered self-determination owes much to how nominalist thinkers envisioned the divine freedom."

casuist period. For example, the only reference to the gifts of the Holy Spirit in the manual of Jone-Adelman comes in reference to what one receives from the Sacraments.[34] In fact, they are completely absent from his moral treatise. While Dominicus Prümmer offers a more extended treatment of the gifts, he describes them as a type of virtue but ignores them during his reflection on specific moral topics.[35] Even this treatment is greatly reduced in Prümmer's one-volume *vademecum* which contains only one reference to the gifts of the Holy Spirit.[36] This truncated view represents a markedly different outlook than that of Aquinas and his most faithful interpreters, who recognize the place of the gifts in the moral life.[37] The gifts of the Holy Spirit were not unknown during the casuist period but were treated almost exclusively as an aspect of ascetical and mystical theology.[38] The difficulty presented by this demarcation between moral and spiritual theology is clear. When one fails to grasp that moral theology encompasses virtues and gifts, one lacks the tools for a full analysis of how the human person flourishes in the Christian life.[39] Specifically, relegating virtues and gifts to ascetical or mystical theology

34. Heribert Jone, OFM Cap., *Moral Theology*, trans. Urban Adelman, OFM Cap., (Westminster, MD: The Newman Bookshop, 1951), §447.

35. Dominicus M. Prümmer, OP, *Manuale Theologiae Moralis: Secundum Principia S. Thomae Aquinatis*, Vol. I (Fribourg: Herder, 1955), §445–55.

36. Dominicus M. Prümmer, OP *Handbook of Moral Theology*, trans. Gerald W. Shelton (Cork: The Mercier Press, 1956), §180.

37. Most notable in this regard is the seventeenth-century Thomistic commentator John of St. Thomas. See his *The Gifts of the Holy Spirit*, trans. Dominic Hughes, OP (New York: Sheed & Ward, 1951). For an excellent exposition of the place of the gifts of the Holy Spirit in Catholic moral thought, see Edwin D. O'Connor, C.S.C., *The Gifts of the Holy Spirit*, vol. 24 of the Blackfriars *Summa* (New York: McGraw-Hill Book Company, 1974), 80–156. For a similarly excellent treatment of the gifts—especially in how they can be distinguished from the infused moral virtues, see Giovanni Kostko, *Doni Dello Spirito Santo E Vita Morale: San Tommaso Nella Somma Teologica* (Roma: Coletti A San Pietro, 1997), 119–28.

38. For an explanation of how this division of moral and ascetical theology arose, especially in the work of the Jesuit Juan Azor at the turn of the seventeenth century, see Kostko, *Doni Dello Spirito Santo E Vita Morale*, 11. For a similar perspective, see Pinckaers, OP, *The Sources of Christian Ethics*, 260–66.

39. For an outstanding treatment of the indispensible place of the gifts of the Holy Spirit in the full flourishing of the Christian life, see Jordan Aumann, OP, *Spiritual Theology* (New York: Continuum, 2006), especially 88–97. Interested readers may also consult Antoine Gardeil, OP, *The Gifts of the Holy Spirit in the Dominican Saints* (Tacoma, WA: Cluny Media, 2017). This 2017 edition includes an excellent introduction by Romanus Cessario, OP, on the place of the gifts of the Holy Spirit in the Christian moral life.

leaves the moral theologian ill-equipped to make a proper exposition of specific moral questions—for example, cooperation with evil.

The approach of moral theology emphasizing man's end in beatitude, acquired and infused virtues, and the gifts of the Holy Spirit has achieved a certain renewal according to the vision of the Second Vatican Council.[40] This view of moral theology received authoritative acceptance in the publication of the *Catechism of the Catholic Church* and the moral encyclical of Pope John Paul II *Veritatis splendor.*[41] It is to an exposition of the works of the Church's Magisterium—and how they relate to the question of moral cooperation—that we now turn.

Magisterial teachings that adopt the language of virtue ethics

The Second Vatican Council's summons to renew moral theology stands in the long tradition of magisterial intervention in moral thought. Even a cursory review of magisterial teaching, especially in the modern period, demonstrates the Church's concern for sound moral instruction.[42] An examination of the interventions of the Magisterium since the time of the Second Vatican Council reveals clear principles for guidance in the moral life. While there may not be a tremendous number of papal interventions specifically regarding issues of moral cooperation, many

40. See Vatican Council II, Decree on Priestly Training, *Optatam totius*, no. 16.

41. For an extended reflection on the treatment of moral questions in the documents of the Magisterium of John Paul II, see Réal Tremblay, *Cristo e la morale in alcuni documenti del Magistero* (Rome: Edizioni Dehoniane, 1996). For appreciative essays on the moral theology of Pope John Paul II, see the volume edited by J. A. DiNoia, OP, and Romanus Cessario, OP, *Veritatis Splendor and the Renewal of Moral Theology* (Chicago: Midwest Theological Forum, 1999). For a far more critical perspective, see Charles E. Curran, *The Moral Theology of Pope John Paul II* (Washington, DC: Georgetown University Press, 2005). For a critical response to Curran's book, see William E. May and E. Christian Brugger, "John Paul II's Moral Theology on Trial: A Reply to Charles E. Curran," *The Thomist* 69 (2005): 279–312.

42. In fact, sound moral theology requires a robust affirmation of the role of the Magisterium in setting forth moral truth. See especially *Veritatis splendor*, no. 110. For further reflection on this point, see Romanus Cessario, OP, *Introduction to Moral Theology*, 16–17. See also, from the Congregation for the Doctrine of the Faith, the Instruction *Donum veritatis*, May 24, 1990, *AAS* 82 (1990): 1550–70; and Benedict M. Ashley, OP, "The Truth Will Set You Free: *Reflections on the* Instruction on the Ecclesial Vocation of the Theologian *of the Congregation for the Doctrine of the Faith, May 24, 1990*," in *The Ashley Reader: Redeeming Reason* (Naples, FL: Sapientia Press, 2006), 89–93.

magisterial documents that address other issues of moral theology offer valuable guidance for questions of cooperation with evil.

In general terms, the post-conciliar Magisterium has repeatedly endorsed an object-based moral inquiry in which an act's object—and not the intention of the agent or the consequences of his acting—plays the primary role in moral analysis. Pope John Paul II outlines this method of moral inquiry in his 1993 encyclical *Veritatis splendor*. The Church utilizes a similar moral system in the *Catechism of the Catholic Church*.[43] Given the Church's responsibility to instruct not only in the doctrine of the faith but also moral teaching, Catholic faithful find in the Church's moral instruction a true source of knowledge about the moral life.[44] In the section which follows, we will examine interventions of the papal Magisterium as well as documents of the Roman Curia and of the United States Conference of Catholic Bishops. We will pay particular attention to the way in which these documents offer guidance for analyzing questions of moral cooperation. By and large, these magisterial interventions avoid the categories of moral casuistry and instead utilize a rigorous object-based method of moral inquiry. In so doing, the Magisterium offers a model for how to address difficult moral questions from the perspective of St. Thomas and his virtue-based moral system.

Pope John Paul II, *Veritatis splendor* (1993)

In the early 1990s word spread throughout the Catholic world that Pope John Paul II was planning an encyclical letter to address fundamental questions of moral theology.[45] Following its proposal at the 1985 Extraordinary Synod of Bishops, work had already begun on the new *Catechism*, and observers anticipated eagerly its treatment of moral matters.

---

43. For a helpful essay demonstrating the continuity between *Veritatis splendor*, the *Catechism of the Catholic Church*, and the work of Servais Pinckaers, see Craig Steven Titus, "Servais Pinckaers and the Renewal of Catholic Moral Theology," *Journal of Moral Theology* 1 (2012): 43–68.

44. See, for example, *Lumen gentium*, no. 25: "In matters of faith and morals, the bishops speak in the name of Christ and the faithful are to accept their teaching and adhere to it with a religious assent." For a helpful commentary on the weight of magisterial interventions, see the Congregation for the Doctrine of the Faith, *Doctrinal Commentary on the Concluding Formula of the* Professio Fidei, June 29, 1998, *AAS* 90 (1998): 544–51.

45. For an evaluation of John Paul II's thought, emphasizing its Thomistic elements, see Jaroslaw Kupczak, OP, *Destined for Liberty: The Human Person in the Philosophy of Karol Wojtyla/John Paul II* (Washington, DC: The Catholic University of America Press, 2000).

Historians now report that the publication of the two texts—*Catechism* and encyclical—were timed to coordinate with one another.[46] Pope John Paul II first promulgated the *Catechism of the Catholic Church*, originally in French, in October 1992. The Holy See issued an English translation the following year.[47] One year later the Pope released the encyclical *Veritatis splendor* on the feast of the Transfiguration, August 6, 1993. Addressed to the bishops of the Catholic world, this encyclical both confronted the challenges of revisionist moral theology and proposed a new way forward for Catholic moral thought.[48]

Often regarded as a response to the revisionist moral theologies of the immediate post-conciliar period, *Veritatis splendor* ultimately provided the foundation for the renewal of moral theology encouraged by the Second Vatican Council. The encyclical indicated the deficiencies in certain revisionist theologies, especially those of consequentialism and proportionalism.[49] It affirmed the existence of intrinsically evil acts and restated the long-standing Catholic belief in the distinction between mortal and venial sin.[50] More than merely this corrective function, however, this landmark encyclical established the way forward for moral theology at the turn of the third Christian millennium. The text did so precisely by reaffirming the venerable tradition of Catholic moral theology grounded in Sacred Scripture, the Fathers of the Church, and especially the moral thought of St. Thomas Aquinas.

46. See George Weigel, *Witness to Hope: The Biography of Pope John Paul II* (New York: Harper Collins, 2004), 691.

47. Pope John Paul II promulgated the *editio typica* of the *Catechism of the Catholic Church* on August 15, 1997. This Latin edition incorporated several revisions from the original French edition which had seen an English translation.

48. For a series of appreciative essays on the importance of this moral encyclical, see J. A. DiNoia, OP, and Romanus Cessario, OP, eds., *Veritatis Splendor and the Renewal of Moral Theology*. For a largely alternative perspective with several essays critical of the encyclical, see John Wilkins, ed., *Understanding Veritatis Splendor: The Encyclical Letter of Pope John Paul II on the Church's Moral Teaching* (London: Society for Promoting Christian Knowledge, 1994).

49. See *VS*, no. 77.

50. For the treatment of intrinsically evil acts, see *VS*, nos. 80–81; and for the distinction between mortal and venial sin, see *Veritatis splendor*, nos. 69–70. For a helpful discussion of venial sin, see Stephen L. Vileo, *A Theological Analysis of Scandal in the Summa Theologiae of St. Thomas Aquinas* (Rome: Pontifical Lateran University Academia Alphonsiana, 1993), 153–56. For an excellent explanation of Aquinas's view of venial sin, see Lawrence Dewan, OP, "St. Thomas, Lying, and Venial Sin: Thomas Aquinas on the Validity of Moral Taxonomy," *The Thomist* 61 (1997): 279–99.

Aquinas begins his moral treatise of the *secunda pars* of the *Summa theologiae* with five questions on beatitude. With this course of inquiry St. Thomas identifies an essential element of Catholic moral theology—its teleological character. Theologians err when they consider the moral life as merely a series of discrete choices. Instead, individual choices both result from and inculcate the virtues that establish human character. Pope John Paul II readily follows Aquinas in this area. The Pope sets his moral encyclical in the context of the Biblical encounter of Christ with the rich young man.[51] In so doing, John Paul II adopts a teleological view of the moral life. *Veritatis* explains: "Consequently the moral life has an essential *'teleological' character*, since it consists in the deliberate ordering of human acts to God, the supreme good and ultimate end (*telos*) of man."[52] The teleological character of the moral life contrasts the teleological ethical theories condemned by the encyclical.[53] The teleological character affirmed by John Paul II refers to the fact that moral choice creates human character. The virtues developed by moral action render one apt for human flourishing and eternal life.[54] A proper understanding of teleology does not permit a choice for evil, but rather guides and directs moral theology to its proper end. Teleology, in this sense, indicates that human actions possess a given character established by their nature. This character can be discovered, but not imposed, by the human mind.

While *Veritatis splendor* does not treat moral cooperation with evil in an explicit manner, it does provide guidance for how one should address such quandaries. In *Veritatis splendor* paragraph 78—the subject of considerable discussion—Pope John Paul II offers guidance on how to specify moral objects.[55] The Pope teaches:

The morality of the human act depends primarily and fundamentally on the "object" rationally chosen by the deliberate will, as is borne out by the insightful analysis, still valid today, made by Saint Thomas. In order to be able to grasp the object of an

---

51. See *VS*, nos. 6–27. For an excellent commentary on this portion of the encyclical, see Livio Melina, "The Desire for Happiness and the Commandments in the First Chapter of *Veritatis splendor*," in *Veritatis Splendor and the Renewal of Moral Theology*, ed. J. A. DiNoia, OP, and Romanus Cessario, OP, 143–60.

52. *VS*, no. 73.

53. See *VS*, no. 75.

54. See *VS*, no. 8.

55. The English edition of *Nova et Vetera* conducted a symposium on this question in 2008. See especially Stephen L. Brock, "*Veritatis Splendor* §78, St. Thomas, and (Not Merely) Physical Objects of Moral Acts," *Nova et Vetera*, English edition, 6 (2008): 1–62.

act which specifies that act morally, it is therefore necessary to place oneself *in the perspective of the acting person*. The object of the act of willing is in fact a freely chosen kind of behavior.... By the object of a given moral act, then, one cannot mean a process or an event of the merely physical order, to be assessed on the basis of its ability to bring about a given state of affairs in the outside world. Rather, that object is the proximate end of a deliberate decision which determines the act of willing on the part of the acting person.[56]

First, one is struck that the Pope speaks of certain kinds of behavior. There really are types of activity, he insists, and not only particular acts which can only later be categorized or put in the same genus to analyze them usefully.[57] The nominalist tendency which does not allow for real types of activity—but only particular instances of acts—finds no place in authentic Catholic moral theology.[58]

The stress on the primary importance of an act's object in analyzing moral questions sheds light on how theologians should address issues of cooperation. If indeed the object of the act—and not the consequences or "state of affairs in the outside world"—takes on the primary concern in sound moral analysis, then theologians should address questions of cooperation in the same fashion. That is, the appropriate question we should ask in a given situation of moral cooperation remains: "What is the object that is chosen here and now?" This differs from an approach where one inquires about how closely the act of the cooperator approaches that of the primary agent. Virtue-based moral inquiry, instead, first addresses the question of what can be said about the particular act of cooperation itself.

Veritatis splendor offers another helpful contribution to moral discourse in its exposition of the role of consequences for determining moral spe-

---

56. *VS*, no. 78. Emphasis in original.

57. For an alternative view largely critical of the moral Magisterium of Pope John Paul II, see Charles E. Curran, *The Moral Theology of Pope John Paul II*. For an eclectic series of articles concerning the moral Magisterium of John Paul II, see Charles E. Curran and Richard McCormick, SJ, eds., *John Paul II and Moral Theology: Readings in Moral Theology* (Mahwah, NJ: Paulist Press, 1998).

58. For a further treatment of the detrimental effect of nominalism on the history of moral theology, see Servais Pinckaers, OP, "A Historical Perspective on Intrinsically Evil Acts," in *The Pinckaers Reader*, 185–235, especially 211–18. For an excellent summary of the specification of moral objects in the thought of William of Ockham, who exercised great influence on the nominalism of the late medieval period, see Thomas M. Osborne, Jr., *Human Action in Thomas Aquinas, John Duns Scotus, and William of Ockham*, 175–84.

cies. While authors of both the proportionalist school as well as some in
the casuist period make ample allusion to foreseeable consequences and
desired effects, *Veritatis* suggests an alternative approach: "The weighing
of the goods and evils foreseeable as the consequence of an action is not
an adequate method for determining whether the choice of that concrete
kind of behavior is 'according to its species,' or 'in itself,' morally good or
bad, licit or illicit."[59] An evaluation of consequences, the Pope explains,
cannot be the ultimate criteria to judge a human action. The moral object
itself—that which is rationally chosen by the deliberate will—offers the
only adequate place to begin a sound moral analysis. This position finds
further support later in the encyclical. The Pope explains:

> The opinion must be rejected as erroneous which maintains that it is impos-
> sible to qualify as morally evil according to its species the deliberate choice of
> certain kinds of behavior or specific acts, without taking into account the in-
> tention for which the choice was made or the totality of the foreseeable conse-
> quences of that act for all persons concerned.[60]

This point is clear. Moral objects themselves must be the criteria for any
decision about what to do in a given situation. The nature of a moral object, the encyclical suggests, can be identified clearly through an analysis according to the method of St. Thomas Aquinas. Foreseeable consequences may alter the circumstances of a given act but cannot transform
a bad act into a good one.[61] This will become crucially important to examine correctly issues of cooperation. Contrary to the guidance of *Veritatis
splendor*, many authors suggest that duress or coercion can fundamentally
alter the nature of an act, transforming an otherwise bad act into a good
one.[62] Following *Veritatis splendor*, on the other hand, moralists can treat
fruitfully issues of cooperation by examining the nature of the proposed
cooperative act itself. They should ask what kind of action the cooperator is doing, as opposed to weighing the effects and consequences of a
given act. While never treating the issue of cooperation with evil directly,
Veritatis splendor provides salutary guidance for how one might establish a
method of inquiry regarding moral cooperation.

---

59. *VS*, no. 77. St. Thomas makes essentially the same point in his treatise on the
moral act. See, for example, *Summa theologiae* Ia–IIae, q. 18, a. 2.
60. *VS*, no. 82.
61. See *VS*, no 81.
62. For one example of an author who holds that a kind of duress can excuse an otherwise moral evil, see, Dominicus M. Prümmer, OP, *Handbook of Moral Theology*, §25–42.

Pope John Paul II, *Evangelium vitae* (1995)

On March 25, 1995 Pope John Paul II signed the eleventh encyclical of his long pontificate. Proving to be among those with the most significant influence, *Evangelium vitae* provided the Church's most comprehensive magisterial defense of the dignity of human life.[63] Following *Veritatis splendor* and the initial publication of the *Catechism of the Catholic Church*, with *Evangelium vitae* John Paul II offered a specific application of the general moral theory of *Veritatis*. In the *Gospel of Life*, John Paul II engages in an object-based moral examination of various threats to the dignity of the human person. He rejects appeals to consequentialist or proportionalist analysis commonly utilized in contemporary moral discourse. The encyclical sustains the thesis of our project as it provides a concrete application to questions of moral cooperation with evil. In addition to treating the topics of abortion, euthanasia, and capital punishment, the encyclical also engages concretely in the question of cooperation with evil acts.

When addressing cooperation in the sin of abortion, the encyclical offers an impassioned plea. Pope John Paul II teaches:

In order to shed light on this difficult question, it is necessary to recall the general principles concerning cooperation in evil actions. Christians, like all people of good will, are called upon under grave obligation of conscience not to cooperate formally in practices which, even if permitted by civil legislation, are contrary to God's law. Indeed, from the moral standpoint, it is never licit to cooperate formally in evil. Such cooperation occurs when an action, either by its very nature or by the form it takes in a concrete situation, can be defined as a direct participation in an act against innocent human life or a sharing in the immoral intention of the person committing it.[64]

---

63. For a sound explanation of the immorality of abortion, see Christopher Kaczor, *The Ethics of Abortion: Women's Rights, Human Life, and the Question of Justice*, 3rd ed. (New York: Routledge, 2022); Francis J. Beckwith, *Defending Life: A Moral and Legal Case Against Abortion Choice* (Cambridge: Cambridge University Press, 2007); and Robert P. George and Christopher Tollefsen, *Embryo: A Defense of Human Life* (Princeton, NJ: Witherspoon Institute, 2011). For a well-known defense of abortion, see David Boonin, *A Defense of Abortion* (Cambridge: Cambridge University Press, 2002). For reflections on the twentieth anniversary of the publication of *Evangelium vitae*, see Nicanor Austriaco, OP, "Mercy of God (Evangelium Vitae §99)," *Nova et Vetera*, English edition, 13 (2015): 1185–1208; David Crawford, "*Evangelium Vitae*, the Rhetoric of Freedom, and *Roe v. Wade's* Totalitarian Implications," *Nova et Vetera*, English edition, 13 (2015): 1209–28; and Aquinas Guilbeau, OP, "Was the Polish Pope a French Personalist?: An Indication from Evangelium Vitae," *Nova et Vetera*, English edition, 13 (2015): 1229–44.

64. *EV*, no. 74.

The Pope makes an important contribution to the debate surrounding moral cooperation when he teaches that an action *"by its very nature"* can cooperate in abortion and therefore should be condemned.[65] The Pope holds that some types of cooperation, by their very nature and regardless of one's intention for doing them, can never be justified. The Pope avoids the error of tying sins of cooperation too closely to the intention of the cooperator. Regardless of good intentions, certain types of cooperation remain unjustifiable. In the encyclical, the Pope explains that there are types of cooperation whose nature does not permit them ever to be employed. This remains true regardless of the further reason one may have for cooperating. The reason a person proposes for his manner of acting—his *finis operantis*—cannot transform the object of the act rationally chosen—the *finis operis*—from a bad act into a good one. The nature of the cooperator's act itself—the kind of thing the cooperator is doing—cannot be rendered a morally good act merely due to his good intention.

In the passage from *Evangelium vitae* cited above, John Paul II treats cooperation in a manner far different from those who would seek to ask how closely one can approach a given crime against human life. The Holy Father does not ask, in this case, about the proximity of an act to evil but rather, about the nature of the act in which one is engaged. Instead, the Pope recognizes that the form an action takes in a concrete circumstance can also render the act *per se malum*.[66] Without reference to the duress in which one finds oneself or the good reasons one may have for acting, the very nature of the act or the form it takes in a given situation can make it the kind of act that should never be chosen.[67]

The Church's law recognizes that acts of cooperation—and not only those of principal malefactors—can be subject to canonical penalties. For

---

65. For an extended treatment of how *Evangelium vitae* deals with cooperation with evil, see Andrew McLean Cummings, *The Servant and the Ladder*, 347–52.

66. St. Thomas Aquinas, for example, explains that the circumstance of place may change the moral species of a given act. See *Summa theologiae* Ia–IIae, q. 18, a. 10: "Place is a circumstance. But place makes a moral action to be in a certain species of evil; for theft of a thing from a holy place is a sacrilege. Therefore, a circumstance makes a moral action to be specifically good or bad."

67. While the presence of duress and other factors may mitigate the application of the canonical penalty, they do not fundamentally change the nature of the act itself. For a treatment of those to whom canonical penalties may apply, including conditions which may mitigate the application of the penalty, see William H. Woestman, O.M.I., *Ecclesiastical Sanctions and the Penal Process: A Commentary on the Code of Canon Law* (Ottawa: St. Paul University, 2003), 23–40.

example, because of the moral gravity of abortion, the 1983 *Code of Canon Law* attaches a canonical penalty to abortion as a crime in the Church's law. This penalty applies both to those who procure an abortion and to those who cooperate in such a way that, without their cooperation, the abortion would not take place.[68] The sole treatment of the *Catechism of the Catholic Church* directly on the issue of so-called formal cooperation with evil deals with cooperation in the sin of abortion. The *Catechism* addresses the issue in the same manner as *Evangelium vitae*. The *Catechism*, both in the 1992 edition and the 1997 typical edition, repeats the canonical penalty attached to assisting in the procurement of an abortion. The *Catechism* teaches:

> Formal cooperation in an abortion constitutes a grave offense. The Church attaches the canonical penalty of excommunication to this crime against human life. "A person who procures a completed abortion incurs excommunication *latae sententiae*," "by the very commission of the offense," and subject to the conditions provided by Canon Law.[69]

As *Evangelium vitae* held, the *Catechism* maintains that the very nature of a given action may make it *per se malum* regardless of the further intention one has for acting.

In this context, one recalls the public dispute over one bishop's invocation of this canonical penalty. In May 2010 in the Diocese of Phoenix, Arizona, Bishop Thomas Olmsted declared that Sister Margaret McBride had incurred a *latae senentiae* excommunication. The bishop explained that during the course of deliberations of a hospital ethics panel on which she served, Sister McBride's decision to vote to permit an abor-

---

68. See *CIC* 1398: "A person who procures a completed abortion incurs a *latae sententiae* excommunication"; and *CIC* 1329, §2: "Accomplices who are not named in a law or precept incur a *latae sententiae* penalty attached to a delict if without their assistance the delict would not have been committed, and the penalty is of such a nature that it can affect them; otherwise, they can be punished by *ferendae sententiae* penalties." This penalty is repeated in the *Catechism of the Catholic Church*, no. 2272. For commentary on this canon, especially for how it differs from the 1917 Code of Canon Law which attempted to delineate various forms of co-delinquency or cooperation, see Ángel Marzoa, *Exegetical Commentary on the Code of Canon Law*, vol. 4/1 (Chicago: Midwest Theological Forum, 2004), 311–16. For commentary on which forms of co-delinquency may or may not receive the canonical penalty, see James A. Coriden, "Canonical Penalties for Abortion as Applicable to Administrators of Clinics and Hospitals," *Roman Replies and CLSA Opinions* (Washington, DC: The Canon Law Society of America, 1986), 80–85.

69. *CCC*, no. 2272.

tion met the conditions to incur the canonical penalty.[70] While one may be inclined to construe a vote of this kind as intending an abortion take place, a perusal of the pertinent documents between the bishop and hospital reveal that never was the sister's intention at issue. Instead, the bishop explained that a public vote for a particular abortion to occur was the kind of action, of its nature, which in principle incurs the canonical penalty. In so doing, the bishop acknowledged that there are types of behavior—indeed types of cooperation—which of their nature are subject to the canonical penalty of excommunication. The action itself—not the reason for one's acting—forms the primary basis of the moral analysis. Obviously to incur the canonical penalty the necessary conditions cannot be absent, e.g., age, awareness of the seriousness of the crime, lack of grave fear, etc. This particular case demonstrates the care with which one bishop chose to provide sound explanation of the canonical issues at play in threats against human life.

Congregation for the Doctrine of the Faith, *Declaration on Euthanasia* (1980)

With the 1980 *Declaration on Euthanasia* the Congregation for the Doctrine of the Faith utilized an object-based approach to moral analysis in order to address a grave threat to the sanctity of human life.[71] In the Con-

---

70. For a fruitful exchange about this matter, see M. Therese Lysaught, "Moral Analysis of a Procedure at Phoenix Hospital," *Origins* 40, no. 33 (January 2011): 537–49; and for a convincing rebuttal, see Edward J. Furton, "Ethics without Metaphysics: A Review of the Lysaught Analysis," *The National Catholic Bioethics Quarterly* 11 (2011): 53–62. For an outstanding treatment of the moral issues at stake in this case, see Thomas A. Cavanagh, "Double-Effect Reasoning, Craniotomy, and Vital Conflicts: A Case of Contemporary Catholic Casuistry," *The National Catholic Bioethics Quarterly* 11 (2011): 453–63; and Kevin L. Flannery, SJ, "Vital Conflicts and the Catholic Magisterial Tradition," *The National Catholic Bioethics Quarterly* 11 (2011): 691–704. Interested readers may also consult the exchange between Christopher O. Tollefsen, "Response to Robert Koons and Matthew O'Brien's 'Objects of Intention: a Hylomorphic Critique of the New Natural Law Theory,'" *American Catholic Philosophical Quarterly* 87 (2013): 751–78; and Steven J. Jensen, "Causal Constraints on Intention: A Critique of Tollefsen on the Phoenix Case," *The National Catholic Bioethics Quarterly* 14 (2014): 273–93. For an interesting reversal of his previous position, see Thomas Berg, "A Revised Analysis of the 'Phoenix Abortion Case' and a Critique of New Natural Law Intentionality," *Nova et Vetera*, English edition, 15 (2017): 365–96.

71. For a thorough examination of the legal and ethical issues involved in the legalization of euthanasia, see Neil M. Gorsuch, *The Future of Assisted Suicide and Euthanasia*

gregation's definition of euthanasia, we discover that certain actions of their very nature and without recourse to further intentions can be considered euthanizing.[72] Resisting efforts to exalt the role of intention in determining the morality of euthanasia, the *Declaration* explains: "By euthanasia is understood an action or an omission which of itself or by intention causes death, in order that all suffering … be eliminated."[73] One thinks of the decision to withhold food and water from a patient who remains able to assimilate them.[74] Regardless of one's further intention

---

(Princeton: Princeton University Press, 2009). For an excellent collection of essays regarding medical, ethical, and legal aspects of the euthanasia debate, see *Last Rights? Assisted Suicide and Euthanasia Debated*, ed. Michael M. Uhlmann (Grand Rapids, MI: Eerdmans, 1998). For an outstanding sustained argument against the legalization of euthanasia, see John Keown, *Euthanasia, Ethics and Public Policy: An Argument Against Legalisation*, 2nd ed. (Cambridge: Cambridge University Press, 2018). For a reflection on the cultural context of the euthanasia debate, see Wesley J. Smith, *Culture of Death: The Assault on Medical Ethics in America* (San Francisco: Encounter Books, 2000).

72. For an extended treatment of Catholic teaching on euthanasia, see William E. May, *Catholic Bioethics and the Gift of Human Life*, 3rd ed. (Huntington, IN: Our Sunday Visitor, 2013); 251–74; Nicanor Pier Giorgio Austriaco, OP, *Biomedicine and Beatitude: An Introduction to Catholic Bioethics*, 2nd. ed. (Washington, DC: The Catholic University of America Press, 2021), 169–224; W.J. Eijk, L.M. Hendriks, J.A. Raymakers, and John I. Fleming, eds., *Manual of Catholic Medical Ethics: Responsible Healthcare from a Catholic Perspective*, trans. M. Regina van den Berg and Janthony Raymakers (Ballarat, VC: Connor Court Publishing, 2014), 561–97; and Elio Sgreccia, *Personalist Bioethics: Foundations and Applications*, trans. John A. Di Camillo and Michael J. Miller (Philadelphia: The National Catholic Bioethics Center, 2012), 663–716. For a reflection on the Biblical foundations of the immorality of euthanasia, see Anthony Fisher, *Catholic Bioethics for a New Millennium* (Cambridge: Cambridge University Press, 2012), 248–71. For a slightly different perspective, specifically regarding nutrition and hydration administered by artificial means, see Benedict M. Ashley, OP, and Kevin D. O'Rourke, OP, *Health Care Ethics: A Theological Analysis*, 4th ed. (Washington, DC: Georgetown University Press, 1997), 411–32.

73. Sacred Congregation for the Doctrine of the Faith, *Declaration on Euthanasia*, no. 3.

74. Two doctoral dissertations offer extended analysis of the morality of providing artificial nutrition and hydration. Completed before the 2004 allocution of Pope John Paul II, the dissertation of Donald Henke offers an outstanding study of the matter. See Donald Edward Henke, *Artificially Assisted Hydration and Nutrition: From Karen Quinlan to Nancy Cruzan to the Present: An Historical Analysis of the Decision to Provide or Withhold/Withdraw Sustenance from PVS Patients in Catholic Moral Theology and Medical Practice in the United States* (Rome: Pontifical Lateran University Academia Alphonsiana, 2004). Completed after the 2004 allocution, the dissertation of Christopher Mahar offers a strong defense of the Pope's teaching. See his *Providing or Withdrawing Artificial Nutrition and Hydration to Patients Diagnosed as Being in the Vegetative State: A Fundamental Investigation into the Underlying Moral-Theological Presuppositions in the Current North American Catholic Ethical Debate* (Leuven: Catholic University of Leuven, 2016).

for keeping a patient comfortable or relieving a burden on a family, this omission of the ordinary care to which a patient is due is by its nature *per se malum*.[75] In a much-debated address in March of 2004, Pope John Paul II offered precision to this moral teaching of the Church. Speaking to participants at the International Congress on Life-Sustaining Treatments and Vegetative State, the Pope explained:

I should like particularly to underline how the administration of water and food, even when provided by artificial means, always represents a *natural means* of preserving life, not a *medical act*. Its use, furthermore, should be considered, in principle, *ordinary* and *proportionate*, and as such morally obligatory, insofar as and until it is seen to have attained its proper finality, which in the present case consists in providing nourishment to the patient and alleviation of his suffering.[76]

Enormous dispute arose following the Pope's allocution.[77] The American bishops inquired with the Congregation for the Doctrine of the Faith about how they should understand the doctrinal weight of the allocution. In response, the Congregation affirmed that nutrition and hydration, even if administered by artificial means, represents "an ordinary and proportionate means of preserving life." For that reason, such care is "therefore obligatory" as long as the food and water can still be assimilated by the patient.[78] The response of the Congregation attests to the fact that certain actions—regardless of one's good intention—cannot be rendered conformable to the truth about the good of the human person.[79]

75. For the definitive study on the distinction between extraordinary means and the ordinary care due to every patient, see Daniel A. Cronin, *Ordinary and Extraordinary Means of Conserving Life: 50th Anniversary Edition* (Philadelphia: The National Catholic Bioethics Center, 2011). Magisterial intervention has clarified that Catholic teaching on the immorality of euthanasia is irreformable. See Congregation for the Doctrine of the Faith, *Doctrinal Commentary on the Concluding Formula of the* Professio Fidei, June 29, 1998.

76. See Pope John Paul II, "Address to the Participants in the International Congress on 'Life-Sustaining Treatments and Vegetative State: Scientific Advances and Ethical Dilemmas,'" March 20, 2004. Emphasis in original.

77. The literature from this dispute is vast. For a representative presentation of the arguments, see Mark S. Latkovic, "The Morality of Tube Feeding PVS Patients: A Critique of the View of Kevin O'Rourke, OP," *The National Catholic Bioethics Quarterly* 5 (2005): 503–13. For an alternative view see, Kevin. D. O'Rourke, OP, "The Catholic Tradition on Forgoing Life Support," *The National Catholic Bioethics Quarterly* 5 (2005): 537–53.

78. See the Congregation for the Doctrine of the Faith, *Responses to Certain Questions of the United States Conference of Catholic Bishops Concerning Artificial Nutrition and Hydration*, August 1, 2007, *AAS* 99 (2007): 820–21.

79. For commentary on the Pope's allocution and the response of the Congregation,

Fifteen years after the *Declaration on Euthanasia,* in 1995 the encyclical *Evangelium vitae* offered without explanation a slightly different definition of euthanasia. *Evangelium vitae* described euthanasia as "an action or omission which of itself and by intention causes death."[80] Both the original 1992 *Catechism* and, more significantly, the 1997 *editio typica* of the *Catechism* released after *Evangelium vitae* employ the previous definition used in the 1980 *Declaration on Euthanasia.* The *editio typica* of the *Catechism* abandons the *Evangelium vitae* rendering "of itself and by intention" and instead reads: "An act or omission which, of itself or by intention, causes death in order to eliminate suffering."[81] The 1997 *Catechism* definition of euthanasia includes any act—regardless of one's intention—that would directly cause the death of a suffering person.[82] This definition ensures that the Church never falls prey to intentionalism which would grant to intention the primary place in the determination of the morality of a given action.

While the Magisterium has not tried to answer every question regarding issues of moral cooperation with evil, it has provided the resources necessary to establish an effective method for addressing such matters. One detects in these magisterial sources a general hermeneutic for approaching questions in this area. Time and again the Magisterium has insisted that the moral object of an act should be the primary locus of investigation to establish the act's moral goodness.[83] Further, one observes the Magisterium exercise an extreme caution at any sign of "intentionalism" where intentions rather than moral objects occupy the principal place in moral analysis. This point will become crucial for analyzing questions of moral cooperation with evil when the temptation to place emphasis on the intention of the cooperator can become very strong.

---

see William E. May, *Catholic Bioethics and the Gift of Human Life,* 276–85. For a more extended treatment of this topic, see Nicanor Pier Giorgio Austriaco, OP, *Biomedicine and Beatitude,* 206–11. For an alternative perspective, see Benedict M. Ashley, OP, *Barefoot Journeying: The Autobiography of a Begging Friar* (Chicago: New Priory Press, 2013), 496–500.

80. Pope John Paul II, *Evangelium vitae,* no. 65. For further analysis of the change in formulation of the definition of euthanasia, see Andrew McLean Cummings, *The Servant and the Ladder,* 221–24.

81. *CCC,* no. 2277.

82. For an alternative perspective, treated below, see Anthony Fisher, *Catholic Bioethics for a New Millennium,* 87.

83. This point is expressed well in *VS,* no. 82: "Furthermore, an intention is good when it has as its aim the true good of the person in view of his ultimate end. But acts whose object is 'not capable of being ordered' to God and 'unworthy of the human person' are always and in every case in conflict with that good."

Pontifical Council for the Family,
Vademecum for Confessors Concerning Some Aspects of Conjugal Life (1997)

In 1997 the Pontifical Council for the Family offered a useful contribution to the question of moral cooperation with evil. The *Vademecum for Confessors* prepared by the Pontifical Council presented guidance to priests for the many challenges they face when hearing the confession of sins against the virtue of chastity. The document balances the need for sound moral counsel when assisting a penitent to make an integral confession with the gentleness required for the delicate cases in which sin is either poorly understood or so habituated as to require special care. When treating the use of contraception within marriage, the document examines how one may or may not cooperate in the sin of contraception with his or her spouse. In so doing, the document provides guidance for understanding how to view cooperation more generally. The Pontifical Council explains:

Special difficulties are presented by cases of cooperation in the sin of a spouse who voluntarily renders the unitive act infecund. In the first place, it is necessary to distinguish cooperation in the proper sense, from violence or unjust imposition on the part of one of the spouses, which the other spouse in fact cannot resist. This cooperation can be licit when the three following conditions are jointly met:

  1. when the action of the cooperating spouse is not already illicit in itself;
  2. when proportionally grave reasons exist for cooperating in the sin of the other spouse;
  3. when one is seeking to help the other spouse to desist from such conduct (patiently, with prayer, charity and dialogue; although not necessarily in that moment, nor on every single occasion).[84]

The text affirms that a cooperating spouse may never choose an act which is evil in itself (*per se malum*) regardless of the reason for his or her acting. Since the *Vademecum* treats the question of the use of contraceptive drugs with an abortifacient effect in the following paragraph, it appears that this section of the document aims to treat those acts which are exclusively

---

84. Pontifical Council for the Family, *Vademecum for Confessors Concerning Some Aspects of the Morality of Conjugal Life*, February 12, 1997, no. 13.

contraceptive.[85] The Pontifical Council refers to the nature of the contraceptive act. This point becomes clear with the footnote to the first bullet point referencing two decrees of the Holy Office.[86] These decrees exclude the possibility that a spouse may engage in a sterilized conjugal act because the other spouse wishes to do so.

The earlier doctrinal decrees recalled in this 1997 text make plain that for a spouse who disapproves of contraception the only permitted acts of conjugal intercourse are those made infecund by the other party. Only those in which one spouse is truly an innocent party to the other spouse's contraceptive choice can be considered morally licit for the non-contracepting spouse. It is not as though when one spouse chooses to sterilize a particular sexual act the other spouse may comply, relying on his or her own good intentions. Rather, moralists must consider the nature of the sterilizing act itself to determine if one spouse can be considered innocent of the other spouse's contraceptive choice.[87] Here again, the nature of the act—or of each spouse's part in the act—as opposed to the intention or reason for acting receives prominence in the Church's recommended moral analysis.

---

85. For guidance on the question of the abortifacient effects of so-called Plan-B contraceptives, see the Congregation for the Doctrine of the Faith, "Instruction *Dignitas Personae* on Certain Bioethical Questions," no. 23: "It is true that there is not always complete knowledge of the way that different pharmaceuticals operate, but scientific studies indicate that *the effect of inhibiting implantation is certainly present*, even if this does not mean that such interceptives cause an abortion every time they are used, also because conception does not occur after every act of sexual intercourse."

86. See DS 2795, Response of the Holy Office, April 6 (19), 1853; and DS 3634, Response of the Sacred Penitentiary, April 3, 1916, both in Heinrich Denzinger, *Enchiridion Symbolorum definitionem et declarationum de rebus fidei et morum*, Latin-English, ed. Peter Hünermann, 43rd ed. (San Francisco: Ignatius Press, 2012). One notes that these decrees are not included in every edition of Denzinger. For example, they cannot be found in the popular thirtieth edition, published in English as *The Sources of Catholic Dogma*. For a further elaboration on this moral topic, see Joseph M. Arias and Basil Cole, OP, "The *Vademecum* and Cooperation in Condomistic Intercourse," *The National Catholic Bioethics Quarterly* 11 (2011): 301–28.

87. For analysis of the related issue of the use of contraceptives in the case of rape, see Martin Rhonheimer, "The Use of Contraceptives under the Threat of Rape: An Exception? Clarifying a Central Teaching of *Veritatis Splendor*," in his *Ethics of Procreation and the Defense of Human Life: Contraception, Artificial Fertilization, and Abortion*, ed. William F. Murphy, Jr. (Washington, DC: The Catholic University of America Press, 2010), 133–50.

*Ethical and Religious Directives for Catholic
Health Care Services* (2009)

In November 2009 the United States Conference of Catholic Bishops issued the fifth edition of the *Ethical and Religious Directives for Catholic Health Care Services.*[88] These directives ensure ethical medical practice at hospitals and other institutions under the Church's care. Since the early part of the twentieth century Catholic theologians in the United States have gathered in various forms moral teaching relevant for health care. After the Second World War, many bishops adopted ethical directives giving them the force of law in their respective dioceses. Only in 1971 did the National Conference of Catholic Bishops oversee a publication for use across the country.[89] Since then these *Directives* have undergone several revisions. The Congregation for the Doctrine of the Faith has followed closely these revisions and has offered particular guidance when it was needed.

The 2009 edition of the *Ethical and Religious Directives* offered guidance on the issue of moral cooperation with evil. The way the 2009 *Directives* addressed moral cooperation differed from the previously promulgated 1995 edition.[90] The 2009 *Ethical and Religious Directives* explain:

This new edition of the *Ethical and Religious Directives* omits the appendix concerning cooperation, which was contained in the 1995 edition. Experience has shown that the brief articulation of the principles of cooperation that was presented there did not sufficiently forestall certain possible misinterpretations and in practice gave rise to problems in concrete application of the principles.[91]

The 2009 *Directives* also maintain that "cooperation, which in all other respects is morally licit, may need to be refused because of the scandal that might be caused."[92] These statements represent a much stronger approach

88. United States Conference of Catholic Bishops, *Ethical and Religious Directives for Catholic Health Care Services: Fifth Edition* (Washington, DC: USCCB Publishing, 2009).

89. See Anthony Fisher, *Catholic Bioethics for a New Millennium,* 74–76.

90. For a firsthand account of the revision of the *Directives* to better accord with Catholic moral principles, see Benedict M. Ashley, OP, *Barefoot Journeying: The Autobiography of a Begging Friar,* 488–95. For further commentary on the revision of the *Ethical and Religious Directives,* see William B. Smith, *Modern Moral Problems: Trustworthy Answers to Your Tough Questions,* ed. Donald Haggerty (San Francisco: Ignatius Press, 2012), 52–54.

91. *Ethical and Religious Directives,* 35–36.

92. *Ethical and Religious Directives,* 71.

to the topic than those found in the earlier 1995 edition.[93] Relying heavily on the category of duress commonly found both in the manuals of the casuist period and utilized by those of the proportionalist school, the 1995 edition of the *Directives* distinguished implicitly formal cooperation from immediate material cooperation. The 1995 *Directives* opined:

Material cooperation is immediate when the object of the cooperator is the same as the object of the wrongdoer. Immediate material cooperation is wrong, except in some instances of duress. The matter of duress distinguishes immediate material cooperation from implicit formal cooperation. But immediate material cooperation—without duress—is equivalent to implicit formal cooperation and, therefore, is morally wrong. When the object of the cooperator's action remains distinguishable from that of the wrongdoer's, material cooperation is mediate and can be morally licit.[94]

This explanation presents a two-fold difficulty. First, it grants too great a capacity to the category of duress to radically change moral objects. Duress may lessen one's culpability for acting but cannot transform a bad act into a good one. Either an act has an object that one should not choose for any reason, or an act does not. If it is the kind of act that should never be chosen—which would be the case in acts involving implicitly formal cooperation with evil—no amount of duress can change the nature of the moral object. Contrary to the implication of the 1995 *Ethical and Religious Directives*, duress cannot change a bad act into a good one.[95]

93. For a more complete treatment of the revision of these *Directives,* with particular attention to the role of the Holy See in the discussion, see Anthony Fisher, *Catholic Bioethics for a New Millennium,* 74–76.

94. National Conference of Catholic Bishops, *Ethical and Religious Directives for Catholic Health Care Services* (Washington, DC: United States Catholic Conference, 1995), as cited in Germain Grisez, *Difficult Moral Questions: The Way of the Lord Jesus,* vol. 3 (Quincy, IL: Franciscan Press, 1997), 894.

95. For a more extended treatment of the controversy over the *Ethical and Religious Directives,* see Benedict M. Ashley, OP, Jean DeBlois, CSJ, and Kevin D. O'Rourke, OP, *Health Care Ethics: A Catholic Theological Analysis,* 5th ed. (Washington, DC: Georgetown University Press, 2006), 57. They explain: "While it is true that the difficulties arising from 'duress' (external pressures) must be taken into consideration in estimating the possible negative effects of non-cooperation, such duress can never justify formal or immediate material cooperation with intrinsically wrong acts. Footnote 44 in the 2001 ERD to Directive 70 quotes a 1974 reply by the Congregation for the Doctrine of the Faith to a question about 'cooperation' that states, 'Any cooperation institutionally approved or tolerated in actions which are in themselves, that is, by their nature and condition, directed to a contraceptive end ... is absolutely forbidden. For the official

The passage of the 1995 *Directives* under consideration presents another difficulty due to its lack of clarity about how best to specify a moral object. The *Directives* do not sufficiently take into account that the separate moral object of the cooperator could itself be the kind of object that can never be chosen. The 1995 *Directives* argue that if a cooperator's action is "distinguishable from that of the wrongdoer's" this fact alone renders the cooperation mediate and therefore possibly justifiable. For most authors in the casuist system, mediate, material cooperation can be justified if a sufficient reason is present.[96] Thus, if an action is distinguishable from that of the principal malefactor, according to the 1995 *Directives*, in principle it can be justified. However, the mere fact of the cooperator's act being distinguishable—or of sufficiently remote proximity to the primary actor's bad act—does not address the nature of the cooperator's action. A "distinguishable" act could still very well be an act that should never be chosen. The category of "distinguishable" of itself fails to render an action as mediate cooperation.

The *Directives* of 1995 raised questions precisely because of their recommended use of proximity to evil in moral judgments. In examining moral cooperation with evil, the *Directives* counsel use of the category of distance from an evil act. The *Directives* explained: "The object of material cooperation should be as distant as possible from the wrongdoer's act."[97] Even though the text went on to allow that "appropriate consideration should also be given to the Church's prophetic responsibility,"[98] still the principal concern was proximity to the act of the principal malefactor. The heavy reliance on proximity to another's bad act presents several difficulties. As the bishops realized in revising this treatment of cooperation in the latter edition of the *Directives*, this manner of proceeding provides a recipe for moral confusion.[99] Physical proximity may not be the

---

approbation of direction sterilization and, *a fortiori*, its management and execution in accord with hospital regulations is a matter which, in the objective order, is by its very nature (or intrinsically) evil.'"

96. See, for example, Henry Davis, SJ, *Moral and Pastoral Theology*, vol. 1 (London: Sheed & Ward, 1958), Ch. VIII, Sec. 1: "Again, some material cooperation in the sin of another is permissible, but it is important to distinguish between immediate and mediate, proximate and remote cooperation, since a more serious excuse is required for immediate than for mediate cooperation, as also for proximate than for remote."

97. National Conference of Catholic Bishops, *Ethical and Religious Directives for Catholic Health Care Services*, as cited in Grisez, *Difficult Moral Questions: The Way of the Lord Jesus*, 894.

98. National Conference of Catholic Bishops, as cited in Grisez, 894.

99. For a more extended critique of the 1995 edition of the *Directives*, see Grisez, *Difficult Moral Questions: The Way of the Lord Jesus*, 893–97.

best judge of the moral quality of the cooperator's act itself. At the same time, the importance of the Church's prophetic voice appears muted in this passage from the *Directives*. In the 1995 version of the *Directives*, however, the Church's prophetic witness appears as a kind of afterthought.[100] This approach contrasts with that of Sydney Archbishop Anthony Fisher who places the highest premium on the Church's prophetic witness in his book *Catholic Bioethics for a New Millennium*. The particular importance of the Church's witness in this area should not be underestimated. Obviously, moral theologians must consider the danger of scandal when any Catholic institution cooperates—even in a possibly legitimate way—with organizations which threaten the dignity of human life or the sanctity of marital love. Christians everywhere—and most especially institutions established and operated by the Church—must be on guard lest their witness be compromised through accommodation to illegitimate government mandates for them to keep their operations open. Unjust mandates or requirements to cooperate unjustly in wrongdoing may prevent some of the Church's good work from continuing. While this is unfortunate, it may be the future for the Church in the twenty-first century.[101]

Some theological efforts directed toward analyzing moral cooperation

To establish a Thomistic approach to address moral cooperation with evil, this chapter began by reviewing the late twentieth-century renewal of moral theology. This renewal sought to ground moral theology more deeply in the virtues and gifts of the Holy Spirit than in a system of moral obligation prevalent in the modern period. The Thomistic, virtue-based approach to moral matters found resonance with the magisterial interventions dealing with cooperation with evil. Unlike the manualist authors of the late nineteenth and early twentieth centuries, the Church's Magisterium has generally avoided the technical categories of moral casuistry. Instead, the Church has presented an object-based approach to

100. See Anthony Fisher, *Catholic Bioethics for a New Millennium*, especially 290–95.

101. In considering the lengths one ought to take to avoid doing evil, one is reminded of the striking words of Pope John Paul II in *VS*, no. 52: "It is always possible that man, as the result of coercion or other circumstances, can be hindered from doing certain good actions; but he can never be hindered from not doing certain actions, especially if he is prepared to die rather than to do evil."

moral analysis while at the same time refusing to afford too great a role
to either intention or consequences in moral consideration.

At this point, it remains necessary to survey how some contemporary
authors have addressed moral cooperation with evil. Three authors in
particular present important work in this area: Steven Long, Anthony
Fisher, and Andrew McLean Cummings. Long's work on the specification of moral objects has received wide notoriety and commentary. A rigorous analysis of moral objects is necessary for a Thomistic approach
to moral cooperation with evil. The argument of this book maintains
that moralists do well to eschew the categories of moral casuistry and in
their place utilize a Thomistic analysis of moral action. Fisher presents
extended case studies of contemporary issues of moral cooperation. He
pays close attention to the magisterial interventions on this topic. Andrew McLean Cummings offers the most extended treatment available of
the history of moral cooperation with evil. His work displays the dangers
of allowing intention to occupy too great a place in moral judgments. Despite the respective strength of each of their contributions, none of these
authors offers an extended consideration of how to cultivate the virtues
necessary to avoid unjust cooperation with evil. Still, each offers clues as
to how such an approach could be developed.

Steven Long and the truth about teleology

Professor of Theology at Ave Maria University Steven A. Long has authored several books on Thomistic philosophy. His *Natura Pura: A Rediscovery of Nature in the Doctrine of Grace* and *Analogia Entis: On the Analogy of Being,
Metaphysics, and the Act of Faith* were acclaimed for their rigorous metaphysical
analysis and recovery of themes in the thought of St. Thomas not widely recognized today.[102] The work which has produced the most commentary, however, treats the area of moral philosophy. His 2007 *The Teleological
Grammar of the Moral Act* initiated intense debate in the philosophical community.[103] This important book provides a fruitful context for current
discussions about action theory in general and cooperation with evil spe-

---

102. See Steven A. Long, *Natura Pura: A Rediscovery of Nature in the Doctrine of Grace* (New
York: Fordham University Press 2010); and, also, his *Analogia Entis: On the Analogy of Being,
Metaphysics, and the Act of Faith* (Notre Dame, IN: University of Notre Dame Press, 2011).

103. See Steven A. Long, *The Teleological Grammar of the Moral Act* (Naples, FL: Sapientia
Press, 2007). The second edition of this book, released in 2015, contains an extensive introduction in which Long responds to his critics.

cifically.[104] Long's work in moral philosophy is not limited to *Teleological Grammar* but, rather, he has authored many scholarly articles on the topic.[105] When examining Long's work, readers discover the crucial role of teleology in the proper specification of moral objects. This proves useful in our search for a virtue-based approach to moral cooperation with evil which requires a rigorous analysis of moral objects.

With *Teleological Grammar* Long undertakes an incisive treatment of moral acts. Long believes he has recovered the underpinnings of St. Thomas's moral theory to provide an account of how St. Thomas specifies moral objects. Unlike other schools of ethical reasoning which analyze moral questions from the perspective of expected consequences or the proportion between good and evil outcomes, Long's approach places prime importance on the moral object itself. His method finds resonance with *Veritatis splendor*. In the 1993 encyclical Pope John Paul II identifies the principal locus of sound moral analysis: "The morality of the human act depends primarily and fundamentally on the 'object' rationally chosen by the deliberate will."[106] The Pope explains that moralists do well to undertake this work of specification of objects with reference to "the insightful analysis, still valid today, made by Saint Thomas."[107] The accurate specification of the moral object of a given act will be of primary importance in determining the act's moral goodness. Neither the circumstances of a given situation nor the remote intention one has for making a particular choice (the *finis operantis*) can transform a fundamentally bad act into a good one.[108] This is

104. The English edition of *Nova et Vetera* dedicated several articles to Long's work in 2010. Interested readers will note the essay by Lawrence Dewan, "St. Thomas, Steven Long, and Private Defense," *Nova et Vetera*, English edition, 8 (2010): 191–205, for its careful criticism of the work as well as the review by Kevin Flannery, *The Thomist* 78 (2008): 322–25, for its thorough analysis. For Long's response to these objections, see his "Engaging Thomist Interlocutors" *Nova et Vetera*, English edition, 9 (2011): 267–95.

105. See, for example, Long's "Natural Law, the Moral Object, and *Humanae Vitae*," in *Ressourcement Thomism: Sacred Doctrine, the Sacraments, and the Moral Life*, ed. Reinhard Hütter and Matthew Levering, 285–311 (Washington, DC: The Catholic University of America Press, 2010); "*Veritatis Splendor* §78 and the Teleological Grammar of the Moral Act," *Nova et Vetera*, English edition, 6 (2008): 139–56; "Regarding the Nature of the Moral Object and Intention: A Response to Steven Jensen," *Nova et Vetera*, English edition, 3 (2005): 101–108; and "A Brief Disquisition Regarding the Nature of the Object of the Moral Act According to St. Thomas Aquinas," *The Thomist* 67 (2003): 45–71.

106. *VS*, no. 78.

107. *VS*, no. 78.

108. See *VS*, no. 81: "Consequently, circumstances or intentions can never transform an act intrinsically evil by virtue of its object into an act 'subjectively' good or defensible

distinct from the situation of a good act done for a bad reason. In this case, a malevolent intention alters what would otherwise be a good act. One who gives alms merely to be praised, for example, commits an act of vainglory.[109] The accomplishment of a good moral act requires both a good moral object and a sound intention. While an evil intention can render an otherwise good act to be a poor moral choice, no good intention can change a bad act into a good one. Some types of acts can never become the kind of act that is choiceworthy. The *Catechism of the Catholic Church* elucidates this truth: "Circumstances of themselves cannot change the moral quality of acts themselves; they can make neither good nor right an action that is in itself evil."[110] An act's moral goodness requires firstly and fundamentally an object rationally chosen which is conformable to the truth about the good of the human person.

In *Teleological Grammar*, Long argues that several aspects of Thomas's analysis of moral objects have been lost in contemporary moral thought. He argues that normative teleology—which is discovered rather than imposed by the human mind—governs human action. Regardless of whatever further reason one may have for performing a particular act, each action itself has an end that is constitutive of its being a given type of act. Each human action possesses a built-in teleology or natural structure. Long explains:

> *The object may be treated merely generically and precisively, apart from any per accidens ordering to a further end*; or it may be treated with its full specification as ordered to the end sought by the agent in a particular act. *This is only possible because the object as such bears a relation and proportion to the end, such that we know the type of the end—otherwise there could be no object which falls by its nature, generically, under negative precept. This again testifies to the truth that there is a per se, normative instance of the moral act for St. Thomas, namely the case wherein the object is per se ordered to the end.*[111]

Long believes that St. Thomas's account of the moral life presumes a teleological order of human action. Long emphasizes that without teleological order—that is, without moral objects *per se* ordered to some end—it

---

as a choice." For a careful treatment of the place of circumstance in the specification of moral objects, see Osborne, Jr., *Human Action in Thomas Aquinas, John Duns Scotus, and William of Ockham*, 149–84. For the distinction between the *finis operis* and the *finis operantis*, see Cessario, OP, *Introduction to Moral Theology*, 167–71.

109. CCC, no. 1753.

110. CCC, no. 1754.

111. Long, *The Teleological Grammar of the Moral Act*, 2nd ed., 149–50. Emphasis in original.

would not be possible to speak sensibly about intrinsically evil acts. Aquinas affirms the existence of objects *malum in se* or evil by means of their object.[112] Only because acts are of a certain type—that a genus of kinds of acts exists at all—can Aquinas reasonably speak of the existence of objects evil in themselves.[113] Long argues that natural teleology ultimately determines what can be included in the moral object of the act. Long explains, "The integral nature and *per se* effects of action are always included in the object of the act."[114] That is, one cannot characterize the nature of the act according to one's wishes but, instead, must include what is given by the very nature of the act and its *per se* effects. For example, according to Long, one cannot rightly describe the use of a condom in a conjugal act by a couple where the husband is HIV positive as an act of disease prevention.[115] Instead, the nature of such an act includes as a *per se* effect of condom use the sterilization of the conjugal act. This act cannot be redefined by one's intention or purpose in performing it. Rather the act is contraceptive by its very nature.[116] For this reason, Long remains leery of any signs of "intentionalism" which would privilege intention instead of object in the specification of a moral act.

Long's analysis provides a particular contribution in his stress on *per se* effects on action. He explains: "When acts of themselves tend toward an end, they are said to be naturally or *per se* ordered to it; likewise, when attainment of an end *by the very nature of the end* requires a certain action, that

112. See, for example, *Summa theologiae*, Ia–IIae, q. 18, a. 2: "And therefore just as the primary goodness of a natural thing is derived from its form, which gives it its species, so the primary goodness of a moral action is derived from its suitable object."

113. For an extended treatment of this question, see Pinckaers, OP, "A Historical Perspective on Intrinsically Evil Acts," *The Pinckaers Reader*, 185–235. For a defense of the existence of intrinsically evil acts although from a different philosophical perspective, see Rhonheimer, "Intrinsically Evil Acts and the Moral Viewpoint: Clarifying a Central Teaching of *Veritatis Splendor*," in *Veritatis Splendor and the Renewal of Moral Theology*, 161–93.

114. Long, "Engaging Thomist Interlocutors," 276.

115. For an enlightening exchange on the debate surrounding the use of condoms by those with HIV or AIDS, see Stephen Napier, "The Missing Premise in the HIV-Condom Debate," *The Linacre Quarterly* 78 (2011): 401–14; and an outstanding rebuttal by Joseph Arias, "'Validity' and 'Liceity' in conjugal acts: A reply to Stephen Napier on the HIV-condom debate," *The Linacre Quarterly* 83 (2016): 330–45.

116. Arguing in a similar fashion, Nicanor Austriaco, OP, explains, "Thus, despite their further intention to prevent the transmission of the AIDS virus, a couple using a condom for prophylactic purposes cannot claim that they are not engaged in a contraceptive act." See Nicanor Pier Giorgio Austriaco, OP, *Biomedicine and Beatitude*, 118.

action is also said to be naturally or *per se* ordered to the end."[117] Long's emphasis on *per se* effects bears no resemblance to the consequentialism condemned by *Veritatis splendor*.[118] Long does not argue that certain effects happen to follow a given act or happen to be consequences of a given action. Rather, natural teleology accounts for the fact that certain effects necessarily follow—by reason of their nature—from a given action. Sound human inquiry discovers this natural teleology; it is not created by the human mind. This distinction will become crucial when dealing with complex acts where an accurate description of the act requires an account of how one act is *per se* ordered to another.

Long holds that when one act is *per se* ordered to another act it is the second act which provides the means of specification for the one complex act which includes both particular acts.[119] It is not as though one can say that any means can be *per se* ordered to some further end, thus justifying any action on the grounds that it is further ordered to a good end. Long holds that a given choice of means if *per se* ordered to an end renders an otherwise complex act simpler to understand. An act in which the choice of means is *per se* ordered to the end is, under one consideration, two acts, but most formally it is only one complex act. Here the given choice of means is *per se* ordered to the further end of the overall act. An example proves useful. A doctor removing a kidney in Pittsburgh for a transplant that will take place in Albuquerque can assert legitimately that his action can be understood properly only with reference to the ill person in New Mexico awaiting the transplant.[120] The doctor's action from out-

117. Long, *The Teleological Grammar of the Moral Act*, 2nd ed., 150.

118. *VS*, no. 77: "But the consideration of these consequences, and also of intentions, is not sufficient for judging the moral quality of a concrete choice. The weighing of the goods and evils foreseeable as the consequence of an action is not an adequate method for determining whether the choice of that concrete kind of behavior is 'according to its species', or 'in itself', morally good or bad, licit or illicit. The foreseeable consequences are part of those circumstances of the act, which, while capable of lessening the gravity of an evil act, nonetheless cannot alter its moral species."

119. See, for example, Long, *The Teleological Grammar of the Moral Act*, 2nd ed., 107–8.

120. For an extended reflection on this topic, see Long, "Natural Law, the Moral Object, and *Humanae Vitae*," in *Ressourcement Thomism: Sacred Doctrine, the Sacraments, and the Moral Life*, 285–311. For the moral issues involved in organ transplantation more generally, see Austriaco, OP, *Biomedicine and Beatitude*, 261–309; and, also, Steven J. Jensen, ed., *The Ethics of Organ Transplantation* (Washington, DC: The Catholic University of America Press, 2011). Interested readers may also consult the influential essay of Gerald Kelly, "The Morality of Mutilations: Towards a Revision of the Treatise," *Theological Studies* 17 (1956): 322–44.

ward appearances could appear like an act of mutilation—surgically removing a healthy kidney. However, the act of removing the kidney by a
trained transplant doctor in Pittsburgh is *per se* ordered to the implanting
of the kidney in Albuquerque. More precisely, the removal of the kidney
is *per se* ordered to the act of the same doctor sending the kidney for implantation to the awaiting patient in Albuquerque. For that reason, the
end of transplantation—rendering a sick person healthy—provides for
the specification of the moral object of the doctor in Pittsburgh. This
moral specification is not the result of the fact that his purpose is to render a sick person healthy. Rendering a sick person healthy does not justify
any means whatsoever to make one healthy. The doctor could not attack
a person on the street to take a healthy kidney for the sick woman in Albuquerque. Presuming the various conditions are met for a morally sound
organ transplantation, the doctor is justified precisely because his removal
of the kidney in Pittsburgh is *per se* ordered to its being sent to the sick patient in Albuquerque.[121]

A large portion of the debate over the proper method of specification of
moral objects surrounds the proper interpretation of St. Thomas's teaching on private defense. In *Summa theologiae* IIa–IIae, q. 64, a. 7, Aquinas argues that one may kill in self-defense. Great debate exists, however, on
how we should understand his account. St. Thomas teaches:

Nothing hinders one act from having two effects, only one of which is intended, while the other is beside the intention. Now moral acts take their species
according to what is intended, and not according to what is beside the intention.... Accordingly the act of self-defense may have two effects, one is the
saving of one's life, the other is the slaying of the aggressor.[122]

This account has given rise to centuries of reflection on what has become
known as the principle of double effect.[123] St. Thomas, however, does not

121. For further reflection on precisely what conditions are required for morally licit
organ transplantation, see *The Ethics of Organ Transplantation*, especially the essay by Romanus Cessario, OP, "Thomistic Moral Theology Confronts the Tide of Relativism,"
195–216.

122. *Summa theologiae*, IIa–IIae, q. 64, a. 7.

123. For the classic articulation of the foundations of this principle, see Joseph T.
Mangan, "A Historical Analysis of the Principle of Double Effect," *Theological Studies* 10
(1949): 41–61. For more recent perspectives, see Lucius I. Ugorji, *The Principle of Double Effect: A Critical Appraisal of its Traditional Understanding and its Modern Reinterpretation* (Frankfurt:
Peter Lang, 1993); and Thomas A. Cavanaugh, *Double-Effect Reasoning: Doing Good and Avoiding Evil* (New York: Oxford University Press, 2006).

establish a principle of double effect as much as he explains a particular instance of his general theory of human action. St. Thomas acknowledges that when a given action has two effects, one effect may be intended and the other beside the intention (*praeter intentionem*).

St. Thomas's treatment of self-defense unfolds in the *secunda-secundae* of his *Summa theologiae*. While in the *prima-secundae* Aquinas offers exposition of the general principles of moral action, here, in the *secunda-secundae*, he applies those general principles to the theological and moral virtues and the acts which flow from them. Thus, when treating self-defense Aquinas does not create a whole new way of approaching moral topics. Rather, it appears more likely that St. Thomas intends this explanation to be an example of the application of his general principles of moral action to the particular instance of an act of self-defense.[124] The type of double-effect reasoning most widely known today does not result from an application of Aquinas's principles. Instead, contemporary accounts of double-effect reasoning represent an alternative to St. Thomas's teaching. Christopher Kaczor has argued convincingly that the modern use of double-effect reasoning has its origins in the manuals of the French Jesuit Jean Pierre Gury (1801–1866).[125] Gury exercised considerable influence as he authored what was most likely the most widely used moral manual of the nineteenth century.[126] This expansion of the use of the principle of double-effect extended to cases of moral cooperation. Authors utilized this principle to justify why one could cooperate with evil despite the resulting evil effects.[127] Instead of examining the act's merits on its own, a primitive consequentialism can develop through extensive use of double-effect reasoning. In fact, throughout the modern period some thinkers have invoked the principle of double effect to justify all manner of evils.[128]

124. See Christopher Kaczor, *Proportionalism and the Natural Law Tradition* (Washington, DC: The Catholic University of America Press, 2002), 26.

125. See Christopher Kaczor, "Double-Effect Reasoning: From Jean Pierre Gury to Peter Knauer," *Theological Studies* 59 (1998): 297–316.

126. See Pinckaers, OP, *Morality: The Catholic View*, trans. Michael Sherwin, OP (South Bend: St. Augustine's Press, 2001), 39. For more information on this period, see Charles E. Curran, *The Origins of Moral Theology in the United States: Three Different Approaches* (Washington, DC: Georgetown University Press, 1997), 54–60.

127. See, for example, Dom Odon Lottin, *Morale Fondamentale* (Paris: Desclée & Co., 1954), 289–90. Lottin treats the issue of cooperation in a section dealing with cases of double-effect reasoning, "Exemples de causes a double effet."

128. For example, the principle of double effect has been invoked to justify therapeutic abortion and craniotomy. Jean Pierre Gury, SJ, for example, initially rejected the permissibility of abortion even if the mother's life was in danger. However, he appeared

In the same article seven of question sixty-four, St. Thomas continues by explaining that not any action may be justified because it falls outside of the intention of the agent. St. Thomas explains: "Therefore this act, since one's intention is to save one's own life, is not unlawful, seeing that it is natural to everything to keep itself in 'being,' as far as possible. And yet, though proceeding from a good intention, an act may be rendered unlawful, if it be out of proportion to the end."[129] Thomas argues that even if preceding from a good intention, an act may be unlawful if it is lacking in proportion to its end. This assertion has yielded abundant commentary on the so-called principle of proportionate reason. It becomes clear from a careful reading of the text, however, that St. Thomas does not argue for interested parties to measure a proportion between positive and negative effects. He does not ask the perplexed moral actor to determine if bad effects outweigh the good which will result from a particular action.[130] Instead, the proportion St. Thomas identifies is precisely of the act *to the end*. Is the given act proportioned or, one could say, *per se ordered by means of natural teleology* to the end of the act?

With proportion in mind one can understand the way in which the choice of means is or is not *per se* ordered to the end of the given act. St Thomas continues:

Wherefore if a man, in self-defense, uses more than necessary violence, it will be unlawful: whereas if he repel force with moderation his defense will be lawful, because according to the jurists "it is lawful to repel force by force, provided one does not exceed the limits of a blameless defense." Nor is it necessary for salvation that a man omit the act of moderate self-defense in order to avoid killing the other man, since one is bound to take more care of one's own life than of another's.[131]

---

to change his view in his *Compendium* of moral theology published the year of his death. This text was published with the assistance of Antonio Ballerini, SJ, and so there exists some question about whether its permission of therapeutic abortion was Gury's position or Ballerini's. Another Jesuit, Augustine Lehmkuhl (1834–1918), also permitted abortion if necessary to save the mother's life as a probable opinion. Lehmkuhl argued explicitly on the grounds of the need to weigh good and evil effects. For an in-depth history of this matter, see John Connery, SJ, *Abortion: The Development of the Roman Catholic Perspective* (Chicago: Loyola University Press, 1977), 214–24.

129. *Summa theologiae*, IIa–IIae, q. 64, a. 7.

130. For an extended reflection on the history and misunderstandings associated with the principle of proportionate reason, see Brian V. Johnstone, CSsR, "The Meaning of Proportionate Reason," *The Thomist* 49 (1985): 223–47.

131. *Summa theologiae*, IIa–IIae, q. 64, a. 7.

Long argues that in the case of self-defense one intends self-defense and chooses means which are *per se* ordered to self-defense. In this case, one may choose lethal means—precisely since these means are *per se* ordered to the end of self-defense.[132] Moralists distinguish this description of self-defense from the celebrated case of a man who steals money in order to commit adultery. In this case, St. Thomas, following Aristotle, affirms: "one who steals to commit adultery is more adulterer than thief."[133] Such a man, however, remains guilty of two sins since there is nothing about thievery that is *per se* ordered to adultery. However, in the case of self-defense, the choice of lethal means is *per se* ordered to the end of self-defense. Thus, the choice of means becomes part of the overall act which takes its object from the end—which in this case is self-defense.

Throughout his work Long adheres to a classical reading of St. Thomas. He argues that some contemporary authors have abandoned Thomistic teleology in favor of an overly intentional account of the human act. Long holds that even some otherwise sound thinkers have adopted the position that one's ultimate reason for acting (*finis operantis*) can play too great a role in specifying a moral object. Elsewhere Long has argued that an unreasonable fear of physicalism has taken hold in some authors who devote insufficient attention to the physicality of what one is actually doing in a given action. Long explains:

There is much talk today of the error of "physicalism"—and of course, the exclusion from the object of the moral act's relation to reason would be an error. Nonetheless, the far more preponderant error today is that of "angelism" or the reduction of the object of the act merely to the relation to reason or to that which makes the act attractive to the agent.[134]

Despite whatever physicalism once may have existed in certain corners of Catholic moral theology, today moralists more commonly commit the error of intentionalism by giving insufficient attention to the nature of the moral object itself.[135] *Veritatis splendor* warns of the dangers of an overly intentional examination of the moral object in its extensive critique of inten-

---

132. For an alternative perspective on this matter, see Stephen L. Brock, *Action and Conduct: Thomas Aquinas and the Theory of Action* (Edinburgh: T&T Clark, 1998), 221–23.

133. *Summa theologiae*, Ia–IIae, q. 18, a. 6.

134. Long, "*Veritatis Splendor* §78 and the Teleological Grammar of the Moral Act," 156.

135. For an excellent treatment of the false charge of physicalism lodged against a Thomistic analysis of the moral act, see Brock, "*Veritatis Splendor* §78, St. Thomas, and (Not Merely) Physical Objects of Moral Acts," 1–62.

tionalist moral theories.[136] The case of craniotomy offers just one example of how an overly intentional reading of a moral object can lead to deleterious consequences for the moral life. Explaining away the act of crushing the skull of a partially born human child by reclassifying the act as reshaping the proportions of the child's skull demonstrates how destructive overly intentional renderings of the moral act can become.

Our effort to establish a virtue-based approach to analyzing moral cooperation with evil requires a careful examination of moral objects. A virtue-based method of moral inquiry demands that perplexed moral actors examine rigorously the objects of their actions. Specifically, in cases of cooperation, attention to the teleology of the cooperative act proves useful. Natural teleology helps to determine whether evil effects follow essentially or accidently from a cooperative act. More than any other author at work today, Steven Long has effectively argued for the need for a robust place for natural teleology in moral action theory. It is not necessary to concur with his analysis in every aspect to recognize that his recovery of natural teleology more generally will prove useful in an object-based account of moral matters.

Anthony Fisher and natural meanings
vs. intended acts

The Dominican Archbishop of Sydney, Australia, Anthony Fisher, stands as one of the great theologian bishops of the early twenty-first century. He has published widely in the area of bioethics and the defense of human life. His 2012 *Catholic Bioethics for a New Millennium* provides a sound account of how to analyze questions of moral cooperation with evil. Fisher's role as a diocesan bishop gives him a unique perspective on the practical nature of the questions involved in institutional cooperation. These cases often involve Catholic hospitals, educational institutions, or social service agencies.[137] A first-rate scholar, Fisher studied at Oxford under the

---

136. See *VS*, especially nos. 76–78.

137. For a helpful collection of essays regarding institutional cooperation, see Edward J. Furton, ed., *Walk as Children of Light: The Challenge of Cooperation in a Pluralistic Society* (Boston: The National Catholic Bioethics Center, 2003). Interested readers may also consult Patrick C. Beeman, "Catholicism, Cooperation, and Contraception," *The National Catholic Bioethics Quarterly* 12 (2012): 283–309; as well as the essays in *The Bishop and the Future of Catholic Health Care: Challenges and Opportunities*, ed. Daniel P. Maher (Boston: Pope John XXIII Medical-Moral Research and Education Center, 1997).

direction of John Finnis and has sympathies for the new natural law approach to moral thinking. Regardless of one's view of the merits of this approach to natural law, Fisher's study represents an important contribution to contemporary discussions of moral cooperation with evil.

Anthony Fisher has been writing about moral cooperation with evil for several decades. In his 1994 essay, "Co-operation in Evil", Fisher poses the fundamental question of moral cooperation. When might someone cooperate with one who is doing wrong? He explains:

The simplest answer is: never. I want to maintain clean hands and a pure heart. I scorn the company of evil-doers. I will not co-operate in their wickedness. I want to set a good example. So it is that some people went to the death camps rather than collaborate in any way with the Nazis. And some people have resigned from the health service, indeed from the healthcare professions, rather than have anything to do with some practice or other which they cannot condone.... These people are either martyrs or fanatics. Those who are martyrs deserve our admiration and respect. But not everyone is called to be a martyr, or at least not all the time.[138]

Fisher rightly gets to the heart of the matter. The answer to the question of how often or how much one should immorally cooperate with evil is never; in no way; no how. Some moralists writing about cooperation with evil give the impression that a little bit of immoral cooperation could be justified in cases of necessity or duress. Instead, Fisher reminds readers that no circumstances justify an action which is evil in itself. When a cooperator's act is the kind of action never to be done, no set of circumstances can alter that fact. No amount of duress or attempts to redefine one's action due to good intentions can transform a bad act into a good one. On the other hand, if a cooperator's action is the type of activity which may be a good act, then he or she must still consider the possibility of scandal. Acts which may not fall under negative precept in some cases still should be avoided due to the risk of scandal.

Fisher provides the context for a discussion of moral cooperation with evil. He offers the traditional list of the types of possible cooperation in this way:

Those of you who were reared on the *Penny Catechism* will be able to recite the nine ways of causing or sharing in the guilt of another's sin: by counsel, by

138. Anthony Fisher, "Co-operation in Evil," *Catholic Medical Quarterly* 44 (1994): 15–16.

command, by consent, by provocation, by praise or flattery, by concealment, by being a partner in the sin, by silence, and by defending the ill done.[139]

These different types of cooperation present a popularized summary of St. Thomas's elaboration of the forms of cooperation. Aquinas delineates these forms of cooperation in his treatment on the necessity of making restitution for sins committed.[140] Each action represents a different manner of activity in which one may classify cooperative acts. Making judicious use of the early twentieth-century moral manuals, Fisher lays out the basic groundwork for a possible response to moral cooperation with evil. Identifying contemporary interventions of the Magisterium, Fisher reviews five cases in which the Holy See has intervened in cases of cooperation. Not surprisingly, Fisher finds the judgments of the Holy See to be both accurate and instructive for how best to think about issues of moral cooperation with evil. A review of his treatment of these cases offers useful data in our effort to establish a virtue-based approach to moral cooperation with evil. In each case Fisher examines, he identifies a principle useful for analyzing moral cooperation more generally. His analysis demonstrates that the praxis of the Church has been to insist that Catholic entities avoid immoral cooperation in every circumstance.[141]

In his first case under consideration Fisher details the controversy surrounding contraceptive sterilizations performed in American hospitals operated by the Catholic Church.[142] Catholic moral teaching condemns sterilization for contraceptive purposes as it represents an act of mutila-

139. Anthony Fisher, "Co-operation in Evil," 16.

140. See *Summa theologiae*, IIa–IIae, q. 62, a. 7: "By command, by counsel, by consent, by flattery, by receiving, by participation, by silence, by not preventing, by not denouncing." "Iussio, consilium, consensus, palpo, recursus, participans, mutus, non obstans, non manifestans."

141. For the most extended statement of the Holy See on the matter, see the Congregation for the Doctrine of the Faith, *Some Principles for Collaboration with Non-Catholic Entities in the Provision of Health Care Services*, as published in *The National Catholic Bioethics Quarterly* 14 (2014): 337–40. This document was never formally promulgated by the Holy See. The text served as a response to bishops regarding the challenges of collaboration with non-Catholic entities. The Congregation granted permission for the document to be published in the *The National Catholic Bioethics Quarterly*.

142. For an extended account of this history, see John P. Boyle, *The Sterilization Controversy: A New Crisis for the Catholic Hospital?* (New York: Paulist Press, 1977). For a helpful treatment of Catholic teaching on this matter, see May, *Catholic Bioethics and the Gift of Human Life*, 3rd ed., 141–44. For an extended review of the history of sterilization, see Elio Sgreccia, *Personalist Bioethics: Foundations and Applications*, 549–80.

tion in violation of the fifth commandment of the Decalogue.[143] In addition, direct sterilization ruptures the intimate connection between the procreative and unitive meanings of human sexuality.[144] However, in the latter part of the twentieth century some theologians began to question Catholic teaching against sterilization.[145] Some theologians claimed physicians could perform such operations in Catholic hospitals if pressured to do so by civil law or for other reasons. Indeed, the *Ethical and Religious Directives for Catholic Health Care Services* issued by the American bishops in both 1977 and again in 1994 appeared to leave room for some possibility of performing sterilizations in Catholic hospitals. Upon careful review, the Congregation for the Doctrine of the Faith found the US bishops' *Directives* to be inadequate on this matter. The Congregation held that these *Directives* were subject to too varied interpretations. For example, the 1994 *Directives* held that immediate material cooperation could be justified in cases of duress.[146] The claim that duress could change implicitly formal (and therefore morally unacceptable) cooperation into immediate material cooperation (and therefore possibly acceptable) fails to address the primary question regarding the nature of the act of sterilization.[147]

143. See *CCC*, no. 2297: "Except when performed for strictly therapeutic medical reasons, directly intended amputations, mutilations, and sterilizations performed on innocent persons are against the moral law."

144. For an elaboration of Catholic teaching about sterilization, see the Congregation for the Doctrine of the Faith, *Responses to Questions Concerning Sterilization in Catholic Hospitals*, March 13, 1975, in particular, from paragraph 1: "Any sterilization which of itself, that is, of its own nature and condition, has the sole immediate effect of rendering the generative faculty incapable of procreation, is to be considered direct sterilization, as the term is understood in the declarations of the pontifical Magisterium, especially of Pius XII. Therefore, notwithstanding any subjectively right intention of those whose actions are prompted by the care or prevention of physical or mental illness which is foreseen or feared as a result of pregnancy, such sterilization remains absolutely forbidden according to the doctrine of the Church."

145. See, for example, Charles E. Curran, "Sterilization: Roman Catholic Theory and Practice," *Linacre Quarterly* 40 (1973): 97–108. For commentary on the context of the debate over sterilization, see Charles E. Curran, *Catholic Moral Theology: A History* (Washington, DC: Georgetown University Press, 2008), 193–95.

146. See Fisher, *Catholic Bioethics for a New Millennium*, 75.

147. Interested readers may also consult the exchange regarding cooperation in sterilization between James F. Keenan, SJ, and Lawrence J. Welch. See James F. Keenan, SJ, "Institutional Cooperation and the Ethical and Religious Directives," *Linacre Quarterly* 64 (1997): 53–76; Lawrence J. Welch, "An Excessive Claim: Sterilization and Immediate Material Cooperation," *Linacre Quarterly* 66 (1999): 4–25; James F. Keenan, SJ, "Not an Excessive Claim, Nor a Divisive One, But a Traditional One: A Response to Lawrence

The Congregation recognized that a situation of duress may affect moral culpability, but it cannot transform a bad act into a good one.

The intervention of the Holy See regarding sterilization at Catholic hospitals offers salutary guidance for our understanding of moral cooperation more generally.[148] In correspondence to the teaching of *Veritatis splendor* and *Evangelium vitae*, the Holy See will not accept the claim that duress can fundamentally change a moral act. Government mandates or financial or legal requirements insisting on such cooperation provide no justification for acting badly. The Holy See rejects the view that the moral law can be jettisoned for an institution to remain in operation. Instead, no one can claim that duress permits what would otherwise be an unjustified act of cooperation with evil.

Examining another case of magisterial intervention regarding cooperation with evil, Fisher treats the dispute over the distribution of condoms to stem the spread of HIV or other sexually transmitted diseases.[149] In the late 1980s, the Catholic bishops of the United States began to draft a document on prevention and treatment of HIV and AIDS. Eventually released in 1989 as *Called to Compassion and Responsibility*, the text spurred contentious debate. An original draft of the pastoral letter had followed the lead of Jesuit theologians Richard McCormick and James Keenan by suggesting that the promotion of condom use would be morally acceptable as the toleration of a lesser evil.[150] A letter from Cardinal Joseph Ratzinger,

---

Welch on Immediate Material Cooperation," *Linacre Quarterly* 67 (2000): 83–88; and Lawrence J. Welch, "Direct Sterilization: An Intrinsically Evil Act—A Rejoinder to Fr. Keenan," *Linacre Quarterly* 68 (2001): 124–30. On the same topic, see also Anthony Zimmerman, "Contraceptive Sterilization in Catholic Hospitals is Intrinsically Evil," *Linacre Quarterly* 68 (2001): 262–73.

148. For a more extended treatment of this question, see Germain Kopaczynski, OFM Conv., "'We Sterilize Instruments, Not People': Catholic Teaching on Direct Sterilization," in *Walk as Children of Light: The Challenge of Cooperation in a Pluralistic Society*, ed. Edward J. Furton, 213–34 (Boston: The National Catholic Bioethics Center, 2003).

149. See Fisher, *Catholic Bioethics for a New Millennium*, 77–80. For a more extended treatment of this question, see Anthony Fisher, "HIV and condoms within marriage," *Communio* 36 (2009): 329–59.

150. For an elaboration of Keenan's support for the distribution of condoms, see James F. Keenan, SJ, "Prophylactics, Toleration and Cooperation: Contemporary Problems and Traditional Principles," *International Philosophical Quarterly* 29 (1989): 205–20. For an alternative view on the use of condoms for the purpose of disease prevention, see Austriaco, OP, *Biomedicine and Beatitude*, 116–20. For a similar perspective, see May, *Catholic Bioethics and the Gift of Human Life*, 3rd ed., 144–47. For another critique of the use of condoms for the purpose of disease prevention, see Robert J. Dempsey, "Condom Use by HIV-Discordant Married Couples," *The National Catholic Bioethics Quarterly* 15 (2015): 91–105.

then Prefect of the Congregation for the Doctrine of the Faith, to Archbishop Pio Laghi, then Apostolic Pro-Nuncio to the United States, persuaded the American bishops to forgo any reference to condom use in the final draft of the pastoral letter.[151]

This example suggests that just as duress cannot transform a bad act into a good one, a particularly challenging situation cannot fundamentally change the nature of a bad act. According to Catholic teaching, the sterilization of the conjugal act remains the kind of thing that can never be choiceworthy.[152] Promoting condom use represents immoral cooperation in fornication, contraceptive sex, or other unchaste acts.[153] Arguments promoting a "lesser evil" expounded by those of the proportionist school fail to add clarity to the issue in question. One distinguishes correctly between tolerating a lesser evil and choosing to commit a lesser sin. One finds no warrant in Catholic moral thought for pursuing the lesser of two sins. Instead, all sin should be avoided. The Church could never counsel one to choose to commit a moral evil, even one less grave than other moral evils. Pope Paul VI addressed the principle of the lesser evil in his 1968 encyclical *Humanae vitae*. Pope Paul explains:

Neither is it valid to argue, as a justification for sexual intercourse which is deliberately contraceptive, that a lesser evil is to be preferred to a greater one, or that such intercourse would merge with procreative acts of past and future to form a single entity, and so be qualified by exactly the same moral goodness as these. Though it is true that sometimes it is lawful to tolerate a lesser moral evil in order to avoid a greater evil or in order to promote a greater good, it is never lawful, even for the gravest reasons, to do evil that good may come of it—in other words, to intend directly something which of its very nature contradicts the moral order, and which must therefore be judged unworthy of man, even though the intention is to protect or promote the welfare of an individual, of a family or of society in general.[154]

151. See Fisher, *Catholic Bioethics for a New Millennium*, 77. Fisher cites the letter of Joseph Cardinal Ratzinger, "Letter to Archbishop Pio Laghi on 'The many faces of AIDS,' 29 May 1988," Origins 18 (July 17, 1988), 117–18.

152. See *Humanae vitae*, no. 14, as cited in *CCC*, no. 2370: "'Every action which, whether in anticipation of the conjugal act, or in its accomplishment, or in the development of its natural consequences, proposes, whether as an end or as a means, to render procreation impossible' is intrinsically evil."

153. For a treatment of offenses against chastity, see *CCC*, nos. 2351–59. For an outstanding overview of this teaching, see also the Sacred Congregation for the Doctrine of the Faith, Declaration on Certain Questions Concerning Sexual Ethics, *Persona humana*.

154. *Humanae vitae*, no. 14. When arguing for the existence of intrinsically evil acts—

Pope Paul teaches that "even for the gravest reasons" one cannot justify the choice for a moral evil. Questions of proportion or weighing of consequences have no place in a sound moral analysis regarding the pursuit of a possible moral evil.[155] No moral justification exists for choosing sin under any circumstance.

Fisher recalls that in the 2010 interview book *Light of the World*, Pope Benedict XVI suggested that there may be cases (such as a male prostitute using a condom) in which his use of a condom may represent the first awakenings of moral responsibility.[156] While Benedict XVI articulated the same principles the Church has always taught on this matter, much discussion ensued suggesting he had changed the teaching of the Church regarding the immorality of contraception. Of course, he had done no such thing. The Pope did not argue that it is better from a moral point of view that such a prostitute in fact use a condom. He asserted only that on a purely psychological level it may (and of course also may not) represent the beginnings of some sense of responsibility on the part of the prostitute. This discussion exists entirely on the level of his subjective consciousness and does not enter into the debate of how it may or may not be better to commit grave sin. It is not that it is better to use a condom as much as its use may represent the first stirrings of moral responsibility.[157]

---

those that can never be ordered to the truth about the good of the human person, Pope John Paul II cites this passage from *Humanae vitae*. See *VS*, no. 80.

155. For a more extended treatment of the sober look of Pope Paul VI at the principle of the lesser of evils, see Robert C. Morlino, *The Principle of the Lesser of Evils in Today's Conflict Situations: New Challenges to Moral Theology from a Pluralistic Society* (Rome: Pontifical Gregorian University, 1990), 39–46.

156. See Pope Benedict XVI and Peter Seewald, *Light of the World: The Pope, the Church, and the Signs of the Times*, trans. Michael J. Miller and Adrian J. Walker (San Francisco: Ignatius Press, 2010), 119. The Pope explained: "There may be a basis in the case of some individuals, as perhaps when a male prostitute uses a condom, where this can be a first step in the direction of a moralization, a first assumption of responsibility, on the way toward recovering an awareness that not everything is allowed and that one cannot do whatever one wants. But it is not really the way to deal with the evil of HIV infection. That can really lie only in a humanization of sexuality."

157. For a more extended treatment of this topic, see David S. Crawford, "Pope Benedict XVI and the Structure of the Moral Act: On the Condoms Controversy," *Communio* 38 (2011): 548–82, specifically 581, where he explains: "Such 'first steps' do not mean that these actions are objectively good, but they do raise them to a certain level of subjective ambiguity. They may very well indeed be a sign of a changing interior disposition. In none of these examples, however, does pointing to a possible changing interior disposition imply a reconstitution of the action itself along the lines provided for by the intentionalist argument."

Even if the use of a condom in a particular case may indicate the begin-nings of some sense of responsibility, its use in an otherwise procreative type act remains an evil that should not be chosen. Unchaste acts of what-ever kind—including sterilizing conjugal acts—are acts which fall short of the full truth about human sexuality.[158] For that reason Fisher holds that the promotion and distribution of condoms represents an immoral cooperation in unchastity. The promotion of condom use fails to advance the truth and beauty of marital love. Pope Benedict XVI himself, in his role as Cardinal Prefect of the Congregation for the Doctrine of the Faith, offered clarity on this matter in his 1988 letter to then-Archbishop Laghi. At that time Cardinal Joseph Ratzinger explained: "The only medical-ly safe means of preventing AIDS are those very types of behavior which conform to God's law and to the truth about man which the Church has always taught and today is still called courageously to teach."[159] Had the Pope's intervention as a Cardinal in 1988 been more widely known, much less misunderstanding would have ensued in 2010. After intense debate surrounding this topic, Fisher aptly explains, "cooperation by Church agencies in condom programmes would still seem to be ruled out."[160] The position of the Holy See remains unchanged. There exists no justification for the promotion of condom use since it represents unjust cooperation in the evil of the sterilization of the conjugal act.[161]

As a third example of possible cooperation with evil, Fisher examines the case of a series of drug injection rooms operated by the Church in Aus-tralia. In the late 1990s, the Sisters of Charity Health Service announced

158. For a reflection on the dignity of human sexuality, see John Paul II, *Man and Woman He Created Them: A Theology of the Body*, trans. Michael Waldstein (Boston: Pauline Books and Media, 2006); and Karol Wojtyla, *Love and Responsibility* (San Francisco: Igna-tius Press, 1993).

159. Ratzinger, "Letter to Archbishop Pio Laghi on 'The many faces of AIDS,' 29 May 1988," 117–18.

160. See Fisher, *Catholic Bioethics for a New Millennium*, 80.

161. For one reflection on the principle of lesser evil, see Sgreccia, *Personalist Bioethics*, 189–90. Sgreccia writes: "When there is a question of two moral evils, the obligation is to refuse both, because evil can never be the object of a choice. This is also true even when a greater evil is brought about as a consequence of refusing the one that appears to be a lesser evil. An often-used example is ordering someone to commit a robbery or tamper with documents on threat of sexual violence or the death of other people. With all the attenuating circumstances that must be considered from the subjective view-point, objectively the robbery should not be committed because it is an evil. If refusal to commit the robbery leads to a form of revenge entailing a more serious moral evil, then this would be imputable solely to the person deciding to commit the evil."

they would begin to operate a facility where those who wish to inject intravenous drugs could do so in a "safe" and medically supervised environment.[162] Some observers raised the question of whether operating such facilities represented formal cooperation in the use of these dangerous and harmful drugs. In this case, the Congregation for the Doctrine of the Faith rejected the claim that aiding drug users to safely administer illegal drugs represented an appropriate exercise of Christian charity. Fisher explains that while the content of the Vatican intervention has never been made public in its entirety, the substance of the position of the Holy See has become clear. Programs aimed at caring for drug users should not provide safe facilities for them to use drugs but instead should establish programs to assist them in ceasing drug use.[163] The intervention of the Holy See was instructive for rejecting the argument that because some action is thought to be inevitable one may cooperate in any way to lessen its evil consequences. The very fact of wishing a situation were otherwise does not provide warrant to render one's cooperation material (as opposed to formal) and therefore possibly licit.[164] Types of cooperation, Fisher argues, can be immoral by their very nature.[165]

In a fourth case of cooperation with evil, Fisher examines the well-known controversy involving German-operated abortion counseling facilities. In the 1990s, the German government began to require that any woman seeking an abortion demonstrate that she had received counseling to determine if this was the course of action she truly desired. At the time, Church-operated facilities continued counseling women not to have abortions. These facilities would provide the requisite document certifying that the pregnant woman had received the necessary counseling. These documents then served as the ticket to a legal abortion.[166]

162. Fisher, *Catholic Bioethics for a New Millennium*, 80.

163. This is essentially the position of the Holy See in its latest interventions. The Church recognizes with admiration those works aimed at assisting those addicted to drugs to be lifted out of addiction. See the Pontifical Council for Health Care Workers, *Nuova Carta Degli Operatori Sanitari* (Vatican City: Libreria Vaticana, 2017), nos. 121–24.

164. For an alternative view, see Daniel P. Sulmasy, OFM, "Catholic Participation in Needle- and Syringe- Exchange Programs for Injection-Drug Users: An Ethical Analysis," *Theological Studies* 73 (2012): 422–41. Sulmasy concludes: "Sponsorship of a needle-exchange program by a Catholic organization would constitute remote, mediate material cooperation, there would be proportionate grounds for acting, and there would be no genuine risk of scandal.... Such cooperation can be judged licit."

165. Fisher, *Catholic Bioethics for a New Millennium*, 83.

166. For more information on this topic, see John L. Allen, Jr., *Cardinal Ratzinger: The*

Considering several letters from Pope John Paul II and the frequent intervention of then-Cardinal Joseph Ratzinger, the German bishops eventually ceased support for these programs.[167] Following the instruction of the Holy See, the German bishops acceded to the assertion that these facilities were cooperating inappropriately in obtaining abortions. The vast majority of the women who received this counseling elected to have an abortion.[168] This case revealed that good motives and consequentialist arguments cannot ultimately provide the criterion to decide if cooperation in an evil act is just or unjust. Rather, the nature of the cooperator's act—in this case, the distribution of the requisite certificate needed to obtain a legal abortion—represents the kind of cooperation that cannot be justified. Fisher offers two possible reasons for the immorality of offering the counseling certificate. He recalls that some theologians held that the distribution of a counseling certificate necessary to obtain an abortion represented formal cooperation with evil. Others held that the cooperation should be considered "impermissible material cooperation" given the gravity of the loss of the life, the need for the bishops to provide clear witness to the sanctity of life, and the corroding effects such work would have on Church employees at such clinics.[169] In either case, the Holy See deemed that granting a certificate necessary to obtain a legal abortion represents an immoral cooperation with evil.

Finally, Archbishop Fisher examines the challenging case of support for an imperfect law. He treats politicians who vote for legislation aimed at limiting the harm done by a particular law, without restricting the evil

---

Vatican's Enforcer of the Faith (New York: Continuum, 2000), 190–92. On page 192 Allen explains: "The debate over the counseling system posed a classic ethical dilemma: is it better to risk facilitating evil for the chance to do good, or to bypass an opportunity for good in order to ensure that evil is not promoted? The controversy also offered a test case for working out the implications of *Gaudium et spes*. Should the church enter into partnership with secular society, accepting that it cannot dictate the terms of that partnership, in order to promote the values of the kingdom of God; or should the church withdraw from such partnerships if they risk doctrinal or moral ambiguity? At both levels, Ratzinger's strong preference was for disengagement."

167. For the interventions of Pope John Paul II, see both his "Letter to the German Bishops, 11 January 1998," *AAS* 90 (1998): 601–7; and his "Letter to the German Bishops, 3 June 1999," *L'Osservatore Romano*, June 26–30, 1999, 2. For further reflection on this topic, see the essay of Robert Spaemann, "Ist die Ausstellung des Beratungsscheins eine «Formelle Mitwirkung» bei der Abtreibung?" in his collection *Grenzen: Zur Ethischen Dimension des Handelns*, 401–6 (Stuggart: Klett-Cotta, 2001).

168. Fisher, *Catholic Bioethics for a New Millennium*, 84.

169. Fisher, *Catholic Bioethics for a New Millennium*, 85.

entirely.[170] The common example in the United States is the practice of voting for a piece of legislation that allows explicitly some instances of abortion. Often legislative proposals to ban abortion allow exceptions for a pregnancy which results from rape. Other bills seek to ban only abortions conducted in the latter months of pregnancy. In either case, morally upright legislators raise the question if they can support a bill which limits abortion but does not criminalize abortion in every instance. Pope John Paul II deals explicitly with this matter in the encyclical *Evangelium vitae*. The Pope explains:

When it is not possible to overturn or completely abrogate a pro-abortion law, an elected official, whose absolute personal opposition to procured abortion was well known, could licitly support proposals aimed at limiting the harm done by such a law and at lessening its negative consequences at the level of general opinion and public morality. This does not in fact represent an illicit cooperation with an unjust law, but rather a legitimate and proper attempt to limit its evil aspects.[171]

The Pope does not affirm the legitimacy of support for legislation that limits but does not completely ban abortion on the basis that this legislation is sufficiently remote from the evil of abortion. Rather, the Pope examines the nature of what the legislator actually is doing. In such a case, a legislator attempts to limit the harm done by a permissive abortion law. A vote for a particular bill does not indicate that one supports everything in the bill but only that this particular proposal provides the best possible means of achieving the desired result at a given time.[172] A legis-

170. For an extended treatment on the responsibility of Catholics in political life, see the Congregation for the Doctrine of the Faith, *Doctrinal Note on Some Questions Regarding the Participation of Catholics in Political Life*, November 24, 2002. The Doctrinal Note specifically addresses the question of voting for an imperfect law. See paragraph 4: "As John Paul II has taught in his Encyclical Letter *Evangelium vitae* regarding the situation in which it is not possible to overturn or completely repeal a law allowing abortion which is already in force or coming up for a vote, «an elected official, whose absolute personal opposition to procured abortion was well known, could licitly support proposals aimed at *limiting the harm* done by such a law and at lessening its negative consequences at the level of general opinion and public morality»."

171. *EV*, no. 73.

172. For an extended reflection on this topic, see Angel Rodríguez Luño, "*Evangelium Vitae* 73: The Catholic Lawmaker and the Problem of a Seriously Unjust Law," *L'Osservatore Romano*, English edition, 18 (September 6, 2002). Luño observes: "It is thus clear that the solution given in *Evangelium vitae* 73 is based on a judgment concerning the moral object of the act by which the lawmaker gives his support to the more restrictive

lator does not cooperate immorally in the evil of abortion by supporting a bill aimed at limiting abortion even if it does not ban it completely. One notes that the Pope insists that legislators make known their "absolute personal opposition" to procured abortion. This public statement of one's opposition to abortion is necessary to avoid the scandal of a legislator voting for a bill that permits abortion in some cases. It is necessary that his or her opposition to abortion be well-known, and therefore the reason for his or her support for the particular bill would be apparent: to limit the harm done by abortion however it is possible.[173]

When examining these cases, Fisher provides a helpful critique of one of the most common claims made when analyzing issues of moral cooperation with evil. Many moralists hold that a situation of duress can fundamentally change the nature of an act, transforming an otherwise bad act into a good one. Fisher recalls that both theologians at work in the casuist period and moralists writing today employ the example of destroying property in grave circumstances.[174] These authors recall Aristotle's description of a man at sea who finds his ship and his crew endangered due to an impending storm. The merchant's ship will sink if he does not lighten the ship's weight by throwing cargo overboard.[175] Aristotle uses the example to show that an act which would ordinarily be contrary to one's desire to preserve material goods can become in this instance a morally good act. This example is crucial from the perspective of virtue ethics to show how such a merchant does not become habituated to the destruction of private property because in this case he throws goods overboard. Instead, the merchant's action represents sound moral

---

law.... The moral object of the lawmaker's act is the elimination of all the unjust aspects of the prior law which here and now he is able to eliminate, without thereby becoming the cause of the retention of the other unjust elements, which he neither wants nor accepts, but which he is unable to eliminate."

173. A related difficulty concerns the regulation of immoral procedures like IVF. A politician's support for a partial banning of this procedure would require that his or her personal opposition to IVF more generally be well-known. For a related argument regarding the distinction between the selective or partial banning of immoral procedures like IVF as opposed to regulating them, which could indicate support for such procedures, see Helen Watt, "Cooperation and Immoral Laws: Preventing without Prescribing Harm," *The National Catholic Bioethics Quarterly* 12 (2012): 241–48.

174. For an argument invoking the example of destroying property under duress, see Keenan, SJ, "Prophylactics, Toleration and Cooperation," 205–20.

175. See Aristotle, *Nicomachean Ethics*, trans. W.D. Ross (London: Oxford University Press, 1925), 1110a.

acting. What is voluntary in the specific case—the choice to be rid of the cargo—is involuntary in the abstract. It goes against the will of the merchant to destroy property in general and that remains unchanged in this situation. In this case the merchant acts well.

Authors from a casuist viewpoint take the example as evidence that there exist certain situations when moral rules governing private property do not apply. The example of the distressed sea merchant, they suggest, shows that duress can change the nature of a moral object. Fisher helpfully points out that no parallel exists between the distressed shipman and one who acts badly out of fear.[176] The seventh commandment itself applies only to the unjust taking of another's goods. Sound theologians will consider the principle of the universal destination of goods and the nature of the goods themselves before making a judgment about the quality of one's action related to property rights. If one borrows a gun from another, for example, he ought not to return it when asked, if he knows the man intends to use it to shoot the borrower.[177]

The claim to private property does not so much admit of exceptions as instead it is conditioned by the factors mentioned above. The merchant does not unjustly destroy private property when he throws cargo overboard to save the ship. Fear has not permitted him to act badly. Rather, in the case described, the merchant acts well. In fact, as an experienced captain, he may suffer no great internal angst. Rather, he makes an intellectual judgment about the best course of action in the given circumstances. He voluntarily does something that in a different instance he would not otherwise do. The nature of the good of private property is such that it is subordinated to the good of human life.[178] When life is threatened, the norm prohibiting stealing is not abrogated—but the act ceases to be stealing. To take what belongs to another to save his life—or to destroy what belongs to another in order to save his ship and crew—does not represent the unjust taking of another's goods. One cannot claim excep-

---

176. See Fisher, *Catholic Bioethics for a New Millennium*, 89: "It is far from clear that such destruction of property would be an objective evil at all, since property rights are not absolute."

177. See Ashley, OP, *Living the Truth in Love*, 337: "Seeming exceptions (such as not giving back a stolen gun to a criminal or a would-be suicide) are not in fact exceptions to the norm, because the one who withholds does not acquire ownership or the right of use but only temporary guardianship of the weapon."

178. In this regard, Catholic theology employs the principle of the universal destination of goods. See, for example, *CCC*, nos. 2402–3.

tion from the truth of the seventh commandment in given situations. Instead, the nature of the claim to private property embraces this nuance.[179]
For this reason, no warrant exists for suggesting duress can fundamentally alter the nature of a moral object. Widespread confusion regarding the category of duress poses serious challenges for Catholic hospitals
and educational or social service institutions. Fisher explains: "the duress exception would ... invite the abandonment of anything distinctively
Catholic in the identity and ethos of Catholic healthcare institutions."[180]
Duress cannot transform a bad act into a good one since it does not fundamentally change the nature of a human act. While duress may have relevance for questions of culpability and subjective responsibility, it ultimately cannot alter the nature of a moral object.

Fisher offers a helpful corrective to many prevailing opinions in a second area of concern for analyzing moral cooperation with evil. Fisher
does not believe that the variety of opinions among moralists can be considered a relevant factor to determine how one ought to act in a given situation. The probabilism utilized during the casuist period emphasized
the importance of what approved authors thought about a given moral
quandary.[181] According to some thinkers a variety of opinions could give
license to act in the way one preferred, as the law could not bind in cases of doubt.[182] Moral theologians of the proportionalist school invoked

179. This explanation follows the teaching of St. Thomas Aquinas. For his treatment of this question, see *Summa theologiae*, IIa–IIae, q. 66, a. 7. St. Thomas explains: "If
the need be so manifest and urgent, that it is evident that the present need must be rem-
edied by whatever means be at hand (for instance when a person is in some imminent
danger, and there is no other possible remedy), then it is lawful for a man to succor his
own need by means of another's property, by taking it either openly or secretly: nor is
this properly speaking theft or robbery." One notes that in *Summa theologiae*, IIa–IIae,
q. 66, a. 5, St. Thomas teaches that "every theft is a sin." This indicates that, for Aquinas, there is never justified theft as much as in a given case taking the goods of another
is not theft.

180. Fisher, *Catholic Bioethics for a New Millennium*, 90.

181. See Pinckaers, OP, *The Sources of Christian Ethics*, 275–76. For a similar critique of
the casuist period, see Cessario, OP, *Introduction to Moral Theology*, 219–32.

182. Romanus Cessario, OP, identifies the tendency to aver to theological disagreement as an essential feature of the probabilism which dates to the late sixteenth century.
Cessario explains: "Probabilism adopted the principle that, if the probity or impropri-
ety of an action is in question, it is lawful to follow a solidly probably opinion favoring liberty, even though the opposing opinion, favoring the law, remains more probable.
Probabilism allowed its adherents to follow a course of action that did not enjoy the
support of a majority of approved authors." See Cessario, OP, *Introduction to Moral Theology*, 225.

this principle in the 1970s in order to support the possibility of providing contraceptive sterilizations in Catholic hospitals.[183] Fisher offers an alternative to this position. He explains: "This pluralism exception, like the duress exception, is a version of what I have called the 'tax-lawyer' morality, according to which the role of the moral advisor is to help people find a way around the law, avoiding as much tax as possible without getting caught."[184] Citing the 1975 declaration of the Congregation for the Doctrine of the faith, Fisher maintains that variety of theological opinion about the issue of sterilization cannot be a valid source from which to make moral judgments.[185] The mere fact that theologians disagree about the liceity of a medical procedure cannot of itself render cooperation in such a procedure morally acceptable.

Marking one significant change in the expression of his thought, in his 1994 essay Fisher prefers to describe formal and material cooperation as "intentional" or "unintentional" cooperation. That language does not appear in his more developed 2012 work, *Catholic Bioethics for a New Millennium*. This change represents a helpful clarification. Wide disagreement surrounds the proper understanding of intention, raising serious questions about the value of making it the primary criterion from which to judge questions of moral cooperation. Still, Fisher remains committed to aspects of the new natural law approach to moral matters. For example, he tends to favor a more intentional—and less physical—reading of how to analyze moral objects. This intentional reading of the moral object generates an unfortunate consequence in Fisher's examination of the definition of euthanasia. While the 1980 *Declaration on Euthanasia* had defined the practice as "an act or omission which of itself or by intention" causes

183. Some authors stress the importance of the variety of theological opinion about a given matter. See, for example, Charles E. Curran, "Cooperation: Toward a Revision of the Concept and Its Application," *Linacre Quarterly* 41 (1974): 152–67. Curran argues in favor of the morality of cooperation in contraceptive sterilization in part based on the theological diversity surrounding the topic of intrinsically evil acts.

184. Fisher, *Catholic Bioethics for a New Millennium*, 91.

185. See the Congregation for the Doctrine of the Faith, *Responses to Questions Concerning Sterilization in Catholic Hospitals*, March 13, 1975, *AAS* 68 (1976): 738–40. In part the Congregation explains: "The Congregation, while it confirms this traditional doctrine of the Church, is not unaware of the dissent against this teaching from many theologians. The Congregation, however, denies that doctrinal significance can be attributed to this fact as such, so as to constitute a 'theological source' which the faithful might invoke and thereby abandon the authentic Magisterium, and follow the opinions of private theologians which dissent from it."

death, the 1995 encyclical *Evangelium vitae* altered this definition to read "an act or omission which of itself and by intention" causes death.[186] Fisher believes in this case the Church adopted what he calls an "intended acts" view of the moral object. He contrasts the "intended acts" view with what he calls a "natural meanings" view of moral objects.[187] Fisher explains: "In this definition and in distinguishing euthanasia from palliative care and from the withdrawal of burdensome treatments the Pope seemed to adopt an intended acts account" of the moral object.[188]

Fisher does not offer a complete explanation for his position on the matter. In my view, he does not sufficiently take into account that both readings—intended acts and natural meanings—remain possible interpretations of the *Evangelium vitae* definition. Defining euthanasia in the way the encyclical does need not preclude the fact that certain actions, by their very nature, have an implicit intention that renders them always euthanizing. Fisher also neglects to point out that the *Catechism*, both in its original 1992 version and its revised 1997 version (issued after *Evangelium vitae*), uses the language of the 1980 *Declaration*. This language expresses

186. See the Congregation for the Doctrine of the Faith, *Declaration on Euthanasia*, May 5, 1980, no. II. See also Pope John Paul II, *Evangelium vitae*, no. 65. This was the same position of the Congregation regarding the administration of food and water to those in a so-called vegetative state. The act is not transformed by one's desire to prevent pain or suffering. It remains the act of providing nutrition/hydration. See Congregation for the Doctrine of the Faith, *Responses to Certain Questions of the United States Conference of Catholic Bishops Concerning Artificial Nutrition and Hydration*, August 1, 2007, *AAS* 99 (2007): 820–21. When asked "if the administration of food and water (whether by natural or artificial means) to a patient in a 'vegetative state' [is] morally obligatory except when they cannot be assimilated by the patient's body or cannot be administered to the patient without causing significant physical discomfort," the Congregation responded in the affirmative: "The administration of food and water even by artificial means is, in principle, an ordinary and proportionate means of preserving life. It is therefore obligatory to the extent to which, and for as long as, it is shown to accomplish its proper finality, which is the hydration and nourishment of the patient. In this way suffering and death by starvation and dehydration are prevented."

187. For a fuller presentation of his position, see Fisher, *Catholic Bioethics for a New Millennium*, 87. He writes: "These two encyclicals would seem to allow, however, at least two accounts of the human act: first, a *natural meanings* account whereby acts have a certain meaning by virtue of their intrinsic object or proximate end, whatever the private intentions or motives of the agent; and second, an *intended acts* account whereby acts can only be assessed 'from the perspective of the acting person' and the proximate ends deliberately willed."

188. Anthony Fisher, *Catholic Bioethics for a New Millennium*, 87. For an alternative view, critical of Fisher's, see Cummings, *The Servant and the Ladder*, 222–24.

clearly that acts by their nature and without reference to any further intention can fall under the negative precept against euthanasia. If indeed the Church has ever adopted a so-called "intended acts" view of the moral object, more evidence than this case of varying definitions of euthanasia seems to be required to demonstrate such a claim.

The criticism should not undermine what remains an outstanding treatment of the issues involved in moral cooperation. In general terms, Archbishop Fisher provides a sound account of how to analyze questions of moral cooperation with evil. Through his judicious use of the examples from the moral manuals, Fisher does not fall subject to the critique of Thomist authors regarding the shortcomings of the casuist period. He likewise rejects the tendency of some revisionist moral theologians to subjugate moral truth to contemporary expediencies. Fisher remains firm in his recognition that accommodation to passing trends falls short of the heroism required of Christians. While he does not purport to offer a fully developed virtue-based approach to moral cooperation, his insights prove helpful in our task to establish such a method. In particular, Fisher's attention to contemporary magisterial interventions regarding cooperation with evil suggests the framework for a virtue-centered approach to these questions. Future theologians remain in his debt for his collection of the Church's interventions in this area.

The Servant and the Ladder and implicitly formal cooperation

At St. Peter's Basilica in Rome, devout pilgrims stop to pray at the various side altars.[189] While the tombs of the holy Popes Pius X, John XXIII, and John Paul II draw many visitors, one altar receives less attention but merits no less interest. A small number of mostly American visitors occasionally offer prayers at the Altar of the Transfiguration adjacent to the Basilica's sacristy. There rests Blessed Pope Innocent XI whose pontificate spanned between 1676 and 1689. In the challenging moral dilemmas that confront twenty-first-century believers, Blessed Innocent XI stands

---

189. A portion of this section was published as my review of Cummings's book. See my "Review: *The Servant and the Ladder: Cooperation with Evil in the Twenty-First Century*," *Studia Moralia* 55 (2017): 211–14. It is used here with permission of *Studia Moralia*. Interested readers may also consult the review of Helen Watt, "Complicity and How to Avoid It: Review: *The Servant and the Ladder: Cooperation with Evil in the Twenty-First Century*," *Faith* 49 (2016): 37–40.

as a model of how to avoid unjust collaboration with evil.[190] In 1679 Pope Innocent XI condemned morally lax propositions prevalent in the seventeenth century. Among the sixty-five propositions he condemned for their moral laxity, one issue concerned whether a servant, without committing mortal sin, could repeatedly hold a ladder for his master to climb into a woman's home to engage in sexual intercourse. At the Pope's direction, the Holy Office condemned the view that such a servant could continue to aid the master to commit sin.[191] Commentary on the condemned proposition occupied the attention of moralists throughout the modern period. This history—with important implications for contemporary issues of cooperation with evil—creates the leitmotif of the work of Andrew McLean Cummings. Any evaluation of cooperation with evil should account for his impressive study.[192] While our attempt to delineate a virtue-based approach to moral cooperation with evil will not mirror his treatment, in many respects this work relies on his historical presentation of the matter.

With *The Servant and the Ladder: Cooperation with Evil in the Twenty-First Century*, Andrew McLean Cummings provides a remarkable account of the history of the theological treatment of cooperation with evil. *The Servant and the Ladder* treats extensively the various positions taken on the above-mentioned condemned proposition and their implications for treating more generally cooperation with evil. The author combines adept historical treatment of moral cooperation with sound theological analysis of the issues involved. Not since Roger Roy's 1968 article, "La coopération selon Saint Alphonse de Liguori," in *Studia Moralia*, has the question of cooperation with evil received such exhaustive treatment.[193] Cummings

190. For a more complete history of the period, see the magisterial treatment of Ludwig Freiherr von Pastor, *The History of the Popes: From the Close of the Middle Ages*, trans. Ernest Graf, OSB, vol. 32 (St. Louis: B. Herder Book, Co., 1957), 423–41. Interestingly, Pastor remarks that the opponents of probabilism failed to obtain a condemnation of the moral theory as such. Instead, only individual conclusions were subjected to condemnation. Pastor writes on page 432: "For one thing it had not been possible to obtain the condemnation of probabilism as such."

191. Strictly speaking the condemnations were the subject of a decree of the Holy Office for the Inquisition. Commentators usually refer to the condemnation of Innocent XI even though he refrained from a solemn pronouncement of the papal office and instead allowed the matter to be resolved by the Holy Office. See Pastor, *The History of the Popes*, 432.

192. See Andrew McLean Cummings, *The Servant and the Ladder: Cooperation with Evil in the Twenty-First Century*.

193. See Roger Roy, CSsR, "La coopération selon Saint Alphonse de Liguori," *Studia*

study unfolds in three parts. The first part contains three chapters chronicling the figures immediately before and after the papal condemnation. The position of St. Alphonsus Liguori looms large in this history. Part Two recounts nineteenth- and twentieth-century proposals regarding cooperation with evil. Cummings also includes in this section an excursus on British moral philosophy which he finds important for understanding the specification of moral objects.[194] The third part assesses the work of contemporary moralists Germain Grisez, Martin Rhonheimer, and Steven Long.[195]

The distinction between material and formal cooperation came into common use only in the eighteenth century. Historians recognize St. Alphonsus Liguori as the first to utilize this distinction. Cummings seeks to retrieve a less recognized—but nonetheless crucial—category of acts of cooperation. He believes that the category of "implicitly formal cooperation" can provide solutions to vexing moral dilemmas. Attention to this category of actions, he explains, enables one to recognize illicit forms of collaboration regardless of the intention of the cooperator.[196] Theologians rarely utilize the category of implicitly formal cooperation. When they do, however, Cummings believes they most often confuse it with

---

Moralia 6 (1968): 377–435. In some respects, Cummings's analysis differs from Roy's. For Cummings's critique, see Cummings, *The Servant and the Ladder*, 64–82.

194. Cummings examines authors such as Jeremy Bentham, Eric D'Arcy, Elizabeth Anscombe, and John Searle. Cummings believes that attention to British moral philosophy can address the challenging question of intention and specifically what effects are intended by a given action. Cummings explains: "[I]t will be of great importance to know if a given negative result of a choice is properly described as an effect, a means, an aspect, or the object chosen itself." See Cummings, *The Servant and the Ladder*, 103.

195. All three authors boast an impressive list of publications. Cummings examines principally their main moral works: Long, *The Teleological Grammar of the Moral Act*; Grisez, *The Way of the Lord Jesus: Vol. 3, Difficult Moral Questions*; Martin Rhonheimer, *Natural Law and Practical Reason: A Thomist View of Moral Autonomy*, trans. G. Malsbary (New York: Fordham University Press, 2000). Cummings also draws heavily upon Rhonheimer's, "Intentional Actions and the Meaning of Object: A reply to Richard McCormick," *The Thomist* 59 (1995): 279–311.

196. Cummings cites the Dominican manual McHugh-Callan for a definition of implicitly formal cooperation. The Dominican moralists explain: "Formal cooperation is implicit, when the cooperator does not directly intend to associate himself with the sin of the principal agent, but the end of the external act (*finis operis*), which for the sake of some advantage or interest the cooperator does intend, includes from its nature or from circumstances the guilt of the sin of the principal agent." See McHugh-Callan, *Moral Theology*, vol. 1, §1511.

immediate material cooperation. The primary difference between these two categories of cooperation can be found in the nature of the moral act itself. An action that is considered an act of material cooperation, at least in principle, could be rendered a morally acceptable act under certain conditions. Most theologians condemn in absolute terms formal cooperation of any type. Cummings argues that even if many theologians retain the category of implicitly formal cooperation, they rarely employ it. Instead, most moralists regard the vast majority of disputed cooperative acts as "material and therefore allowable for sufficient reason."[197]

During the casuist period, the majority of authors rendered a cooperator's action material so long as he did not share the evil intention of the principal sinful actor.[198] In order to determine if the cooperation should be considered licit, casuist authors examined whether the cooperator possessed a sufficient reason for his collaboration.[199] Cummings argues convincingly, on the other hand, that there are types of cooperation that, regardless of why one engages in them, directly participate in the evil action of the principal malefactor. According to Cummings, such acts can best be described as implicitly formal cooperation with evil. He explains:

Implicitly formal cooperation is cooperation in which the *finis operis* of the cooperator will be wrong due to direct participation in the evil activity of the principal agents. The "directness" of the contribution and the correspondingly disordered proximate intention of the cooperator, will be determined neither by an exaggerated first-person stance (focusing on the cooperator's goals or proposal) nor by an exaggerated third-person stance (focusing on the causal effects of his action) but by a consideration of the natural teleology or intrinsic meaning of the behavior itself.[200]

Cummings holds that neither proximity to an evil act nor the possible consequences from one's cooperation present the most helpful points of departure for a moral analysis of cooperation with evil. Instead, careful attention to the act of the cooperator—what type of thing he actually is

197. Cummings, *The Servant and the Ladder*, xii.

198. See, for example, the manual of Thomas Slater, SJ. Slater maintains that formal cooperation is "the concurrence in the bad action of another and in the bad intention with which it is performed." See Thomas Slater, SJ, *A Manual of Moral Theology*, vol. 1 (New York: Benziger Brothers, 1925), Bk. IV, Ch. VII, §1. Slater, like many of his contemporaries, does not mention the category of implicitly formal cooperation.

199. For one list of the degrees of sufficient or grave reason necessary to justify various types of cooperative acts, see McHugh-Callan, *Moral Theology*, vol. 1, §1519–22.

200. Cummings, *The Servant and the Ladder*, 398–99.

doing—remains the best way to determine whether his act is a good one.

As we saw in the examination of the authors from the casuist period, rarely did they invoke the category of implicitly formal cooperation.[201] Instead, so long as a cooperator did not share the evil intention of the sinful actor, the vast majority of authors treated the question as if the cooperator's action must certainly be material cooperation. In this case, moralists most often raise questions of proximity and sufficient reason in order to determine the moral acceptability of cooperating. On the other hand, Cummings argues that this category of implicitly formal cooperation more accurately accounts for the nature of the moral object. From an alternative perspective, some moral theologians suggest the category of duress can transform what would otherwise be formal cooperation into material cooperation.[202] Even the Catholic bishops of the United States appear to have adopted this view in the mid-1990s *Ethical and Religious Directives for Catholic Health Care Services*.[203] Those directives have since been revised precisely on this point. The difficulty of this way of pursuing moral inquiry quickly becomes obvious. Cummings explains:

> Duress does not turn implicitly formal cooperation into immediately [*sic*] material cooperation.... [Likewise] the proximate-remote gradations do not enter into the question of the directness of participation. Consequently, cooperative actions that are essentially ordered to bringing about the evil (formal) and those that do so accidentally (material) will both admit of being more or less significant contributors to the harm.[204]

201. A survey of early twentieth-century moral manuals shows that Dominican authors were more likely to utilize the category of implicitly formal cooperation, as they tended to analyze more rigorously the nature of the moral act. Henry Davis, SJ, for example, makes no use of this category of implicitly formal cooperation whereas McHugh-Callan make ready use of it. Others, as Cummings points out, collapsed the category with immediate material cooperation; see Jone-Adelman, *Moral Theology*, §147. For a more robust use of this category of cooperation, see McHugh-Callan, *Moral Theology*, vol. 1, §§1511–12.

202. See, for example, the view of James F. Keenan, SJ, regarding Catholic hospitals performing contraceptive sterilizations when legally required to do so. He leaves to the judgment of individual bishops whether this may be morally acceptable. For Keenan, a situation of duress alters considerably the moral calculus. See James F. Keenan, SJ, "Institutional Cooperation and the Ethical and Religious Directives," *Linacre Quarterly* 64 (1997): 53–76. For a general history of this debate, see Boyle, *The Sterilization Controversy: A New Crisis for the Catholic Hospital*.

203. For a more complete discussion of these points, see Fisher, *Catholic Bioethics for a New Millennium*, 74–76.

204. Cummings, *The Servant and the Ladder*, 399.

A preoccupation with the category of duress represents a failure to appreciate fully the nature of moral action. Extenuating circumstances possess no ability to change fundamentally the nature of a moral act.

A large portion of Cummings's work deals with a direct treatment of the case of the servant and the ladder. While Pope Innocent's 1679 decree condemned the position that the servant's cooperation could be morally acceptable, the debate surrounding this question continued throughout the modern period. Moralists disagreed on the reason for the Pope's condemnation.[205] While all concurred the servant acted badly, some held that the servant failed to present a sufficiently grave reason for cooperating. Others maintained that the cooperating act itself was, of its nature, an unjust act.[206] Cummings offers a critique of the solution proposed to this question by St. Alphonsus Liguori. St. Alphonsus had originally held that the servant's cooperation represented the type of action that of its nature was always wrong. In the later editions of his *Theologia Moralis*, however, St. Alphonsus maintained that the servant's cooperation cannot be considered intrinsically evil. The holy doctor concluded that the servant's action would represent only material cooperation since the servant does not share in the bad will of the master. For St. Alphonsus, the circumstances of the case, specifically, the lack of a sufficient reason for the servant to cooperate, render the cooperation unacceptable.[207] The condemnation of the Holy Office established that in the case of the servant and the ladder the servant acts badly. However, the saintly doctor remains unwilling to call that type of cooperation necessarily formal. According to Cummings, the servant's action can best be described as implicitly formal cooperation.[208] The servant's action, regardless of whether he shares

205. Cummings chronicles the views on the condemned proposition of François Genet, Patritius Sporer, the Salmanticenses, Claude Lacroix, Juan Cardenas and Johann Kugler, Dominicus Viva, Constantino Roncaglia, Benjamin Elbel, Honoré Tournely and Pierre Collet, Pio Tommaso Milante, and Nicolò Mazzotta before treating extensively the position of St. Alphonsus. See Cummings, *The Servant and the Ladder*, 51–82.

206. Cummings credits the French canon-theologian François Genet with being the first to distinguish adequately scandal from cooperation. Cummings explains: "Genet is the first author to intuit that more is at stake in cooperation than scandal. The main sin is not against the master, whom one confirms in sin, but against the girl, the victim of his design." See Cummings, *The Servant and the Ladder*, 53.

207. For fuller treatment of the position of St. Alphonsus, see Roy, CSsR, "La coopération selon Saint Alphonse de Liguori," 420–23.

208. Cummings holds that St. Alphonsus does not allow for a category of implicitly formal cooperation. Cummings explains: "For Alphonsus, this possibility is ruled out

the malevolent intention of his master, is of its nature the kind of action that directly participates in the evil committed. Holding a ladder for one to enter a home to commit a grave sin must be considered an unjust act. Cummings explains that, regardless of the servant's intention, holding the ladder cooperates in an implicitly formal way in the master's evil action. He credits Blessed Innocent XI for observing and condemning the moral laxity of the period.[209]

Cummings argues that the category of implicitly formal cooperation helps to avoid confusion in moral inquiry. If the servant's action, regardless of whether he shares the ill will of his master, is of its nature the kind of action that participates in the evil committed, it must be considered implicitly formal cooperation and, therefore, a bad act. Cummings holds that the confusion surrounding the place of intention in moral analysis will disappear if theologians employ this category of cooperation. He argues that theologians both long past and in the present day neglect the use of this category of acts. Cummings explains:

Germain Grisez and Martin Rhonheimer make essentially the same error of "putting the cart before the horse" as was made by St. Alphonsus in applying his formal/material distinction. Just as the saint reasoned (in modern terms) that the lack of intention of the servant to harm the girl implied that his choice was simply to hold the ladder, so Grisez and Rhonheimer emphasize the role of intention in constituting the object of the act without paying sufficient attention to whether the matter can receive such a form.[210]

Both authors of the casuist period and contemporary theologians who emphasize to an inordinate degree the role of intention in determining the nature of the moral object appear to confuse the *finis operis* with the *finis operantis*.[211] The fact that one does not wish a certain action to bring about its

by definition: the kind of cooperative action with which we are concerned is not formal because that has been defined as intending (explicitly) the principal agent's goal, and it is not illicit material cooperation as it is not evil 'in-itself' (apart from the master's crime). Conceptually, there is no room for implicitly formal cooperation." See Cummings, *The Servant and the Ladder*, 70.

209. For an outstanding history of the period and an assessment of the contribution of St. Alphonsus, see Louis Vereecke, *Da Guglielmo d'Ockham a sant'Alfonso de Liguori: Saggi di storia della teologia morale moderna 1300–1787* (Milan: Edizioni Paoline, 1990), 715–57.

210. Cummings, *The Servant and the Ladder*, 397.

211. For a helpful summary of the distinction between the *finis operis* and the *finis operantis*, see Servais Pinckaers, OP, *Le renouveau de la morale* (Tournai: Casterman, 1964), 139–41. For the historical perspective on how this distinction appears more frequently

per se result does not alter what *per se* follows from that action. An action's natural teleology cannot be jettisoned by one's wishing it so. For example, in the late nineteenth century the Holy Office identified the dangers of theologians failing to recognize that craniotomy terminates in the crushed skull—and therefore killing—of a partially-born child. Because one wishes the child would not die, does not mean that the act of craniotomy can be reconstituted as an act of changing the dimensions of the child's skull.[212] Similarly, just because a husband uses a condom for the purpose of disease prevention does not make the use of a condom in a conjugal act any less an act of sterilizing sexual intercourse. These acts have an integral nature which the mere wishes of a moral agent cannot alter. The fact that one who has engaged in an act may have a certain remote intention or reason for performing the act does not change fundamentally the nature of the action.[213] Attention to the category of implicitly formal cooperation makes clear that there are certain actions that, of their nature, represent formal cooperation with evil and therefore can never be justified under any circumstance. Implicitly formal cooperation offers an important distinction from immediate material cooperation which traditionally theologians permit under very grave circumstances.

Readers find particular interest in the practical consequences of Cummings's approach. He explains, for example, that he believes a cashier ringing up the purchase of pornographic material cooperates in an implicitly formal way in the sin of the distribution of pornography. While some moralists may instruct a cashier in such a situation to consider seeking other work to avoid even this remote material cooperation, Cummings argues that "such a person should be considered in a situation of venial sin until he did make such a change."[214] In Cummings's view, a number of ac-

---

in Aquinas's early works, see Pinckaers, OP, *The Pinckaers Reader*, 209–10. Here Pinckaers argues that the extensive use of this distinction is itself the result of the nominalist influences on moral theology.

212. See DS 3258. For a defense of the liceity of craniotomy, see John Finnis, Germain Grisez, and Joseph Boyle, "'Direct' and 'Indirect': A Reply to Critics of Our Action Theory," *The Thomist* 65 (2001): 1–44. For a critique of their position, see Long, *The Teleological Grammar of the Moral Act*, 2nd ed., 169–70; and Flannery, *Acts Amid Precepts*, 173–76 and 223–26. For an excellent history of the controversy surrounding the issue of craniotomy, see John Connery, SJ, *Abortion: The Development of the Roman Catholic Perspective*, 225–303.

213. See, in particular, Long, *The Teleological Grammar of the Moral Act*, 2nd ed., 170–80.

214. See Cummings, *The Servant and the Ladder*, 400 where Cummings explains: "For instance, a cashier who has to handle pornographic magazines would usually be told that this is remote material cooperation, but that he has an obligation to look for another

tivities common in today's world represent implicitly formal cooperation in evil. Such cooperation cannot be justified under any circumstance.[215] Students of St. Thomas Aquinas will wonder why the Angelic Doctor does not play a larger role in Cummings's study. The answer is simple. The virtue-based moral reasoning employed by St. Thomas garnered little support during the casuist debates of the early modern period. The renewal of moral theology according to the virtues—given papal approbation with the 1993 encyclical letter *Veritatis splendor*—offers a new perspective on these old questions. One wonders if some of the casuist categories themselves introduce as much difficulty as they do clarity. Thomists consider the possibility of moving away from the casuist categories more completely. Instead, theologians could provide a moral analysis based on the natural teleology of human action and its *per se* effects. Cummings hints at the possibility of this approach but, in the end, remains committed to the usefulness of the classical categories of cooperation with evil.

Conclusion

In a virtue-based approach to moral cooperation, theologians will inquire about what *per se* follows a given act and what *kind of act* one is doing. Broadly speaking, this has been the method utilized by the Holy See in its interventions in cases of moral cooperation. Instead of obscuring issues of cooperation through the imposition of extrinsic ethical categories, this approach will offer clarity about what types of cooperation should be avoided. By and large, the documents of the Magisterium have avoided the use of the technical terms of moral casuistry. Despite not making extensive use of the distinctions, i.e., implicitly formal, remote, immediate, etc., the Holy See has been able to achieve clarity about disputed cases of cooperation. While there have been occasions in which the Holy See has

---

kind of work. In light of our proposals, such a person should be considered in a situation of venial sin until he did make such a change. As we pointed out before, but underline again, a proper understanding of venial sin reminds us that most people commit venial sins every day. Is it surprising that in our evil world, many people should find themselves in jobs where they are asked to do so?"

215. Cummings does not hesitate to draw conclusions from this thesis. He recognizes that such a radical approach to cooperation with evil will require dramatic witness for the sake of moral truth. Cummings includes an appendix on two martyrs, Blessed Michael Nakashima and Blessed Franz Jägerstatter whom he exalts as "Witnesses to Non-Cooperation." The example of the martyrs plays an important role in a robust explanation of refusal to cooperate with evil. See Cummings, *The Servant and the Ladder*, 403–7.

employed these categories, it has done so to a much more limited degree than one finds in the casuist authors.[216] It remains, however, the contention of the present study that a moral analysis of cooperation based on natural teleology and a robust place for the virtues in the moral life ultimately will bear more fruit than reliance on the casuist categories.

The present work proposes that this Thomist virtue-based analysis finds resonance in the approach advanced in recent magisterial teaching, especially the encyclical letter *Veritatis splendor*. In addition, the work of Steven A. Long, Archbishop Anthony Fisher, and Andrew McLean Cummings provides us with the tools to evaluate cooperation with evil based on the nature of human action and its natural teleology. An approach to cooperation with evil grounded in virtue-ethics avoids the pitfalls to which the casuist method remains prone. Drawing upon the resources of the virtue-based tradition and relying on the guidance of the Church's Magisterium, in the following chapter we outline how virtue-based theologians will analyze cooperative acts.

216. For example, see *Worthiness to Receive Holy Communion*, the letter of Cardinal Joseph Ratzinger to the Archbishop of Washington, DC in July 2004: "When a Catholic does not share a candidate's stand in favor of abortion and/or euthanasia, but votes for that candidate for other reasons, it is considered remote material cooperation." There is a way in which this is the exception that proves the rule. The number of times the Holy See utilizes these distinctions of cooperation is relatively small. Rather, as Archbishop Fisher was able to show, the Holy See tends to analyze rigorously the nature of the moral act—especially in light of *Veritatis splendor*—instead of forcing human actions into extrinsic categories of cooperation.

CHAPTER FOUR

A New Way Forward

The Virtuous Person Faces
a Moral Dilemma

In the previous three chapters we outlined the resources available from the Catholic tradition useful to establish a virtue-based approach to the challenge of moral cooperation with evil.[1] It remains for us to demonstrate how such an approach would unfold in practice. In the chapter which follows we sketch the contours of a virtue-based approach to moral cooperation with evil. The elements of the method below rely upon an account of the moral life as outlined by St. Thomas Aquinas. In the final chapter we will apply this method of moral reasoning to disputed contemporary issues of moral cooperation. Before we can embark on this project, however, we must describe the elements of our virtue-based method. In what follows we remain attentive to the way in which each element of the virtue-based approach to moral cooperation with evil differs from the method utilized by authors of the casuist tradition.

In the sections which follow, we outline several aspects of our proposed method for addressing issues of cooperation with evil. We have chosen to describe this method as "virtue-based" even though the terms "Thomistic" or "object-based" could also describe accurately our project. The approach we propose is Thomistic insofar as we adopt the method of moral reasoning utilized by St. Thomas Aquinas. We prefer to speak of this method as "virtue-based" for several reasons. The method we outline here is not merely the one utilized by Aquinas but also by many of his commentators. Likewise, it is not a method which contemporary moralists should relegate to the thirteenth century. This is not principally an

---

1. Specifically, we examined the texts of St. Thomas himself, the work of his interpreters Jean Capreolus, Thomas de Vio Cajetan, and John of St. Thomas, and the magisterial texts of the post-conciliar period.

exercise of historical scholarship. Rather, as we demonstrated in the first chapter, Thomist authors throughout the centuries have adopted and utilized a similar approach to moral matters. In addition, our virtue-based approach finds resonance both with the texts of the recent Magisterium and the work of certain contemporary authors. That is to say, Aquinas, his commentators old and new, and texts of the Magisterium all employ the method we propose in order to address questions of cooperation with evil.

The first several sections below refer to the aspects of our method related to the specification of moral objects. Aquinas's moral method requires a careful exposition of moral objects.[2] At the same time, his moral framework unfolds within the theological and moral virtues. Reflection on the virtues represents the aspect of our method which will prove most crucial for the execution of sound moral action. For that reason, we have chosen to adopt the label "virtue-based" for our project. Virtue-based moral reasoning relies upon and demands careful analysis of moral objects. Since virtues develop by means of—and sustain the exercise of—particular moral actions, it will be necessary to analyze rightly human acts in order to establish a virtue-based method of moral reasoning. The first four sections of this chapter delineate the proper specification of moral objects. We will treat the teleological nature or essential character of moral acts; the *per se* effects or necessarily intended results of certain acts; the deficiency of the category of physical proximity to evil for analyzing cooperative acts; and the importance of context to comprehend properly species of acts. The following three sections highlight pitfalls for such a sound specification. We will examine the extrinsicism of imposed categories upon actions by casuist treatments of the topic; the challenge posed by recourse to duress for sound moral analysis; and the deficiencies of certain casuist treatments of cooperation with abortion. Only after completing this necessary work regarding the mechanics of human acts can we outline the exercise of the cardinal virtues regarding cases of moral cooperation. While this final section is most crucial for our project, its success will depend upon the adequate analysis of moral acts outlined in the first seven sections of the chapter.

---

2. See, for example, Aquinas's exposition of human acts in *Summa theologiae*, Ia–IIae, qq. 6–21.

A teleological analysis of the moral act

For moralists to analyze properly cooperative acts requires their attention to the intelligible character of human action.[3] An act of cooperation receives its status as a cooperative act by its connection to some other act. Cooperative acts, therefore, unfold within the framework of the teleology of human action. When Aquinas asks whether one can borrow money from a known usurer, he scrutinizes the teleology of the act of borrowing. St. Thomas allows one to borrow from one known to practice usury because nothing about the act of borrowing implies usury.[4] Aquinas explains: "He who borrows for usury gives the usurer an occasion, not for taking usury, but for lending; it is the usurer who finds an occasion of sin in the malice of his heart."[5] With this proposal Aquinas grounds his teaching in the essential character of the act of borrowing. Rather than examine how close the evil of usury approaches the borrowing of money, Aquinas attends to the nature of the act of borrowing. One could say that St. Thomas offers a teleological analysis of the act of borrowing money.

A moralist following the example of St. Thomas recognizes that teleology occupies an important place in virtue theory. The development of a given virtue requires one's conscious attention to the acts one chooses. As Aquinas observes, the mere repetition of acts does not alone suffice to increase a habit.[6] In order to develop the virtues necessary to eschew immoral

3. For a sustained treatment of the teleology of human action, see Steven A. Long, *The Teleological Grammar of the Moral Act*, 2nd ed. (Naples, FL: Sapientia Press, 2015). For a slightly different perspective but one that still emphasizes the teleology of human acts, see Steven J. Jensen, *Good and Evil Actions: A Journey through St. Thomas Aquinas* (Washington, DC: The Catholic University of America Press, 2010). Interested readers should also consult several important essays of Steven A. Long and Steven J. Jensen. Long's essays include: "*Veritatis Splendor* §78 and The Teleological Grammar of the Moral Act," *Nova et Vetera*, English edition, 6 (2008): 139–56; "Regarding the Nature of the Moral Object and Intention: A Response to Steven Jensen," *Nova et Vetera*, English edition, 3 (2005): 101–108; and "A Brief Disquisition Regarding the Nature of the Object of the Moral Act According to St. Thomas Aquinas," *The Thomist* 67 (2003): 45–71. Jensen's articles include: "A Long Discussion Regarding Steven A. Long's Interpretation of the Moral Species," *The Thomist* 67 (2003): 623–43; "Do Circumstances Give Species?" *The Thomist* 70 (2006): 1–26; and "A Defense of Physicalism," *The Thomist* 61 (1997): 377–404.

4. *Summa theologiae*, IIa–IIae, q. 78, a. 4.

5. *Summa theologiae*, IIa–IIae, q. 78, a. 4.

6. See *Summa theologiae*, Ia–IIae, q. 52, a. 3: "So, too, repeated acts cause a habit to grow. If, however, the act falls short of the intensity of the habit, such an act does not dispose

cooperation with evil requires that one examine the intelligible character of one's action. A perplexed cooperator will ponder several matters before forming a judgment about the moral quality of a proposed cooperative act. Each relevant question concerns the essential character of the proposed action. Before making a judgment about a course of action, a perplexed would-be cooperator must consider the following questions: what necessarily follows a given act of cooperation? What effects are necessarily included in the choice of a given act? How do these effects differ from what merely happens to result from a given act? Can one reasonably describe the cooperator's proposed course of action apart from the evil effects which may follow? In contrast to what interested many authors of the casuist period, these questions occupy the attention of moralists who seek to establish a virtue-based approach to moral cooperation with evil.

By and large, moralists of the casuist period judged issues of cooperation with evil in terms of a neutral or good act in some proximity to a bad act. For example, the nineteenth-century Italian Jesuit Aloysius Sabetti argued that material cooperation "can be licit with the presence of a just cause, proportionate to the gravity of the other's sin, and depending on how proximate it is to the execution of the sin."[7] The casuists' analysis focused disproportionately on a certainly evil act and the proximity of a neutral act of cooperation to this evil act.[8] At the same time, these authors tended to refrain from treating sufficiently the act of cooperation itself, irrespective of its proximity to the principal evil act.[9] Instead,

---

to an increase of that habit, but rather to a lessening thereof." On the nature of *habitus* and the quality of its growth, see Romanus Cessario, OP, *The Moral Virtues and Theological Ethics* (Notre Dame, IN: University of Notre Dame Press, 1991), 34–44. On the place of virtuous *habitus* in the Christian moral life, see Romanus Cessario, OP, *Introduction to Moral Theology*, rev. ed. (Washington, DC: The Catholic University of America Press, 2013), 184–96.

7. See Aloysius Sabetti, SJ, *Compendium Theologiae Moralis* (New York: Frederick Pustet Co., 1931), 190: "materialis vero potest evadere licita, si adsit causa justa et proportionata gravitati peccati alterius, et proximitati concursus ad peccati executionem."

8. See, for example, the manual of John A. McHugh, OP, and Charles J. Callan, OP, *Moral Theology: A Complete Course*, vol. 1 (New York: Joseph F. Wagner, Inc., 1958), 619: "Mediate cooperation is also subdivided into *proximate* and *remote*. (a) It is proximate or remote by reason of nearness, according as the act of sin will follow closely or otherwise on the act of cooperation."

9. See, for example, Henry Davis, SJ, *Moral and Pastoral Theology*, vol. 1. (London: Sheed and Ward, 1958), 341. Davis holds that "cooperation … is concurrence with another in a sinful act." The act of cooperation is judged relative to some other obviously sinful act as opposed to examining it more directly on its own.

moralists of the casuist period often judged an act of cooperation almost exclusively in reference to the other certainly bad act. Might we describe more accurately issues of cooperation not so much in terms of proximity to evil but as to whether or not the act of cooperation represents an independently bad act?

An example proves helpful in this regard. A nurse hands a suction device to a doctor performing an abortion. Any attempt to analyze this action based exclusively on its proximity to the intrinsically evil act of a direct abortion fails to describe accurately the nurse's action.[10] Rather, the act of assisting in an abortion in this manner can be the subject of an analysis in its own right. Moralists would describe such an act as directly assisting in a procured abortion. For that reason, the nurse's action falls under negative precept. We are able to render this judgment before making any analysis about how closely this act stands relative to the actual abortion. This judgment does not depend upon the proximity in time or space to the abortion. Instead, the moral quality of the act hinges on what type of act the nurse performs. From our analysis of *Veritatis splendor* we recall the emphasis Pope John Paul II placed on intrinsically evil acts.[11] The Pope's teaching presupposes that there are in fact species of acts which may be subjected to moral analysis. Assisting in an actual abortion represents a type of human activity. In fact, it denotes a type of activity which always embodies a violation of human dignity.

One may argue that this distinction introduces a matter of hair-splitting. After all, many moral theologians agree that the act of handing a

10. On the immorality of abortion, see, for example, *Evangelium vitae*, no. 62: "Therefore, by the authority which Christ conferred upon Peter and his Successors, in communion with the Bishops—who on various occasions have condemned abortion and who in the aforementioned consultation, albeit dispersed throughout the world, have shown unanimous agreement concerning this doctrine—I declare that direct abortion, that is, abortion willed as an end or as a means, always constitutes a grave moral disorder, since it is the deliberate killing of an innocent human being."

11. See *VS*, no. 80: "Reason attests that there are objects of the human act which are by their nature 'incapable of being ordered' to God, because they radically contradict the good of the person made in his image. These are the acts which, in the Church's moral tradition, have been termed 'intrinsically evil' (*intrinsece malum*): they are such *always and per se*, in other words, on account of their very object, and quite apart from the ulterior intentions of the one acting and the circumstances. Consequently, without in the least denying the influence on morality exercised by circumstances and especially by intentions, the Church teaches that 'there exist acts which *per se* and in themselves, independently of circumstances, are always seriously wrong by reason of their object.'"

suction device to an abortionist is always a bad act. Many casuist authors argue in this way because handing to a doctor instruments utilized in abortion represents such close, proximate, immediate cooperation with the taking of innocent human life.[12] A method of moral reasoning which relies on proximity to evil presents the difficulty of necessarily becoming a matter of drawing a line of how close one wants to get to an abortion. The more rigorous the moralist the further one would want to be from abortion. The more lax moralist, however, would be more willing to tolerate some proximity to abortion.

A virtue-based approach to moral cooperation offers an alternative path. The garbage collector who discovers an abortion clinic on his assigned route does not have to analyze his proximity to the abortion industry. Instead, he should ask whether one could describe accurately his activity as assisting in abortion. If, in fact, one describes more accurately his work as fulfilling the worthy civil purpose of garbage collection, he need not worry that he is violating a precept of the moral law. For the purposes of this example, we prescind from the question of what justice requires in regard to care for fetal remains. One could construe a situation where a new moral object—namely, the appropriate care of fetal remains—presents the garbage collector with a new moral quandary.[13] For the purposes of this example, however, it is only necessary to demonstrate that ordinary garbage collection represents a worthy civil service. Nothing about this work is *per se* ordered to evil things.

One may—and in some cases must—choose to abandon even morally licit activity in order to avoid the possibility of scandal. In describing scandal as "something less rightly done," St. Thomas Aquinas sought to include both evil acts and those that had the appearance of evil.[14] One should refrain from otherwise morally licit activity which would induce another to sin. In a similar fashion, one may wish to serve as a witness to

12. However, not all the authors of this period believed assistance to an abortion could never be justified. As examined above, see Bernhard Häring, CSsR, *The Law of Christ*, trans. Edwin G. Kaiser (Westminster, MD: Newman Press, 1961), 505.

13. In this regard, see the guidance of the Congregation for the Doctrine of the Faith, Instruction *Donum vitae*, I, 4: "The corpses of human embryos and fetuses, whether they have been deliberately aborted or not, must be respected just as the remains of other human beings."

14. See *Summa theologiae*, IIa-IIae, q. 43, a. 1, ad. 2: "[Scandal] is therefore fittingly described as something done 'less rightly,' so as to comprise both whatever is sinful in itself, and all that has an appearance of evil."

the value of human life in the refusal to be in any way associated with the abortion industry.[15] In light of his particular circumstances the perplexed garbage collector will need to discover his most prudent course of action. However, the categories of proximity to evil will not serve his analysis of whether there exists an obligation to abandon his work of garbage collection. The teleology of what one is really doing—rather than how closely it approaches some other act—presents a better way to analyze the moral quality of one's actions.

Per se ordering to an end and what necessarily follows from certain acts

To analyze properly the essential character of a human act, moralists must attend to the natural or *per se* ordering of a given moral action. *Per se* order refers to the inherent teleology of human activity. The object of one's moral choice should be ordered to the end or intention one seeks. In such a case, the object of one's action can be said to be *per se* ordered to the end of a given human activity.[16] For example, the act of eating is *per se* ordered to health. Eating is for the sake of health, broadly understood. Unhealthy eating or food consumption that is truly unhealthy carries with it a disordered quality. Attention to the *per se* as opposed to *per accidens* ordering of human activity constitutes a crucial distinction between the virtue-based approach to analyzing moral cooperation from the methods utilized by other schools of moral inquiry.[17] Steven A. Long offers the most notable recent work regarding the ordering of human action with his *The Teleological Grammar of the Moral Act*.[18] The characteristics of this method of

15. For a rousing call for Christians to bear witness to the dignity of human life, see *Evangelium vitae*, especially nos. 78–101.

16. Steven Long explains the matter succinctly: "The essential element constituting the intelligibility and simplicity of human action is *per se* order; that is to say, either the object is such by nature that it tends toward the end, or the end is such by nature that it requires the object." See Steven A. Long, "Natural Law, the Moral Object, and *Humanae Vitae*," in *Ressourcement Thomism: Sacred Doctrine, the Sacraments, and the Moral Life*, ed. Reinhard Hütter and Matthew Levering, 285–311 (Washington, DC: The Catholic University of America Press, 2010).

17. For an extended treatment of the difference between *per se* and *per accidens* ordering of moral acts in Aristotle, see Kevin L. Flannery, SJ, *Action and Character according to Aristotle: The Logic of the Moral Life* (Washington, DC: The Catholic University of America Press, 2013), especially 139–72.

18. See chapter three above for an extended treatment of this work. Action theory

moral analysis include, first of all, a strong account of teleology. Ends are not imposed by human actors but rather are intrinsic to the acts themselves. The act of eating is naturally ordered to health and cannot be changed by human will. Discovering the right measure of food to eat may be a challenging dilemma. However, identifying the reason for eating— and the natural teleology of eating—as the preservation of health broadly speaking poses no special challenge.

Long offers a cogent explanation of the teleological method of moral inquiry. Given its importance for our project, it is worth quoting in full:

> When acts of themselves tend toward an end, they are said to be naturally or *per se* ordered to it; likewise, when attainment of an end *by the very nature of the end* requires a certain action, that action is also said to be naturally or *per se* ordered to the end. In cases wherein the object is *per se* ordered to the end sought by the agent, the moral species derived from the end sought is most formal, most defining, and most containing, and the species derived from the object is merely—in relation to the species derived from the end—an accidental specification of the latter.[19]

The debate over the use of condoms by a married couple in which one partner is HIV positive offers a clear example of how natural teleology functions in moral theology. Some authors argue that in a case where one spouse is HIV positive, the husband may use a condom for the purpose of preventing disease. According to Martin Rhonheimer, a notable proponent of this view, an HIV positive husband's use of a condom renders what would otherwise be an act of contraception in this case an act of disease prevention.[20] Other theologians hold that conjugal acts which make use of a condom render the acts necessarily contraceptive regardless of the reason the condoms are employed.[21]

The difference of views between those who permit the use of condoms

---

has become a notoriously difficult area of moral inquiry. Universal agreement eludes even thinkers who share similar first premises. See the careful, although critical, review of the book by Kevin Flannery, SJ, *The Thomist* 78 (2008): 322–25. For Long's response to these objections, see his "Engaging Thomist Interlocutors," *Nova et Vetera*, English edition, 9 (2011): 267–95.

19. Long, *The Teleological Grammar of the Moral Act*, 2nd ed., 150. Emphasis in original.

20. See Martin Rhonheimer, "The Truth about Condoms" *The Tablet*, July 10, 2004. For an extended exchange, see Benedict Guevin, OSB, and Martin Rhonheimer, "On the Use of Condoms to Prevent Acquired Immune Deficiency Syndrome," *The National Catholic Bioethics Quarterly* 5 (2005): 37–48.

21. See, for example, Long, *The Teleological Grammar of the Moral Act*, 2nd ed., 170–80.

by an HIV infected husband and those who grant no exception to the prohibition of sterilizing a conjugal act does not depend principally on moral intuition or fidelity to Church teaching.[22] Rather, the two schools of thought hold alternate positions about how best to analyze moral acts. The more an author allows intention—that is, the agent's stated reason for acting—to shape the understanding of the moral object rationally chosen, the more the purpose of disease prevention can shape the description of the use of a condom in a conjugal act. On the other hand, authors who allow natural teleology and *per se* order to shape their method of moral inquiry recognize the reason for the use of a condom in a conjugal act as irrelevant to what remains essentially a contraceptive choice.[23] In this way, natural teleology yields a very different moral analysis than intention-based moral theories.

Natural teleology will play a crucial role in a virtue-based approach to moral cooperation. While authors of the casuist school ponder the proximity of a cooperative act to some evil action, virtue ethicists attend to the teleology of the given cooperative act itself. In order to determine the quality of a particular cooperative act, an essential element which moralists must consider remains whether the evil effects follow necessarily—or merely accidently—from the cooperator's action. Moralists' attention to natural teleology and *per se* order ensures that the enterprise of analyzing moral cooperation does not descend into relativism. For example, a scrupulous mail carrier who frets about the moral content of the mail he delivers can be consoled by reflecting on the teleology of mail distribution. Nothing in the worthy civil service of mail distribution implies fraud. However, in the course of a day's mail route, one can imagine that some piece of mail contains a lie or plans for fraudulent activity. The mail car-

---

22. For the teaching of the Catholic Church on the morality of the regulation of births, see Pope Pius XI, *Casti connubii*; Second Vatican Council, *Gaudium et spes*, nos. 50–51; Pope Paul VI, *Humanae vitae*; and *CCC*, nos. 2366–72.

23. Long, *The Teleological Grammar of the Moral Act*, 2nd ed., 170–80. See especially 173–74, where Long explains: "The essential point, however, is simple: that the fundamental teleological analysis of object and species in the moral act does not discriminate the use of the condom and the condom's contraceptive character within the venereal act as a mere 'consequence' of seeking a good end through an object *per se* ordered to that end. For the object of such an act is 'uniting conjugally in the procreative act while using a means that is objectively contraceptive for the sake of avoiding the transmission of AIDS.' This object is not *per se* ordered to the end of procreation. The introduction of contraceptive means severs the order of the act performed toward procreation. It is precisely this which falls under negative precept and may never be done."

rier does not cooperate immorally in this fraud. The reason for his inno-
cence lies not in his wish to avoid contributing to fraud but in the nature
of his activity itself.[24] The teleology of mail carrying is not *per se* ordered to fraud. Immoral activity does not necessarily follow the delivery
of mail. Instead, the reception of illicit mail remains a *per accidens* result of
the noble public good of mail distribution.[25]

The deficiency of the "proximity to evil" argument

A method of analyzing cooperative acts which relies heavily on the
category of proximity to evil—literally how close an act of cooperation
stands in relation to some evil act—will always remain extrinsic to the
act itself. Moralists can only utilize a proximity-based method of moral
analysis when they analyze cases based on extrinsic laws and obligations.
A particular law, extrinsic to the human person, will draw the line of just
how closely one can approach bad acts before one's cooperation becomes
illicit. In the second chapter of this project, we observed the great variety
of judgments moralists rendered during the casuist period. In part, the
importance casuists placed on the judgment of proximity to evil caused
the disagreement about the liceity of certain forms of cooperation.[26]

When the determining factor for judging the morality of a cooperative act is its proximity to another bad act, it is difficult to know why one
act of cooperation is good and another bad. When proximity occupies a
prominent place in moral analysis, the judgments inevitably will appear
arbitrary. Why draw the line precisely here and not there? At the same
time, when the judgment regarding the morality of a given act depends
primarily on how close it stands to some other act, the whole deliberation remains extrinsic to the human person. The question is not what the

24. Steven Long explains: "Because when the object is *per se* ordered to the end the
most formal, defining, and containing moral species is derived from the end, it is also
true that to determine the species of an act one must refer to natural teleology.... It follows that natural teleology provides the grammar for the constitution of the species of
the moral act, and also for the constitution of the object of the moral act." See Long,
The Teleological Grammar of the Moral Act, 2nd ed., 151.

25. For extended reflection on the difference between *per se* and *per accidens* ordering
of human acts, see Long, 42–50.

26. For further treatment of the deleterious effects of an extrinsic understanding
of the moral law, see Servais Pinckaers, OP, *Les Actes Humains*. Ia–IIae, Questions 18–21,
Somme Théologique, Notes et Appendices (Paris: Descleé & Cie, 1966), especially the section "*Loi et liberté: l' «extrinsécisme»*," 227–33.

agent is doing but how closely his act approaches someone else's act. On the other hand, if one judges habitually the goodness of an act on the basis of whether it naturally implies good or evil things, one can recognize more easily the nature of a good act. As Kevin Flannery observes: "Determining that certain acts of cooperation are too close to the bad acts and so impermissible is not a question of the relationship of cooperator (or cooperators) to malefactor (malefactors) but rather of the nature of the situation in which various parties find themselves."[27] When one judges the liceity of a cooperative act according to its natural teleology, one employs a method of moral analysis where moral truth is intrinsic to human acting.[28] For this reason, the virtuous person possesses the capacity to appreciate the natural teleology of his actions.

One's consciousness regarding the type of activity in which one is engaged makes one more aware of what is naturally implied from one's activity, that is, what are an act's *per se* effects. In this way, one can develop a connaturality toward virtuous cooperation. So long as a person asks how closely he or she can move toward bad acts, such a person will never develop a connaturality toward the good. Likewise, such a person will never overcome the tendency for this judgment of proximity to be arbitrary and, indeed, one that tends towards laxism. Whenever the predominant question in moral analysis is how close we can get to an evil act or how an extrinsic law does or does not apply in a given case, the tendency of moral judgment veers toward a lax approach.[29] Such an approach might be rule-upholding but hardly virtue-inducing.

St. Thomas himself avoids grounding his arguments of the moral liceity of cooperative acts upon judgments regarding proximity to evil. When he

27. Kevin L. Flannery, SJ, *Cooperation with Evil: Thomistic Tools of Analysis* (Washington, DC: The Catholic University of America Press, 2019), 213–14.

28. For an extended treatment of the intrinsic nature of the moral law based on the natural inclinations, see Servais Pinckaers, OP, *The Pinckaers Reader: Renewing Thomistic Moral Theology*, ed. John Berkman and Craig Steven Titus, trans. Sr. Mary Thomas Noble, OP, Craig Steven Titus, Michael Sherwin, OP, and Hugh Connolly (Washington, DC: The Catholic University of America Press, 2005), 369–84, and, by the same author, *Morality: The Catholic View*, trans. Michael Sherwin, OP (South Bend, IN: St. Augustine's Press, 2001), especially 96–111.

29. For a further treatment of the minimalism that an obligation-based morality can induce, see Servais Pinckaers, OP, *Le renouveau de la morale* (Tournai: Casterman, 1964), 26–31. For more information on laxism, see Cessario, OP, *Introduction to Moral Theology*, 224; McHugh-Callan, *Moral Theology*, vol. 1, 249; and Jonsen and Toulmin, *The Abuse of Casuistry: A History of Moral Reasoning*, 231–49.

addresses the production of objects whose sole use rests in immoral activities, Aquinas teaches that no one may licitly produce such objects. He teaches that this kind of cooperation with evil stands under negative precept not because it approaches too closely the evil action. Instead, St. Thomas explains the unlawful production in terms of the nature of the act itself. St. Thomas teaches:

> In the case of an art directed to the production of goods which men cannot use without sin, it follows that the workmen sin in making such things, as directly affording others an occasion of sin; for instance, if a man were to make idols or anything pertaining to idolatrous worship. But in the case of an art the products of which may be employed by man either for a good or for an evil use, such as swords, arrows, and the like, the practice of such an art is not sinful.[30]

One thinks of an instrument used solely for abortions or some other crime against human life. The question we need to ask is not how closely this object approaches the sin of abortion.[31] Other objects could be used for an abortion which, in such a case, would render them equally close to the procedure. However, the use of this second class of objects not specifically designed for abortion would represent a *per accidens* and not *per se* use of the instrument. In such a case, the producers of instruments used in abortion—but which have many other licit purposes—would not necessarily be morally culpable for the instruments' production. Rather, the nature of the thing produced—and the *per se* effects which follow from it—constitute the sole criterion to render the production of an object immoral. An instrument used exclusively for abortion is teleologically ordered to abortion. Therefore, its production falls under negative precept. The production and distribution of such an instrument could never be a good act.

The appropriate question moralists should ask about the production of certain objects, weapons, or other tools used for immoral activities is whether there is something in the production of the object itself which points towards immoral activity. Gloves can be used by thieves to protect their anonymity. Nothing about a glove, however, suggests it is *per se* ordered to thievery. A glove-maker, therefore, need not fret that he has ma-

---

30. *Summa theologiae*, IIa–IIae, q. 169, a. 2, ad. 4.

31. For a strong and clear condemnation of abortion, see the Congregation for the Doctrine of the Faith, *Declaration on Procured Abortion*, June 28, 1974. See also *CCC*, nos. 2270–75, as well as the landmark encyclical of Pope John Paul II, *Evangelium vitae*.

terially cooperated in burglary. Even if the gloves he produced were used in a theft, the glove-maker is not morally responsible for the thievery. The point at issue is one of moral methodology. It is not that the glove-maker has produced something that is sufficiently removed from the sin of thievery. Rather, there is nothing in the nature of glove-producing that implies thievery. It is not one's proximity to an evil act that requires moral analysis but instead the nature of the activity in which one is engaged that should be the subject of moral inquiry.[32]

The context of a moral act

In order to determine an act's moral quality, some actions require an especially careful analysis. The context in which a moral decision unfolds can play an important role in understanding the nature of a moral choice.[33] For example, one who manufactures weapons knows what he produces sometimes will be used for immoral means. Such is the case in an unjust war or an intentional homicide.[34] At the same time, it may very well be the case that the weapons he produces are used ordinarily for just and moral purposes. These could include legitimate defense or recreational hunting.[35] The context of the moral activity is of great importance. Producing or distributing weapons in a place where they are almost certainly to be used for immoral ends would order one's production of them to the immoral activ-

---

32. See *Summa theologiae*, IIa–IIae, q. 169, a. 2, ad. 4.

33. For an insightful reflection on the rich context of the moral act, beyond merely its physical components, see Stephen L. Brock, "*Veritatis Splendor* §78, St. Thomas, and (Not Merely) Physical Objects of Moral Acts," *Nova et Vetera*, English edition, 6 (2008): 1–62.

34. For Catholic teaching on just war, see *CCC*, nos. 2307–17. See also George Weigel, *Tranquillitas Ordinis: The Present Failure and Future Promise of American Catholic Thought on War and Peace* (New York: Oxford University Press, 1987). See also Paul Ramsey, *War and the Christian Conscience: How Shall Modern War Be Conducted Justly?* (Durham, NC: Seeman Printery, 1961). Interested readers may also consult a 2012 symposium of the English edition of *Nova et Vetera*. See, for example, Joseph W. Koterski, SJ, "Just War and the Common Good," *Nova et Vetera*, English edition, 10 (2012): 1031–48; Robert John Araujo, SJ, "Roman Catholic Teachings on the Use of Force: Assessing Rights and Wrongs from World War I to Iraq," *Nova et Vetera*, English edition, 10 (2012): 1049–72; Gregory M. Reichberg, "Discontinuity in Catholic Just War Teaching? From Aquinas to the Contemporary Popes," *Nova et Vetera*, English edition, 10 (2012): 1073–97; and James Turner Johnson, "Holy War," *Nova et Vetera*, English edition, 10 (2012): 1099–1113.

35. For the duties for those responsible for the common good regarding legitimate defense, see *CCC*, nos. 2263–2367. Regarding hunting, for the use of animals for food and clothing, see *CCC*, no. 2417.

ity.[36] The teleology of human action is discovered and not imposed, but it is discovered within a certain context. Man does not "produce weapons" in the abstract; he does so always in a given context. The Jesuit philosopher Kevin Flannery offers salutary counsel on this question. Flannery explains the importance of context or culture in moral analysis. He explains: "In order to understand an act, we have to set it within the culture within which it is performed. It is culture whence comes an act's meaning."[37] Attention to culture does not relativize moral truth, but rather helps us to understand moral truths more clearly. Weapons production in one time and place means something different than it does in another context. Far from the accusation of physicalism, a rigorous analysis of the moral object must take into account a certain context which gives the act its specificity.

While the object of the moral act provides the primary means of analyzing an act's moral goodness, certain circumstances can alter the correct moral analysis. Romanus Cessario observes: "The Scholastic theologians acknowledged that certain weighty circumstances may affect the composition of the moral object. A circumstance, they argued, can pass over into the condition of the object."[38] In the area of moral cooperation, circumstances can render an otherwise choiceworthy act an evil one. For example, certain forms of cooperation that may not of themselves be evil, under some circumstances could become an act a virtuous person should avoid. Shopping for groceries at an establishment which invests in immoral activity does not necessarily represent an unjust collaboration with evil. Manualists would categorize such an act as remote material cooperation. In the casuist framework, such cooperation could be justified without much difficulty. However, one could envision a case in which a community boasted only two grocery stores. In this small village perhaps, it became known that one store invested heavily in immoral activities whereas the other was known to donate to worthy charitable causes. In such circumstances, procuring goods from the charitable grocer offers an attractive moral choice. Attention to an act's natural teleology and *per se* effects does not promise to make every case of moral inquiry easy. Complexities remain. However, this method does ensure that one can become a virtuous

36. One finds a similar analysis in the treatment of arms production in the *Catechism of the Catholic Church*. See *CCC*, no. 2315.

37. Kevin L. Flannery, *Acts Amid Precepts: The Aristotelian Structure of Thomas Aquinas's Moral Theory*, xiii.

38. Cessario, *Introduction to Moral Theology*, 174.

cooperator. A person can develop connatural knowledge of which forms of cooperation he must avoid.[39] The cooperator's awareness of the teleology of his actions proves indispensable for the development of the capacity to avoid vicious cooperation.

The intrinsic nature of virtue ethics as contrasted with the extrinsicism of the law

A particular danger we identified in the casuist system results from authors counseling the application of extrinsic laws to particular disputed cases.[40] In such a moral landscape, the cultivation of habitual dispositions toward sound moral action remains challenging. Virtue-based moral theory, on the other hand, allows one's moral judgments to be based on what is intrinsic to human acting. Virtue-based moralists avoid the appearance of applying extrinsic laws to concrete human situations. Instead, they identify the shape of moral truth concretized in a given moral choice. For that reason, those who utilize virtue-based reasoning can develop a habitual disposition to avoid unjust cooperation with evil.

Some thinkers recognize that the category of participation provides a useful tool for an adequate moral analysis. As a participation in God's eternal law, human action is ordered to a particular end. Only with reference to its teleological character can one provide a full account of a human act. Understood in this sense, human action, far from merely submitting to external and imposed laws, truly participates in God's governing of the universe and in His divine wisdom. John Rziha affirms: "When God legislates morality, this legislation is in accord with His divine wisdom, and when humans know moral truth, their knowledge participates in divine knowledge."[41] Pope John Paul II referred to this participated nature of hu-

---

39. For the clear teaching of St. Thomas Aquinas on this matter, see *Summa theologiae*, IIa–IIae q. 45, a. 2: "Now rectitude of judgment is twofold: first, on account of perfect use of reason, secondly, on account of a certain connaturality with the matter about which one has to judge. Thus, about matters of chastity, a man after inquiring with his reason forms a right judgment, if he has learnt the science of morals, while he who has the habit of chastity judges of such matters by a kind of connaturality."

40. Servais Pinckaers has written eloquently about the dangers of viewing the moral law as extrinsic to human nature. See, for example, his *The Sources of Christian Ethics*, especially 408. See also Servais Pinckaers, OP, "A Historical Perspective on Intrinsically Evil Acts," in *The Pinckaers Reader*, 185–235.

41. John Rziha, *Perfecting Human Actions: St. Thomas Aquinas on Human Participation in Eternal*

man action as "theonomy or participated theonomy."[42] In the context of
cooperation, this means that only when a person acts consciously in accord with the truth about human nature can he be said to participate fully in the divine wisdom. This *habitus* becomes more difficult to cultivate
when one tries merely to observe an external law.[43] The category of proximity to evil—as opposed to natural teleology—presents this danger in
the area of moral cooperation with evil. To understand more completely
the sense in which participation shapes St. Thomas's moral discourse, it is
necessary to recall his understanding of analogy.[44] While a full treatment
of analogy exceeds the scope of this study, one can recognize that the use
of analogous and not only univocal concepts of action, goodness, and nature are necessary to grasp the full truth about human acting. Specifically,
a robust concept of analogy and participation—often lacking in authors
prone to voluntarism or extrinsicism—is required to grasp how human
action habituates one to become a virtuous or vicious person. This concept provides an account of human flourishing in which acts of cooperation either aid or hinder in this development.

Challenges posed by the consideration of duress and the possibility of involuntary acts

Classical Thomism has utilized the term "enemies of the voluntary"
to refer to those factors which threaten the full knowledge and freedom
that characterize properly human acting.[45] In the beginning of his moral

---

Law (Washington, DC: The Catholic University of America Press, 2009), 2. For an insightful review of this work highlighting its broad implications in moral theology, see
the review of Aquinas Guilbeau, OP, and Romanus Cessario, OP, *Nova et Vetera*, English
edition, 10 (2012): 877–79.

42. See *VS*, no. 41: "Others speak, and rightly so, of *theonomy*, or *participated theonomy*,
since man's free obedience to God's law effectively implies that human reason and human will participate in God's wisdom and providence."

43. This becomes clear in light of the express teaching of St. Thomas that acts are
good and evil in themselves not based merely on the imposition of law. See *Summa Contra
Gentiles* III, q. 129, trans. Vernon J. Burke (Notre Dame, IN: University of Notre Dame
Press, 1975): "Therefore, it is clear that good and evil in human activities are based not
only on the prescription of law, but also on the natural order."

44. For an excellent presentation of the importance of the debate surrounding the
concept of analogy, see the collection of essays edited by Thomas Joseph White, OP,
The Analogy of Being: Invention of the Antichrist or Wisdom of God? (Grand Rapids, MI: Eerdmans, 2010).

45. See Cessario, *Introduction to Moral Theology*, 104–10. For further treatment of the

treatise, St. Thomas explains how violence, fear, lust, and ignorance affect human activity.[46] Aquinas holds that violence can be done to the external act of the will such that a man is said to act involuntarily.[47] The presence of fear, on the other hand, does not by itself render an action involuntary. It can, however, explain why an action was, in a certain sense, against the will of the actor. In this regard, Aquinas recognized the distinction between *metus*, an estimative judgment of danger, and *timor*, the passion or feeling of fear. The presence of one type of fear does not necessarily indicate the presence of the other.

By and large, authors of the casuist period do not offer a complete treatment of the enemies of the voluntary. In the rare cases when casuists invoke the enemies of the voluntary, they utilize them to excuse from obligation, rather than to offer an account of human action.[48] In the place of the enemies of the voluntary, these authors most often employ the category of duress to demonstrate how outside influences can affect the freedom of human action.[49] In the casuist system, the value that the category the "enemies of the voluntary" affords the analysis of human action is limited to the degree of praise or blame that one should place on an individual human actor. The invocation of the "enemies of the voluntary" cannot determine the moral goodness of an action as such. Contemporary authors join those of the casuist period when they invoke the category of duress in order to address cooperation with evil. According to these thinkers, actions committed under duress describe those acts which one does under a certain compulsion.[50] A person can be morally responsible only for those actions he

---

enemies of the voluntary, see Romanus Cessario, OP, "Sacramental Confession and Addictions," in *Addiction and Compulsive Behaviors*, ed. Edward J. Furton, 125–39 (Philadelphia: The National Catholic Bioethics Center, 2000). For an excellent treatment of Aquinas's use of *liberum arbitrium*, often misleadingly rendered "free will," see Wojciech Giertych, OP, "Free Will, Addiction, and Moral Culpability," in *Addiction and Compulsive Behaviors*, ed. Edward J. Furton, 113–24 (Philadelphia: The National Catholic Bioethics Center, 2000).

46. See *Summa theologiae*, Ia–IIae, q. 6, a. 4–8.

47. See *Summa theologiae*, Ia–IIae, q. 6, a. 5.

48. For example, see Dominicus M. Prümmer, OP, *Handbook of Moral Theology*, trans. Gerald W. Shelton (Cork: The Mercier Press, 1956), 16: "Grave fear or, as is commonly said, grave inconvenience excuse a man from compliance with positive law (whether human or divine)."

49. For an account of the history of the use of duress in casuist authors, see Cummings, *The Servant and the Ladder*, 168–72.

50. For a fruitful exchange on the place of duress in moral analysis, see Thomas Kopfensteiner, "The Meaning and Role of Duress in the Cooperation in Wrongdoing,"

does knowingly and willingly, not all those in which he might materially play a part. For example: one may consider the case of one who is thrown out of a window and falls onto a table, breaking it. This person cannot be held morally responsible for the broken table. Indeed, the person cannot be said to have broken the table by means of a properly human act. St. Thomas Aquinas distinguishes rightly between properly human acts and those which are merely acts of man. Human acts are those which proceed from a deliberate will, while acts of man are those lacking any moral weight. An act of man might be a physical reflex, or an act done without any deliberation whatsoever.[51]

Only those acts which proceed from a deliberate will and with a knowledge of what one is doing classify as voluntary actions.[52] However, this fact does not mean that everyone who finds himself under some kind of pressure to act or fears the consequences of inaction can be said to act involuntarily. Instead, absent real violence done to the person—as in the case of one being thrown out of a window—one's actions still classify as voluntary.[53] In his treatment of St. Thomas's moral philosophy, Ralph McInerny explains: "There are certain kinds of act that can never be performed well even when we fear the consequences of non-performance."[54] No matter the reason for one's action nor the level of fear or duress experienced, certain actions remain unjustifiable. McInerny continues: "Aristotle wisely said we feel pity and pardon for those who perform demeaning acts out of fear."[55] While we may feel badly for someone who acted in a certain way, indeed the person himself may regret acting the way he did, it does not change the fact that he committed a bad act. The presence of duress does not transform a bad act into a good one. The category

---

Linacre Quarterly 70 (2003): 150–58; and Anthony Zimmerman, "Duress and Contraceptive Sterilization: A Reply to Prof. Thomas Kopfsteiner," *Linacre Quarterly* 70 (2003): 210–17.

51. See *Summa theologiae*, Ia–IIae, q. 6, a. 1.

52. See *Summa theologiae*, Ia–IIae, q. 6, a. 1: "Therefore, since man especially knows the end of his work, and moves himself, in his acts especially is the voluntary to be found."

53. For an excellent treatment of how violence and fear can affect one's capacity to consent to marriage, see Paolo Bianchi, *When is Marriage Null? Guide to the Grounds of Matrimonial Nullity for Pastors, Counselors, and Lay Faithful*, trans. Michael J. Miller (San Francisco: Ignatius Press, 2015), 35–46.

54. Ralph McInerny, *Ethica Thomistica: The Moral Philosophy of Thomas Aquinas*, rev. ed. (Washington, DC: The Catholic University of America Press, 1997), 64.

55. McInerny, 64. For a more extended treatment of Aquinas's teaching on human action, see Ralph McInerny, *Aquinas on Human Action: A Theory of Practice* (Washington, DC: The Catholic University of America Press, 1992).

of duress may be useful in assessing the culpability or merit of one's action. Attention to the presence of duress might help to answer the question of how much a person should receive praise or blame for what he did. However, duress cannot ultimately excuse acting badly. One who committed an evil act under grave duress could be subject to a lesser penalty for his bad acting. Nevertheless, a bad act remains bad acting regardless of whether it was done under duress. Pope John Paul II taught: "It is possible that the evil done as the result of invincible ignorance or a nonculpable error of judgment may not be imputable to the agent; but even in this case it does not cease to be an evil, a disorder in relation to the truth about the good."[56] An act which does not conform to the truth about the good of the human person remains a bad act even if it is performed under duress.

In cases of moral cooperation with evil, often a cooperator claims he lacks an alternative course of action. "My hand was forced," the cooperator under duress asserts. Sometimes those who engage in immoral cooperative acts allege they had no choice but to cooperate with the evil act of another. This contention requires the strictest scrutiny. Is the cooperator truly no longer free to act in a different way? Has the cooperator's freedom truly been compromised? Has someone else done violence to the cooperator's will such that he is no longer capable of free human action? Allowing even for a broad interpretation of psychological violence done to another where the will may be coerced into acting in a certain way, still the category of duress does not justify acting badly because one does not like the consequences of refusing cooperation.[57] If the government were to make a law that said one must commit adultery or kill a first-born child, one may not do so under the guise of duress. Rather, one remains free to refuse to commit immoral behavior. In the same vein, if a government were to require a certain participation in the taking of innocent human life or bodily mutilation, one would not be justified in engaging

---

56. *VS*, no. 63

57. For a useful primer on the limits of duress as a moral category, see Fisher, *Catholic Bioethics for a New Millennium*, 89–90. Fisher refers to the duress exception contained in the 1994 US Bishops' *Ethical and Religious Directives* to be "at best muddled thinking." For an alternative perspective, see Kopfensteiner, "The Meaning and Role of Duress in the Cooperation in Wrongdoing," 150–58. Kopfensteiner prefers to speak of a grammar of responsibility. He maintains that this manner of expression "would provide a broader and more adequate context in which to weigh the goods and evils involved in any application of the principle [of cooperation], especially though when the element of duress is a morally relevant factor in our deliberations." See Kopfensteiner, 156.

in such activity under the claim "the state made me do it."[58] Even if the consequence of refusing compliance with such a law were the loss of business revenue or large state-imposed fines, if the cooperation is *per se malum* it does not become licit because of the situation of duress.[59]

During the ongoing debate in the United States over the mandate of the Department of Health and Human Services that all health care providers fund contraception, sterilization, and abortion-inducing drugs, some involved in the debate have invoked arguments based on duress in their moral analysis.[60] While it is true that those who do not wish to fund these so-called "services" may find themselves in a situation of duress after a government mandate, they remain free moral actors who are not in an involuntary state. For that reason, their acting remains worthy of praise or blame based on the merits of the acts themselves. Put simply, duress does not change whether a particular cooperative act is a good act or a bad one. The moral quality of funding these procedures depends on the kind of thing one who chooses to fund them is doing.[61] While duress may be a useful category of moral inquiry to analyze the culpability of one's action, it cannot fundamentally change the nature of what one is doing.

The consequences of this truth are widespread and life changing. Once

58. For more information on responses to government mandates for immoral services, see three essays by Elliott Louis Bedford, "The Reality of Institutional Conscience," *The National Catholic Bioethics Quarterly* 16 (2016): 255–72; "The Concept of Institutional Conscience," *The National Catholic Bioethics Quarterly* 12 (2012): 409–20; and "Catholic Social Teaching and the Women's Preventative Health Services Mandate," *Nova et Vetera*, English edition, 10 (2012): 909–22. See also Long, *The Teleological Grammar of the Moral Act*, 2nd ed., 208–25.

59. Arguing in a similar fashion, the American Bishops maintained that compliance with the 2012 contraceptive mandate of the Department of Health and Human Services of the Obama Administration cannot be justified. See "United for Religious Freedom: A Statement of the Administrative Committee of the United States Conference of Catholic Bishops," March 14, 2012; and "Our First, Most Cherished Liberty: A Statement on Religious Liberty," of the United States Conference of Catholic Bishops Ad Hoc Committee for Religious Liberty, March 2012.

60. See, for example, news reports which indicate that the well-known opponent of contraception Janet Smith held that compliance with government mandates requiring health insurance providers cover contraception could be licit under duress. See David Gibson, "Behind scenes, Catholic bishops seek an exit strategy for Obamacare mandate," *Religion News Service*, November 22, 2013.

61. Peter Cataldo argues that cooperation with contraceptive mandates would be "licit remote mediate material cooperation." See Peter Cataldo, "Compliance with contraceptive insurances mandates: licit or illicit cooperation in evil?" *The National Catholic Bioethics Quarterly* 4 (2004): 103–30.

we grasp that some actions cannot be chosen without sin, we recognize that no set of circumstances can make a bad act a good one. With a kind of prophecy for what may lie in store for Christians who confront hostile elements in their culture, Pope John Paul II offers the following: "[I]t is always possible that man, as the result of coercion or other circumstances, can be hindered from doing certain good actions; but he can never be hindered from not doing certain actions, especially if he is prepared to die rather than to do evil."[62] The state may enact laws which render it impossible for Christians to perform certain good works. For example, some state and local governments have forced Catholics to close Church-operated adoption agencies when those organizations refused to comply with a mandate to place children to be adopted with those in same-sex partnerships.[63] At the same time, while the state may inhibit good activity, it can never force Christians to do immoral things. Christians can always choose—or refuse—to participate in those activities. The results of such refusal may prove unfortunate but may nonetheless be what fidelity requires of Christians during times of hostility toward the practice of their faith.[64]

The category of duress will not occupy a prominent place in virtue-based moral reasoning. Duress suits a moral theory in which theologians ask whether a given act is right or wrong. These thinkers ponder whether a given act violates some extrinsic moral law. In these circumstances, grave situations of duress may reduce to a minimum one's moral culpability. Duress functions as a category of moral analysis in a law-based system where, authors opine, duress could make a law cease to apply. On the other hand, for virtue-based moral theologians, good and bad—more than right and wrong—represent the operative categories for moral analysis.[65]

62. *VS*, no. 52.

63. For more information about this matter, see the Congregation for the Doctrine of the Faith, *Considerations regarding proposals to give legal recognition to unions between homosexual persons*, March 28, 2003.

64. For further reflection on the challenges posed to the practice of Catholic faith in contemporary Western culture, see an outstanding volume of essays of The National Catholic Bioethics Center, *Urged on by Christ: Catholic Health Care in Tension with Contemporary Culture*, ed. Edward J. Furton (Philadelphia: The National Catholic Bioethics Center, 2007).

65. Lawrence Welch explains: "The Holy See is concerned that the current form of the Appendix to the ERD [the 1995 *Ethical and Religious Directives*] can be used to conclude that instrinsically evil acts could be considered permissible if duress were present. The Holy See cautions that such a position cannot be reconciled with the Church's teaching

This manner of thinking—virtue-based as opposed to rule-oriented—sees little place for extended reflection on the category of duress and its claim on moral reasoning.

Modern moral casuistry: a brief excursus on cooperation with abortion

Casuist authors address frequently the difficult case of one's employment at an organization that performs intrinsically evil acts. While the Catholic tradition—unlike some religious sects—has not mandated a complete retreat from society, Catholic moralists have cautioned against participation in any employment which does harm to the human person. One case in particular has generated significant discussion. Pro-life nurses who oppose abortion but find themselves asked to assist in performing abortions present a particular difficulty. The case of a nurse's assistance at a procured abortion challenges moralists to ground their analysis in the truth about human acting.

One such moralist who takes up the challenge of the perplexed nurse, Germain Grisez (1929–2018), offers counsel that may surprise those accustomed to his customarily rigorous conclusions.[66] Grisez describes a nurse employed at a community hospital who is required to assist in performing an abortion. The nurse must "prepare the patient, assist in surgery, and provide aftercare." The nurse has made moral objections to assisting in abortions known to the hospital administrators but remains required to assist when on duty. The hospital offers no accommodation for conscientious objection.[67] Grisez argues that while finding alternative employment may be admirable, it is not required. Rather, in response to one who asks if a nurse must resign the position to avoid providing assistance for abortions, Grisez explains:

---

in *Evangelium vitae*, no. 74 and *Veritatis splendor*, nos. 71–83. The category of duress is also a concern of the Holy See.... The Holy See in its correspondence objects to the 'position that a form of cooperation that otherwise would be considered formal could be considered material and licit if the category of duress is present.'" See his "Direct Sterilization: An Intrinsically Evil Act—A Rejoinder to Fr. Keenan," *Linacre Quarterly* 68 (2001): 124–30.

66. See, for example, the rigor with which he addresses the morality of reusing uncanceled postage stamps. See Germain Grisez, *Difficult Moral Questions: The Way of the Lord Jesus*, vol. 3, 629–31.

67. Grisez, 355.

Some faithful Catholic moralists—ones who did not dissent from any teaching of the Church—held that in such a case a nurse's assisting in abortion
could be morally acceptable material cooperation. It seems to me that if recent
teachings were meant to exclude that opinion, they would have done so more
clearly. Therefore, it is reasonable to suppose that your question remains to be
answered.[68]

This passage contains a footnote to the work of the famed Jesuit Gerald
Kelly (1902–1964). Kelly argues that nurses could assist in illicit operations
so long as they had a sufficient reason for doing so.[69] Kelly explains: "Most
authors would agree that the danger of losing one's position without the
hope of getting another would certainly be a sufficient reason to justify
material cooperation at the illicit operations."[70] In the case described, the
assistance the nurse provides constitutes direct assistance in a procured
abortion. Kelly describes the case of a nurse "handing instruments to doctors." The assistance the nurse provides in such a case goes beyond the ordinary care given to patients at any medical facility. In many cases, operations require the assistance of nurses and others to ensure their successful
completion. The handing of instruments to one performing an abortion
could even fall within the parameters of the Church's canonical jurisprudence. According to the 1983 Code of Canon Law, one incurs a canonical
penalty if he or she provides assistance without which the abortion would
not take place.[71]

The counsel Gerald Kelly gives in this case stands in contrast to his
otherwise strict interpretation of moral questions.[72] One recognizes in his
analysis of this example a heavy emphasis on the weighing of consequences to determine the nurse's best course of action. While some argue that

68. Grisez, 357.

69. Gerald Kelly, SJ, *Medico-Moral Problems* (St. Louis: The Catholic Hospital Association of the United States and Canada, 1958), 332–35.

70. Kelly, 334.

71. See the *CIC* 1398: "A person who procures a completed abortion incurs a *latae sententiae* excommunication"; and *CIC* 1329, §2: "Accomplices who are not named in a law or
precept incur a *latae sententiae* penalty attached to a delict if without their assistance the
delict would not have been committed, and the penalty is of such a nature that it can affect them; otherwise, they can be punished by *ferendae sententiae* penalties."

72. Along with John C. Ford, SJ, with whom he authored several books, Kelly
achieved prominence for his defense of the moral teaching of Pope Pius XII. Kelly is
remembered for his overall rigorous approach to moral questions. See, for example,
the description of Charles E. Curran, *Catholic Moral Theology in the United States: A History*
(Washington, DC: Georgetown University Press, 2008), 39–42.

a nurse must accept other employment when available, Kelly holds that the good work a Catholic nurse can accomplish in a non-Catholic hospital may outweigh the negative effects of the nurse's assistance at immoral procedures. Kelly explains:

We should not be too ready to insist or suggest that Catholic nurses leave public institutions merely because they could get equally good or ever better positions elsewhere. The conscientious and exemplary nurse can do much spiritual good in these institutions; and this good more than compensates for occasional and unavoidable material cooperation in evil.[73]

While Catholic nurses have offered valuable service at secular institutions, this cannot justify positive assistance to a procured abortion. Difficult cases exist in which clarity about the nature of a cooperating act eludes even skilled theologians. Still, the question moralists should ask concerns the nature of the act of cooperation, not a weighing of consequences which may result.

Grisez's treatment of the nurse assisting at an abortion follows that of Gerald Kelly. Grisez argues that one may provide positive assistance to a particular abortion without intending that such an abortion take place. He describes certain forms of assistance, such as handing "such-and-such an instrument" as "behavior you could perform without making any choice regarding abortion."[74] He grants that certain acts—"[using] your judgment in selecting implements" or "administer[ing] medication to induce labor" represent unjustifiable cooperation.[75] Grisez holds that cooperation may be formal—and not merely material—even when the cooperator abhors the act that will follow. He explains that one who contracts with an agency of temporary workers cooperates formally with the evil of prostitution if this is one of the so-called employments for which the agency contracts. One struggles to understand how this example differs from that of the nurse who assists at an abortion. In both cases, one's ordinary work requires some cooperation in facilitating evil activity. Grisez permits the nurse's abortion assistance but forbids a temporary work agency to contract for prostitution on the grounds that the latter is unable not to will the evil being done. He explains: "She intends that Cadillac Escorts un-

73. Kelly, SJ, *Medico-Moral Problems*, 334.

74. Grisez, *Difficult Moral Questions: The Way of the Lord Jesus*, vol. 3, 358. For an extended treatment of Grisez's position on moral cooperation—in light of his action theory more generally, see Cummings, *The Servant and the Ladder*, 224–49.

75. Grisez, *Difficult Moral Questions: The Way of the Lord Jesus*, vol. 3, 357.

dertake and carry out its part of the arrangement—that is, meet UA's requirements for hostesses who will provide sexual services. So she formally cooperates in prostitution."[76] It seems, for Grisez, it is less the nature of the work itself than the fact that the work cannot be done without engaging one's intention in the work that renders certain activities necessarily formal cooperation with evil. Grisez relies here on the definition of material and formal cooperation established by St. Alphonsus Liguori. Readers will recall that St. Alphonsus defined formal cooperation as that which "concurs in the bad will of the other."[77] This definition fails to specify whether it is the cooperator or the cooperator's act which must concur in the bad will of another. That is to say, are there types of activity which, of their nature, necessarily concur in the bad will of another?

Grisez, for his part, grants that some actions necessarily entail willing certain things. For example, he does not allow the nurse to assist the abortionist if her assistance requires her to choose which instrument is needed for the next step in a given abortion. He believes this kind of cooperation requires that the nurse intend the abortion to take place. However, Grisez does not believe that the handing of instruments, selected by the abortionist, requires such an engagement of the nurse's will. Grisez explains: "Suppose you were assisting at a surgical abortion and were required to use your judgment in selecting implements or regulating a machine in order to help bring about the abortion. You could not carry out such directives without intending to effect the abortion."[78]

One wonders if this is not a distinction without a moral difference. While a nurse's handing of pre-selected instruments to an abortionist may appear mechanical, the cooperation itself remains indispensable for the abortion to take place. Even in Grisez's own logic, one must will that the doctor receives the instrument—that the device not harm him in the transfer from one hand to the other or that it not be dropped on the floor. The reason for Grisez's position on this matter relies less on his particular moral judgments than on his overall theory of moral action.[79] While Grisez tries to distance himself from what he describes as classical moral

76. Grisez, 875.

77. Grisez, 873, citing St. Alphonsus Liguori, *Theologia moralis*, ed. L. Gaudé, 4 vols. (Rome: Ex Typographia Vaticana, 1905–12), 1:357 (lib. II, §63): "illam esse formalem, quae concurrit ad malam voluntatem alterius."

78. Grisez, *Difficult Moral Questions: The Way of the Lord Jesus*, vol. 3, 357.

79. For a critical review of Grisez's action theory, see Benedict Ashley, OP, "Integral Human Fulfillment According to Germain Grisez," in *The Ashley Reader: Redeeming Reason* (Naples, FL: Sapientia Press, 2006), 225–69.

theology, he retains the majority of the categories utilized by the casuist authors.[80] Grisez organizes his moral theology textbook around the categories of conscience, law, and sin. By and large he remains committed to the casuist framework of a law-based approach to moral thought.

The role of the cardinal virtues in addressing cooperation with evil

Unlike authors from either the casuist period or those of the proportionalist school, moralists of the Thomist tradition will address matters of cooperation with evil according to the virtues. These thinkers seek to articulate those virtues which prove helpful for virtuous participation in social life. Virtuous involvement in the social order obviously precludes immoral forms of cooperation with evil. In the section which follows we examine the role of the four cardinal virtues in addressing matters of moral cooperation with evil. Prudence, justice, fortitude, and temperance each occupy a crucial place in the virtue-based approach to moral cooperation.[81] Those who cultivate these virtues stand ready to address the manifold issues of cooperation which face twenty-first-century believers.

Prudence

Francis II, Duke of Brittany, died in 1488. Laid to rest in the Cathedral church of Nantes, his tomb stands as a monument to the virtue tradition. The four corners of his tomb are adorned by statues of the four cardinal virtues. Erected prior to the eclipse of virtue-based reasoning in the modern period, the tomb of this fifteenth-century Duke recalls the place of the moral virtues in the Christian life. Representing prudence, one statue holds a mirror. This depiction of the first of the cardinal virtues portrays prudence as the power to look over one's actions in the light of the truth of the moral law. Given the centuries of the practice of moral casuistry one cannot help but note the absence of artistic monuments to its practice.

80. See Germain Grisez, *The Way of the Lord Jesus: Christian Moral Principles*, vol. 1 (Chicago: Franciscan Herald Press, 1983), 12–13.

81. Catholic moral theology boasts much recent literature in the virtue-based tradition. Interested readers will welcome the recent publication of the course-notes of Michel Labourdette, OP. See, in particular, his *La Prudence: Grand cours de théologie morale/ 11* (Paris: Parole et Silence, 2016).

The statue of lady prudence holding a mirror establishes the virtue's basic parameters. For virtue-based moral theology, the operation of prudence remains indispensable. Romanus Cessario explains: "Prudence, then transforms knowledge of moral truth into specific virtuous actions which are not burdensome, that is, which do not include friction, internal strife, forcing oneself."[82] For the virtue-based moral theologian, prudence more than conscience provides the help necessary for determining the best course of action in a particular instance of cooperation with evil. Prudence also ensures that one actually pursues virtuous action.[83] Cessario continues: "Whenever conscience plays an autonomous role in the moral life, even with the due insistence on the obligation to inform it, the importance of a rational measure harmoniously directing and shaping the movement of appetite towards the authentic ends of human nature vanishes."[84] Conscience-based moral theories pose a special challenge for dealing with cases of cooperation with evil. This method attempts to impose ready-made answers to complicated cases.[85] The application of an imposed law to a particular case suggests a certain extrinsicism. Such a moral theory fails to pay sufficient attention to the way in which the norm arises from the nature of the activity itself. Prudence, on the other hand, offers the help needed to discover the right manner of moral acting in a given circumstance.

Far from relativizing decision-making in the moral life, prudence provides its concrete direction. Whenever theologians raise the question of

82. Cessario, *The Moral Virtues and Theological Ethics*, 80.

83. For an insightful look at the role of prudence (as distinct from conscience) in sound moral action, see John Dominic Corbett, OP, *Sacra Doctrina and the Discernment of Human Action* (Washington, DC, n/p, 1999), 348–63. For a further treatment of this distinction, see McInerny, *Ethica Thomistica*, chapter 7, "Prudence and Conscience," 103–13. For a slightly more technical analysis, see Servais Pinckaers, OP, "Conscience and the Virtue of Prudence," in *The Pinckaers Reader: Renewing Thomistic Moral Theology*, 342–55. For an excellent treatment of Aquinas's teaching on conscience, see Cajetan Cuddy, OP, "St. Thomas Aquinas on Conscience," in *Christianity and the Laws of Conscience: An Introduction*, ed. Jeffrey B. Hammond and Helen M. Alvare, 112–31 (Cambridge: Cambridge University Press, 2021).

84. Cessario, *The Moral Virtues and Theological Ethics*, 81.

85. For an excellent treatment of the placement of the treatise on conscience in the moral manuals, as it relates to St. Thomas's treatise on prudence, see Benoît-Henri Merkelbach, OP, "Quelle place assigner au traité de la conscience?" *Revue des Sciences Philosophiques et Théologiques* 12 (1923): 170–83. For a useful summary of Merkelbach's reflections on conscience and prudence, see Matthew Levering, *The Abuse of Conscience: A Century of Catholic Moral Theology* (Grand Rapids, MI: Eerdmans, 2021), 86–92.

whether or not a moral law applies in a particular case, their responses
will tend towards laxism. In the casuist system, moral theologians can
proffer themselves as those who can demonstrate when laws do not apply.[86] An example of this approach can be found in the heavy reliance in
casuist and proportionalist thinking on the category of duress to demonstrate that a law restricting cooperation does not apply in a given case.
On the other hand, when theologians recognize moral norms as intrinsic
to human flourishing—and not as extrinsic laws imposed from the outside—they generally remain unwilling to grant exceptions to a norm forbidding immoral cooperation.

   Some theologians misunderstand the role of prudence in the moral
life. These thinkers describe prudence as a kind of "pure-knowing" which
provides a theoretical answer to the question of how one ought to act in
each circumstance.[87] Alternatively, Thomists recognize that the principal
act of prudence is to command.[88] For that reason, prudence represents a
genuine source of moral activity.[89] Romanus Cessario affirms: "Only the
virtue of prudence shapes practical reason in accordance with authentic
moral knowledge and, therefore, renders it capable of conforming human
behavior towards the achievement of virtuous ends already in a sense possessed by rectified appetites."[90] Aquinas maintains, especially in his later
works, that prudence, more than conscience, stands as the true source of
virtuous acting.[91] Prudence does not provide a simple knowledge of what

86. A recent example of this approach can be found in those authors relying heavily
on casuist categories who find compliance with government contraceptive mandates to
be morally licit. They argue that so long as proportionately grave reasons are present,
such cooperation is "licit remote mediate material cooperation." See Cataldo, "Compliance with contraceptive insurances mandates: licit or illicit cooperation in evil?," 103–30.

87. Romanus Cessario, OP, observes: "The Thomist claim about the function of
prudence differs from that, for instance, of John Duns Scotus (c. 1264–1308), who taught
that prudence remains a kind of pure knowing. By defining it as a simple intellectual
virtue that provides direction for the moral life, but not formation of the powers of the
soul, Scotists effectively suspended what moral realists refer to as prudence's unitive
function." See his *Introduction to Moral Theology*, 125.

88. See *Summa theologiae*, IIa–IIae, q. 47, a. 8: "The practical reason, which is directed
to action, goes further, and its third act is 'to command,' which act consists in applying
to action the things counselled and judged. And since this act approaches nearer to the
end of the practical reason, it follows that it is the chief act of the practical reason, and
consequently of prudence."

89. For a helpful treatment of the role of prudence in the moral life, see Livio Melina, *Sharing in Christ's Virtues: For the Renewal of Moral Theology in Light of Veritatis Splendor*, 88–91.

90. Cessario, *The Moral Virtues and Theological Ethics*, 82.

91. For a demonstration of the connection between conscience and objective truth in

is to be done in the abstract but represents a real source of right moral acting in a given circumstance. As the French Dominican Ambroise Gardeil (1859–1931) astutely observes, "There is no prudence that is written on paper."[92] A prudent moral action depends, in large part, on rectified appetites. These desires for a good, together with the knowledge of how to achieve it, allow one to accomplish a prudent act.

Some authors needlessly worry that assigning prudence a prominent place in the moral life will leave one with moral knowledge at only the most universal level.[93] They fear that without ready-made casuist solutions to moral problems, interested parties will be left with only vague and abstract moral principles. However, those who object to the reliance on prudence in virtue-based moral theology misunderstand the nature of this first of the moral virtues. Josef Pieper aptly observes: "Prudence, however, is not concerned directly with the ultimate—natural and supernatural— ends of human life, but with the means to these ends."[94] The virtue of prudence provides knowledge of particulars, not just universal principles.[95] Again Pieper explains: "The special nature of prudence is its concern with the realm of 'ways and means' and down-to-earth realities."[96] Put simply, prudence extends to each particular of life.[97] Since prudence is a virtue—

---

the thought of St. Thomas Aquinas, see Brian Mullady, OP, "The Virtue of Prudence and the Primacy of Conscience," *Angelicum* 92 (2015): 425–45. For an alternative view on the place of conscience in the moral life, see James T. Bretzke, SJ, "Conscience and *Veritatis Splendor* in the Church Today," *Studia Moralia* 55 (2017): 271–95.

92. Ambroise Gardeil, OP, *The True Christian Life: Thomistic Reflections on Divinization, Prudence, Religion, and Prayer*, trans. Matthew K. Minerd (Washington, DC: The Catholic University of America Press, 2022), 89.

93. See, for example, the remark of Basil Cole, OP, in his review of a work purporting to offer a virtue approach: "The title of this profound work provokes skepticism because the phrase 'virtue approach' seems to suggest a way to avoid moral principles, redefine moral objects based on one's motives, the trumping of subjectivity over objectivity, or simply a lack of realism." See Basil Cole, OP, "Review: *Vital Conflicts in Medical Ethics: A Virtue Approach to Craniotomy and Tubal Pregnancies*," *The Thomist* 74 (2010): 160–64.

94. Josef Pieper, *The Four Cardinal Virtues* (New York: Harcourt, Brace & World, Inc., 1965), 11.

95. See *Summa theologiae*, IIa–IIae, q. 47, a. 3: "To prudence belongs not only the consideration of the reason, but also the application to action, which is the end of the practical reason. But no man can conveniently apply one thing to another, unless he knows both the thing to be applied, and the thing to which it has to be applied. Now actions are in singular matters: and so it is necessary for the prudent man to know both the universal principles of reason, and the singulars about which actions are concerned."

96. Pieper, *The Four Cardinal Virtues*, 11.

97. See Labourdette, OP, *La Prudence*, 24–26.

a firm disposition to do the good—it represents a genuine source of moral action. Human action necessarily comes to fruition in particular acts, not only in universal principles. St Thomas teaches: "Prudence is the right reason about things to be done (and this, not merely in general, but also in particular)."[98] All that is to say, the virtue of prudence terminates in a good action accomplished in the here and now.

One fear which can cripple moral action lies in seeking a false certitude before executing a particular activity. How often do we encounter those who cannot get beyond the first—but only preliminary step—of seeking counsel before deciding upon a course of action? This error in the moral life can be overcome only through a well-developed prudence. No amount of consultation or recourse to approved authorities can replace the virtue of prudence which ultimately will command a good action in a timely manner.[99] Insufficient attention to the development of prudence will lead to crippling effects on effective human action. Josef Pieper rightly observes that decisions subject to moral reasoning deal with realities "concrete, contingent, and future" and thus "there cannot be that certainty which is possible in a theoretical conclusion."[100] Insisting upon such a mathematical or logical certitude before initiating moral choice cannot promise error-free acting. Instead, such a hesitation will hinder the promptness and ease proper to virtuous living. Practically speaking, no one can wait for apodictic certainty before making a moral decision when it depends upon so many future contingents.[101] Here again a well-developed prudence proves indispensable to sound moral acting.

What St. Thomas calls *providentia* or foresight plays an important part in moral decisions involving cooperation with evil. This quasi-integral part of prudence reveals how a person here and now will actually complete a particular moral action. For St. Thomas, foresight can be called

98. *Summa theologiae*, Ia–IIae, q. 58, a. 5.

99. This approach stands in contrast to that of the moral manuals. Their reliance on the consultation of authorities can stifle the development of prudence. Romanus Cessario, OP, opines: "As casuistry involves the weighing of collected moral opinions in order to arrive at a course of action, a certain mathematical approach to morality emerges in this approach to the moral life. In fact, the various schools of casuistry arose because of the different opinions scholars held concerning how to settle the case of the perplexed conscience." See his *Introduction to Moral Theology*, 224.

100. Pieper, *The Four Cardinal Virtues*, 18.

101. Interested readers will find helpful Thomas Gilby's "Prudence and Certainty," appendix 4 of *Prudence*, vol. 36 of the Blackfriars *Summa Theologiae* (New York: McGraw-Hill Book Company, 1974), 182–84.

the principle of all parts of prudence.[102] Foresight establishes the proper means to a given end by ensuring that a given choice of means will engender a particular end.[103] In the ordinary circumstances of life we encounter people who lack such foresight about their given choice of means. How often do we pity the imprudent man who should have known that a given choice of means—however noble in and of itself—would be very unlikely to render a given end? For example, a politician who delivers an aggressive and outspoken address to a legislative assembly known to hold an alternative view should not be surprised when the vote is cast against his cause. While some may admire the come-what-may attitude of such a political figure, the more prudent statesman possesses the foresight to know beforehand the likely outcome of a fiery discourse. In this case, the prudent legislator would seek an alternative choice of means—perhaps having recourse to diplomatic or parliamentary procedures—to prevent such a vote in the first place.[104] Foresight, then, remains an indispensable part of prudence that results in sound acting.

One who eschews the place of prudence in the moral life assures unfortunate results when trying to determine how to avoid vicious forms of cooperation. Again, Pieper explains: "Hence, we do not achieve the good by slavishly and literally following certain prescriptions which have been blindly and arbitrarily set forth."[105] Instead, a well-developed prudence is required to enact sound moral action. Seeking the counsel of respected authors in a given field will prove a necessary but insufficient foundation for the execution of a prudent moral choice. The English Dominican Thomas Gilby aptly infers:

102. See *Summa theologiae*, IIa–IIae, q. 49, a. 6, ad. 1: "Hence it is that the very name of prudence is taken from foresight as from its principal part."

103. *Summa theologiae*, IIa–IIae, q. 49, a. 6.

104. In the modern period, several ecclesial figures have been recognized for their prudence in matters of Church and state. One thinks, for example, of the work of Cardinal Ercole Consalvi and Cardinal Rafael Merry del Val. Interested readers should consult John Martin Robinson, *Cardinal Consalvi: 1757–1824* (New York: St. Martin's Press, 1987); and Bernetta M. Quinn, *Give Me Souls: A Life of Raphael Cardinal Merry del Val* (Westminster, MD: Newman Press, 1958) for detailed descriptions of their prudence in action. The Church's Magisterium has offered guidance on the participation of Catholics in political life. See the Congregation for the Doctrine of the Faith, *Doctrinal Note on some questions regarding The Participation of Catholics in Political Life*, November 22, 2002. See also the apostolic exhortation concerning the role of the lay faithful in the Church and the world, Pope John Paul II, *Christifideles laici*, December 30, 1988.

105. Pieper, *The Four Cardinal Virtues*, 24.

Yet, it is well to recognize that casuistry alone will never quite meet a given case, that it is more a directive art than an explicative science, a method of giving advice not of issuing edicts, and that it may be pragmatically justified so long as it is not used to shelve personal responsibility and leave one's own thinking to another, in other words, as a substitute for the virtue of prudence.[106]

No one should conflate the consultation of reliable authorities in moral theology with the execution of a prudent moral choice. One challenge presented by much of the casuist tradition is that the guidance of moral manuals remains necessarily in the abstract. The case studies of a manual of moral theology can never capture the intricacies of an actual situation. Only prudence grasps the particularity of a concrete moral dilemma. Josef Pieper explains:

The statements of moral theology, including those of casuistry, necessarily remain general. They can never take hold of a real and whole "here and now" for the reason that only the person really engaged in the decision experiences (or at least *can* experience) the concrete situation with its need for concrete action. He alone.[107]

No one should fear needlessly that such a robust account of prudence will lead to relativism in the moral life. In fact, quite the contrary obtains. A person who executes a genuinely prudent action can never contravene right reason. A prudent choice can never be for a *malum in se*, or in other words, for an intrinsically evil act.[108] Far from avoiding the specification of moral objects, virtue-based moral theology remains in possession of the necessary tools for such an analysis. Theologians who rely on virtue in making moral judgments insert themselves squarely in the Thomist tradition ready to analyze rigorously the nature of moral objects. In the area of moral cooperation with evil, the choice of some moral objects will never

---

106. Thomas Gilby, OP, "Prudence and Casuistry," appendix 2 of vol. 36 of the Blackfriars *Summa Theologiae* (New York: McGraw-Hill, 1974), 178.

107. Pieper, *The Four Cardinal Virtues*, 28. Emphasis in original.

108. For an extended reflection on what, following St. Thomas, he calls counterfeit prudence, see Cessario, OP, *The Virtues, or the Examined Life*, 120–22. On page 121 Cessario explains: "For prudence can also appear in false guises. This happens either when a person develops prudence-like qualities in order to achieve an end that does not conduce to true happiness (for instance, when one makes bodily comfort an ultimate goal), or when a person wittingly adopts improper means in order to achieve a good goal. Because persons with uncontrolled wants easily substitute their own providence for the guidance that reflects the eternal law, the tradition names avarice as the capital vice responsible for turning a person away from the designs of divine providence."

conform to the truth about the good of the human person.[109] Direct assistance to an abortion, for example, falls under the category of a *malum in se* or an intrinsically evil act. The choice to commit such an act never conforms to the truth about the good. No doubt, some authors hold an alternative view. Bernhard Häring, for example, permits a form of cooperation in the procurement of an abortion. His view seems impossible to reconcile with both right reason and ecclesial discipline.[110]

Following Aristotle, St. Thomas Aquinas holds that prudence "regards contingent matters of action."[111] For that reason, St. Thomas explains: "a man can be directed, not by those things that are simply and necessarily true, but by those which occur in the majority of cases."[112] All that is to say, the prudent man cannot rely on ready-made solutions alone to every moral problem. The particularity and contingency of human life demand a prudence ready to act—and indeed ready to command to act—without extended recourse to extrinsic solutions. In the area of moral cooperation with evil, other than the choice for a *malum per se*, which may never be the object of a moral choice, the challenge of what to do here and now often perplexes the would-be cooperator. A great many cases of cooperation do not admit of easy solutions. Only one with a well-developed prudence will be prepared to face such moral challenges.

The Thomist tradition acknowledges that the proper exercise of prudence requires the presence of rectified appetites.[113] Indeed, the habitual execution of sound moral action requires sense appetites ordered by right reason. Alternatively, voluntarist moral theories tend to neglect the perennial wisdom of this insight.[114] To varying degrees voluntarists have ignored the importance of rightly ordered appetites for the regular exe-

---

109. See *VS*, no. 63.

110. See Bernhard Häring, CSsR, *The Law of Christ*, trans. Edwin G. Kaiser (Westminster, MD: Newman Press, 1961), 505. For the alternative view, rejecting direct assistance in an abortion, see Pope John Paul II, *EV*, no. 74; and the 1983 *Code of Canon Law*, CIC 1329 and CIC 1398.

111. *Summa theologiae*, IIa–IIae, q. 49, a. 1.

112. *Summa theologiae*, IIa–IIae, q. 49, a. 1.

113. See, for example, *Summa theologiae*, Ia–IIae, q. 59, a. 5; and *Summa theologiae*, IIa–IIae, q. 45, a. 2.

114. Thomas M. Osborne, Jr. observes: "Scotus differs from Thomas by stating that prudence is like technical skill insofar as it has distinct and separable species. According to Scotus, prudence is one as a genus, but the absence of one of its species does not affect the other species." See his *Human Action in Thomas Aquinas, John Duns Scotus and William of Ockham*, 83–84.

cution of good acts. In a similar vein, figures in the Franciscan tradition by and large have denied the existence of infused moral virtues.[115] On this matter, however, the Thomistic tradition offers clarity: "Pleasure and sadness, and likewise a spirit of warfare, are corruptive of the principle of prudence, as is clear from Book VI of the Ethics. But these belong to appetite. Therefore prudence depends on appetite."[116]

In order to reach a sound moral choice regarding possible cooperation with evil, rectified sense appetites prove indispensable. One who loves the good and is willing to suffer for it stands ready to eschew immoral forms of cooperation. Loving the truth about human sexuality prepares one to refuse cooperation in the sale or distribution of contraception. Sense appetites given over to lust, however, make one a much less likely martyr for the truth about human love. An educator habitually given over to cutting pedagogical corners will not likely perceive the educational harm in permitting students to present themselves in a manner contrary to their biological sex.[117] Only in mythology could man habitually commit dry acts of the will. No one routinely will command himself to behave in ways that he in no way desires. Instead, virtuous moral action requires rightly ordered appetites.[118] The desire for the right amount of food and drink, for example, are necessary for the habitual eating and drinking in the proper measure.

A sound account of connaturality constitutes an indispensable piece of our efforts to understand the development of virtuous cooperation.[119]

115. For the differences between Aquinas and Bonaventure on this matter, see Cessario, OP, *Introduction to Moral Theology*, 194.

116. Thomas de Vio Cajetan, *Commentary on Summa Theologiae 1a–2ae, q. 58, a. 5, Sancti Thomae de Aquino Opera omnia*, Leonine edition, vol. 6 (Rome, 1882), 377.

117. A more complete virtue-based treatment of these issues of cooperation can be found in chapter five of the present work.

118. For an outstanding treatment of the role of the passions in the moral life, see Paul Gondreau, "The Passions and the Moral Life: Appreciating the Originality of Aquinas," *The Thomist* 71 (2007): 419–50. Gondreau observes: "In practical terms, this means the more virtuous a person becomes, the more he can trust his emotional reactions to persons and events around him, and the less he will struggle with his lower animal-like impulses. There is a greater likelihood that his emotions will incline him to what is morally good for him" (450).

119. For an extended treatment of the issue of connaturality, see the excellent essay by Antonio Moreno, OP, "The Nature of St. Thomas' Knowledge 'Per Connaturalitatem,'" *Angelicum* 47 (1970): 44–62. For a more extended treatment of the issue, see Craig Steven Titus, *The Development of Virtue and "Connaturality" in Thomas Aquinas' Works* (STL thesis, University of Fribourg, 1990). Titus incorporates many insights from this earlier

Aquinas explains that connaturality allows the virtuous man to know the right manner of acting in a given case, without strained efforts to impose extrinsic or ready-made rules. St. Thomas teaches: "Now rectitude of judgment is twofold: first, on account of perfect use of reason, secondly, on account of a certain connaturality with the matter about which one has to judge."[120] Connaturality does not provide a vague sense of what one ought to do, but represents a true source of moral knowledge.[121] The importance of connaturality in virtue-based moral theory follows from the attention Aquinas gives to rectitude of appetite in his moral treatise. For St. Thomas, the appetites do not constitute forces merely to be controlled but instead over time, and even more so under the influence of grace, can become rightly-ordered sources of moral knowledge. In the order of grace, the infused moral virtues enter precisely into the appetites. For Aquinas and the Thomist tradition, the sense appetites themselves become fonts of moral wisdom.

The English Dominican and celebrated editor of the Blackfriars edition of the *Summa theologiae* Thomas Gilby highlights the importance of connaturality for the exercise of the moral life. He explains: "The knowledge which results [from love] is called a sympathy, a *connaturalitas* or *compassio* ... love can enter into the very constitution of knowledge."[122] One develops this connaturality through prudent acting, for example, prudent moral cooperation. One fears the possibility that knowledge by connatu-

---

work in his *Resilience and the Virtue of Fortitude: Aquinas in Dialogue with the Psychological Sciences* (Washington, DC: The Catholic University of America Press, 2006).

120. *Summa theologiae*, IIa–IIae, q. 45, a. 2. This passage is cited explicitly in *Veritatis splendor*, no. 64: "Knowledge of God's law in general is certainly necessary, but it is not sufficient: what is essential is a sort of 'connaturality' between man and the true good. Such a connaturality is rooted in and develops through the virtuous attitudes of the individual himself: prudence and the other cardinal virtues." Footnote no. 110 provides a reference to St. Thomas Aquinas, *Summa theologiae*, IIa–IIae, q. 45, a. 2.

121. For an insightful treatment of the precise nature of moral knowledge by connaturality, see Jacques Maritain, *The Range of Reason* (New York: Charles Scribner's Sons, 1952), especially 22–29. For a positive appraisal of Maritain's contribution, see Donald F. Haggerty, *Jacques Maritain and the Notion of Connaturality: The Valid Role of Nonconceptual Moral Knowledge in the Existential Order* (Rome: Pontificia Universitas Lateranensis Accademia Alphonsiana, 1995).

122. Thomas Gilby, OP, *Between Community and Society* (London: Longmans, Green and Co., 1953), 182. For a comprehensive treatment of the interrelationship between knowledge and love in Aquinas's moral thought, see Michael S. Sherwin, OP, *By Knowledge and by Love: Charity and Knowledge in the Moral Theology of St. Thomas Aquinas* (Washington, DC: The Catholic University of America Press, 2011).

rality could remain underdeveloped in those who utilize theories of analyzing moral cooperation which do not pay sufficient attention to the nature of the acting itself. Those who rely on the extrinsic categories of proximity to another's evil action will struggle to develop a connaturality toward virtuous cooperation.[123]

Justice

When addressing questions of cooperation with evil, modern moralists have not always examined adequately the obligations of the virtue of justice. Because theologians of the casuist period most often treated cooperation with evil as a subspecies of scandal, these authors understood sins of cooperation as violations of the virtue of charity.[124] For example, in the celebrated case of the servant and the ladder, most manualist theologians argued that the servant's cooperation represented unjust collaboration with his master. They opined that the servant—under the obligations of charity—should attempt to prevent the master's sin. Since casuist authors considered the case under the matrix of scandal (a sin against charity), the whole matter would unfold with reference to the charity the servant owed the master. Unfortunately, concern for the woman whom the master intended to violate appears absent from their treatment. Their analysis would benefit from a deeper penetration of the virtue of justice.[125] In the case of the servant and the ladder, in justice what is due the woman?[126] This case offers just one example of why a virtue-based

123. Pope John Paul II refers also to knowledge by connaturality in his 1998 encyclical on faith and reason. See *Fides et ratio*, no. 44: "From the first pages of his *Summa Theologiae*, Aquinas was keen to show the primacy of the wisdom which is the gift of the Holy Spirit and which opens the way to a knowledge of divine realities. His theology allows us to understand what is distinctive of wisdom in its close link with faith and knowledge of the divine. This wisdom comes to know by way of connaturality; it presupposes faith and eventually formulates its right judgement on the basis of the truth of faith itself."

124. See, for example, Aloysius Sabetti, *Compendium Theologiae Moralis* (New York: Frederick Pustet Co., 1931), §194–99; Thomas Slater, SJ, *A Manual of Moral Theology for English Speaking Countries*, vol. 1 (New York, Benziger Brothers, 1925), Bk. V, Ch. VII, §1–2; John A. McHugh, OP, and Charles J. Callan, OP, *Moral Theology: A Complete Course*, vol. 1 (New York: Joseph F. Wagner, Inc., 1929), §1506–46.

125. For an extended treatment of the virtue of justice, see Romanus Cessario, OP, *The Virtues, or the Examined Life*, 127–56.

126. Andrew McLean Cummings shares this perspective. He observes: "The concern ignored by the holy doctor is that a servant, by helping his master commit this

treatment of cooperation with evil requires a robust account of the place of justice in the moral life.

When St. Thomas defines the virtue of justice, he adopts the definition of Justinian. Justice is "the perpetual and constant will to render to each one his right."[127] Aquinas elaborates further as he describes justice as "a habit whereby a man renders to each one his due by a constant and perpetual will."[128] Aquinas explains that this definition corresponds to that of Aristotle: "justice is a habit whereby a man is said to be capable of doing just actions in accordance with his choice."[129] The virtue of justice occupies a crucial place in a sound analysis of cooperation since cooperative acts either aid another or participate in the action of another. Due to its quality as relating to another—*ad alterum*—the virtue of justice governs the morality of cooperative acts. St. Thomas explains "justice is concerned only about our dealings with others."[130] The virtue of justice governs relations between individuals in an effort to obtain some equality between them.[131] Virtuous participation related to issues of moral cooperation aims to ensure this equality is not violated.[132] Justice then proves crucial in our analysis of cooperation with evil.

Moral agents must possess the virtue of justice to navigate the complexities of relations between individuals and families and families and society.[133] Contemporary questions of cooperation with evil most often concern issues of either marriage and family or relations between individuals and states. Debates surrounding cooperation with evil frequently involve the essentially procreative nature of human sexuality, the payment of taxes, voting for political candidates who oppose aspects of the

---

crime, risks violating not a positive commandment to 'help thy neighbor' but the negative commandment, 'do not rape.'" See Cummings, *The Servant and the Ladder*, 69.

127. *Summa theologiae*, IIa–IIae, q. 58, a. 1.

128. *Summa theologiae*, IIa–IIae, q. 58, a. 1.

129. *Summa theologiae*, IIa–IIae, q. 58, a. 1.

130. *Summa theologiae*, IIa–IIae, q. 58, a. 2.

131. See *Summa theologiae*, IIa–IIae, q. 57, a. 1: "It is proper to justice, as compared with the other virtues, to direct man in his relations with others: because it denotes a kind of equality, as its very name implies; indeed we are wont to say that things are adjusted when they are made equal, for equality is in reference of one thing to some other."

132. For an extended reflection on justice as aiming at some equality, see Jean Porter, *Justice as a Virtue: A Thomistic Perspective* (Grand Rapids, MI: Eerdmans, 2016), 116–46.

133. For an extended treatment of this aspect of the virtue of justice, see Cessario, OP, *The Virtues, or the Examined Life*, 136–37. See also Jean Porter, *Justice as a Virtue: A Thomistic Perspective*. For a highly readable account, see Pieper, *The Four Cardinal Virtues*, 43–113.

common good, and legislative mandates against the dignity of the human person. Aquinas teaches that "all the precepts of the Decalogue pertain to justice."[134] The precepts of justice govern relations between individuals and groups, and, *mutatis mutandis*, between individuals and God.[135] Moral theologians employ profitably the precepts of the Decalogue when analyzing issues of moral cooperation. Collaboration with false worship, offenses against the dignity of human life, violations of the sanctity of marriage, all occupy the attention of moralists concerned with cooperation with evil. Indeed, moral cooperation with evil largely falls under the virtue of justice. Readers will recall that the Belgian Dominican Benoît-Henri Merkelbach treated cooperation with evil as a sin against justice.[136] This classification represented a departure from its customary treatment during the casuist period as a sin against charity.

As part of his treatise on justice, Aquinas identifies the virtue of *epikeia* as a potential part of justice.[137] *Epikeia* will occupy an important place in establishing a virtue-based approach to moral cooperation.[138] Perplexed moral actors require this capacity to recognize and adjust to particular instances when a positive law does not obtain. Theologians refer to this capacity as the virtue of *epikeia*. As one author observes, a person possessed of the virtue of *epikeia* "is well supplied with the inner resources with which to act rightly even without the guidance afforded by the letter of the law."[139] Only positive human or ecclesiastical law can be subject to *epikeia*.[140] In no

---

134. *Summa theologiae*, IIa–IIae, q. 122, a. 1.

135. For a reflection on the formation of virtuous and harmonious relations between individuals and between individuals and states, see Pope John Paul II, *Sollicitudo rei socialis*, especially nos. 38–39. In this regard, see also the important social encyclical of Pope John Paul II, *Centesimus annus*.

136. See Benoît-Henri Merkelbach, *Summa Theologiae Moralis ad mentem D. Thomae et ad normam juris novi*, vol. 2 (Bruges: Desclée de Brouwer, 1956), §309–19.

137. See *Summa theologiae*, IIa–IIae, q. 120, a. 2.

138. For a comprehensive treatment of *epikeia* and its use in moral theology, see Lawrence Joseph Riley, *The History, Nature and Use of Epikeia in Moral Theology* (Washington, DC: The Catholic University of America Press, 1948).

139. See Romanus Cessario, OP, "Epieikeia and the Accomplishment of the Just," in *Aquinas and Empowerment: Classical Ethics for Ordinary Lives*, ed. G. Simon Harak, 170–205 (Washington, DC: Georgetown University Press, 1996), 193.

140. For a reflection on how the virtue of *epikeia* can be misused, see Angel Rodriguez Luño, "Can Epikeia Be Used in the Pastoral Care of the Divorced and Remarried Faithful?" *L'Osservatore Romano*, English edition, 9 February 2000. See also Joseph Ratzinger, "Concerning some objections to the church's teaching on the reception of holy communion by divorced and remarried members of the faithful," in the volume of the

circumstance does the natural law cease to bind.[141] Instead, the principles of the natural law govern human life without exception. On the other hand, those who promulgate positive law cannot account for every instance to which a given law may apply. For that reason, in particular cases, following the law as proscribed may be contrary to justice. For example, when a husband drives to the hospital his pregnant wife while in labor, the virtue of *epikeia* affords him the knowledge to observe safe driving but likely beyond that of the posted speed limit. St. Thomas Aquinas reminds his readers that should a madman come to collect his sword from a depository, a just man—by reason of *epikeia*—would refuse him.[142] The dictates of justice specified in the seventh commandment do not mean that a madman should receive a weapon. Certain individuals scrupulous in observing laws as proscribed would benefit from the knowledge that a virtue exists to ensure that in no instance does the keeping of the positive law contradict the mind of the lawgiver.

The virtue of *epikeia* can be employed profitably within St. Thomas's realist moral philosophy. As T. C. O'Brien observes: "St. Thomas's theology approaches every moral situation as it presents itself to the man of virtue; the problematic is the placing of a virtuous act, not of avoiding sin or evading the extrinsic strictures of law."[143] Aquinas affirms the

---

Congregation for the Doctrine of the Faith, "Documenti e Studi", vol. 17, *On the Pastoral Care of the Divorced and Remarried* (Vatican City: Libreria Editrice Vaticana, 1998), 20–29. Ratzinger observes: *"Epikeia* and *aequitas canonica* exist in the sphere of human and purely ecclesiastical norms of great significance, but cannot be applied to those norms over which the Church has no discretionary authority. The indissoluble nature of marriage is one of these norms which goes back to Christ Himself and is thus identified as a norm of divine law. The Church cannot sanction pastoral practices—for example, sacramental pastoral practices—which contradict the clear instruction of the Lord."

141. See Cessario, OP, "Epieikeia and the Accomplishment of the Just," 170–205.

142. See *Summa theologiae*, IIa–IIae, q. 120, a. 1. Aquinas teaches: "Thus the law requires deposits to be restored, because in the majority of cases this is just. Yet it happens sometimes to be injurious—for instance, if a madman were to put his sword in deposit, and demand its delivery while in a state of madness, or if a man were to seek the return of his deposit in order to fight against his country. On these and like cases it is bad to follow the law, and it is good to set aside the letter of the law and to follow the dictates of justice and the common good. This is the object of 'epikeia' which we call equity. Therefore it is evident that 'epikeia' is a virtue."

143. T. C. O'Brien, *Virtues of Justice in the Human Community*, appendix 2: "Epieikeia," vol. 41 of the Blackfriars *Summa Theologiae* (New York: McGraw-Hill Book Company, 1972), 323.

existence of exceptionless moral norms.[144] Particular circumstances cannot alter the dictates of justice.[145] However, individual cases may require examination of whether or not a given case is in fact an instance bound by an exceptionless moral norm.[146] Those seeking a virtue-based response to challenging issues of moral cooperation profitably call upon the virtue of *epikeia*. This virtue proves useful when facing the requirements of civil law. We can envision cases in which the civil law does not account for the particularities of today's secular proclivities. While in certain cases a civil law may contradict the natural moral law—such as a requirement to fund abortion—one can envision a civil requirement which in principle enshrined a just standard but in a particular case should not be followed. Travelling faster than the posted speed limit under some grave circumstance serves as the standard example. Authors of the Thomist tradition refer to infused justice as the virtue which ensures the due owed both to God and the Church.[147] When addressing matters of moral cooperation, Christians worry about the possibility of scandal by their collaboration with immoral activity. Infused justice helps believers to render due regard for the Church and the purity of her moral teaching. That is to say, only

144. For a review of Aquinas as an interpreter of Aristotle, see Jeffrey Hause, "Aquinas on Aristotelian justice: defender, destroyer, subverter, or surveyor?" in *Aquinas and the Nicomachean Ethics*, ed. Tobias Hoffmann, Jörn Müller, and Matthias Perkams, 146–64 (Cambridge: Cambridge University Press, 2013). For an insightful examination of the place of exceptionless moral norms in Aquinas's commentary on the *Nicomachean Ethics*, see Christopher Kaczor, "Exceptionless Norms in Aristotle?: Thomas Aquinas and Twentieth-Century Interpreters of the *Nicomachean Ethics*," *The Thomist* 61 (1997): 33–62. For a careful review of Aquinas's treatment of exceptionless moral norms, see Kevin L. Flannery, SJ, and Thomas V. Berg, "*Amoris Laetitia*, Pastoral Discernment, and Thomas Aquinas," *Nova et Vetera*, English edition, 16 (2018): 81–111.

145. For further reflection on the precepts of justice, see Jean Porter, *Justice as a Virtue: A Thomistic Perspective*, 172–73.

146. The literature regarding the existence of moral absolutes is vast. See, for example, John Finnis, *Moral Absolutes: Tradition, Revision, and Truth* (Washington, DC: The Catholic University of America Press, 1991); William E. May, *Moral Absolutes: Catholic Tradition, Current Trends, and the Truth* (Milwaukee: Marquette University Press, 1989); Martin Rhonheimer, "Intrinsically Evil Acts and the Moral Viewpoint: Clarifying a Central Teaching of *Veritatis Splendor*," in *Veritatis Splendor and the Renewal of Moral Theology*, 161–93; and Romanus Cessario, OP, "Moral Absolutes in the Civilization of Love," in *Veritatis Splendor and the Renewal of Moral Theology*, 195–208.

147. For an outstanding treatment of infused justice according to St. Thomas Aquinas, see Markus Christoph, SJM, *Justice as an Infused Virtue in the Secunda Secundae and Its Implications for Our Understating of the Moral Life* (Doctoral dissertation, University of Fribourg, 2011).

infused justice given in grace and aided by the gift of piety can ensure that a believer will grasp what is truly due to God and His Church.

Fortitude

While prudence ensures that the intellect is capable of making sound moral decisions and justice habituates one to give to others their due, the proper exercise of these virtues requires the presence of the cardinal virtues of fortitude and temperance. St. Thomas affirms the connection of the virtues when he explains that the full exercise of each virtue requires the presence of the other virtues.[148] Fortitude and temperance support the proper exercise of prudence and justice. The virtue of fortitude orders the irascible appetite whereas temperance deals with its concupiscible counterpart.[149] Both virtues are needed to draw the emotions into right reason to achieve sound moral acting. Romanus Cessario observes: "Unruly emotions pose the most serious threat to maintaining a watchful prudence."[150] Only pure mythology would envision that the mere knowledge of ready-made solutions to complex moral problems would produce the full flourishing of the moral life. Instead, only the presence of all the moral virtues can promise sound moral action.

Thomists recognize that fortitude proves necessary for virtuous acting in the area of moral cooperation with evil. Given the difficult situations which abound in the contemporary cultural context it is no wonder that there will be a special need for courageous acting. In a particular way, in the area of moral cooperation, from government mandates to act unjustly or grave economic and cultural pressure to assist in threats to the dignity of human life or offenses against chastity, there will be a need to exercise fortitude to act well under such conditions. The need for fortitude to act well in situations of moral cooperation with evil recalls a lacuna in the casuist approach to moral cooperation. As Servais Pinckaers has observed, fortitude occupied an important place in moral theology of the

---

148. See *Summa theologiae*, Ia–IIae, q. 65, a. 1: "But the perfect moral virtue is a habit that inclines us to do a good deed well; and if we take moral virtues in this way, we must say that they are connected."

149. For the relation of fortitude to the irascible appetite, see *Summa theologiae*, IIa-IIae, q. 123, a. 4: "Fortitude is a virtue of the irascible faculty." For the relation of temperance to the concupiscible appetite, see *Summa theologiae*, IIa–IIae, q. 141, a. 3, ad. 1.

150. See Cessario, OP, *The Virtues, or the Examined Life*, 162.

patristic and medieval period.[151] Casuist authors, however, who organized their manuals around the commandments instead of the virtues, most often failed to provide an extensive treatment of the place of the virtue of fortitude in the moral life.[152]

In his treatise on fortitude Aquinas identifies martyrdom as the virtue's supreme act of perfection.[153] Pope John Paul II concludes his encyclical *Veritatis splendor* with an extended reflection on martyrdom.[154] The martyrs represent the supreme witness to the truth of the moral law.[155] The connection of martyrdom to courage on the battlefield more generally has been the subject of scholarly inquiry.[156] If battlefield courage and martyrdom share a kind of continuity, it suggests that courage in small things will prepare for courage needed in more difficult affairs.[157]

151. See Pinckaers, OP, *The Sources of Christian Ethics*, especially 24–27 and 178–81.

152. See, for example, the moral manual of Heribert Jone, OFM Cap. The only reference to fortitude in the entire manual is when he lists the four cardinal virtues. See Heribert Jone, OFM Cap., *Moral Theology*, §112.

153. See *Summa theologiae*, IIa–IIae, q. 124, a. 3: "And from this point of view it is clear that martyrdom is the most perfect of human acts in respect of its genus, as being the sign of the greatest charity, according to John 15:13: 'Greater love than this no man hath, that a man lay down his life for his friends.'"

154. See the section entitled "Martyrdom, the exaltation of the inviolable holiness of God's law," *Veritatis splendor*, nos. 90–94.

155. See *Veritatis splendor*, no. 93: "Although martyrdom represents the high point of the witness to moral truth, and one to which relatively few people are called, there is nonetheless a consistent witness which all Christians must daily be ready to make, even at the cost of suffering and grave sacrifice. Indeed, faced with the many difficulties which fidelity to the moral order can demand, even in the most ordinary circumstances, the Christian is called, with the grace of God invoked in prayer, to a sometimes heroic commitment. In this he or she is sustained by the virtue of fortitude, whereby—as Gregory the Great teaches—one can actually 'love the difficulties of this world for the sake of eternal rewards.'"

156. For a treatment of battlefield courage and martyrdom as the principal acts of acquired and infused fortitude respectively, see Gregory M. Reichberg, "Aquinas on Battlefield Courage," *The Thomist* 74 (2010): 337–68. For a more complete treatment of Aquinas's teaching on martyrdom, see Patrick M. Clark, *Perfection in Death: The Christological Dimension of Courage in Aquinas* (Washington, DC: The Catholic University of America Press, 2015), especially 181–244.

157. Reichberg maintains: "[Aquinas] is not thereby affirming that every death in a just war would count as martyrdom, nor that the battlefield is a typical setting for martyrdom, but only how, on his understanding, there exists sufficient commonality between the two sorts of death—the soldier's and the martyr's—that the same virtue can be predicated of each without equivocation." See Gregory M. Reichberg, "Aquinas on Battlefield Courage," *The Thomist* 74 (2010): 339n7.

This seemingly obvious point apparent to anyone familiar with the principles of virtue-ethics nonetheless offers sage counsel for those considering matters of moral cooperation. A small accommodation in one area only makes resisting a further unjust accommodation elsewhere more difficult. Fortitude plays an important role in the area of moral cooperation because it concerns primarily the ability to endure difficulties. Following Aristotle, Aquinas holds that the chief activity of courage is not attacking but enduring.[158] Aquinas affirms that it is a greater challenge "to allay fear than to moderate daring, since the danger which is the object of daring and fear, tends by its very nature to check daring, but to increase fear."[159] Twenty-first-century believers need fortitude to overcome the fear of offending secular sensibilities.

The cardinal virtue of fortitude differs from the false courage of the foolhardy. The courageous person does not seek danger for its own sake. Instead, one possessed of fortitude seeks the good and is willing to overcome dangers to achieve it.[160] However, the virtue of fortitude does not induce courageous persons to seek dangers. Rather, fortitude allows them to strive for the good despite the presence of difficulties. This distinction proves helpful in matters of moral cooperation with evil. Virtuous persons do not seek dangers or conflicts for their own sake. Rather, they remain willing to pursue the good despite challenges.[161] Virtuous individuals would rather avoid public confrontations that could be costly to their businesses or reputations in the community. At the same time, they are prepared and willing to suffer these challenges when necessary to avoid immoral cooperation with evil.

The foolhardy offer an alternative to this account of true courage. Foolhardy persons seek dangers and difficulties for their own sake. While believers should avoid unjust collaboration with evil, they should seek ways to remain engaged in the community and in their respective businesses.

---

158. See *Summa theologiae*, IIa–IIae, q. 123, a. 6.

159. *Summa theologiae*, IIa–IIae, q. 123, a. 6.

160. For more detail on this matter, see Pieper, *The Four Cardinal Virtues*, 122–23. See also Clark, *Perfection in Death: The Christological Dimension of Courage in Aquinas*, especially 146–80.

161. Josef Pieper aptly observes: "The virtue of fortitude has nothing to do with a purely vital, blind, exuberant, daredevil spirit.... The man who recklessly and indiscriminately courts any kind of danger is not for that reason brave; all he proves is that, without preliminary examination or distinction, he considers all manner of things more valuable than the personal intactness of which he risks for their sake." See Pieper, *The Four Cardinal Virtues*, 124.

The courageous do not seek dangers—economic, political, or otherwise. Rather, they consent to undergo them to pursue a good. Those who lack the virtuous mean of fortitude fail in either of two extremes. Some cower in the face of danger while others seek dangers for their own sake. Aquinas assigns the vice of daring to this latter group.[162] In questions of moral cooperation, the relevant capacity of the virtuous cooperator is not so much his willingness to attack those who seek his unjust collaboration. Instead, the virtuous cooperator stands possessed of the capacity to endure the difficulties which follow the refusal to cooperate immorally. For that reason, fortitude proves indispensable in discovering and embodying virtuous cooperation in the world today.[163] Absent a well-developed fortitude, discussion of moral cooperation with evil easily dissipates into a merely intellectual exercise of either casuistic justification for one's actions or theoretical refusals to collaborate that do not come to fruition in a virtuous moral choice. The truly courageous person does not hesitate to accept whatever difficulties result from refusing to cooperate with evil.

Temperance

Casuist treatments of moral cooperation with evil routinely neglect to examine the role of the virtue of temperance in ensuring sound moral action. This lacuna proves unfortunate since absent a well-developed temperance few moral agents will be able to avoid unjust collaboration with evil.[164] A basic principle of virtue-based moral analysis lies in the intimate connection between the virtues.[165] Since sometimes a just or temperate act can be arduous, a moral agent requires a full measure of fortitude to complete such an act. In a similar fashion, one given over to intemperate sense

---

162. See *Summa theologiae*, IIa–IIae, q. 127, a. 2.

163. For an excellent summary of the virtue of fortitude and the related virtues of magnanimity, generosity, and patience, see Ashley, OP, *Living the Truth in Love: A Biblical Approach Introduction to Moral Theology*, 247–68.

164. For an extended treatment of the virtue of temperance, see Cessario, OP, *The Virtues, or the Examined Life*, 177–97; as well as Pieper, *The Four Cardinal Virtues*, 145–206.

165. See *Summa theologiae*, Ia–IIae, q. 65, a. 1. For an excellent treatment of the connection between virtues, see Craig Steven Titus, "Moral Development and Connecting the Virtues: Aquinas, Porter, and the Flawed Saint," in *Ressourcement Thomism: Sacred Doctrine, the Sacraments, and the Moral Life*, 330–52. For an outstanding essay on the relationship between the acquired and infused moral virtues, see Michael S. Sherwin, OP, "Infused Virtue and the Effects of Acquired Vice: A Test Case for the Thomistic Theory of Infused Cardinal Virtues," *The Thomist* 73 (2009): 29–52.

pleasure will not be well-suited to avoid collaborations in intemperate activity. In the contemporary context, many issues of cooperation with evil involve matters of temperance, specifically chastity.[166] The admission and education of students who present themselves as transgendered present challenges to schools today.[167] The legal recognition of civil marriage between those of the same sex likewise can pose difficulties for virtuous living in the twenty-first century. The Christian understanding of marriage and family life has witnessed a dramatic transformation in recent decades.[168] All of these factors have led to the quandary of the present moment. Only those with a developed virtue of chastity are likely to eschew unjust collaborations with unchaste relationships.

Just as those who may be required to avoid collaboration with government mandates regarding contraception need a well-developed fortitude, so too will they require a developed temperance.[169] Those given over to unchastity themselves will be unlikely to perceive and adequately access when their cooperative acts sin against chastity. For example, those unwilling to live married life in a faithful and fruitful manner are not well-equipped to oppose a redefinition of marriage to include those of the same sex. Moral and legal arguments against the redefinition of marriage notwithstanding, those committed to heterosexual unchastity cannot long oppose unchastity of other types.[170] While it belongs to the vir-

---

166. St. Thomas identifies chastity as a subjective part of the virtue of temperance. See *Summa theologiae*, IIa–IIae, q. 151, a. 2.

167. For a useful primer on the challenges to religious liberty regarding issues of sexual orientation and gender identity, see John Corvino, Ryan T. Anderson, and Sherif Girgis, *Debating Religious Liberty and Discrimination* (Oxford: Oxford University Press, 2017). Interested readers should also consult Ryan T. Anderson, *When Harry Became Sally: Responding to the Transgender Movement* (New York: Encounter Books, 2018).

168. For an attempt to integrate personalist phenomenology with the requirements of civil and canon law regarding marriage, see Cormac Burke, *The Theology of Marriage: Personalism, Doctrine, and Canon Law* (Washington, DC: The Catholic University of America Press, 2015).

169. For an extended reflection on the challenge of contraceptive mandates, see Marie T. Hilliard, "Contraceptive Mandates and Immoral Cooperation," in *Catholic Health Care Ethics: A Manual for Practitioners*, 2nd ed., ed. Edward J. Furton with Peter J. Cataldo and Albert S. Moraczewski, OP, 275–81 (Philadelphia: The National Catholic Bioethics Center, 2009).

170. For another perspective which allows for a stronger divide between personal sexuality morality and one's ability to recognize the government's role in regulating marriage law, see Sherif Grigis, Ryan T. Anderson, and Robert P. George, *What is Marriage?: Man and Woman: A Defense* (New York: Encounter Books, 2012); Patrick Lee and Robert P.

tue of chastity and the related capacity of continence to moderate sexual
appetite, the subjective parts of the virtue of temperance must moderate
all the sense appetites. Just as abstinence and sobriety which concern food
and drink are parts of temperance, so too temperance must moderate the
desire of the mind for knowledge. Aquinas describes the virtue of *studiositas* or studiousness as a potential part of temperance.[171] He contrasts the
virtue of *studiositas* with the vice of *curiositas*.[172] On this matter, St. Thomas
relies on the teaching of St. Augustine: "We are forbidden to be curious:
and this is a great gift that temperance bestows."[173] While Aquinas treats
acedia, often translated as sloth, as a vice contrary to charity, he renders
curiositas as a sin of intemperance.[174] Nonetheless, the twin vices of *acedia*
and *curiositas* are interrelated.[175] St. Thomas identifies curiosity as a consequence of *acedia*.[176] The mind of the restless individual wanders in curiosity and thus can fail to grasp the truth necessary to confront a moral
dilemma.

To tackle challenging cases of moral cooperation with evil, moral agents
must examine rigorously the quality of their actions. Those who desire to
live virtuously must avoid two extremes in their deliberation. On the one
hand, moral agents must avoid careless activity in which they fail to consider the extended consequences of their cooperative acts. In the twenty-
first century unreflective activity could very likely involve unjust collabo-

---

George, *Conjugal Union: What Marriage Is and Why It Matters* (Cambridge: Cambridge University Press, 2014); and Ryan T. Anderson, *Truth Overruled: The Future of Marriage and Religious
Freedom* (Washington, DC: Regnery Publishing, 2015).

171. See *Summa theologiae*, IIa–IIae, q. 166, a. 1. For a further reflection on the virtue of
studiousness, see Ashley, OP, *Living the Truth in Love: A Biblical Introduction to Moral Theology*, 231–34. For the classic reflection on the virtue of study, see A. G. Sertillanges, OP,
The Intellectual Life: Its Spirit, Conditions, Methods, trans. Mary Ryan (Washington, DC: The
Catholic University of America Press, 1998). Interested readers may also consult James
V. Schall, *The Life of the Mind: On the Joys and Travails of Thinking* (Wilmington, DE: Intercollegiate Studies Institute, 2008).

172. See *Summa theologiae*, IIa–IIae, q. 166 and q. 167.

173. *Summa theologiae*, IIa–IIae, q. 166, a. 2. St. Thomas quotes Augustine's chapter 21 of
De Moribus Ecclesiae Catholicae.

174. For an extended reflection on the vice of *acedia*, see both R. J. Snell, *Acedia and Its
Discontents: Metaphysical Boredom in an Empire of Desire* (Kettering, OH: Angelico Press, 2015);
and Dom Jean-Charles Nault, *The Noonday Devil: Acedia, the Unnamed Evil of Our Times* (San
Francisco: Ignatius Press, 2015).

175. For the connection between *acedia* and *curiositas*, see Pieper, *The Four Cardinal Virtues*, 198–202.

176. See *Summa theologiae*, IIa–IIae, q. 35, a. 4, ad. 3.

ration with evil. At the same time, a moral actor must not be crippled by the thought of how many possible effects flow from his action. The purchase of an ice cream cone could lead one to consider where the money goes from the ice cream proprietor to his own purchases, and from there to sundry other establishments. This extended reflection at the window of an ice cream vendor could leave one crippled in inaction. Only the virtuous mean of *studiositas* will avoid these extremes. The virtuous mean ensures that the perplexed moral actor examines with appropriate rigor the nature of his action and at the same time avoids crippling scrupulosity about its unforeseen consequences.[177]

Virtue-based moral thought identifies two integral parts of temperance. According to the classical exposition, temperance includes both shame or *verecundia* and honesty or *honestas*.[178] Romanus Cessario explains that shame "causes the temperate person to recoil from what is dishonorable and disgraceful."[179] In order to avoid unjust collaboration with evil, a moral agent must possess a certain shame or disgrace at sin. For example, the temperate person will experience shame or disgrace when considering a cooperative act that would aid the procurement of an abortion. In a similar fashion, one possessed of a well-developed temperance would shun displays of unchastity or celebrations aimed at undermining the truth about marriage. Aquinas explains that while the virtuous do not have shame actually, they do possess the capacity for it. Regarding virtuous persons, St. Thomas, following Aristotle, observes "that if there were anything disgraceful in them they would be ashamed of it. Wherefore the Philosopher says (Ethic. iv, 9) that 'shame is in the virtuous hypothetically.'"[180] In

---

177. Germain Grisez offers an alternative perspective. He insists on fastidious consideration of the consequences of some actions which others would deem rigorist. For example, he maintains that one's charitable giving should account for others in need to whom one chooses not to donate. See his *The Way of the Lord Jesus: Difficult Moral Questions*, vol. 3, 436: "For instance, one should not supply a few hungry people with choice and expensive food rather than many with a palatable diet or provide one institution with sumptuous facilities rather than several with serviceable ones."

178. See *Summa theologiae*, IIa–IIae, q. 143, a. 1: "A cardinal virtue may have three kinds of parts, namely integral, subjective, and potential. The integral parts of a virtue are the conditions the concurrence of which are necessary for virtue: and in this respect there are two integral parts of temperance, 'shamefacedness,' whereby one recoils from the disgrace that is contrary to temperance, and 'honesty,' whereby one loves the beauty of temperance."

179. Cessario, OP, *The Virtues, or the Examined Life*, 186.

180. *Summa theologiae*, IIa–IIae, q. 144, a. 4.

the field of moral cooperation with evil no substitute exists for a healthy shame in response to actions which would cooperative with sin. No set of guidelines can replace the proper appetitive response to overt unchastity or other sins of intemperance.

In a related way, one endowed with *honestas* would naturally draw near to the good and beautiful. Pockets of economic and social life which consciously eschew collaboration with vice will draw those possessed of *honestas*. Put simply, temperate persons are drawn to virtuous activity and flee vicious collaboration with evil. The success of projects styled on the so-called "Benedict option" in the United States and around the world can only be explained with reference to *honestas*.[181] Those who possess a well-developed temperance recognize immediately and without the need for extended reflection healthy pockets of social life. Such virtuous persons not only recognize these oases of healthy living but are drawn to them. *Verecundia* and *honestas* play a crucial role in addressing matters of moral cooperation with evil. Twenty-first-century Americans routinely observe violations of the moral law throughout political and economic life. They confront offenses against the dignity of the human person and the procreative nature of human sexuality. Without a perception of the ugliness or shame of these cultural phenomena, no ready-made list of prohibited activities will supply the necessary capacity to eschew immoral cooperation with evil.[182]

181. For one effort to explain how Christians can avoid collaboration in a secular world, see Rod Dreher, *The Benedict Option: A Strategy for Christians in a Post-Christian Nation* (New York: Sentinel, 2017). For an account of one successful effort at contemporary monastic observance, see Francis Bethel, OSB, *John Senior and the Restoration of Realism* (Merrimack, NH: Thomas More College Press, 2016). For a related perspective, see Anthony Esolen, *Out of the Ashes: Rebuilding American Culture* (Washington, DC: Regnery Publishing, 2017). Interested readers may also consult the celebrated texts of John Senior. See his *The Death of Christian Culture* (Norfolk, VA: IHS Press, 2008); and *The Restoration of Christian Culture* (Norfolk, VA: IHS Press, 2008).

182. For a helpful summary of this difficulty, see Romanus Cessario, OP, *The Virtues, or the Examined Life*, 186. Cessario writes: "Unfortunately, since people easily develop a preference for the morally ugly instead of what comprises the morally beautiful, these component elements of temperance easily fall dormant in human consciousness, resulting in a deformed moral conscience. Those who are brazen about vice no longer recognize the difference between the morally aesthetic and the ugly; and such people are said in fact to lack all shame.... In any case, shamelessness, except among the saints, leaves a person liable to making gross misjudgments concerning what is proper and fitting in matters dealing with temperance."

Conclusion

In this chapter we outlined the contours of a virtue-based approach to moral cooperation with evil. This method of moral reasoning, faithful to the teaching of St. Thomas, takes seriously the teleology of the moral act. Unlike schools of moral theology which allow intention to shape moral objects, our approach attends to the natural species of human acts.[183] In order for one to develop the virtues necessary to confront challenges of moral cooperation, one must examine the nature of any proposed action and its *per se* effects. That is, one must possess the prudence to look over one's actions and acknowledge what is likely to result from them.

Each of the four cardinal virtues proves indispensable in meeting the challenge of cooperation with evil. Only those possessed of prudence have the foresight to know something of the results of their actions. Who other than just persons stand willing to render what is due to another? How could one without sufficient fortitude be willing to suffer to avoid immoral cooperation? Only those possessed of a sufficient shame or *verecundia* will flee immoral cooperative acts. That is to say, temperance too will be irreplaceable in order to face the challenges of the twenty-first century. While a full delineation of how the moral and theological virtues as well as the gifts of the Holy Spirit operate extends beyond the scope of the present study of the principles analyzing the nature of moral cooperation with evil, it is sufficient to establish that the approach presented here provides the framework for virtuous—and not merely rule-abiding—moral cooperation.

---

183. See *VS*, no. 78: "The morality of the human act depends primarily and fundamentally on the 'object' rationally chosen by the deliberate will, as is borne out by the insightful analysis, still valid today, made by Saint Thomas."

CHAPTER FIVE

Some Applications to Contemporary Issues of Moral Cooperation

In the present work I propose a method for analyzing questions of moral cooperation grounded in the tradition of St. Thomas Aquinas. After both demonstrating the need for such an approach in chapters one and two and outlining its basic contours in chapters three and four, I hope now to apply this virtue-based method of analysis to contemporary issues of moral cooperation. In the chapter that follows we examine five issues of moral cooperation with evil that are the subject of debate by contemporary moral theologians. We will examine the nature of the moral cooperation involved in the following situations: (1) voting in political elections; (2) paying taxes when some funds will be used for immoral ends; (3) celebrating or participating in same-sex civil marriages; (4) complying with government mandates to fund contraception, sterilization, or abortion; and (5) dealing with challenges in schools regarding those who present themselves as transgendered. In each case, we will present a virtue-based reading of the moral quandary paying particular attention to the method of reasoning we undertake. In each instance, we identify the resources from the virtue tradition which aid those who face these moral challenges.

Voting and choosing: cooperating at the ballot box

Ethical challenges faced by voters in contemporary democracies represent a moral quandary for nearly every adult in most countries throughout the world. Even those who have never heard of the ethical debates surrounding cooperation with evil recognize that their vote in a democratic election plays a role in the unfolding of political life for good or ill.[1] That

---

1. See, for example, the statement of the United States Conference of Catholic Bishops, *Forming Consciences for Faithful Citizenship: A Call to Political Responsibility from the Catholic Bishops of the United States with Introductory Note* (Washington, DC: United States Conference

is to say, voters cooperate to one degree or another with democratically elected officials. Despite this widespread experience, the moral implications of voting in civil elections have received surprisingly limited attention. The noted American moralist William B. Smith suggests the reason for this lacuna. Smith observes: "Manuals of moral theology that predate the Second Vatican Council are not a great help in this question. Those manuals regarded voting as a privilege, which citizens were free to exercise or not. When not seen as a positive duty, there was not much mention of moral obligation."[2] Despite offering extended reflection on the obligations of policemen, domestic servants, tavern proprietors, and artisans, modern moral manuals offer limited counsel regarding participation in political life. Virtue-based moral reasoning can offer a useful contribution to the moral challenges faced by voters.

The ethics of voting in civil elections stands as just one of many challenges at the nexus of church and state.[3] Both legislators and ordinary citizens have responsibilities according to their state in life. The Church's Magisterium has offered guidance on the participation of Catholics in public life.[4] The Church has spoken of the need to exercise one's right to

---

of Catholic Bishops, 2015), and, in particular, no. 34: "Catholics often face difficult choices about how to vote. This is why it is so important to vote according to a well-formed conscience that perceives the proper relationship among moral goods. A Catholic cannot vote for a candidate who favors a policy promoting an intrinsically evil act, such as abortion, euthanasia, assisted suicide, deliberately subjecting workers or the poor to subhuman living conditions, redefining marriage in ways that violate its essential meaning, or racist behavior, if the voter's intent is to support that position. In such cases, a Catholic would be guilty of formal cooperation in grave evil. At the same time, a voter should not use a candidate's opposition to an intrinsic evil to justify indifference or inattentiveness to other important moral issues involving human life and dignity."

2. See William B. Smith, *Modern Moral Problems: Trustworthy Answers to Your Tough Questions*, ed. Donald Haggerty (San Francisco: Ignatius Press, 2012), 269.

3. For an excellent overview of the complexities of relations between church and state, see Russell Hittinger, "Introduction to Modern Catholicism," in *The Teachings of Modern Roman Catholicism: On Law, Politics, and Human Nature*, ed. John Witte Jr. and Frank S. Alexander, 1–38 (New York: Columbia University Press, 2007). For further reflection on Catholic participation in public life, see Charles J. Chaput, *Render unto Caesar: Serving the Nation by Living Our Catholic Beliefs in Political Life* (New York: Doubleday, 2008).

4. See especially the Congregation for the Doctrine of the Faith, *Doctrinal Note on Some Questions Regarding the Participation of Catholics in Political Life*, November 24, 2002. See also the declaration of St. Thomas More as patron saint of statesmen of Pope John Paul II, Apostolic Letter, *Moto Proprio*, Proclaiming Saint Thomas More Patron of Statesmen and Politicians, October 31, 2000.

vote.[5] At various times, Catholics have recognized that particular political movements or parties represent an antithetical position hostile to the exercise of Catholic faith. In the post-World War II period, for example, the Church forbad Catholics from participation in or support for the Communist party.[6] Catholic social thought extends to a variety of issues, including the protection of human life and the public recognition of the sanctity of marriage. In recent years theologians have debated the nuances of Catholic teaching on the use of the death penalty.[7] Other concerns of Catholic social thought include the promotion of a robust economy to safeguard family life, the promotion of peace and security around the world, and the protection of the environment.

While authors of the manualist period did not provide a full treatment of the responsibilities of voters in political elections, some proffered general counsel. Bernhard Häring's *The Law of Christ*, published in 1954, offers a representative treatment of the ethics of voting from the pre-conciliar period.[8] Häring holds that a voter "must choose that group or individual who, everything considered, is the most favorable to faith and morals or is the least hostile."[9] In a similar fashion, he explains that a legislator who votes for legislation "hostile to faith or morals" may do so only to prevent still greater evil. In this case, the legislator "must make very clear that his vote in favor of a bill is not approval of the evil ... but only the choice of the lesser evil."[10]

Many American bishops have addressed the ethical challenges that con-

5. See *CCC*, no. 2240: "Submission to authority and co-responsibility for the common good make it morally obligatory to pay taxes, to exercise the right to vote, and to defend one's country."

6. See DS 3865, Decree of the Holy Office, June 28 (July 1), 1949, *AAS* 41 (1949): 334.

7. For a strong defense of capital punishment according to Catholic moral principles, see Edward Feser and Joseph M. Bessette, *By Man Shall His Blood Be Shed: A Catholic Defense of Capital Punishment* (San Francisco: Ignatius Press, 2017). For an alternative perspective, see E. Christian Brugger, *Capital Punishment and Roman Catholic Moral Tradition* (Notre Dame, IN: University of Notre Dame Press, 2003). Both texts were composed prior to the 2018 Rescript of Pope Francis altering the treatment of the death penalty in the *Catechism*. See the August 2, 2018 Rescript, "New revision of number 2267 of the Catechism of the Catholic Church on the death penalty."

8. For a positive appraisal of Häring's influence on moral theology, see James F. Keenan, SJ, "Bernard Häring's Influence on American Catholic Moral Theology," *Journal of Moral Theology* 1 (2012): 23–42.

9. Bernhard Häring, CSsR, *The Law of Christ*, trans. Edwin G. Kaiser (Westminster, MD: Newman Press, 1961), 514.

10. Häring, 515.

front Catholic voters in contemporary democracies. While some prelates
have restricted their pronouncements to encouraging voters to reflect on
issues of Catholic social doctrine, others have entered into an analysis of
voting as a moral act. For example, John J. Myers, former Archbishop of
Newark, NJ, argued that at least in the contemporary American context
there is no justification to vote for a candidate who supported the right
to abortion.[11] In the United States the 2004 Democrat nominee for President, John Kerry, a professed Catholic, maintained he was personally opposed to abortion. However, Kerry supported virtually unlimited access
to abortion, including the public funding of abortion.[12] Several American
bishops questioned publicly his suitability to receive Holy Communion.[13]
Others raised the question of whether Catholics could vote for the Massa-
chusetts Senator despite his support for abortion rights. In a 2004 letter to
the Archbishop of Washington, DC, Cardinal Joseph Ratzinger, Prefect
of the Congregation for the Doctrine of the Faith, addressed the worthy
reception of Holy Communion. Ratzinger also identified how voting for a
candidate who supported abortion related to the question of cooperation
with evil. Ratzinger explained:

A Catholic would be guilty of formal cooperation in evil, and so unworthy
to present himself for Holy Communion, if he were to deliberately vote for
a candidate precisely because of the candidate's permissive stand on abortion
and/or euthanasia. When a Catholic does not share a candidate's stand in fa-

11. See John J. Myers, "A Voter's Guide: Pro-choice candidates and church teaching," *Wall Street Journal*, September 17, 2004. Myers argues that no issue could justify a
vote for a politician who supported the right to abortion. He writes: "What evil could
be so grave and widespread as to constitute a 'proportionate reason' to support candidates who would preserve and protect the abortion license and even extend it to publicly
funded embryo-killing in our nation's labs? Certainly policies on welfare, national security, the war in Iraq, Social Security or taxes, taken singly or in any combination, do not
provide a proportionate reason to vote for a pro-abortion candidate."

12. For one response to the challenge of Catholic politicians who support access to
abortion, see Smith, *Modern Moral Problems*, 264–66. See also Francis J. Connell, CSsR,
Morals in Politics and Professions: A Guide for Catholics in Public Life (Westminster, MD: The
Newman Bookshop, 1946), 10–22.

13. See, for example, the statement of then-Archbishop Raymond L. Burke, Archbishop of St. Louis: "I would have to admonish him not to present himself for communion.... I might give him a blessing or something.... If his archbishop has told him he
should not present himself for communion, he shouldn't. I agree with Archbishop (Sean
P.) O'Malley (of Boston)," as quoted by Patricia Rice, "Burke Would Refuse Communion to Kerry," *St. Louis Post-Dispatch*, January 30, 2004.

vor of abortion and/or euthanasia, but votes for that candidate for other reasons, it is considered remote material cooperation, which can be permitted in the presence of proportionate reasons.[14]

The Ratzinger letter recognizes the role of the reason why someone chooses to vote for a particular candidate in determining the moral quality of such a vote. If a vote represents an effort to advance an immoral agenda, then casting a ballot in such circumstances stands as a positive effort to bring about an evil end. On the other hand, it is possible that a vote cast even for the same candidate by a different voter for a different reason could represent a good moral act. In this case, the reason for the vote (a desire to limit the harm done and to promote the common good) actually specifies the nature of the moral act. In the same way as cutting open a person's chest by a surgeon may appear to be the same moral act as when done in torture, in fact, they have different formal objects. The reason for the activity (restoration of health on the one hand and vengeance on the other hand) specifies the nature of the act.[15] In the same way, one's sincere desire for his or her vote in a civil election to bring about the common good helps to shape the physical act of pulling a ballot or punching a voting card. A vote cast for a pro-choice candidate because the candidate is pro-choice is a different moral act than a vote cast for him because he is less pro-abortion than his opponent.

In the encyclical *Evangelium vitae* Pope John Paul II instructs the Catholic world about ethical voting.[16] The Pope addressed specifically the obligations of legislators in regard to laws which seek to protect innocent human life.[17] Against those who claimed that a political figure who voted

14. Joseph Cardinal Ratzinger, *Worthiness to Receive Holy Communion*, letter to the Archbishop of Washington, DC, July 2004.

15. For a longer reflection on the nature of the moral act performed by a surgeon, see chapter three above of the present work. For further treatment of natural teleology in the specification of moral objects, see Steven A. Long, "Natural Law, the Moral Object, and *Humanae Vitae*," in *Ressourcement Thomism: Sacred Doctrine, the Sacraments, and the Moral Life*, ed. Reinhard Hütter and Matthew Levering, 285–311 (Washington, DC: The Catholic University of America Press, 2010).

16. For extended commentary on *Evangelium vitae* from a diversity of theological perspectives, see *Choosing Life: A Dialogue on Evangelium Vitae*, ed. Kevin Wm. Wildes, SJ, and Alan C. Mitchell (Washington, DC: Georgetown University Press, 1997). See also an excellent collection of essays from the Pontifical Academy for Life, *Evangelium Vitae: Five Years of Confrontation with the Society*, ed. Juan de Dios Vial Correa and Elio Sgreccia (Città del Vaticano: Libreria Editrice Vaticana, 2001).

17. For an exposition of the moral principles that should guide Catholic politicians,

for a bill that would allow some abortion, while limiting other abortions perhaps in the late term of a pregnancy, committed a moral evil, Pope John Paul II offers clear guidance. He teaches:

When it is not possible to overturn or completely abrogate a pro-abortion law, an elected official, whose absolute personal opposition to procured abortion was well known, could licitly support proposals aimed at limiting the harm done by such a law and at lessening its negative consequences at the level of general opinion and public morality. This does not in fact represent an illicit cooperation with an unjust law, but rather a legitimate and proper attempt to limit its evil aspects.[18]

The case of a political official voting for a so-called "imperfect law" demonstrates the dynamics of the morality of voting.[19] While in this instance we are concerned principally with the responsibilities of citizens in democratic elections, an examination of the duties of legislators proves useful. Indeed, a legislator's vote for a particular piece of legislation represents a real participation in whatever proposals the legislation advances.[20] Catholic legislators recognize the need for the civil law to reflect moral principles as no warrant exists for the adoption of a civil law which promotes injustice.[21] The Pope's charge for one's "personal opposition to

see Anthony Fisher, *Catholic Bioethics for a New Millennium* (Cambridge: Cambridge University Press, 2012), 304–27.

18. *Evangelium vitae*, no. 73. For a review of the reception of *Evangelium vitae*, see John Berkman, "Has the Message of *Evangelium vitae* Been Missed? An Analysis and a Future Direction for Catholic Biomedical Ethics," *The Thomist* 63 (1999): 461–80.

19. For a careful exposition of the challenge Catholics face in supporting so-called "imperfect laws," see Tarcisio Bertone, "Catholics and pluralist society: 'imperfect laws' and the responsibility of legislators," in Pontifical Academy for Life, *Evangelium Vitae: Five Years of Confrontation with the Society*, 206–22. For a thoughtful exchange on the possibility of voting for legislation which limits abortion only partially, see Colin Harte, "Problems of principle in voting for unjust legislation," in *Cooperation, Complicity & Conscience: Problems in healthcare, science, law and public policy*, ed. Helen Watt, 179–208 (London: The Linacre Centre, 2005); John Finnis, "Restricting legalized abortion is not intrinsically evil," in *Cooperation, Complicity & Conscience: Problems in healthcare, science, law and public policy*, 209–45; Colin Harte, "The opening up of a discussion: a response to John Finnis," in *Cooperation, Complicity & Conscience: Problems in healthcare, science, law and public policy*, 246–68; and John Finnis, "'A vote decisive for … a *more* restrictive law,'" in *Cooperation, Complicity & Conscience: Problems in healthcare, science, law and public policy*, 269–95.

20. For further reflection on the type of cooperation involved in the vote cast by a legislator, see Kevin L. Flannery, SJ, *Christian and Moral Action* (Arlington, VA: The Institute for Psychological Sciences, 2012), 50–55.

21. On the requirement of the civil law to respect the moral law, see the Congregation for the Doctrine of the Faith, the Instruction *Donum vitae*, III, "Moral and Civil Law."

procured abortion [to be] well-known" averts the challenge of scandal. Scandal could ensue if one could interpret a legislator's support for a particular bill as evidence that he or she supported some immoral measure in the piece of legislation when in fact the legislator voted for the bill precisely to limit the occurrence of still further evils.[22]

The fundamental question regarding the morality of voting in civil elections is what is the object of the act of voting?[23] In what sort of act is a citizen engaged when he or she casts a ballot? If the candidate for whom one votes is elected, is the teleology of casting a ballot *per se* ordered to every action of the newly elected official?[24] Most basically, when casting a ballot, a voter adds to the number of votes that a particular candidate receives. In some cases, this vote contributes to his or her victory. However, in some cases—in US elections one thinks of certain third-party candidates about whom there is moral certainty they will not be elected—it is more accurate to assert that one's vote contributes to this losing candidate's number of votes. The voter, however, can be morally certain the candidate will not win. He casts his vote for this candidate not so much in hopes of a victory but rather with the hope that the candidate may receive greater name recognition or additional funding for the next election. Put simply, a voter's ballot contributes to the number of votes a candidate receives.

One's vote for a particular candidate is not *per se* ordered to every act an elected official undertakes. The simple fact that one action follows upon

---

22. See *Summa theologiae*, IIa–IIae, q. 43. For commentary on the sin of scandal, see Matthew Levering, *The Betrayal of Charity: The Sins that Sabotage Divine Love* (Waco: Baylor Univesity Press, 2011), 127–42. For an overview of the concept of scandal in the *Catechism of the Catholic Church* and the *Code of Canon Law*, see Patrick Connolly, "The Concept of Scandal in a Changed Ecclesial Context," *Studia Canonica* 51 (2017): 135–48.

23. We recall the teaching of Pope John Paul II in *VS*, no. 78: "The morality of the human act depends primarily and fundamentally on the 'object' rationally chosen by the deliberate will." For an outstanding commentary on this passage, see Stephen L. Brock, "*Veritatis Splendor* §78, St. Thomas, and (Not Merely) Physical Objects of Moral Acts," *Nova et Vetera*, English edition, 6 (2008): 1–62. From a slightly different perspective, interested readers may also consult Martin Rhonheimer, "Intrinsically Evil Acts and the Moral Viewpoint: Clarifying a Central Teaching of *Veritatis Splendor*," in *Veritatis Splendor and the Renewal of Moral Theology*, ed. J. A. DiNoia, OP, and Romanus Cessario, OP, 161–93 (Chicago: Midwest Theological Forum, 1999).

24. Steven A. Long explains that *per se* order refers to what follows a given act according to its natural teleology. He distinguishes correctly the *per se* order from the *per accidens* ordering of human action. See his *The Theological Grammar of the Moral Act*, 2nd ed. (Naples, FL: Sapientia Press, 2015), especially 42–50.

another (i.e., after receiving sufficient votes to be elected, a legislator chooses to cast a vote on a particular bill) does not mean that the subsequent action (the legislator's vote) follows the first action (the citizen's vote for the politician) in a *per se* manner. It does not represent a reconstitution of the object of the act of voting to recall that every action of an elected official does not fall under the object of the act of voting for such an official. The natural teleology of voting for a politician does not include moral responsibility for each and every one of the politician's subsequent actions.[25]

In the 1996 US Presidential election, some committed to the pro-life cause refused to vote for the Republican nominee US Senator Robert Dole. A small number of voters even cast their ballots for the incumbent Democrat and supporter of abortion rights President Bill Clinton. The rationale for such a vote would lie in an effort to show the Republican Party that it needed to nominate a more conservative—and more deeply pro-life—candidate in the next election. In part due to evangelical Christians and some Catholics abstaining from voting altogether or even voting for President Clinton in 1996, this strategy succeeded. It persuaded the Republican Party to nominate a candidate more committed to the pro-life cause in the next election. While this strategy helped to bring about a Clinton victory, one could argue it actually brought about the best long-term result for the pro-life movement. Namely, after four years of a Clinton presidency, a much stronger pro-life President followed.[26] In such a scenario, we are not reconstituting the object of voting. Instead, one may believe that a Clinton victory would, in the long term, most effectively promote the common good and even the pro-life cause.

The above example does not demonstrate that Catholic voters can choose candidates based on any set of criteria. Rather, voters should con-

25. Steven A. Long remains the great exponent of the natural teleology of human action. Long writes: "It follows that natural teleology provides the grammar for the constitution of the species of the moral act, and also for the constitution of the object of the moral act." See Long, *The Theological Grammar of the Moral Act*, 2nd ed., 151.

26. For one account of the consolidation of the Republican Party around pro-life principles and the nomination of pro-life candidates, see Ramesh Ponnuru, *The Party of Death: The Democrats, the Media, the Courts, and the Disregard for Human Life* (Washington, DC: Regnery Publishing, 2006). For a treatment of the 1996 US elections, see Harvey L. Schantz, *Politics in the Era of Divided Government: The Election of 1996 and its Aftermath* (New York: Routledge, 2001). For more information on George Bush's move to the right on the issue of abortion in the 2000 election, see Frank Bruni, "The 2000 Campaign: The Platform, Bush Says He Supports the Party's Strong Anti-Abortion Stand," *New York Times*, January 23, 2000.

sider how best to achieve the common good. An upstanding voter eschews purely personal interest or economic gain for some minority of citizens. Instead, the virtuous voter knows and seeks the good common to all. The Jesuit philosopher Kevin Flannery explains:

The question comes down, in other words, to the moral character of the elector. If he genuinely does make his choice with the common good as his reason for choosing, he is acting prudently and morally. If the common good is not his reason for choosing, then he has acted immorally by giving preference to something other than the common good.[27]

Flannery recalls that Aquinas teaches that respect of persons opposes distributive justice. Justice requires that goods—and by extension votes—go to those most deserving, those to whom they are due. According to Aquinas, one who "respects persons," that is, who chooses to render to someone not according to their merit but based upon a biased judgement or self-interested rationalization, fails to act according to the norms of distributive justice.[28] It is all partially a guess as to what will happen if a particular candidate wins an election. A candidate may assert a pro-life position, but one may reasonably conclude that such a candidate will accomplish nothing regarding the protection of human life. One's vote will give that candidate more votes, generally contributing to his or her victory. While political prudence is not consequentialist, the act of voting engages what one believes the best political outcome to be.[29] This is not reconstituting the object of voting. Instead, this describes accurately the moral object of casting a ballot in a political election.

This example serves to demonstrate how crucial it is for voters to recognize the consequences of their actions without succumbing to consequentialism. St. Thomas Aquinas identifies the virtue of foresight as a quasi-integral part of prudence necessary to complete a sound moral ac-

27. Kevin L. Flannery, SJ, "Voting, Intrinsic Evil, and Commensuration," *The American Journal of Jurisprudence* 60 (2015): 195–96. For a response to Flannery and his convincing rejoinder, see Cathleen Kaveny and Kevin L. Flannery, SJ, "Response and Rejoinder: On Voting, Intrinsic Evil, and Ranking of Political Issues," *The American Journal of Jurisprudence* 61 (2016): 259–73. For the background to this debate, see Cathleen Kaveny, *Law's Virtues: Fostering Autonomy and Solidarity in American Society* (Washington, DC: Georgetown University Press, 2012); and a largely critical review by Kevin L. Flannery, SJ, "Voting Conscience: A Review of *Law's Virtues*," *First Things* (June/July 2015): 54–55.

28. See *Summa theologiae*, IIa–IIae, q. 63, a. 1.

29. For Aquinas's treatment of political prudence, see *Summa theologiae*, IIa–IIae, q. 50, a. 2.

tion.[30] Good consequences cannot justify an evil action.[31] However, the moral quality of some actions depends upon a sound judgment about what such an action will accomplish. In the act of casting a ballot in a political election, voters make a judgment about what will occur should a particular candidate receive more votes. By voting, a citizen hopes to see some end achieved. What is the relationship between what a candidate purports to believe and what he or she may actually accomplish? To what extent will the election of a particular candidate serve the common good? No rule book exists for determining how a candidate will exercise his or her office if elected. Only the virtuous voter knows connaturally the goods of political life and stands ready to seek them promptly and habitually.

Render unto Caesar: paying taxes to fund immoral activities

In December 1985 the daily Vatican bulletin announced that Donald Wuerl, a priest of the Diocese of Pittsburgh, Pennsylvania who had served as secretary to Cardinal John Wright, Prefect of the Congregation for the Clergy in Rome, had been appointed auxiliary bishop of Seattle.[32] The announcement—and the subsequent months of controversy about his nomination—revealed the reasons behind the unusual appointment. Not only had the Pope appointed a priest from across the country as auxiliary bishop of a large archdiocese, but the Pope had given Wuerl special responsibilities to make final decisions regarding a series of issues of pastoral concern. While the principal issues over which the Pope had given then-Bishop Wuerl responsibility concerned the governance of the Diocese on a variety of moral questions, another issue of concern to the

---

30. See *Summa theologiae*, IIa–IIae, q. 49, a. 6.

31. See, for example, *VS*, no. 77: "But the consideration of these consequences, and also of intentions, is not sufficient for judging the moral quality of a concrete choice. The weighing of the goods and evils foreseeable as the consequence of an action is not an adequate method for determining whether the choice of that concrete kind of behavior is 'according to its species,' or 'in itself,' morally good or bad, licit or illicit. The foreseeable consequences are part of those circumstances of the act, which, while capable of lessening the gravity of an evil act, nonetheless cannot alter its moral species."

32. For a history of then-Bishop Wuerl's service in the Archdiocese of Seattle, see Ann Rodgers and Mike Aquilina, *Something More Pastoral: The Mission of Bishop, Archbishop and Cardinal Donald Wuerl* (Pittsburgh: The Lambert Press, 2015) 40–53.

Holy See was the refusal of Seattle Archbishop Raymond Hunthausen to pay federal income taxes. Hunthausen claimed that because money would go toward the creation of nuclear weapons, he could not in conscience pay federal taxes.[33]

For many centuries theologians have tackled the moral issues involved in the levying and payment of taxes. The Pharisees asked our Lord Himself to pronounce on the ethics of the payment of taxes.[34] The Church has recognized consistently the moral duty to pay a justly levied tax. The Second Vatican Council affirmed the need to pay just taxes.[35] More recently, the Church's Magisterium has reiterated the moral obligation of the payment of taxes.[36] The question of the payment of taxes proves useful as an example of moral cooperation with evil, as it helps to identify different approaches to examining moral matters. Employing the casuist categories, the payment of taxes fits neatly in the category of remote material cooperation. The casuist system considers such cooperation licit for nearly any sufficient reason. The legal requirement to pay taxes—or suffer a penalty for refusing to pay them—would suffice easily as a reason to justify this remote material cooperation.[37]

33. For one account of this matter, albeit sympathetic to Hunthausen and not to the Holy See, see John A. McCoy, *A Still Quiet Conscience: The Archbishop Who Challenged a Pope, a President, and a Church* (Maryknoll, NY: Orbis Books, 2015), especially 165–218. On pages 184–85 McCoy cites theologian Peter Chirico's assertion that the refusal to pay taxes was the principal concern of the Holy See: "[Chirico] became convinced that the motivation behind the Vatican investigation—despite Rome's protestations to the contrary—was Hunthausen's stand on unilateral disarmament and his tax resistance. In the minds of many American Catholics withholding taxes to protest nuclear weapons was unpatriotic and tantamount to treason, a crime far worse than heresy."

34. See Matthew 22: 16–22. For an analysis of the Biblical texts which deal with the payment of taxes, see Raymond F. Collins, *Wealth, Wages, and the Wealthy: New Testament Insight for Preachers and Teachers* (Collegeville, MN: Liturgical Press, 2017), 297–99.

35. See the Pastoral Constitution on the Church in the Modern World, *Gaudium et spes*, no. 30: "Many in various places even make light of social laws and precepts, and do not hesitate to resort to various frauds and deceptions in avoiding just taxes or other debts due to society."

36. See *CCC*, no. 2240: "Submission to authority and co-responsibility for the common good make it morally obligatory to pay taxes, to exercise the right to vote, and to defend one's country." See also the *Compendium of the Social Doctrine of the Church*, no. 355: "Public spending is directed to the common good when certain fundamental principles are observed: the payment of taxes as part of the duty of solidarity; a reasonable and fair application of taxes; precision and integrity in administering and distributing public resources." For commentary on the duties of citizens in paying taxes, see Smith, *Modern Moral Problems*, 237–40.

37. For one exposition of the conditions necessary for licit material cooperation, see

In his 1997 manual *Difficult Moral Questions* the American moralist Germain Grisez offers an extended reflection on the morality of paying taxes. Grisez responds to an inquiry of a perplexed man who wonders whether citizens of what they consider to be an unjust government may evade paying income tax.[38] The inquirer is troubled by his government's promotion of abortion, nuclear weapons, and population control. He wonders whether these moral ills justify his evading paying taxes. Grisez holds that tax evasion is illicit. He explains that "prolonged tax evasion is hardly likely to succeed without lying."[39] According to Grisez, lying is always wrong.[40] Grisez also instructs the perplexed on how he might limit his income so as to pay less in taxes. He suggests that if the man "gathered, begged, and produced ...on a small subsistence farm," he would have such a low income as to avoid paying taxes.[41] In the course of these counsels making up his extended reply, Grisez makes no reference to the virtue of justice. The entire exercise unfolds without reference to the cardinal virtue which governs this area of the moral life. Those grounded in the virtue-based tradition, on the other hand, would utilize an alternative method for analyzing the same example. Thomists recognize that the payment of taxes represents an act of the virtue of justice. The Dominican Benedict Ashley organizes his moral text around the theological and moral virtues. He considers the payment of taxes as an act which falls under the virtue of justice.[42] Ashley observes that the payment of taxes

---

John A. McHugh, OP and Charles J. Callan, OP, *Moral Theology: A Complete Course*, vol. 1 (New York: Joseph F. Wagner, Inc., 1958), §1520.

38. Germain Grisez, *Difficult Moral Questions: The Way of the Lord Jesus*, vol. 3, 725–30.

39. Grisez, 727.

40. See Germain Grisez, *Living a Christian Life: The Way of the Lord Jesus*, vol. 2 (Quincy, IL: Franciscan Press, 1993), 405: "Lying and other deception in communication are always wrong."

41. German Grisez, *Difficult Moral Questions: The Way of the Lord Jesus*, vol. 3, 730: "One [way] would be to limit the net income you earn each year to a sum that, with legitimate deductions and exemptions, would fall just below the minimum that is subject to income taxes. Could you subsist on so little income? Perhaps, if you gathered, begged, and produced for yourself—perhaps on a small subsistence farm—many of the necessities of life. Then too, you would qualify for various public programs to aid the poor, and you could justly take advantage of them provided you bore clear witness by your lifestyle against the government's wrongdoing and used a substantial part of your time and energy in serving the nation's common good—for example, by working to mitigate some of the injustice you rightly deplore."

42. See Benedict M. Ashley, OP, *Living the Truth in Love: A Biblical Introduction to Moral Theology* (Staten Island: Alba House, 1996), 346–47. For further reflection on the virtue of justice as related to the state, see Romanus Cessario, OP, *The Virtues, or the Examined Life*

represents an "obligation that is not merely penal (i.e. to avoid the penalty imposed for failing to pay a tax) but a moral obligation in social justice."[43] The state possesses a due, which, in justice, citizens owe toward the common good. A citizen paying a justly levied tax exercises this virtue of justice toward the state. Nothing in the payment of taxes is *per se* ordered to the rendering of vice. Natural teleology proves useful for one's understanding what sort of act is involved in the payment of taxes.

In the 1980s, theologians debated the liceity of paying taxes to the US government during a period of nuclear deterrence.[44] Many authors taught the immorality of the development of these weapons which they believed could never be employed for a moral purpose.[45] Some who hold even the production of these weapons to be immoral raise the question of whether one may legitimately pay taxes to a government committed to the production of such weapons.[46] A similar question arises regarding the payment of taxes when a government commits to funding abortion. In the United States, since the 1976 adoption of the Hyde Amendment, federal dollars have generally not been spent on abortions. However, Medicaid funded abortions from pregnancies which result from rape or incest, abortion on military bases and on Native American reservations have all been hot-

---

(New York: Continuum, 2002), 137–39, especially page 137, where he observes: "Because it possesses a distinct formal object, namely, the human community ordered towards the common good as such, general justice represents an authentic form of justice. Just as a hand naturally defends the whole body-person, so a virtuous citizen defends and promotes the good of his or her 'city,' the state."

43. Ashley, OP, *Living the Truth in Love*, 347.

44. For more information on this matter, see John Finnis, Joseph Boyle, and Germain Grisez, *Nuclear Deterrence, Morality and Realism* (Oxford: Oxford University Press, 1987), 352. They argue: "For taxes, in Western democracies, are paid into a single fund; no payment is earmarked for expenditure on any particular governmental project. Hence, one can intend that one's tax payments be spent on worthy projects which one is morally bound, as a citizen, to support, and merely accept, as an unwanted side-effect, that some portion of these payments will be diverted to immoral purposes."

45. For the classic account of the moral objection to obliteration bombing of civilian populations, see John C. Ford, SJ, "The Morality of Obliteration Bombing," *Theological Studies* 5 (1944): 261–309.

46. For an overview of the question of production and use of nuclear weapons which faced the American bishops in the 1980s, see John Langan, SJ, "The American Hierarchy and Nuclear Weapons," *Theological Studies* 43 (1982): 447–67. For a view more sympathetic to the pacifist position, see David Hollenbach, SJ, "Nuclear Weapons and Nuclear War: The Shape of the Catholic Debate," *Theological Studies* 43 (1982): 577–605. For an alternative perspective, see Joseph P. Martino, *A Fighting Chance: The Moral Use of Nuclear Weapons* (San Francisco: Ignatius Press, 1988).

ly contested in recent decades.[47] The payment of taxes to a government committed to some immoral practice raises the question of whether the payment of taxes could represent an immoral cooperative act.

Theological dispute has centered on the precise nature of the obligation of paying taxes. St. Antoninus of Florence, for example, considered justly levied tax laws binding "in virtue of commutative justice."[48] Theologians grounded in the virtue tradition recognize the payment of a justly levied tax as an exercise of piety, a potential part of the virtue of justice.[49] In the early twentieth century, authors sparred over what sort of obligation a tax imposed. While some theologians considered the obligation merely penal, the more probable opinion held that it bound citizens under legal justice.[50] Authors of this period disputed the precise nature of the obligation. Some held that when citizens evaded a justly levied tax they violated a norm of commutative justice.[51] In so doing these citizens were bound to make restitution, the particular act of commutative justice.[52] Other more lax theologians held only that tax laws bound in penal justice, which is to say, violators must pay any penalties should government officials discover the evasion but are not bound to make restitution for the full amount of the evasion.[53]

47. For an account of the political and legislative disputes regarding abortion, see Anne Hendershott, *The Politics of Abortion* (New York: Encounter Books, 2006).

48. See Martin T. Crowe, CSsR, *The Moral Obligation of Paying Just Taxes* (Washington, DC: The Catholic University of America Press, 1944), 42. For more information on the life of St. Antoninus and his teachings, see Bede Jarrett, OP, *S. Antonino and Medieval Economics* (London: The Manresa Press, 1914).

49. See *Summa theologiae*, IIa–IIae, q. 101, a. 1,

50. See Connell, CSsR, *Morals in Politics and Professions*, 68.

51. For example, Martin Timothy Crowe, CSsR, lists St. Antoninus, Molina, Suarez, Bonacina, Lugo, St. Alphonsus, and Gury, among others, as proponents of the view that taxes bind in commutative justice. See Crowe, CSsR, *The Moral Obligation of Paying Just Taxes*, 42–72.

52. See *Summa theologiae*, IIa–IIae, q. 62, a. 1: "Hence restitution is an act of commutative justice, occasioned by one person having what belongs to another, either with his consent, for instance on loan or deposit, or against his will, as in robbery or theft." For further information about this matter, see Cessario, OP, *The Virtues, or the Examined Life*, 142.

53. For an account of the various opinions of whether the payment of taxes obliges under commutative justice, legal justice, or merely as a penal law, see Dominicus M. Prümmer, OP, *Manuale Theologiae Moralis: Secundum Principia S. Thomae Aquinatis*, vol. 1 (Fribourg: Herder, 1955), §288–94. For one account of the ethics of tax evasion, see Henry Davis, SJ, *Moral and Pastoral Theology*, vol. 2 (London: Sheed and Ward, 1958), Tr. VI, Ch. VIII, Sec. 7, §2, b, ii, 6. For a related presentation of the nature of the obligation to pay taxes, see McHugh-Callan, *Moral Theology*, vol. 2, §2640–42. For the distinction between

During the casuist period manualist authors said very little about the challenge of taxes being used for immoral ends. Some authors utilized the categories of virtue but only to organize their list of obligations. Many authors expressed significant concern about whether the evasion of taxes required restitution. They discussed the distinctions between commutative and distributive justice only to determine if the evasion necessitated restitution. This recalls Servais Pinckaers's observation about Dominican moralists in the early to middle part of the twentieth century. Writing about the Fribourg Dominican Dominicus Prümmer, Pinckaers observed: "But the virtues never furnished him with anything more than a different framework; the material itself was still oriented to obligations and sins."[54] In a similar manner, disputes about which part of the virtue of justice tax evaders violated provided the framework for what was essentially a discussion of the obligation of restitution. The virtues did not form the fundamental structure of the casuist moral analysis.

When faced with the challenge of a government using tax revenue for immoral ends, a citizen should be consoled to know that the payment of taxes does not in principle represent immoral cooperation with evil. The case parallels St. Thomas's treatment of borrowing money from one known to practice usury. Aquinas teaches that one who borrows from a known usurer does not commit an evil act. Instead, the good act of borrowing money presents an occasion for lending which the usurer misuses due to his own malice.[55] In the same manner, Aquinas considers the judge who sentences an innocent man to death according to the evidence presented at trial. St. Thomas recognizes that the judge fulfills his civic role and the false witnesses—not the judge—are responsible for the unjust sentence.[56] In much the same way, a citizen who pays a tax levied by a legit-

---

commutative, distributive, and legal or general justice, see Josef Pieper, *The Four Cardinal Virtues* (New York: Harcourt, Brace & World, Inc., 1965), 70–75. For the distinction between a legal debt and a moral debt according to St. Thomas, see T.C. O'Brien, *Virtues of Justice in the Human Community*, appendix 1: "Legal Debt, Moral Debt," vol. 41 of the Blackfriars *Summa Theologiae* (New York: McGraw-Hill Book Company, 1972), 316–20.

54. Servais Pinckaers, OP, "Dominican Moral Theology in the 20th Century," in *The Pinckaers Reader: Renewing Thomistic Moral Theology*, ed. John Berkman and Craig Steven Titus, trans. Sr. Mary Thomas Noble, OP, Craig Steven Titus, Michael Sherwin, OP, and Hugh Connolly (Washington, DC: The Catholic University of America Press, 2005), 76.

55. See *Summa theologiae*, IIa–IIae, q. 78, a. 4, ad. 2.

56. *Summa theologiae*, IIa–IIae, q. 64, a. 6, ad. 3: "[The judge] does not sin if he pronounce sentence in accordance with the evidence, for it is not he that puts the innocent man to death, but they who stated him to be guilty."

imate government exercises the virtue of justice. Nothing about tax paying is *per se* ordered to immoral activity. Rather, the good act of tax paying is misused by imprudent, confused, or immoral government officials.

This example serves to demonstrate how crucial it is for moral actors to recognize the virtue they employ in a particular action. Knowledge of obligations and prohibitions proves insufficient if one cannot also understand the particular virtue he or she utilizes in a given case. The inability of some moralists to attend to the dynamics of virtue—but instead remain in the realm of obligation—cripples their ability to analyze correctly difficult moral topics.[57] Only when theologians break free from an obligation-based moral framework can they observe and invoke the virtues necessary for sound acting in each circumstance. Both theologians grounded in the virtue tradition and those committed to the system of moral casuistry agree that in principle citizens may pay taxes despite some portion of the funds being used for immoral ends. However, we seek to demonstrate the relative superiority of the virtue-based system even in cases when both virtue-based theologians and casuists agree upon the appropriate course of action. When we move to more disputed cases of possible moral cooperation with evil, our commitment to the virtue-based approach will prove useful.

Wedding cakes and flowers: navigating the civil redefinition of marriage

On September 29, 2015, American news outlets reported that Pope Francis conducted a meeting with potentially significant consequences for political life in the United States. The initial reporting—and ensuing controversy—did not involve the Pope's meeting at the White House with President Barack Obama or his address at the US Capitol before a joint assembly of Congress. Nor did the consternation result from the Holy Father's address at the United Nations in New York. Instead, the

---

57. What Servais Pinckaers, OP calls the "manuals of moral theology" suffer from several deficiencies. He observes: "Comparing this structure [of the manuals] with the structure of St. Thomas' *Summa theologiae*, one notes immediately the disappearance of the treatise on happiness and the ultimate end, as well as the absence of a treatment of the virtues and the gifts.... At the core of this conception of morality, monopolizing all its energy, is the idea and sentiment of *obligation*." See Servais Pinckaers, OP, *Morality: The Catholic View*, trans. Michael Sherwin, OP (South Bend, IN: St. Augustine's Press, 2001), 33–34.

controversy surrounded a private audience the Pope granted to a simple county clerk from Rowan County, Kentucky. Her name was Kim Davis. On June 26, 2015 the United States Supreme Court ruled in *Obergefell v. Hodges* that the US Constitution guaranteed the right of same-sex couples to marry.[58] In the weeks that followed, Davis, a born-again Christian, had refused to sign marriage licenses for those who had civilly contracted same-sex marriages. She believed that her attestation of the civil marriage represented an immoral cooperation in what she believed to be the fiction of a purported marriage.

The Pope's greeting Kim Davis does not solve the complex matter of what set of actions represent immoral cooperation with the celebration of same-sex marriage. Challenging questions remain for those who ac-knowledge the error of the civil redefinition of marriage. The Church has offered guidance on the immorality of unchaste acts.[59] The Church's Magisterium has given further instruction on the impossibility of equiv-ocating a same-sex union with a marriage between a man and a woman. The Church's opposition to this equivocation also excludes the possibil-ity of so-called civil unions.[60] Indeed, the Church opposes any civil rec-ognition of same-sex relationships which would place them on par with marriage.[61] This teaching is based not merely on Sacred Scripture and Tradition but, the Church maintains, on what human reason can grasp about the nature of the human person, the complementarity of men and women, and their capacity to love and beget life.[62] Regarding issues of

58. See United States Supreme Court, *Obergefell et al. v. Hodges, Director, Ohio Department of Health, et al.*, (2015) No. 14–556, June 26, 2015.

59. See *CCC*, nos. 2357–59. See also the Congregation for the Doctrine of the Faith, *Persona Humana*, December 29, 1975, and by the same Congregation, *Letter to the Bishops of the Catholic Church on the Pastoral Care of Homosexual Persons*, October 1, 1986. For an alternative perspective, see the volume edited by Robert Nugent, *A Challenge to Love: Gay and Lesbian Catholics in the Church* (New York: The Crossroad Publishing Company, 1983).

60. Congregation for the Doctrine of the Faith, *Considerations regarding proposals to give le-gal recognition to unions between homosexual persons*, June 3, 2003, *AAS* 96 (2004): 41–57. For a re-flection on the anthropological errors at work in the gay marriage debate, see David S. Crawford, "Public Reason and the Anthropology of Orientation: How the Debate over 'Gay Marriage' Has Been Shaped by some Ubiquitous but Unexamined Propositions," *Communio* 43 (2016): 247–73.

61. Congregation for the Doctrine of the Faith, *Considerations regarding proposals to give le-gal recognition to unions between homosexual persons*, no. 4. The Congregation explains: "There are absolutely no grounds for considering homosexual unions to be in any way similar or even remotely analogous to God's plan for marriage and family."

62. Alternatively, Mark D. Jordan has argued that the Christian teaching on the

moral cooperation with evil, several questions arise related to the public recognition of same-sex relationships and civil marriage. First, we must review briefly the reasons why individuals or ecclesial communities might oppose the celebration of same-sex marriage. Second, we will examine the nature of the cooperation of attending or assisting in the celebrations of these unions. Third, we will consider how employers should address the allocation of benefits normally reserved to married couples.

To understand why persons and institutions oppose cooperation that would assist or promote same-sex marriages, it is necessary to identify the reasons why they would object to the celebration of these unions. As Western nations in rapid succession have redefined marriage to include couples of the same sex, one wonders if everyone involved correctly identifies the question at the heart of these discussions. Many who support a redefinition of marriage to include those of the same sex believe the issue involves principally the economic benefits to be afforded by employers or the state to the individuals concerned. Unfortunately, they fail to appreciate the full scope of the question. The frustration of Christian believers and others does not result from concern about what benefits employers or states afford individuals but about the nature of the institution of marriage.[63] Those who oppose a redefinition of marriage to include unions of those of the same sex acknowledge that marriage is the friendship of a man and woman bonded together for life. Marriage is uniquely the kind of union that brings new life into the world. Based on the natural complementarity of husband and wife, marriage is—of its nature—ordered

---

immorality of homosexual acts is not of biblical origin. See Jordan's, *The Invention of Sodomy in Christian Theology* (Chicago: The University of Chicago Press, 1998). For a refutation of this position, see Innocent Himbaza, Adrien Schenker, and Jean-baptiste Edart, *The Bible on the Question of Homosexuality*, trans. Benedict M. Guevin, OSB (Washington, DC: The Catholic University of America Press, 2012). For a convincing argument against the claim that the works of Aquinas could be read to justify homosexual acts, see Fr. Bernhard Blankenhorn, OP, Sr. Catherine Joseph Droste, OP, Fr. Efrem Jindracek, OP, Fr. Dominic Legge, OP, Fr. Thomas Joseph White, OP, "Aquinas & Homosexuality: Five Dominicans Respond to Adriano Oliva, OP," *Angelicum* 92 (2015): 297–302.

63. For example, the position of the bishops of the United States regarding universal access to affordable health care is well-known. See, for example, the document of the United States Catholic Conference, *Health and Healthcare: A Pastoral Letter of the American Catholic Bishops* (Washington, DC: United States Catholic Conference, 1982). At the same time, the American bishops have insisted that employers and states ensure that healthcare and other benefits be afforded to every individual but not by reason of a commitment to an ongoing homosexual relationship.

to new life. Put simply, lovemaking and life-making go together.[64] Many who oppose a redefinition of marriage may be religious believers, but they are not by that very fact bigoted. In fact, to maintain that believing in the biblical definition of marriage ipso facto makes one a bigot, reveals a frightening bias against religion.[65] If we understand that this conversation is not principally about the rights to be afforded individuals but rather about the nature of marriage itself, that shifts the discussion.

The Catholic Church teaches that every human person possesses an inviolable dignity. Each life is sacred, and no person is excluded from God's mercy. For that reason, the Church recognizes that the union that brings new life into the world deserves a special name and special status in the law. That view is not a "No" to anybody but a "Yes" to the sanctity of human life and marital love.[66] Pope Benedict XVI offered instruction on this matter. He explained:

If there is no pre-ordained duality of man and women in creation, then neither is the family any longer a reality established by creation.... When the freedom to be creative becomes the freedom to create oneself, then necessarily the Maker himself is denied and ultimately man too is stripped of his dignity as a creature of God.[67]

The definition of marriage as the union of a man and woman bonded together for life does not discriminate against anyone. Rather, this definition describes what marriage is and how it is distinct from other friendships. This background undergirds the belief of many persons that celebrating

64. For an excellent treatment of the connection between the procreative and unitive ends of marriage, see Paul Gondreau, "The 'Inseparable Connection' between Procreation and Unitive Love (*Humanae Vitae*, §12) and Thomistic Hylemorphic Anthropology," *Nova et Vetera* 6 (2008): 731–64. For an alternative perspective, see Bernard Häring, CSsR, "The Inseparability of the Unitive-Procreative Functions of the Marital Act," in *Readings in Moral Theology, No. 8: Dialogue about Catholic Sexual Teaching*, ed. Charles E. Curran and Richard A. McCormick, SJ, 153–67 (New York: Paulist Press, 1993).

65. For the challenges a redefinition of marriage poses to religious freedom, see Ryan T. Anderson, *Truth Overruled: The Future of Marriage and Religious Freedom*, especially 85–104. For a more general treatment of contemporary challenges to religious freedom, see Mary Eberstadt, *It's Dangerous to Believe: Religious Freedom and Its Enemies* (New York: Harper Collins, 2016).

66. See *Dignitas personae*, no. 37: "Behind every 'no' in the difficult task of discerning between good and evil, there shines a *great 'yes' to the recognition of the dignity and inalienable value of every single and unique human being called into existence.*"

67. Pope Benedict XVI, *Address of His Holiness Benedict XVI on the Occasion of Christmas Greetings to the Roman Curia*, December 21, 2012.

or supporting same-sex marriage could represent an immoral cooperation in these unions.[68]

The legal recognition of same-sex marriage raises important questions regarding moral cooperation. The Congregation for the Doctrine of the Faith cautions against immoral cooperation with unjust laws related to marriage. The Congregation observes: "One must refrain from any kind of formal cooperation in the enactment or application of such gravely unjust laws and, as far as possible, from material cooperation on the level of their application."[69] The Congregation continues: "In this area, everyone can exercise the right to conscientious objection."[70] While a Catholic's cooperation in the celebration of homosexual unions represents a relatively recent question for Catholic moral theology, the issue of participation in a union the Church recognizes as invalid has a longer history. For example, theologians of the early twentieth century took up the question of whether a Catholic judge could officiate at a civil wedding that would constitute an invalid sacramental or natural marriage.[71] In Catholic theology, a valid marriage is one where both parties are free to marry and exchange consent according to a lawful form. In principle, Catholics are required to marry according to canonical form before a minister of the Church or receive a dispensation from this obligation which is necessary for them validly to contract a marriage.[72]

Catholic moralists have treated the matter of whether Catholics could attend celebrations of invalid marriages.[73] The noted American moralist Germain Grisez takes a strict view. He holds that a Catholic may not at-

---

68. For an alternative perspective, see Stephen J. Pope, "The Magisterium's Arguments against 'Same-Sex Marriage': An Ethical Analysis and Critique," *Theological Studies* 65 (2004): 530–65. For a broader critique of magisterial teaching on homosexuality, see James F. Keenan, SJ, "The Open Debate: Moral Theology and the Lives of Gay and Lesbian Persons," *Theological Studies* 64 (2003): 127–50.

69. See the Congregation for the Doctrine of the Faith, *Considerations regarding proposals to give legal recognition to unions between homosexual persons*, no. 5.

70. Congregation for the Doctrine of the Faith, no. 5.

71. For one response to the challenges faced by Catholic judges, especially regarding divorce law and officiating at invalid marriages, see Connell, CSsR, *Morals in Politics and Professions*, 29–33.

72. See *CCC*, no. 1631. See also *CIC* 1108, §1: "Only those marriages are valid which are contracted before the local ordinary, pastor, or a priest or deacon delegated by either of them, who assist, and before two witnesses according to the rules expressed in the [succeeding] canons."

73. See Grisez, *Difficult Moral Questions: The Way of the Lord Jesus*, vol. 3, 171–74.

tend a ceremony or reception for any civil wedding which would constitute an invalid sacramental or natural marriage. He likewise opposes the giving of gifts or recognition of the anniversary of the invalid union.[74] Regarding one who attempts remarriage after a valid sacramental or natural marriage (without recourse to an ecclesial declaration that one is free to marry), Grisez explains: "To act as if an attempted remarriage after divorce were a real marriage is to belie the truth; to refuse to be involved is necessary to proclaim your faith about this matter."[75] On the other hand, former Dunwoodie professor and celebrated moral theologian William B. Smith permits one to attend a reception for such a union but not the marriage ceremony itself.[76]

Participation in the celebration of a homosexual union raises serious questions regarding scandal and cooperation with evil. Some of these issues are unique to same-sex unions. Unlike an irregular marriage between a man and a woman—for example an attempted marriage between two Catholics outside of canonical form—the union of those of the same sex could never be regularized in the Church.[77] It is clear to all involved that a union of those of the same sex is not a marriage recognized by the Catholic Church. A union of a man and woman celebrated outdoors or when one party has a previous bond could in fact be a valid marriage. In this case, one or both of the parties could have received a declaration of nullity from a previous marriage. They also could have received a dispensation from the obligation to marry according to canonical form.[78] If one of the

74. Grisez, 172: "I do not think you should give the couple a wedding gift, attend the ceremony, or do anything else that would be inappropriate if they were simply setting up housekeeping together without any pretense of marrying. Why? Because in this situation, as in all others, you should bear witness to the faith, which includes the truth about marriage's indissolubility."

75. Grisez, 172.

76. See Smith, *Modern Moral Problems*, 125–29.

77. See the *Responsum* of the Congregation for the Doctrine of the Faith to a *dubium* regarding the blessing of the unions of persons of the same sex, March 15, 2021.

78. For an excellent treatment of the canonical issues involved in marriage, see Paolo Bianchi, *When is Marriage Null? Guide to the Grounds of Matrimonial Nullity for Pastors, Counselors, and Lay Faithful*, trans. Michael J Miller (San Francisco: Ignatius Press, 2015). For another outstanding treatment of the theological and canonical questions regarding marriage, see Cormac Burke, *The Theology of Marriage: Personalism, Doctrine, and Canon Law* (Washington, DC: The Catholic University of America Press, 2015). For a collection of essays on Pope Francis's changes to the process of declaration of nullity, see the volume edited by Kurt Martens, *Justice and Mercy Have Met* (Washington, DC: The Catholic University of America Press, 2017).

parties is non-Catholic, dioceses regularly grant a dispensation from canonical form when requested to do so.[79] Attempted marriages outside of
canonical form when at least one party is Catholic and celebrated without dispensation could later be validated according to the prescriptions of
Canon Law.[80] All that is to say, it is not always immediately clear if the
union of a man and woman is a valid marriage. And, if not, such a union
could be validated in the future. On the other hand, standard Catholic
teaching recognizes that the union of those of the same sex is not and
could never become a valid sacramental or natural marriage.

Serving as an official witness, electing to assist at the marriage as an
officiant or in any formal capacity represents an objectively scandalous
act which cooperates immorally in the invalid union. Under normal circumstances, attendance at such a union would represent support for such
a celebration. The celebrated formula known to all movie viewers recalls
the expectation that one's attendance at the event indicates consent for the
union: "If anyone here present objects to this union, speak now or forever
hold your peace." Those who serve in an official capacity for the civil government stand in a unique position related to the administration of marriage. On the one hand to avoid scandal, an official's personal opposition
to same-sex marriage should be widely known. At the same time, there is
a difference between one who elects to officiate at an irregular union and
one whose position in civil government requires the recording or process-
ing of such unions. Similarly, photographers, cake-bakers, florists, and the
like face challenging questions of whether their participation represents
an immoral cooperation in the celebration of unchastity. It is not so much
that the Church has formulated defined norms against such cooperation
as it is the case that virtuous persons will flee instinctually from these cooperative acts.[81] For those who attend carefully to the teleology of moral
acts, the key question is whether an action can reasonably be construed

79. See *CIC* 1127, §2.

80. For commentary on the canonical form of a marriage, see John McAreavey, *The
Canon Law of Marriage and the Family* (Dublin: Four Courts Press, 1997), 137–51; and for
commentary on the possibility of validation of a marriage, from the same volume, see
171–78.

81. For reflection on Pope John Paul II's treatment of shame in the "Theology of
the Body," see Jaroslaw Kupczak, OP, *Gift & Communion: John Paul II's Theology of the Body*
(Washington, DC: The Catholic University of America Press, 2014), 52–59. For commentary on the concept of shame in the Theology of the Body, see William E. May,
Theology of the Body in Context: Genesis and Growth (Boston: Pauline Books & Media, 2010),
92–97.

apart from participation in the immoral union. For example, one whose job it is to sweep the floor of an event hall can assert reasonably that this work bears no teleological relationship to any immoral activity or celebration which takes place in the event hall. The activity of a wedding-cake maker who is asked to produce a cake with artistic representations of unchastity stands more clearly as an immoral participation in the celebration.

The issue of scandal occupies an important place in discussions surrounding same-sex marriage. Those who acknowledge that the public recognition of same-sex marriage is detrimental to the common good seek to ensure that their actions never give the impression that they approve of such unions. The actions of both individuals and institutions can give scandal if their actions appear to condone immoral activity. For Catholic institutions, the judgment for bishops occupies the principal place in questions related to the presence of scandal.[82] Bishops should ensure that no Catholic institution allows the solemnization of a same-sex union nor cooperates with its celebration. Bishops should likewise insist that those employed at Catholic schools or other institutions do not by their public behavior give the impression of support for acts of unchastity. Proper pastoral care requires speaking the truth. As the Church's Magisterium instructs its pastors, silence regarding fundamental truths of the moral life does not represent authentic pastoral care.[83] Bishops and others charged with the care of souls should make clear the truth about human love and the sanctity of marriage.

A particularly challenging question regarding the civil recognition of same-sex marriage involves the benefits normally afforded to civilly mar-

---

82. For reflection on the theology of the episcopacy, see Michael G. Sirilla, *The Ideal Bishop: Aquinas' Commentaries on the Pastoral Epistles* (Washington, DC: The Catholic University of America Press, 2017). For careful treatment of the question of the unique character of episcopal consecration, see three essays by Guy Mansini, OSB, "Episcopal *Munera* and the Character of Episcopal Orders," *The Thomist* 66 (2002): 369–94; "Sacerdotal Character at the Second Vatican Council," *The Thomist* 67 (2003): 539–77; and "A Contemporary Understanding of St. Thomas on Sacerdotal Character," *The Thomist* 71 (2007): 171–98.

83. See the Congregation for the Doctrine of the Faith, *Letter to the Bishops of the Catholic Church on the Pastoral Care of Homosexual Persons*, no. 15: "No authentic pastoral program will include organizations in which homosexual persons associate with each other without clearly stating that homosexual activity is immoral. A truly pastoral approach will appreciate the need for homosexual persons to avoid the near occasions of sin."

ried couples. Both employers and state and federal governments often afford financial benefits to those who have entered civil marriages. The common good of marriage for children and all society serves as the reason for the state's privileging of marriage in the law. Benefits should not be afforded to anyone based on the commitment to engage in unchaste acts.[84] Nothing is to prevent a state from granting certain benefits previously reserved to spouses to other non-marital partners. For example, a state which previously restricted hospital visitation rights to spouses could allow a patient to designate one or more people the privilege of visitation, for example, allowing the designation of a single caregiver. On the other hand, granting financial benefits on the condition that one enter an immoral union serves as an unjust cooperation with that union. Any action which would suggest that marriage is equivalent to an immoral relationship represents an immoral cooperative act.[85]

The Congregation for the Doctrine of the Faith observes that in justice no individual or group should act as if marriage is equivalent to any other union.[86] No one should maintain that the friendship of siblings or between two or three friends is equivalent to the life-long and life-giving bond of husband and wife. For one to assert that any persons who love each other can enter a marriage demonstrates that one has failed to grasp fully what marriage is.[87] The suggestion that the gender of those seeking marriage has no bearing on the character of their union neglects to observe what nature reveals about human dignity. The claim that the possibility of creating new life is an accidental quality of marital relations— and not constitutive of what marriage is—reveals a blindness to the gift of human life. A culture that values life will only flourish when communi-

---

84. See the Congregation for the Doctrine of the Faith, *Some Considerations Concerning the Response to Legislative Proposals on the Non-Discrimination of Homosexual Persons*, no. 14.

85. See the Congregation for the Doctrine of the Faith, *Considerations regarding proposals to give legal recognition to unions between homosexual persons*, no. 11. "Legal recognition of homosexual unions or placing them on the same level as marriage would mean not only the approval of deviant behavior, with the consequence of making it a model in present-day society, but would also obscure basic values which belong to the common inheritance of humanity."

86. Congregation for the Doctrine of the Faith, no. 15.

87. For St. Thomas's teaching on the natural law foundation for the indissolubility of marriage, see *Summa theologiae*, Sup., q. 67, a. 1. For a historical study of the formulation of the decrees of the Council of Trent on the indissolubility of marriage, see E. Christian Brugger, *The Indissolubility of Marriage & the Council of Trent* (Washington, DC: The Catholic University of America Press, 2017).

ties and their laws esteem the relationship from which life springs. Those who claim that any two people who love each other ought to be able to get married demonstrate a lack of sustained reflection on the topic. What about two people who are in love when one of them is already married? What about three people who claim to love one another? Anyone who is willing to grant that the number of persons makes a difference in a relationship (that for a marriage you need two—not one or three) can in principle grant that the gender of those in the relationship matters as well.[88] The natural complementarity of a husband and wife—a relationship of its nature ordered to new life—is what we call marriage.[89]

The definition of marriage as the union of a man and woman bonded together for life does not endorse nor permit unjust discrimination against anyone. Regarding persons who identify as homosexual, the *Catechism of the Catholic Church* warns against "any sign of unjust discrimination."[90] However, laws which observe that the relationship of a brother and sister or between two or three friends is not the same as the life-long and life-giving bond between a husband and wife do not represent unjust discrimination.[91] Indeed, the relationship of marriage—by its very nature ordered to new life—is a unique bond. For that reason, the Church believes that marriage should retain a special name and receive unique status in the law. Marriage advocates have long argued that the best place—not the

88. For Aquinas's careful treatment of the natural law foundation for monogamy, see *Summa theologiae*, Sup., q. 65, a. 1. For an excellent commentary on Aquinas's treatment of law more generally, see J. Budziszewski, *Commentary on Thomas Aquinas's Treatise on Law* (New York: Cambridge University Press, 2014).

89. For an extended exposition of this topic, albeit from the perspective of the new natural law, see Sherif Grigis, Ryan T. Anderson, and Robert P. George, *What is Marriage?: Man and Woman: A Defense* (New York: Encounter Books, 2012). For an excellent collection of essays on disputed issues of the natural law, see the volume edited by Lawrence S. Cunningham, *Intractable Disputes about the Natural Law: Alasdair MacIntyre and His Critics* (Notre Dame: University of Notre Dame Press, 2009).

90. See *CCC*, no. 2358: "The number of men and women who have deep-seated homosexual tendencies is not negligible. This inclination, which is objectively disordered, constitutes for most of them a trial. They must be accepted with respect, compassion, and sensitivity. Every sign of unjust discrimination in their regard should be avoided. These persons are called to fulfill God's will in their lives and, if they are Christians, to unite to the sacrifice of the Lord's Cross the difficulties they may encounter from their condition."

91. For a series of essays on public policy related to marriage, see *The Meaning of Marriage: Family, State, Market, and Morals*, ed. Robert P. George and Jean Bethke Elshtain (Dallas: Spence Publishing Company, 2006).

only place but the best place—to raise a child is between a mother and father bonded together for life. Children are more likely to perform well in school and avoid poverty when they are raised by a mother and father.[92] Efforts to redefine marriage undermine this truth confirmed by sociological data. Those who struggle with same-sex attraction are not the ones primarily to blame for the now widespread rejection of the truth about marriage. When a culture misunderstands marriage, rejecting indissolubility and embracing a near ubiquitous practice of contraception, it is much harder to observe the truth about marital love. A culture that does not value the uniqueness of the relationship from which life comes will be hard pressed to build a solid foundation for the culture of life.[93]

This example serves to demonstrate the importance of the virtue of chastity for those confronting questions of cooperation with the redefinition of marriage. Only those with a healthy *verecundia* or shame toward acts of unchastity will shun cooperation with celebrations of such acts.[94] The unwillingness of Christians to mount opposition to widespread divorce and the practice of contraception does not render them ready to argue persuasively against a redefinition of marriage to include couples of the same sex.[95] More precisely, one given over to unchastity of any kind will not recognize and shun cooperative acts which participate in celebrations of unchaste relationships. While the moral manuals of the early to mid-twentieth century offered some guidance on these matters, they could not ensure that one actually possessed the capacity to enact a sound moral choice.[96] Only growth in virtue safeguards effective and habitual moral action.

---

92. For an insightful reflection on the benefits of marriage for child-rearing, see Maggie Gallagher, "(How) Does Marriage Protect Child Well-Being?" in *The Meaning of Marriage: Family, State, Market, and Morals*, 197–212.

93. For guidance on challenges that arise after a civil redefinition of marriage, see Smith, *Modern Moral Problems*, 247–57.

94. See *Summa theologiae*, IIa–IIae, q. 144, a. 4.

95. For the difficulties for individuals and society generated from the widespread practice of divorce, see Jennifer Roback Morse, "Why Unilateral Divorce Has No Place in a Free Society," in *The Meaning of Marriage Family, State, Market, and Morals*, 74–99.

96. For a more positive portrayal of the moral manuals on cooperation with evil, see Julie Hanlon Rubio, "Cooperation with Evil Reconsidered: The Moral Duty of Resistance," *Theological Studies* 78 (2017): 96–120.

Keeping body healthy and soul holy:
contraceptive "mandates" and other government
regulations in health care

In January 2012 the United States Department of Health and Human Services (HHS), a cabinet agency of the Obama administration, issued a mandate that all health insurance providers offer coverage for contraception, which could include abortifacient drugs, and procedures aimed at contraceptive sterilization.[97] The American bishops responded with firm opposition. They insisted that Catholic institutions and others should not abide by this mandate.[98] In recent decades, state governments had issued similar mandates, but this was the first time the federal government delivered such a blanket regulation. While religious bodies received a narrow exception, the relief would not apply to religious institutions working in education, health care, or social service. Thus, the whole network of Catholic schools, hospitals, and charitable organizations would not be exempt from the mandate. The moral status of compliance with this contraception mandate stands as one of the most controversial and challenging matters in the field of moral cooperation in recent years. Several studies in the Catholic moral tradition have provided sound guidance in biomedical ethics generally.[99] The Church's Magisterium has also in-

97. The text of the regulation was published in the Federal Register on February 15, 2012. See 77 Fed. Reg. 8725.

98. United States Conference of Catholic Bishops, Ad Hoc Committee on Religious Liberty, *Our First, Most Cherished Liberty: A Statement on Religious Liberty* (April 2012). The bishops explain: "It is a sobering thing to contemplate our government enacting an unjust law. An unjust law cannot be obeyed. In the face of an unjust law, an accommodation is not to be sought, especially by resorting to equivocal words and deceptive practices. If we face today the prospect of unjust laws, then Catholics in America, in solidarity with our fellow citizens, must have the courage not to obey them. No American desires this. No Catholic welcomes it. But if it should fall upon us, we must discharge it as a duty of citizenship and an obligation of faith. It is essential to understand the distinction between conscientious objection and an unjust law. Conscientious objection permits some relief to those who object to a just law for reasons of conscience—conscription being the most well-known example. An unjust law is 'no law at all.' It cannot be obeyed, and therefore one does not seek relief from it, but rather its repeal."

99. In recent years, the field of Catholic bioethics has been enriched by many thoughtful publications. Interested readers should consult: Nicanor Pier Giorgio Austriaco, OP, *Biomedicine and Beatitude: An Introduction to Catholic Bioethics*, 2nd. ed. (Washington, DC: The Catholic University of America Press, 2021); Elio Sgreccia, *Personalist Bioethics: Foundations and Applications*, trans. John A. Di Camillo and Michael J. Miller

tervened to offer counsel about a host of bioethical matters.[100] Scientific, moral, and legal issues abound in this area, making sensible discourse both crucial and challenging. In what follows, we will review briefly Catholic teaching on contraception and contraceptive sterilization. Second, we will examine the morality of health insurance providers offering coverage which includes these so-called "services." Third, we will address arguments that a government mandate to offer such coverage might alter the moral evaluation of providing funds for this purpose.

The Church's teaching on the immorality of contraception is well-known. This does not mean, however, that it is necessarily well-understood. Few teachings of the Church have been as roundly criticized and ignored as Catholic belief regarding the immorality of contraception. The fundamental tenants of this teaching were expressed in the 1968 encyclical letter *Humanae vitae*. In the encyclical Pope Paul VI declared: "Similarly excluded is any action which either before, at the moment of, or after sexual intercourse, is specifically intended to prevent procreation—whether as an end or as a means."[101] While with this affirmation Pope Paul VI reiterated previous Catholic teaching, immediate reaction to the encyclical varied widely across the globe.[102] Some bishops' conferences

---

(Philadelphia: The National Catholic Bioethics Center, 2012); Dionigi Tettamanzi, *Nuova Bioetica Cristiana* (Segrete: Piemme, 2000); and W. J. Eijk, L. M. Hendriks, J. A. Raymakers, and John I. Fleming, eds., *Manual of Catholic Medical Ethics: Responsible Healthcare from a Catholic Perspective*, trans. M. Regina van den Berg and Janthony Raymakers (Ballarat: Connor Court Publishing, 2014). Reflecting the perspective of the new natural law, the volume of William E. May, *Catholic Bioethics and the Gift of Human Life*, 3rd ed. (Huntington: Our Sunday Visitor, 2013) offers generally sound instruction. For a good collection of essays on issues of bioethics and Catholic social doctrine, see the volume compiled by the Associazione scienza & vita, *Vita, Ragione, Dialogo: Scitti in onore di Elio Sgreccia* (Siena: Cantagalli, 2012).

100. See two documents of the Congregation for the Doctrine of the Faith, the *Instruction* Donum vitae *on Respect for Human Life in its Origin and on the Dignity of Procreation*, February 22, 1987: *AAS* 80 (1988):70–102; and the *Instruction* Dignitas Personae *on Certain Bioethical Questions*, September 8, 2008: *AAS* 100 (2008): 858–87; DeS 24 (2010).

101. See Pope Paul VI, *Humanae Vitae*, no. 14. For exposition and commentary, see the volume edited by Janet E. Smith, *Why Humanae Vitae Was Right: A Reader* (San Francisco: Ignatius Press, 1993). And, by the same author, *Humanae Vitae: A Generation Later* (Washington, DC: The Catholic University of America Press, 1991). For an alternative perspective, see the volume of essays edited by Charles E. Curran, *Contraception: Authority and Dissent* (New York: Herder and Herder, 1969).

102. For previous iterations of Catholic teaching on the immorality of contraception, see, for example, Pope Pius XI's encyclical letter *Casti Connubii*, December 31, 1930.

even attempted to distance themselves from the rigor of this pronounce-ment.[103] On the other hand, recent authors have added clarity to the wis-dom of this teaching. In this regard, one thinks especially of the work of Pope John Paul II.[104] Catholic belief can be expressed simply: the choice to sterilize a conjugal act impedes the complete self-giving expressed in conjugal love. From a teleological perspective, the use of the sexual fac-ulty while impeding its procreative capacity represents a perversion of its natural end.[105] This stands in contrast to the regulation of conception by natural means, specifically by recourse to infertile periods.[106]

In addition to contraception, government mandates for health insur-ance have included coverage for contraceptive sterilization and certain abortifacient drugs. Medical coverage for either sterilization or abortion-inducing drugs presents serious moral problems. Theologians and others

103. Reaction to the encyclical varied widely. For an account of the reception of the document, see the responses from national bishops' conferences collected in the volume *Humanae Vitae and the Bishops: The Encyclical and the Statements of the National Hierarchies*, ed. John Horgan (Shannon, Ireland: Irish University Press, 1972). For the well-known defense of the infallibility of the teaching of *Humanae vitae*, see John C. Ford, SJ, and Germain Gri-sez, "Contraception and the Infallibility of the Ordinary Magisterium," *Theological Studies* 39 (1978): 258–312. From a similar perspective, see Russell Shaw, "Contraception, Infalli-bility and the Ordinary Magisterium," in *Why Humanae Vitae Was Right: A Reader*, ed. Janet E. Smith, 343–61 (San Francisco: Ignatius Press, 1993).

104. See his Wednesday audience catecheses compiled as the "Theology of the Body," most recently published as *Man and Woman He Created Them: A Theology of the Body*, trans. Mi-chael Waldstein (Boston: Pauline Books and Media, 2006). For the philosophical foun-dations of this work, see the volume published during his time as a bishop, *Love and Re-sponsibility* (San Francisco: Ignatius Press, 1993). Commentary on these works abounds in recent years. Especially helpful in emphasizing the Thomistic foundations of these works, see Thomas Petri, OP, *Aquinas and the Theology of the Body: The Thomistic Foundations of John Paul II's Anthropology* (Washington, DC: The Catholic University of America Press, 2016).

105. For an outstanding expression of this argument, see Edward Feser, "In Defense of the Perverted Faculty Argument," in his *Neo-Scholastic Essays* (South Bend: St. Augus-tine Press, 2015), 378–415. For an argument from the phenomenological perspective, see Josef Seifert, "The Problem of the Moral Significance of Human Fertility and Birth Control Methods: Philosophical Arguments against Contraception?" in *"Humanae Vi-tae": 20 Anni Dopo, Atti del II Congresso Internazionale di Teologia Morale* (Milan: Edizioni Ares, 1989), 661–72.

106. For a clear presentation of the Church's teaching on the immorality of con-traception, see Pope John Paul II, *Familiaris consortio*, no. 32. For a thoughtful examina-tion of the difference between contraception and Natural Family Planning, see John S. Grabowski, *Sex and Virtue: An Introduction to Sexual Ethics* (Washington, DC: The Catholic University of America Press, 2003), 142–54.

have long argued that certain forms of contraception can also serve an abortifacient purpose. While scientists and theologians may continue to debate this matter, the necessity of erring always on the side of protecting human life remains clear.[107] In the 2008 instruction *Dignitas personae,* the Holy See insisted upon this position.[108] This case is not dissimilar to pharmacists who may be called to conscientious objection if asked to supply pharmaceuticals used for immoral ends.[109] In similar fashion, debates over contraceptive sterilization raged within the Church during the post-conciliar period. In 1975 the Congregation for the Doctrine of the Faith gave definite answer to this dispute. The Congregation affirmed that contraceptive sterilizations may not be performed in Catholic hospitals as such procedures represent unjust mutilations and serve a contraceptive purpose.[110] Catholic moral theology holds that recourse to contraception, sterilization, or abortifacient drugs does not correspond to the truth about the good of the human person.[111]

Even among those who acknowledge the immorality of contraception,

107. For trustworthy guidance on questions of emergency contraception, the use of contraception in acts of fornication, and related topics, see Smith, *Modern Moral Problems,* 136–53.

108. *Dignitas personae,* no. 23: "It is true that there is not always complete knowledge of the way that different pharmaceuticals operate, but scientific studies indicate that the effect of inhibiting implantation is certainly present, even if this does not mean that such interceptives cause an abortion every time they are used, also because conception does not occur after every act of sexual intercourse. It must be noted, however, that anyone who seeks to prevent the implantation of an embryo which may possibly have been conceived and who therefore either requests or prescribes such a pharmaceutical, generally intends abortion." For further reflection on this matter, see Nicanor Pier Giorgio Austriaco, OP, *Biomedicine and Beatitude,* 120–24.

109. See the address of Pope Benedict XVI, *Address to Members of the International Congress of Catholic Pharmacists,* October 29, 2007: "In the moral domain, your Federation is invited to address the issue of conscientious objection, which is a right your profession must recognize, permitting you not to collaborate either directly or indirectly by supplying products for the purpose of decisions that are clearly immoral such as, for example, abortion or euthanasia." For further reflection on this matter, see Grisez, *Difficult Moral Questions: The Way of the Lord Jesus,* vol. 3, 374–80. For an extended study on the ethics of conscientious objection regarding contraceptive and abortifacient drugs, see Pau Agulles Simó, *La objeción de conciencia farmacéutica en España* (Rome: Edizioni Università della Santa Croce, 2006).

110. See the Congregation for the Doctrine of the Faith, *Responses to Questions Concerning Sterilization in Catholic Hospitals,* March 13, 1975. For more information on this teaching, see chapter three above.

111. See *VS,* no. 61.

many disagree about the nature of the cooperation involved in compliance with a contraception mandate. The regulation requiring coverage of contraception in health insurance presents a serious question of cooperation with evil. What is the nature of the act of offering health insurance? This question arises in hospital mergers, health care collaboration among those of opposing ethical systems, as well as in the case of any employer who offers health insurance coverage.[112] It is not unrelated to the moral quandary of doctors who wonder if they can prescribe contraception to their clients.[113] The moral question concerns the nature of the cooperative acts related to assisting a person who wishes to use contraception. Compliance with a government mandate for health insurance to cover immoral practices presents a serious challenge of cooperation with evil.

Some might suggest that complying with a contraceptive mandate differs little from Americans paying taxes which provide limited coverage for abortion, traditionally limited to pregnancies arising from cases of rape, incest, or when the mother's life or health may be threatened. However, there is nothing about paying taxes that implies payment for abortion. In fact, the paying of taxes represents an act of the virtue of justice. The payment of taxes is not *per se* ordered to the act of abortion. Thus, a taxpayer is not morally responsible for everything a government chooses to fund.[114] Using the common terminology, the payment of taxes to a government which funds immoral acts represents remote material cooperation, licit for a sufficient reason. In a similar fashion, some wonder if an individual may purchase health insurance which includes coverage of vicious services. They conjecture that this act might not differ from an employer complying with the government mandate. However, the acts differ considerably. An individual may purchase health insurance even if it covers immoral procedures. The virtuous employee who purchases such health insurance

---

112. For a reflection on ecumenical collaboration in health care, see the National Catholic Bioethics Center Ethicists, "Cooperating with Non-Catholic Partners," in *Catholic Health Care Ethics: A Manual for Practitioners*, 2nd ed., ed. Edward J. Furton with Peter J. Cataldo and Albert S. Moraczewski, OP, 265–70 (Philadelphia: The National Catholic Bioethics Center, 2009). For further reflection on health care collaboration, see Peter J. Cataldo, "Models of Health Care Collaboration," in *Catholic Health Care Ethics: A Manual for Practitioners*, 2nd ed., 271–73.

113. For one response to the question of whether physicians may prescribe contraceptives or participate in medical groups that offer immoral services, see Grisez, *Difficult Moral Questions: The Way of the Lord Jesus*, vol. 3, 308–18.

114. See the first section of this chapter above for a full treatment of the ethics of the payment of taxes.

knows he or she will never use these vicious services. No acts of contraception, sterilization, or use of abortifacient drugs will follow from the employee's purchase of health insurance. The employer who complies with the mandate, on the other hand, agrees to contract for vice.[115] The employer chooses the evil of payment for another's vice without any knowledge that the employees will refrain from making use of these so-called services. In fact, insofar as these services are part of the employee's contract, the employer presents them as a benefit of employment.

Even among those theologians who recognize the immorality of contraception and the inadvisability of providing for contraception in health insurance, still some disagree about how to respond to a government mandate to offer such coverage.[116] Some employers might suggest that their compliance with the mandate is justified under the condition of duress. While Catholic and other conscientiously objecting employers may not wish to fund these services, their decision to comply with the mandate remains an exercise of free choice. Duress does not change whether funding these services represents good or bad acting. That judgment should be based on the kind of thing one funding the services is doing. The offer and contract to pay for vice can never be a good act. Duress may be a useful category to analyze the culpability for one's action, but it cannot fundamentally change the nature of what one is doing. As Pope John Paul II explained: "[I]t is always possible that man, as the result of coercion or other circumstances, can be hindered from doing certain good actions; but he can never be hindered from not doing certain actions, especially if he is prepared to die rather than to do evil."[117] At the heart of the moral debate about compliance with a contraception mandate is the nature of the act of offering health insurance. What happens when an employer offers health insurance coverage (including for vicious services) as part of a benefits package provided with employment? If this is the sort of act that should never be chosen, no set of circumstances can transform this bad act into a good one.

---

115. Steven A. Long maintains that an employer's offering coverage for what he aptly calls "vicious services" represents an immoral cooperative act. He explains: "It is immoral deliberately, voluntarily, and directly to contribute to the object of the external act of achieving a gravely evil action; and to provide the essential means for the performance of an evil act cannot be done." See his *The Teleological Grammar of the Moral Act*, 2nd ed., 217.

116. For one perspective, see Long, 208–25.

117. *VS*, no. 52.

Steven Long has offered an extended reflection on this matter applying a Thomistic analysis to specific issues of cooperation with evil. Long
maintains that compliance with government mandates to fund contraception, sterilization, or abortion represents immoral cooperation with
evil.[118] Long explains that to offer the coverage of vicious services as part
of a contract of employment represents an immoral cooperation with
vice.[119] Long distinguishes between "the *most* formal cooperation which
would consist in actually sharing the intention of the end" and the formal cooperation of compliance with the mandate.[120] Compliance remains, in his view, "formal cooperation because it is direct, essential aid
given voluntarily and deliberately to gravely sinful action."[121]

Government mandates to ensure coverage of immoral procedures affect
both individuals and institutions.[122] Institutional compliance presents serious challenges both on the level of scandal and cooperation with evil.[123]
For example, if a Catholic hospital were to merge with a secular health
care facility, a government mandate which previously granted an exception
to the Catholic hospital may not apply to the new merged institution.[124] A

118. See Long, *The Theological Grammar of the Moral Act*, 2nd ed., 208–25.

119. See Long, 225: "The view that cooperation with the HHS mandate is merely ma-
terial cooperation with evil seems to presuppose an intentionalist analysis of operation.
But it is far from obvious that such accounts are easily reconcilable with the Roman
Catholic doctrinal tradition."

120. Long, 221.

121. Long, 221.

122. For the norms governing partnerships between Catholic and non-Catholic
health care agencies, see the United States Conference for Catholic Bishops, *Ethical and
Religious Directives for Catholic Health Care Services*, 5th ed. (Washington, DC: United States
Conference of Catholic Bishops, 2009), 34–37, especially directive no. 70: "Catholic
health care organizations are not permitted to engage in immediate material cooperation in actions that are intrinsically immoral, such as abortion, euthanasia, assisted suicide, and direct sterilization."

123. For a treatment of the issues involved with institutional compliance, see Elliott
Louis Bedford, "The Reality of Institutional Conscience," *The National Catholic Bioethics
Quarterly* 16 (2016): 255–72; and by the same author, "The Concept of Institutional Con-
science," *The National Catholic Bioethics Quarterly* 12 (2012): 409–20. On the same topic, inter-
ested readers should also consult Bedford's "Catholic Social Teaching and the Women's
Preventative Health Services Mandate," *Nova et Vetera*, English edition, 10 (2012): 909–22.
For treatment of some of the necessary qualities of Catholic hospitals, see Dionigi Tettamanzi, *Nuova Bioetica Cristiana* (Segrete, Italy: Piemme, 2000), 377–84.

124. For the canonical issues involved in hospital mergers, see Nick P. Cafardi, "Canonical Concerns in Catholic Health Care," in *The Splendor of Truth and Health Care*, ed.

government mandate may require this new and merged institution to perform contraceptive sterilizations or to distribute abortifacient drugs. Solutions to these types of dilemmas may not be readily apparent. One possibility would be for a merged institution to require immoral procedures to be performed exclusively on certain separated sections of the merged facility.[125] While one can doubt the long-term viability of such collaborations, the effort to restrict immoral action to a portion of a facility or institution to which common funds may not be directed is not completely futile. Like the distinction moralists make between lying and the use of discreet language, these strict segregations are not insignificant. While they can appear to be a matter of hair-splitting, in fact, these efforts indicate an attempt to keep an institution's work distinct from immoral activity. However, the strong possibility of the likelihood of scandal remains. Most probably, even in situations when the Catholic portion of a facility will not perform an immoral cooperative act, it may be impossible for those collaborating to avoid confusion and scandal in the community.[126]

This example demonstrates the importance of a would-be cooperator to possess the capacity to recognize the natural teleology of a moral act. Some actions are extremely complex, such as an employer's decision to contract for health insurance. Only when paying sufficient attention to

---

Russell E. Smith, 87–97 (Braintree, MA: The Pope John Center, 1995). For a useful exchange on the principles involved in evaluating questions of moral cooperation in hospital mergers, see Russell E. Smith, "The Principles of Cooperation and their Application to the Present State of Health Care Evaluation," in *The Splendor of Truth and Health Care*, 217–31; and two responses to Smith's essay, Frances Marie Masching, O.S.F., "Response to 'The Principles of Cooperation and their Application to the Present State of Health Care Evaluation,'" in *The Splendor of Truth and Health Care*, 232–37; and Patricia A. Cahill, "Response to 'The Principles of Cooperation and their Application to the Present State of Health Care Evaluation,'" in *The Splendor of Truth and Health Care*, 238–42. For a helpful reflection on hospital mergers more generally, see Russell E. Smith, "Ethical Quandary: Forming Hospital Partnerships," in *The Gospel of Life and the Vision of Health Care*, ed. Russell E. Smith, 109–23 (Braintree, MA: The Pope John Center, 1996).

125. For useful principles for avoiding immoral cooperation in health care mergers, see the statement of the Ethicists of The National Catholic Bioethics Center, "Avoiding Formal Cooperation in Health Care Alliances," in *Ethical Principles in Catholic Health Care: Selections from 25 Years of Ethics and Medics* (Boston: The National Catholic Bioethics Center, 1999), 139–46.

126. See the United States Conference for Catholic Bishops, *Ethical and Religious Directives for Catholic Health Care Services*, 5th ed., 37, directive no. 71: "Cooperation, which in all other respects is morally licit, may need to be refused because of the scandal that might be caused."

what is necessarily included in the object of a particular action can one determine accurately the moral quality of a complex act. Rigorous examination of the act of contracting for health insurance precludes overemphasis on either the intention of the employer or the dangers to one's business which could result from denying such coverage. This example also reveals the need for a robust fortitude for those who attempt to live the truth of the moral law. The dramatic consequences of the refusal to comply with government mandates, for example, crippling fines or incarceration, demonstrates the need for fortitude when dealing with challenging matters of cooperation with evil in an increasingly secular environment.[127]

Principals seeking principles: avoiding scandal in Catholic education

In the fall of 2016, a fourteen-year-old girl was set to begin studies at Camden Catholic High School in New Jersey. Upon the conclusion of her eighth-grade year, the student had been admitted to the private high school operated under the leadership of the Catholic Diocese of Camden. In fact, she had been awarded a scholarship. However, when the student's family informed the school that their daughter had "transitioned" over the summer—now identifying as a male and would present herself as such—the school explained that it could not accommodate the family's demands.[128] Michael Walsh, Diocese of Camden Director of Communications, defended the school's position: "Adhering to its Catholic principles, the school concluded that it could not accommodate the family's requests without compromising some of the basic tenets of our faith."[129] In the twenty-first century, school administrators face the challenge of car-

---

127. For a sound treatment of how Catholic institutions can navigate the challenge of providing health care in a pluralistic society, see Nicanor Pier Giorgio Austriaco, OP, *Biomedicine and Beatitude*, 362–399. For a more general reflection on the challenge of living Catholic faith in a secular world, see Carl A. Anderson, "A Mandate for All Seasons: Catholic Conscience and Secular Society," *The National Catholic Bioethics Quarterly* 12 (2012): 597–609.

128. See Jessica Chasmar, "Transgender teen forced out at Catholic school that won't recognize student's new gender identity," *Washington Times*, September 14, 2016, https://www.washingtontimes.com/news-/2016/sep/14/nj-high-school-sticks-to-catholic-prin ciples-wont-/, accessed November 16, 2017.

129. Chasmar.

ing for parents who request their children be permitted to present themselves as transgendered in a school setting. Robust moral virtue will prove necessary to eschew both immoral cooperative acts and the danger of scandal when navigating these challenging waters.

Since the middle of the nineteenth century, Catholic schools in the United States have played a crucial role in the Church's evangelical success. At the present moment, however, Catholic education in American society faces manifold challenges. Not least among these trials is the burden of maintaining a school's Catholic identity in a culture often at odds with Catholic moral teaching. Fortunately, the Church's Magisterium has offered guidance in this area.[130] An essential principle of magisterial teaching in this regard concerns how schools should teach clearly the truth about disputed moral questions. One such area where the conflict between Catholic moral teaching and secular culture arises is in caring for those who present themselves as transgendered. In recent years debate about transgender issues across the United States has focused on whether elementary and high schools—including those based in the Catholic moral tradition—should accommodate those who present themselves as transgendered.[131] While much of this commentary has surrounded practical concerns about bathrooms, locker rooms, and shower facilities, theologians and others have devoted limited attention to the underlying moral questions at stake. In what follows we review briefly Catholic belief regarding sex and gender. Second, we examine how transgender ideology fails to correspond to this teaching. Third, we address how schools

---

130. See, for example, the Apostolic Constitution of Pope John Paul II, *Ex corde Ecclesiae*, August 15, 1990. While this document applies directly to Catholic universities, the principles of the document extend to other Catholic schools and educational institutions. For a collection of essays regarding the issues surrounding the implementation of *Ex corde Ecclesiae*, see *Catholic Universities in the Church and Society: A Dialogue on Ex Corde Ecclesiae*, ed. John P. Langan, SJ (Washington, DC: Georgetown University Press, 1993). For responses to common objections to *Ex corde Ecclesiae*, see Michael J. Baxter, CSC, "Notes in Defense of *Ex corde Ecclesiae*: Three Replies to Three Typical Objections," *The Thomist* 63 (1999): 629–42. For a useful collection of ecclesial documents dealing with Catholic universities, see United States Conference of Catholic Bishops Committee on Education, *Catholic Identity in Our Colleges and Universities* (Washington, DC: United States Conference of Catholic Bishops, 2006). Interested readers may also consult the address of Pope Benedict XVI on the topic of Catholic education delivered during his 2008 visit to the United States, Pope Benedict XVI, *Meeting with Catholic Educators*, April 17, 2008.

131. See, for example, the 2016 controversy at the Rhode Island Catholic school Mt. St. Charles Academy. See Linda Borg, "Mt. St Charles policy not to accept trans students decried," *Providence Journal*, March 4, 2016.

should approach those who present themselves as transgendered to avoid immoral cooperation with evil.

According to the Catholic moral tradition, the existence of men and women reflects God's creative design.[132] This complementarity is built into nature and does not result merely from social engineering. In his encyclical letter *Laudato Si'*, Pope Francis explains:

Learning to accept our body, to care for it and to respect its fullest meaning, is an essential element of any genuine human ecology. Also, *valuing one's own body in its femininity or masculinity* is necessary if I am going to be able to recognize myself in an encounter with someone who is different. In this way we can joyfully accept ... the work of God the Creator.[133]

Catholics believe, in accord with right reason, that the human person is a composite of body and soul. Unlike the angels who are pure spirits, human beings are necessarily embodied.[134] Thus, sexual difference does not result from cultural imposition but rather reflects the will of the Creator.

A fundamental principle of Catholic social teaching is that everyone deserves the love and affection of the ecclesial community. Every person is called to holiness of life, to reject sin, and to embrace Gospel teaching. No one is excluded from the invitation to conversion. Those who pres-

---

132. See, for example, the letter of the Congregation for the Doctrine of the Faith, *Letter to the Bishops of the Catholic Church on the Collaboration of Men and Women in the Church and in the World*, May 31, 2004. For the history and development of the understanding of women, interested readers may consult the monumental three volume work of Sister Prudence Allen, RSM, *The Concept of Woman: The Aristotelian Revolution, 750 B.C.–1250* (Grand Rapids: Wm. B. Eerdmans Publishing Company, 1997); *The Concept of Woman: The Early Humanist Reformation, 1250–1500* (Grand Rapids: Wm. B. Eerdmans Publishing Company, 2002); and *The Concept of Woman: The Search for Communion of Persons, 1500–2015* (Grand Rapids: Wm. B. Eerdmans Publishing Company, 2017). For both a biblical and ethical defense of the essential differences between men and women, see John S. Grabowski, *Sex and Virtue*, 96–126.

133. Pope Francis, *Laudato Si'*, no. 155. Emphasis in the original.

134. For a masterful reflection on human person as necessarily embodied, see Benedict M. Ashley, OP, *Theologies of the Body: Humanist and Christian* (Braintree, MA: National Catholic Bioethics Center, 1985). For further reflection on the same matter, see Benedict M. Ashley, OP, *Healing for Freedom: A Christian Perspective on Personhood and Psychotherapy* (Arlington, VA: The Institute of Psychological Sciences Press, 2013). This latter book was reviewed positively by the present author. See my, "Review: *Healing for Freedom: A Christian Perspective on Personhood and Psychotherapy*," *Nova et Vetera*, English edition, 14 (2016): 1345–49. Alternatively, for an outstanding account of angels, see Serge-Thomas Bonino, OP, *Angels and Demons: A Catholic Introduction*, trans. Michael J. Miller (Washington, DC: The Catholic University of America, 2016).

ent themselves as transgendered should not be subject to ridicule or unjust discrimination. Catholic theology acknowledges, however, that insofar as they present themselves publicly in this way, they have not embraced the fullness of Christian teaching. The point is not to moralize about the origin of questions surrounding gender identity. People who struggle with all manner of psychological and social difficulties deserve love, support, and patience. No one should feel excluded from the Church's loving concern. The issue at hand though is why administrators of a Catholic school might feel that they could not accommodate those who present themselves in this way.

The transgender movement rejects the natural duality of male and female. Those who espouse a gender ideology believe biological sex does not determine one's gender.[135] Instead, the determination of whether one should identify as male or female is left to the free choice of the individual, not tethered to biological and chromosomal reality. For that reason, those who present themselves as transgendered have not embraced Catholic belief about the nature of the human person. Transgender ideology can claim little connection to debates over biological anomalies related to those considered intersex.[136] In such cases when doctors find biological sex difficult to determine, their recourse to surgical or chemical methods to restore what they believe to be the underlying physiological sex bears no resemblance to transgender ideology. Transgenderism, on the other hand, rejects specifically the biological conclusion that an anatomical male is in fact a male. One who presents himself as transgendered does not suffer from an intersex anomaly. Rather, such a person rejects the fact that his male anatomy determines that he is in fact a man.

Some who adopt the label "transgendered" do nothing more than dress and present themselves as a different biological sex than in fact they are.[137] Without judging the struggles that motivate those individuals to present themselves in this way, we can classify behavior of this kind as a sin

135. For the canonical challenges which transgender surgery presents, see Urbano Cardinal Navarrete, SJ, "Transsexualism and the Canonical Order," *The National Catholic Bioethics Quarterly* 14 (2014): 105–18.

136. For the distinction between intersex conditions and gender identity disorder, see Nicholas Tonti-Filippini, "Sex Reassignment and Catholic Schools," *The National Catholic Bioethics Quarterly* 12 (2012): 85–97.

137. For an examination of the related issue of identification with same-sex desire, see Daniel C. Mattson, *Why I Don't Call Myself Gay: How I Reclaimed My Sexual Reality and Found Peace* (San Francisco: Ignatius Press, 2017).

against the eighth commandment of the Decalogue forbidding lying.[138] Attempting to deceive others into believing something that is not true—namely, that one is a different biological sex than in fact is the case—fails to present the truth. Human communities only flourish in the truth. Other persons take a further step in gender reorientation when they resort to chemical or surgical procedures. Such medical interventions represent sins against the fifth commandment of the Decalogue which forbids mutilation and sterilization.[139] Such procedures could not be conducted licitly at Catholic hospitals and, in fact, violate the respect due to the human body.[140] Public identification as transgendered does not accord with Catholic moral teaching. Catholic schools have a duty to present the fullness of Catholic truth and would struggle to do so if they were to admit without qualification students who refuse even to attempt to live by these standards. Those who insist on identifying publicly as transgendered are not dealing with a private struggle or sin. Instead, they refuse even to endeavor to comport themselves according to Catholic moral teaching. Members of the Church desire correctly to be a welcoming community. For his part, Pope Francis has reminded the world that Christians seek to welcome everyone to embrace the fullness of the truth of the Gospel—without corner-cutting. The joy of the Gospel will only come from embracing its challenge, not accommodating moral confusion.

In July 2016 ten states across the United States announced that they would sue the federal government over the Obama administration rule insisting that schools permit students to use bathrooms and locker rooms according to their gender of choice. At that time, the ten states joined elev-

---

138. See *CCC*, nos. 2485–86.

139. See *CCC*, no. 2297: "Except when performed for strictly therapeutic medical reasons, directly intended amputations, mutilations, and sterilizations performed on innocent persons are against the moral law." See also the Congregation for the Doctrine of the Faith, *Responses to Questions Concerning Sterilization in Catholic Hospitals*, March 13, 1975, *AAS* 68 (1976): 738–40. And from the same Congregation, see *Responses to questions proposed concerning uterine isolation and related matters*, July 31, 1993, *AAS* 86 (1994): 820–21. Here the Congregation explains: "The end of avoiding risks to the mother, deriving from a possible pregnancy, is thus pursued by means of a direct sterilization, in itself always morally illicit, while other ways, which are morally licit, remain open to free choice." For a treatment of the ethics of sex-change procedures, see W. J. Eijk, L. M. Hendriks, J. A. Raymakers, and John I. Fleming, eds., *Manual of Catholic Medical Ethics*, 460–67.

140. For an anthropological argument against sex reassignment surgery, see Jacob Harrison, "Karol Wojtyla, Sex Reassignment Surgery, and the Body-Soul Union," *The National Catholic Bioethics Quarterly* 17 (2017): 291–302.

en others that had already filed similar suits.[141] In May of 2016, the United States Departments of Justice and Education issued federal guidance to all public-school districts in the country insisting they allow students to use bathrooms and locker rooms according to their chosen gender—not their biological sex. In response to this controversy, the chairman of the United States Bishops Committee for Laity, Marriage, Family Life, and Youth, and the chairman of the United States Bishops Committee on Catholic Education issued a joint statement condemning the federal regulation. The bishops explained:

Children, youth, and parents in these difficult situations deserve compassion, sensitivity, and respect.... All of these can be expressed without infringing on legitimate concerns about privacy and security. The federal regulatory guidance ... does not even attempt to achieve this balance.... We pray that the government make room for more just and compassionate approaches and policies in this sensitive area.[142]

Pope Francis has expressed disappointment when governments fail to achieve the balance between compassion for individuals and the need for sensible policies which account for the truth about the human person. The Pope explicitly rejected gender ideology when he taught: "The complementarity of man and woman, the pinnacle of divine creation, is being questioned by the so-called *gender ideology*, in the name of a more free and just society."[143] The Pope has further questioned how gender ideology would "fall into the sin of trying to replace the Creator."[144]

141. See Jess Bidgood, "10 More States Sue U.S. Over Transgender Policy for Schools," *New York Times*, July 8, 2016. For an evaluation of issues related to transsexuality, see W. J. Eijk, L. M. Hendriks, J. A. Raymakers, and John I. Fleming, eds., *Manual of Catholic Medical Ethics*, 462–66.

142. United States Conference of Catholic Bishops' statement, "USCCB Chairmen Respond to Administration's New Guidance Letter on Title IX Application," May 16, 2016.

143. Pope Francis, *Address to the Bishops of the Episcopal Conference of Puerto Rico on their Ad Limina Visit*, June 8, 2015. For reflection on both the origins and ramifications of gender ideology, see Michele M. Schumacher, "Gender Ideology and the 'Artistic' Fabrication of Human Sex: Nature as Norm or the Remaking of the Human?" *The Thomist* 80 (2016): 363–423. For a more popular presentation of these challenges, see Ashley McGuire, *Sex Scandal: The Drive to Abolish Male and Female* (Washington, DC: Regnery Publishing, 2017).

144. See Pope Francis, *Amoris laetitia*, no. 56: "Yet another challenge is posed by the various forms of an ideology of gender that 'denies the difference and reciprocity in nature of a man and a woman and envisages a society without sexual differences, thereby eliminating the anthropological basis of the family. This ideology leads to educational programs and legislative enactments that promote a personal identity and emotional

In a school environment, several questions arise concerning possible
immoral cooperation with those who present themselves as transgendered.
Sexual education, the distribution of contraception, vaccination against
sexually transmitted disease, and accommodation of students who present themselves as transgendered all offer instances of conflict between prevailing cultural sensibilities and Catholic moral teaching. In each case, the
Church has established general guidance regarding the truth of the moral
issues involved.[145] Precisely how individuals and institutions should—or
should not—cooperate with these new realities remains a more challenging question. Among the fundamental goals of Catholic education stands
the task of leading students out of error and into the truth. Teachers and
administrators, therefore, can never teach falsehood.[146] In recent years,
communities have seen efforts to mandate the teaching of sexual education in public schools that falls short of the full truth about the human
person. The effort to promote instructing young children in how to perform acts of unchastity offers just one example of the ways in which contemporary sexual education does not afford students exposure to the truth
about human love.[147]

intimacy radically separated from the biological difference between male and female.
Consequently, human identity becomes the choice of the individual, one which can also
change over time.' It is a source of concern that some ideologies of this sort, which seek
to respond to what are at times understandable aspirations, manage to assert themselves
as absolute and unquestionable, even dictating how children should be raised. It needs
to be emphasized that 'biological sex and the socio-cultural role of sex (gender) can be
distinguished but not separated.' ... It is one thing to be understanding of human weak-
ness and the complexities of life, and another to accept ideologies that attempt to sun-
der what are inseparable aspects of reality. Let us not fall into the sin of trying to replace the Creator. We are creatures, and not omnipotent. Creation is prior to us and
must be received as a gift. At the same time, we are called to protect our humanity, and
this means, in the first place, accepting it and respecting it as it was created."

145. For the general principles of Catholic moral teaching regarding matters of sexual morality, see the document of the Congregation for the Doctrine of the Faith, *Persona
humana*, December 29, 1975.

146. See, for example, what St. Thomas teaches about how the immorality of lying
admits of no exceptions. See *Summa theologiae*, IIa–IIae, q. 110, a. 3.

147. See, for example, the document of the Pontifical Council for the Family, *The
Truth and Meaning of Human Sexuality: Guidelines for Education within the Family* (Città del Vaticano: Libreria Editrice Vaticana, 1995). Interested readers may also consult the previous text of the Congregation for Catholic Education, *Educational Guidance in Human Love:
Outlines for Sexual Education*, November 1, 1983. For an excellent overview of the challenges
which face young people after the sexual revolution, see Mary Eberstadt, *Adam and Eve
after the Pill: Paradoxes of the Sexual Revolution* (San Francisco: Ignatius Press, 2012).

Amidst these cultural challenges, teachers remain duty-bound to lead students to the truth. Despite the misgivings of some moralists, the Catholic moral tradition does not allow for lying even in so-called "difficult cases."[148] While the prohibition against lying applies to everyone, a special responsibility follows from the relationship of student and teacher. When dealing with those who present themselves as transgendered, a teacher is obliged to instruct students in the truth. Educators bear special responsibility to help students understand the truth about themselves. Any action which would positively affirm a student in a gender identity different than what biology has determined would fall short of the moral standards appropriate for the relationship between teacher and student. For the same reasons, those schools which have created standards for the admission of students who insist on presenting themselves as transgendered act reasonably when they express concern about scandal and the possibility of immoral cooperation in erroneous self-presentation.[149] School administrators' praiseworthy concern for students in these situations should not become a Trojan horse for schools to admit presentations of unchastity or falsehood which would confuse the young about the truth about the human person.

This example demonstrates the necessary connection of the virtues in order to enact a sound moral decision.[150] Only those with a well-developed temperance will be well-equipped to navigate the complicated issues regarding chastity which are manifold in the contemporary cultural context.[151] Those persons who possess a healthy sense of shame at displays of

148. See *CCC*, no. 2485: "By its very nature, lying is to be condemned." For an exposition of the Catholic tradition on the absolute prohibition against lying, see Lawrence Dewan, OP, "St. Thomas, Lying and Venial Sin: Thomas Aquinas and the Validity of Moral Taxonomy," *The Thomist* 61 (1997): 279–99. Janet E. Smith has argued against this view, maintaining that the position of St. Thomas is flawed. See her "Fig Leaves and Falsehoods," *First Things* June/July 2011: 45–49. For a convincing rebuttal to Smith's claims, see Thomas Petri, OP, and Michael A. Wahl, "Live Action and Planned Parenthood: A New Test Case for Lying," *Nova et Vetera*, English edition, 10 (2012): 437–62.

149. See, for example, the instruction of the Diocese of Marquette, *Created in the Image and Likeness of God: An Instruction on Some Aspects of the Pastoral Care of Persons with Same-Sex Attraction and Gender Dysphoria*, July 29, 2021.

150. On the connection of the virtues, see Romanus Cessario, OP, *The Moral Virtues and Theological Ethics* (Notre Dame, IN: University of Notre Dame Press, 1991), 138–46.

151. See the outstanding reflection of Josef Pieper on the deleterious effects of unchastity on the exercise of the virtue of prudence. See Pieper, *The Four Cardinal Virtues*, 159–60: "Unchastity most effectively falsifies and corrupts the virtue of prudence. All that conflicts with the virtue of prudence for the most part stems from unchastity;

unchastity stand ready to confront the challenge of transgender ideology.[152] In a similar fashion, those with a deep love of the truth will shun instinctually the untruths necessary to enter the ideology's myth. The development of precise norms for Catholic schools to guard against scandal and immoral cooperative acts falls to bishops in their respective sees. This example demonstrates that no set of norms, however, can substitute for the necessary shame virtuous persons experience before displays of unchastity or untruth. Only virtue supplies the solution to these challenging moral quandaries.

Conclusion

The five case studies we have considered in this chapter demonstrate both the value and relative superiority of the virtue-based approach for addressing moral matters. The present work is principally a study in moral methodology. More than the particular conclusions we have reached in these cases, our aim has been to show the usefulness of our method of inquiry. The level of disagreement among moralists varies considerably in the cases we have treated. Near universal agreement exists, for example, regarding the morality of the payment of taxes even when some portion of the funds may be used for immoral ends. In that example, our aim was not to confirm the wide agreement about the conclusion regarding the topic but rather to demonstrate the relative superiority of the virtue-based approach to that of moral casuistry. While both casuists and virtue-based thinkers agree that one may pay taxes even when funds may be used for immoral purposes, only those grounded in the virtue tradition stake their claim on the fact that tax-paying is an act of the virtue of justice. When we moved to more controversial matters, such as the morality of compliance with government mandated funding of contraception, our commitment to a methodology of virtue and rigorous analysis of moral objects was able to yield clear conclusions. The purpose of this chapter, however, does not regard principally the particular conclusions reached in the case studies as much as it is an effort to demonstrate the quality of the virtue-based method and its ability to reach particular and reasonable answers to disputed moral topics.

---

unchastity begets a blindness of spirit which practically excludes all understanding of the goods of the spirit; unchastity splits the power of decision."

152. For theological reflection on the dynamics of shame, see Pope John Paul II, *Man and Woman He Created Them,* 171–73 and 236–46.

Conclusion

In the present work we have undertaken a study in moral methodology. More than particular conclusions about disputed moral matters, we have sought to establish a general method for analyzing questions of moral cooperation with evil. Unlike authors of either the casuist or proportionalist school, we have utilized the moral method of St. Thomas Aquinas. While the late twentieth century saw renewed attention to Aquinas's moral theory, only in a limited fashion have scholars applied his moral method to questions of cooperation with evil. In fact, moralists disagree about the prospects of such research. Some authors express hesitation about the value of the application of a virtue-based approach to moral matters.[1] In particular, cooperation with evil represents an area of moral inquiry hitherto dominated by casuist treatments. In the present study, however, we have demonstrated that virtue-based moral theology can render definitive conclusions in challenging cases and avoid the laxism to which rule-based moral theories are prone.

In the first chapter we identified the passages in St. Thomas Aquinas's *Summa theologiae* useful to establish a method for analyzing cooperative acts. We recalled that rather than utilizing extrinsic categories of types of cooperation, Aquinas analyzed rigorously the nature of the moral act of the would-be cooperator. He eschewed an analysis based on the proximity of the cooperator's act to that of the principal malefactor. Instead, Aquinas focused his attention on the nature of the cooperator's act itself. In particular, St. Thomas's permission for one to borrow money from one known to practice usury demonstrates his commitment to an object-based moral inquiry.[2] St. Thomas did not undertake a consequentialist evaluation of the effects of the cooperation. Instead, he limited his attention to the act of borrowing itself. Because nothing about the act of borrowing money implies usury, but instead the usurer misuses the good act

---

1. See, for example, the defense of manualist authors by Brian Besong, "Reappraising the Manual Tradition," *American Catholic Philosophical Quarterly* 89 (2015): 557–84.

2. See *Summa theologiae*, IIa–IIae, q. 78, a. 4.

of the borrower, Aquinas allows one to borrow from a known usurer. He does not resort to the imposed categories of formal and material cooperation *ante litteram*, nor does he inquire extensively about the intentions of the borrower. Instead, St. Thomas restricts his examination to the act of borrowing. The best method for analyzing the cooperative act of borrowing money from a usurer is to look closely at the act of borrowing itself.

In the first chapter we also gathered resources from the Thomist tradition useful for our project. St. Thomas Aquinas remains our principal guide in the effort to establish a virtue-centered approach to moral cooperation. At the same time, aspects of his moral method have been utilized fruitfully through the centuries. While by no means exhaustive, our research did uncover contributions of Thomist authors from the Catholic tradition. The fifteenth-century Dominican Jean Capreolus argued for the position of St. Thomas—against that of John Duns Scotus—on the need for the moral virtues for the proper exercise of prudence.[3] When addressing issues of cooperation with evil, moral theologians' goal is not merely the acquisition of a theoretical knowledge of what should be done in a given case. Rather, moralists hope to guide the perplexed individual to enact a sound moral action. In order to do so they must attend to how one can grow in moral virtue. For example, only those who possess a robust temperance will identify correctly and be willing to avoid immoral cooperation with sins of unchastity. Capreolus's defense of the connection between prudence and the moral virtues has important implications for how moralists can aid the perplexed to avoid unjust cooperative acts. For one to shun an immoral cooperative act requires the possession of the moral virtues, not merely a theoretical knowledge of what should be done in a given case.

The work of the sixteenth-century Dominican Cardinal Thomas de Vio Cajetan as well as that of the seventeenth-century Dominican John of St. Thomas offer resources from the Thomist tradition useful for our inquiry. From Cardinal Cajetan's work we were able to appreciate again the dependence of the exercise of prudence on rectified appetite. We also saw how Cajetan utilized an object-based moral inquiry when he addressed Aquinas's treatment of borrowing from one known to practice usury. John of St. Thomas remains the principal exponent of the place of the gifts

---

3. See John Capreolus, *On the Virtues*, translated with an Introduction and Notes by Kevin White and Romanus Cessario, OP (Washington, DC: The Catholic University of America Press, 2001), 325–76.

of the Holy Spirit in the Christian moral life. He expounds on Aquinas's treatment of the gifts, elucidating their particular role in disputed moral questions. Only those who cultivate the gifts in their own lives stand ready to face the multifarious forms of cooperation which confront modern-day believers. All that is to say, any approach to cooperation with evil which neglects the role of the gifts of the Holy Spirit cannot promise a full account of how Christians should actually address these challenges.[4]

In the second chapter we recounted in broad strokes the efforts to analyze moral cooperation in the period preceding the Second Vatican Council. The authors we examined took seriously questions of moral cooperation, and, in general terms, provided sound counsel for how a perplexed cooperator ought to proceed in individual cases. The authors we examined—the most commonly used manuals available in either Latin or English in the late nineteenth and early twentieth centuries—generally followed the method in use since the latter part of the eighteenth century. Following St. Alphonsus Liguori, these authors distinguished formal and material cooperation and then made further efforts to show which types of material cooperation would be licit or illicit. The judgment of the liceity of material cooperation most often would depend on some sort of proximity to the evil action with which one was cooperating. These authors most often treated cooperation as a sub-species of the sin of scandal. They considered it a sin against the charity owed one's neighbor, specifically the obligation in charity to attempt to prevent the sin of another. The juxtaposition of the treatise on cooperation with the casuist treatment of scandal proved unfortunate. Instead of analyzing cooperative acts in their own right, moralists of the period tended to examine the matter from the perspective of the obligations of charity. They evaluated the moral quality of the cooperative act relative to the obligation of charity to prevent the sin of the principal malefactor. In so doing, these moralists neglected the moral quality of the cooperative act in its own right.

Each author we examined bears significance for our project. The Italian Jesuit Aloysius Sabetti authored the most influential manual in the United States in the nineteenth century. The English Jesuit Thomas Slater produced the first English language casuist manual. The Dominicans Dominicus Prümmer and Benoît-Henri Merkelbach composed two sig-

---

4. For an excellent treatment of the place of the gifts of the Holy Spirit in the Christian life, see Walter Farrell, OP, and Dominic Hughes, OP, *Swift Victory: Essays on the Gifts of the Holy Spirit* (Providence, RI: Cluny Media, 2021).

nificant—and broadly speaking Thomist—moral manuals. The German Jesuits Noldin-Schmitt authored the most widely used manual in US seminaries in the first half of the twentieth century. The American Dominicans McHugh-Callan composed the first English language manual designed for American readers. In their moral text, the Franciscans Jone-Adelman considered a large corpus of examples of cooperation with evil. The English Jesuit Henry Davis remains known in the English-speaking world for his work in moral and sacramental theology. Finally, the German Redemptorist Bernhard Häring stands as one of the most influential moralists of the twentieth century and a bridge between casuistry and proportionalism. Despite the merits of their work, a careful reading of these authors reveals certain deficiencies in their approach and thus prompted our investigation of an alternative moral method.

Those committed to St. Thomas's vision of the moral life find inadequate the restricted view of moral theology adopted by the casuist authors. By and large, moralists of that period often paid insufficient attention to the role of the virtues and the gifts of the Holy Spirit when they sought to determine how to navigate difficult questions of cooperation with evil. We recalled the English Jesuit Thomas Slater's truncated view of the task of moral theology. Slater held that moral manuals "are not intended for edification, nor do they hold up a high ideal of Christian perfection." They are, he explained, "books of moral pathology." While not every manualist author taught explicitly in this manner, most did share this basic outlook. The Second Vatican Council called for a renewal of moral theology precisely on this point. The work of moral theology, the Council taught, is to "shed light on the loftiness of the calling of the faithful in Christ."

Contrary to what is often assumed to be a general consensus among casuist authors, one discovers disagreement over just what types of cooperation could be justified. Questions such as the sale of contraception and the assistance given during a procured abortion were justified by some authors so long as moral agents could claim a grave or proportionate reason to cooperate. Equally frustrating for those seeking answers to their moral questions, authors of this period often left a perplexed reader in a state of uncertainty about the nature of the cooperative act itself. Far from answering all questions related to cooperation, a perplexus was often left to determine whether his particular circumstances justified a particular act of material cooperation. Manualist authors considered crucial the judgment of whether a situation presented a serious, grave, still more grave, or proportionate reason for cooperating. Despite the efforts to elucidate these terms, both disagreement among authors and lack of resolution for the perplexed remained during this period.

The method of moral casuistry contrasts with an approach to moral matters based in the essential character or natural teleology of the act. According to this approach, to determine whether a type of cooperation can be a good act, moral agents need to determine the nature of the cooperative act itself. Put simply, what is the cooperator doing? What *per se* follows from his act? Leaving aside the question of just how closely his action comes into contact with the malfeasant act of another, what can the cooperator be said to be doing? To make a thorough evaluation of the cooperator's action, one needs to understand the context in which he is acting and what necessarily or *per se* follows from the action.

In chapter three we demonstrated that this object-based analysis finds resonance in the approach advanced in recent magisterial teaching, especially the encyclical letter of Pope John Paul II, *Veritatis splendor*. Both the revised version of the *Ethical and Religious Directives for Catholic Health Care Services* of the American bishops as well as recent documents of the Holy See propose this type of moral analysis. By and large the documents of the Magisterium have avoided use of the technical terms of moral casuistry. Instead, these instructions have cautioned readers about the dangers of affording too great a place in moral reasoning to the intention or consequences of a particular action. Three contemporary authors offered guidance for our work in their efforts to utilize recent magisterial teaching as well as a robust object-based approach to analyzing questions of moral cooperation. The work of Steven A. Long, Archbishop Anthony Fisher, and Andrew McLean Cummings have provided us with the tools to ground an approach to moral cooperation in the nature of human action and its natural teleology. In so doing, we discover a method that grounds analysis of moral cooperation in the truth about human acting and human flourishing.

In the fourth chapter we set to describe the contours of the virtue-based approach to cooperation with evil. Drawing upon the resources of the Thomist tradition and relying on the guidance of the Church's Magisterium, we outlined how virtue-based theologians will analyze cooperative acts. The imposition of extrinsic categories upon cooperative acts—formal, material, remote, proximate—failed to reach consensus about disputed cases. More seriously, moral agents struggle to determine easily which extrinsic category to apply in difficult circumstances. Alternatively, the approach we advocate makes possible connatural knowledge of which types of cooperation to avoid. As opposed to seeking a ready-made category into which a challenging cooperative act may fit, moral agents may be better served through attention to the act itself. If one possesses sufficient moral virtue, he can also rely on an appropriate appetitive response to the case in question.

Confusion surrounding the merits of a virtue-based approach to moral cooperation results principally from misunderstanding the virtue of prudence. Those who reduce prudence to a purely theoretical knowing fail to grasp the power of this virtue. Those possessed of prudence possess knowledge of what to do in a particular case. By means of prudence they also enjoy the power to enact a sound moral choice. Issues of cooperation with evil involve what justice requires in the relations of familial and political life. Those persons possessed of the virtue of justice stand ready to recognize the due to be rendered to family or state. The challenges of the twenty-first century will require of Christians a robust fortitude to avoid immoral cooperation with evil. Like the other moral virtues, acquired fortitude grows through actions large and small. That means small accommodations to questionably licit cooperative acts will not bode well for persons seeking the courage to refuse to cooperate in more difficult cases. Challenging issues related to chastity and gender ideology represent common questions of cooperation with evil for Christians in the twenty-first century. No one will effectively shun vicious forms of cooperation without a healthy *verecundia* or shame toward evils.[5] Similarly, only those with a developed *honestas* will intuitively draw near to pockets of virtuous social and political life.[6]

While it extends beyond the scope of this study to apply this approach to every contemporary question of moral cooperation, in chapter five we offered some particular conclusions for the beginnings of such work. We emphasized the place of the moral virtues in ensuring the execution of good acts in this area. There can be no dispute that it is difficult work to analyze rigorously the nature of a particular human action in a given context. We cannot guarantee that the virtue-based method will achieve universal agreement in application to every case. However, among those

5. See *Summa theologiae*, IIa–IIae, q. 144, a. 4.
6. See *Summa theologiae*, IIa–IIae, q. 145, a. 2.

committed to a morally serious way of approaching these questions one can hope that greater consensus could be built precisely because this approach is grounded in virtuous acting. That is, virtuous cooperation requires a sound method for analyzing questions of moral cooperation with evil in order that the cooperator remain conscious of the nature of the acts he executes and what *per se* follows from what he is doing.[7] In this way, moral agents can develop the virtues needed to act well in instances of possible cooperation with evil. As elements of contemporary Western culture ignore the truth about the good of the human person, the need for courageous resistance to immoral cooperation becomes even more necessary. Avoiding vicious cooperation will not be easy. However, Catholic moral theology possesses well-founded hope that a clear conception of how to live the truth about cooperative acts will make our embracing virtuous—and so eschewing vicious—cooperation possible in our time.

7. For an insightful expression of the same point, see Kevin L. Flannery, SJ, *Cooperation with Evil: Thomistic Tools of Analysis* (Washington, DC: The Catholic University of America Press, 2019), 216. "The primary advantage of a genuinely Thomistic approach to cooperation with evil—besides, for instance, the avoidance of confusion regarding act indifference and the resulting emphasis on intention, understood in a particular way—is that, when the approach is adopted by those tasked with determining what is immoral cooperation and what is not, they know what they are doing. They have the proper tools for their particular task."

Bibliography

Magisterial Documents

Benedict XVI, *Address of His Holiness Benedict XVI on the Occasion of Christmas Greetings to the Roman Curia*. December 22, 2012. *AAS* 98 (2006): 40–53.

———. General Audience. August 1, 2012.

———. General Audience. March 30, 2011.

———. General Audience. June 2, 2010.

———. *Meeting with Catholic Educators*. April 17, 2008.

———. *Address to Members of the International Congress of Catholic Pharmacists*. October 29, 2007.

Congregation for Catholic Education. *Educational Guidance in Human Love: Outlines for Sexual Education*. November 1, 1983.

———. *Document on the Theological Formation of Future Priests*. February 22, 1976.

Congregation for the Doctrine of the Faith. *Responsum* to a *dubium* regarding the blessing of the unions of persons of the same sex. March 15, 2021.

———. *Note on the morality of using some anti-Covid-19 vaccines*. December 21, 2020.

———. *Some Principles for Collaboration with Non-Catholic Entities in the Provision of Health Care Services*, as published in *The National Catholic Bioethics Quarterly* 14 (2014): 337–40.

———. Instruction *Dignitas Personae* on Certain Bioethical Questions. September 8, 2008. *AAS* 100 (2008) 858–87; *DeS* 24 (2010).

———. *Responses to Certain Questions of the United States Conference of Catholic Bishops Concerning Artificial Nutrition and Hydration*. August 1, 2007. *AAS* 99 (2007): 820–21.

———. *Letter to the Bishops of the Catholic Church on the Collaboration of Men and Women in the Church and in the World*. May 31, 2004. *AAS* 96 (2004): 671–87.

———. *Considerations regarding proposals to give legal recognition to unions between homosexual persons*. June 3, 2003. *AAS* 96 (2004): 41–57.

———. *Doctrinal Note on Some Questions Regarding the Participation of Catholics in Political Life*. November 24, 2002.

———. *Doctrinal Commentary on the Concluding Formula of the* Professio Fidei. June 29, 1998. *AAS* 90 (1998): 544–51.

———. *Responses to questions proposed concerning uterine isolation and related matters*. July 31, 1993. *AAS* 86 (1994): 820–21.

———. *Some Considerations Concerning the Response to Legislative Proposals on the Non-Discrimination of Homosexual Persons*. *L'Osservatore Romano*. July 24, 1992.

———. Instruction *Donum Veritatis: On the Ecclesial Vocation of the Theologian*. May 24, 1990. *AAS* 82 (1990): 1550–70.

————. Instruction *Donum vitae* on Respect for Human Life in its Origin and on the Dignity of Procreation. February 22, 1987. *AAS* 80 (1988): 70–102.

————. *Letter to the Bishops of the Catholic Church on the Pastoral Care of Homosexual Persons*. October 1, 1986. *AAS* 79 (1987): 543–54.

————. *Declaration on Euthanasia*. May 5, 1980. *AAS* 72 (1980): 542–52.

————. *Persona humana*. Declaration on Certain Questions Concerning Sexual Ethics. December 29, 1975. *AAS* 68 (1976): 77–96.

————. *Responses to Questions Concerning Sterilization in Catholic Hospitals*. March 13, 1975. *AAS* 68 (1976): 738–40.

————. *Declaration on Procured Abortion*. June 28, 1974. *AAS* 66 (1974): 730–47.

Francis. *Amoris Laetitia*. March 19, 2016. *AAS* 108 (2016): 311–446.

————. *Address to the Bishops of the Episcopal Conference of Puerto Rico on their Ad Limina Visit*. June 8, 2015.

————. *Laudato si'*. May 24, 2015. *AAS* 107 (2015): 847–945.

John Paul II. *Man and Woman He Created Them: A Theology of the Body*. Translated by Michael Waldstein. Boston: Pauline Books and Media, 2006.

————. Apostolic Letter. *Moto Proprio*. Proclaiming Saint Thomas More Patron of Statesmen and Politicians. October 31, 2000.

————. *Fides et ratio*. September 14, 1998. *AAS* 91 (1999): 5–88.

————. *Ut Unum Sint*. May 25, 1995. *AAS* 87 (1995): II, 921–82.

————. *Evangelium vitae*. March 25, 1995. *AAS* 87 (1995): I, 401–522.

————. *Veritatis splendor*. August 6, 1993. *AAS* 85 (1993): II, 1134–1228.

————. *Centesimus annus*. May 1, 1991. *AAS* 83 (1991): II, 793–867.

————. *Ex corde Ecclesiae*. August 15, 1990. *AAS* 82 (1990): II, 1475–1509.

————. *Christifideles laici*. December 30, 1988. *AAS* 81 (1989): 393–523.

————. *Sollicitudo rei socialis*. December 30, 1987. *AAS* 80 (1988): 513–86.

————. *Spiritus Domini*, Apostolic Letter for the Bicentenary of the death of St. Alphonsus de'Liguori. August 1, 1987. *AAS* 79 (1987): 1365–75.

Paul VI. *Humane vitae*. *AAS* 60 (1968): 481–503.

Pius XI. *Casti connubii*. *AAS* 22 (1930): 579–81.

————. *Mortalium animos*. *AAS* 20 (1928): 5–16.

Sacra Congregatio S. Officii, "*De Participatione Catholicorum*." *AAS* 11 (1919): 312–16.

Second Vatican Council. Declaration on Christian Education, *Gravissimum educationis*. October 28, 1965. *AAS* 58 (1966): 728–39.

————. Decree on Priestly Training, *Optatam totius*. October 28, 1965. *AAS* 58 (1966): 713–27.

————. Decree on Ecumenism, *Unitatis redintegratio*. November 21, 1964. *AAS* 57 (1965): 90–112.

Other Ecclesial Documents

Diocese of Marquette, Instruction, *Created in the Image and Likeness of God: An Instruction on Some Aspects of the Pastoral Care of Persons with Same-Sex Attraction and Gender Dysphoria*. July 29, 2021.

Pontifical Academy for Life. "Moral Reflections on Vaccines Prepared from Cells Derived from Aborted Human Fetuses." June 9, 2005.

———. *Evangelium Vitae: Five Years of Confrontation with the Society*. Edited by Juan de Dios Vial Correa and Elio Sgreccia. Vatican City: Libreria Editrice Vaticana, 2001.

Pontifical Council for the Family. *Vademecum for Confessors Concerning Some Aspects of the Morality of Conjugal Life*. Vatican City: Libreria Editrice Vaticana, 1997.

———. *The Truth and Meaning of Human Sexuality: Guidelines for Education within the Family*. Vatican City: Libreria Editrice Vaticana, 1995.

Pontifical Council for the Pastoral Care of Health Care Workers. *Nuova Carta degli Operatori Sanitari*. Vatican City: Libreria Editrice Vaticana, 2017.

United States Catholic Conference. *Health and Healthcare: A Pastoral Letter of the American Catholic Bishops*. Washington, DC: United States Catholic Conference, 1982.

United States Conference of Catholic Bishops. "USCCB Chairmen Respond to Administration's New Guidance Letter on Title IX Application." May 16, 2016.

———. *Ethical and Religious Directives for Catholic Health Care Services: Fifth Edition*. Washington, DC: USCCB Publishing, 2009.

United States Conference of Catholic Bishops, Ad Hoc Committee on Religious Liberty. *Our First, Most Cherished Liberty: A Statement on Religious Liberty*. April 2012.

United States Conference of Catholic Bishops Committee on Education. *Catholic Identity in Our Colleges and Universities*. Washington, DC: United States Conference of Catholic Bishops, 2006.

Other Sources

Aertnys, Joseph, CSsR, and C. A. Deman, CSsR. *Theologia Moralis*. 11th Edition. Rome: Marietti, 1928.

Agulles Simó, Pau. *La objeción de conciencia farmacéutica en España*. Rome: Edizioni Università della Santa Croce, 2006.

Allen, John L., Jr. *Cardinal Ratzinger: The Vatican's Enforcer of the Faith*. New York: Continuum, 2000.

Allen, Prudence, RSM. *The Concept of Woman: The Search for Communion of Persons, 1500–2015*. Grand Rapids, MI: Eerdmans, 2017.

———. *The Concept of Woman: The Early Humanist Reformation, 1250–1500*. Grand Rapids, MI: Eerdmans, 2002.

———. *The Concept of Woman: The Aristotelian Revolution, 750 B.C.–1250*. Grand Rapids, MI: Eerdmans, 1997.

Anderson, Carl A. "A Mandate for All Seasons: Catholic Conscience and Secular Society." *The National Catholic Bioethics Quarterly* 12 (2012): 597–609.

Anderson, Ryan T. *When Harry Became Sally: Responding to the Transgender Movement*. New York: Encounter Books, 2018.

———. *Truth Overruled: The Future of Marriage and Religious Freedom*. Washington, DC: Regnery Publishing, 2015.

Angelini, Guiseppe, and Ambrogio Valsecchi. *Disegno storico della teologia morale*. Bologna: Dehoniane, 1972.

Anscombe, G. E. M. "Modern Moral Philosophy." *Philosophy* 33 (1958). Reprinted in *Ethics, Religion, and Politics*. Minneapolis: University of Minnesota Press, 1982.

———. *Intention*. Oxford: Basil Blackwell, 1957.

Araujo, Robert John, SJ. "Roman Catholic Teachings on the Use of Force: Assessing Rights and Wrongs from World War I to Iraq." *Nova et Vetera*, English edition, 10 (2012): 1049–72.

Arias, Joseph M. "'Validity' and 'Liceity' in conjugal acts: A reply to Stephen Napier on the HIV-condom debate." *The Linacre Quarterly* 83 (2016): 330–45.

Arias, Joseph M., and Basil Cole, OP. "The *Vademecum* and Cooperation in Condomistic Intercourse." *The National Catholic Bioethics Quarterly* 11 (2011): 301–28.

Ashley, Benedict M., OP. *Barefoot Journeying: The Autobiography of a Begging Friar*. Chicago: New Priory Press, 2013.

———. *Healing for Freedom: A Christian Perspective on Personhood and Psychotherapy*. Arlington, VA: The Institute for Psychological Sciences, 2013.

———. "The Truth Will Set You Free: *Reflections on the* Instruction on the Ecclesial Vocation of the Theologian *of the Congregation for the Doctrine of the Faith, May 24, 1990*." In *The Ashley Reader: Redeeming Reason*, 89–93. Naples, FL: Sapientia Press, 2006.

———. "Integral Human Fulfillment According to Germain Grisez." In *The Ashley Reader: Redeeming Reason*, 225–69. Naples, FL: Sapientia Press, 2006.

———. *Living the Truth in Love. A Biblical Introduction to Moral Theology*. Staten Island, NY: Alba House, 1996.

———. *Theologies of the Body: Humanist and Christian*. Braintree, MA: National Catholic Bioethics Center, 1985.

Ashley, Benedict M., OP, Jean K. DeBlois, CSJ, and Kevin D. O'Rourke, OP. *Health Care Ethics: A Catholic Theological Analysis*, 5th ed. Washington, DC: Georgetown University Press, 2006.

Associazione scienza & vita. Ed. *Vita, Ragione, Dialogo: Scitti in onore di Elio Sgreccia*. Siena: Cantagalli, 2012.

Aumann, Jordan, OP. *Spiritual Theology*. New York: Continuum, 2006.

———. "Spiritual Theology in the Thomistic Tradition." *Angelicum* 51 (1974): 571–98.

Austriaco, Nicanor Pier Giorgio, OP. *Biomedicine and Beatitude: An Introduction to Catholic Bioethics*, 2nd. ed. Washington, DC: The Catholic University of America Press, 2021.

———. "Mercy of God (Evangelium Vitae §99)." *Nova et Vetera*, English edition, 13 (2015): 1185–1208.

Baum, William W. *The Teaching of Cardinal Cajetan on the Sacrifice of the Mass: A Study in Pre-Tridentine Theology*. Rome: Pontificium Athenaeum "Angelicum" De Urbe, 1958.

Baxter, Michael J., CSC. "Notes in Defense of *Ex corde Ecclesiae*: Three Replies to Three Typical Objections." *The Thomist* 63 (1999): 629–42.

Beckwith, Francis J. *Defending Life: A Moral and Legal Case Against Abortion Choice*. Cambridge: Cambridge University Press, 2007.

Bedford, Elliott Louis. "The Reality of Institutional Conscience." *The National Catholic Bioethics Quarterly* 16 (2016): 255–72.

———. "The Concept of Institutional Conscience." *The National Catholic Bioethics Quarterly* 12 (2012): 409–20.

———. "Catholic Social Teaching and the Women's Preventative Health Services Mandate." *Nova et Vetera*, English edition, 10 (2012): 909–22.

Beeman, Patrick C. "Catholicism, Cooperation, and Contraception." *The National Catholic Bioethics Quarterly* 12 (2012): 283–309.

Benedict XVI and Peter Seewald. *Light of the World: The Pope, the Church, and the Signs of the Times*. Translated by Michael J. Miller and Adrian J. Walker. San Francisco: Ignatius Press, 2010.

Berg, Thomas. "A Revised Analysis of the 'Phoenix Abortion Case' and a Critique of New Natural Law Intentionality." *Nova et Vetera*, English edition, 15 (2017): 365–96.

Berkman, John. "Has the Message of *Evangelium vitae* Been Missed? An Analysis and a Future Direction for Catholic Biomedical Ethics." *The Thomist* 63 (1999): 461–80.

Bertone, Tarcisio. "Catholics and pluralist society: 'imperfect laws' and the responsibility of legislators." In Pontifical Academy for Life, *Evangelium Vitae: Five Years of Confrontation with the Society*, edited by Juan de Dios Vial Correa and Elio Sgreccia, 206–22. Vatican City: Libreria Editrice Vaticana, 2001.

Besong, Brian. "Reappraising the Manual Tradition." *American Catholic Philosophical Quarterly* 89 (2015): 557–84.

Bethel, Francis, OSB. *John Senior and the Restoration of Realism*. Merrimack, NH: Thomas More College Press, 2016.

Bianchi, Paolo. *When is Marriage Null? Guide to the Grounds of Matrimonial Nullity for Pastors, Counselors, and Lay Faithful*. Translated by Michael J. Miller. San Francisco: Ignatius Press, 2015.

Bidgood, Jess. "10 More States Sue U.S. Over Transgender Policy for Schools." *New York Times*. July 8, 2016.

Blankenhorn, Fr. Bernhard, OP, Sr. Catherine Joseph Droste, OP, Fr. Efrem Jindracek, OP, Fr. Dominic Legge, OP, Fr. Thomas Joseph White, OP. "Aquinas & Homosexuality: Five Dominicans Respond to Adriano Oliva, OP." *Angelicum* 92 (2015): 297–302.

Bonino, Serge-Thomas, OP. "St. Thomas Aquinas in the Apostolic Exhortation *Amoris Laetitia*." *The Thomist* 80 (2016): 499–519.

———. *Angels and Demons: A Catholic Introduction*. Translated by Michael J. Miller. Washington, DC: The Catholic University of America, 2016.

———, ed. *Surnaturel: A Controversy at the Heart of Twentieth-Century Thomistic Thought*. Translated by Robert Williams, translation revised by Matthew Levering. Naples, FL: Sapientia Press, 2009.

Boonin, David. *A Defense of Abortion*. Cambridge: Cambridge University Press, 2002.

Bouquillon, Thomas J. "Moral Theology at the End of the Nineteenth Century."

In *The Historical Development of Fundamental Moral Theology in the United States, Readings in Moral Theology, No. 11,* edited by Charles E. Curran and Richard A. McCormick, SJ, 91–114. New York: Paulist Press, 1999.

Bouscaren, Timothy L., SJ. *The Ethics of Ectopic Pregnancy: Catholic Ethics Regarding Ectopic and Pathological Pregnancies.* Rouchas Sud, France: Tradibooks 1933.

Bouthillon, Fabrice. "Le diable, probablement: Le P. Mandonnet, les Jésuites et le probabilisme (1901–1903)." In *Saint Thomas au XXᵉ siècle: Actes du colloque du Centenaire de la "Revue thomiste,"* edited by Serge-Thomas Bonino, 53–76. Toulouse: Éditions Saint-Paul, 1994.

Boyle, John P. *The Sterilization Controversy: A New Crisis for the Catholic Hospital?.* New York: Paulist Press, 1977.

Brennan, Robert Edward, OP. *Thomistic Psychology: A Philosophic Analysis of the Nature of Man.* Tacoma, WA: Cluny Media, 2016.

Bretzke, James T., SJ. "Conscience and *Veritatis Splendor* in the Church Today." *Studia Moralia* 55 (2017): 271–95.

Brock, Stephen L. "*Veritatis Splendor* §78, St. Thomas, and (Not Merely) Physical Objects of Moral Acts." *Nova et Vetera,* English edition, 6 (2008): 1–62.

———. *Action and Conduct: Thomas Aquinas and the Theory of Action.* Edinburgh: T&T Clark, 1998.

Brugger, E. Christian. *The Indissolubility of Marriage & the Council of Trent.* Washington, DC: The Catholic University of America Press, 2017.

———. *Capital Punishment and Roman Catholic Moral Tradition.* Notre Dame, IN: University of Notre Dame Press, 2003.

Budziszewski, J. *Commentary on Thomas Aquinas's Treatise on Law.* New York: Cambridge University Press, 2014.

Burke, Cormac. *The Theology of Marriage: Personalism, Doctrine, and Canon Law.* Washington, DC: The Catholic University of America Press, 2015.

Cafardi, Nicholas. "Canonical Concerns in Catholic Health Care." In *The Splendor of Truth and Health Care,* edited by Russell E. Smith, 87–97. Braintree, MA: The Pope John Center, 1995.

Cahill, Patricia A. "Response to 'The Principles of Cooperation and Their Application to the Present State of Health Care Evolution'." In *The Splendor of Truth and Health Care,* edited by Russell E. Smith, 238–42. Braintree, MA: The Pope John Center, 1995.

Capps, Charles F. "Formal and Material Cooperation with Evil." *American Catholic Philosophical Quarterly* 89 (2015): 681–98.

Capreolus, Jean, Ceslaus Paban, and Thomas Pègues. *Defensiones theologiae divi Thomae Aquinatis.* 7 vols. Turonibus: Cattier, 1900.

Capreolus, John. *On the Virtues,* Translated with an Introduction and Notes by Kevin White and Romanus Cessario, OP. Washington, DC: The Catholic University of America Press, 2001.

Carola, Joseph, SJ. *Engaging the Church Fathers in Nineteenth-Century Catholicism: The Patristic Legacy of the Scuola Romana.* Steubenville, OH: Emmaus Academic, 2023.

———. "La metodologia patristica nella teologia preconciliare dell'Ottocento." *Gregorianum* 97 (2016): 605–17.

Cataldo, Peter J. "Models of Health Care Collaboration." In *Catholic Health Care Ethics: A Manual for Practitioners*. 2nd ed., edited by Edward J. Furton with Peter J. Cataldo and Albert S. Moraczewski, OP, 271–73. Philadelphia: The National Catholic Bioethics Center, 2009.

———. "State-Mandated Immoral Procedures in Catholic Facilities: How Is Licit Compliance Possible?" In *Live the Truth: The Moral Legacy of John Paul II in Catholic Health Care*, edited by Edward J. Furton, 253–67. Philadelphia: The National Catholic Bioethics Center, 2006.

———. "Compliance with contraceptive insurances mandates: licit or illicit cooperation in evil?" *The National Catholic Bioethics Quarterly* 4 (2004): 103–30.

Cavanaugh, Thomas A. "Double-Effect Reasoning, Craniotomy, and Vital Conflicts: A Case of Contemporary Catholic Casuistry." *The National Catholic Bioethics Quarterly* 11 (2011): 453–63.

———. *Double-Effect Reasoning: Doing Good and Avoiding Evil*. New York: Oxford University Press, 2006.

Cessario, Romanus, OP, and Cajetan Cuddy, OP. *Thomas and the Thomists: The Achievement of Thomas Aquinas and His Interpreters*. Minneapolis: Fortress Press, 2017.

———. *Introduction to Moral Theology*, rev. ed. Washington, DC: The Catholic University of America Press, 2013.

———. "*After Virtue*, Thirty Years After: Laudatio for Alasdair MacIntyre." *Nova et Vetera*, English edition, 10 (2012): 895–900.

———. "Scripture as the Soul of Moral Theology." *The Thomist* 76 (2012): 165–88.

———. "On the Place of Servais Pinckaers (†7 April 2008) in the Renewal of Moral Theology." *The Thomist* 73 (2009): 1–27.

———. *A Short History of Thomism*. Washington, DC: The Catholic University of America Press, 2005.

———. *The Virtues, or the Examined Life*. New York: Continuum, 2002.

———. "Sacramental Confession and Addictions." In *Addiction and Compulsive Behaviors*, edited by Edward J. Furton, 125–39. Philadelphia: The National Catholic Bioethics Center, 2000.

———. "John Poinsot: On the Gift of Counsel." In *The Common Things: Essays on Thomism and Education*, edited by Daniel McInerny, 163–78. Mishawaka: American Maritain Association, 1999.

———. "*Epieikeia* and the Accomplishment of the Just." In *Aquinas and Empowerment: Classical Ethics for Ordinary Lives*, edited by G. Simon Harak, 170–205. Washington, DC: Georgetown University Press, 1996.

———. *The Moral Virtues and Theological Ethics*. Notre Dame, IN: University of Notre Dame Press, 1991.

———. "Casuistry and Revisionism: Structural Similarities in Method and Content." In *"Humanae Vitae": 20 Anni Dopo. Atti del II Congresso Internazionale di Theologia Morale*, 385–409. Milan: Edizioni Ares, 1990.

Chaput, Charles J. *Render unto Caesar: Serving the Nation by Living Our Catholic Beliefs in Political Life*. New York: Doubleday, 2008.

Cole, Basil, OP. "Review: *Vital Conflicts in Medical Ethics: A Virtue Approach to Craniotomy and Tubal Pregnancies*." *The Thomist* 74 (2010): 160–64.

Collins, Raymond F. *Wealth, Wages, and the Wealthy: New Testament Insight for Preachers and Teachers*. Collegeville, MN: Liturgical Press, 2017.

Connell, Francis J., CSsR. *Morals in Politics and Professions: A Guide for Catholics in Public Life*. Westminster, MD: The Newman Bookshop, 1946.

Connery, John, SJ. *Abortion: The Development of the Roman Catholic Perspective*. Chicago: Loyola University Press, 1977.

Connolly, Patrick. "The Concept of Scandal in a Changed Ecclesial Context." *Studia Canonica* 51 (2017): 135–48.

Connors, Ryan. "Review: *The Servant and the Ladder: Cooperation with Evil in the Twenty-First Century*." *Studia Moralia* 55 (2017): 211–14.

————. "Review: *Healing for Freedom: A Christian Perspective on Personhood and Psychotherapy*." *Nova et Vetera*, English edition, 14 (2016): 1345–49.

Corbett, John Dominic, OP. *Sacra Doctrina and the Discernment of Human Action*. Washington, DC, 1999.

Coriden, James A. "Canonical Penalties for Abortion as Applicable to Administrators of Clinics and Hospitals." *Roman Replies and CLSA Opinions*. Washington, DC: The Canon Law Society of America, 1986: 80–85.

Corvino, John, Ryan T. Anderson, and Sherif Girgis. *Debating Religious Liberty and Discrimination*. Oxford: Oxford University Press, 2017.

Crawford, David S. "Public Reason and the Anthropology of Orientation: How the Debate over 'Gay Marriage' Has Been Shaped by some Ubiquitous but Unexamined Propositions." *Communio* 43 (2016): 247–73.

————. "*Evangelium Vitae*, the Rhetoric of Freedom, and *Roe v. Wade*'s Totalitarian Implications." *Nova et Vetera*, English edition, 13 (2015): 1209–28.

————. "Pope Benedict XVI and the Structure of the Moral Act: On the Condoms Controversy." *Communio* 38 (2011): 548–82.

Cronin, Daniel A. *Ordinary and Extraordinary Means of Conserving Life: 50th Anniversary Edition*. Philadelphia: The National Catholic Bioethics Center, 2011.

Crowe, Martin Timothy, CSsR. *The Moral Obligation of Paying Just Taxes*. Washington, DC: The Catholic University of America Press, 1944.

Cuddy, Cajetan, OP. "St. Thomas Aquinas on Conscience." In *Christianity and the Laws of Conscience: An Introduction*, edited by Jeffrey B. Hammond and Helen M. Alvare, 112–31. Cambridge: Cambridge University Press, 2021.

Cummings, Andrew McLean. *The Servant and the Ladder: Cooperation with Evil in the Twenty-First Century*. Leominster: Gracewing, 2014.

Cunningham, Lawrence S., ed. *Intractable Disputes about the Natural Law: Alasdair MacIntyre and His Critics*. Notre Dame: University of Notre Dame Press, 2009.

Curran, Charles E. *Catholic Moral Theology in the United States: A History*. Washington, DC: Georgetown University Press, 2008.

————. *Loyal Dissent: Memoir of a Catholic Theologian.* Washington, DC: Georgetown University Press, 2006.

————. *The Moral Theology of Pope John Paul II.* Washington, DC: Georgetown University Press, 2005.

————. *The Origins of Moral Theology in the United States: Three Different Approaches.* Washington, DC: Georgetown University Press, 1997.

————. "The Manual and Casuistry of Aloysius Sabetti." In *The Context of Casuistry,* edited by James F. Keenan, SJ, and Thomas A. Shannon, 161–87. Washington, DC: Georgetown University Press, 1995.

————. "The Inseparability of the Unitive-Procreative Functions of the Marital Act." In *Readings in Moral Theology, No. 8: Dialogue about Catholic Sexual Teaching,* edited by Charles E. Curran and Richard A. McCormick, SJ, 153–67. New York: Paulist Press, 1993.

————. *The Living Tradition of Catholic Moral Theology.* Notre Dame, IN: University of Notre Dame Press, 1992.

————. *Toward an American Catholic Moral Theology.* Notre Dame, IN: University of Notre Dame Press, 1987.

————. "Cooperation: Toward a Revision of the Concept and Its Application." *Linacre Quarterly* 41 (1974): 152–67.

————. "Sterilization: Roman Catholic Theory and Practice." *Linacre Quarterly* 40 (1973): 97–108.

————. Ed. *Contraception: Authority and Dissent.* New York: Herder and Herder, 1969.

Curran, Charles E., and Richard McCormick, SJ, eds. *John Paul II and Moral Theology: Readings in Moral Theology.* Mahwah, NJ: Paulist Press, 1998.

Davis, Henry, SJ. *Moral and Pastoral Theology.* 4 vols. London: Sheed and Ward, 1958.

De Franceschi, S.H. "La rénovation de la théologie morale catholique à l'époque préconciliaire." *Revue thomiste* 116 (2016): 383–419.

DeCosse, David, and Kristin E. Heyer. *Conscience & Catholicism: Rights, Responsibilities, and Institutional Responses.* Maryknoll, NY: Orbis Books, 2015.

Deman, Thomas, OP. *Aux origines de la théologie morale.* Paris: Librairie J. Vrin, 1951.

————. "Probabilisme." In the *Dictionnaire de théologie catholique,* 417–619. Paris: Letouzey et Ane, 1936.

Dempsey, Robert J. "Condom Use by HIV-Discordant Married Couples." *The National Catholic Bioethics Quarterly* 15 (2015): 91–105.

Dewan, Lawrence, OP. "St. Thomas, Steven Long, and Private Defense." *Nova et Vetera,* English edition, 8 (2010): 191–205.

————. "St. Thomas, Lying and Venial Sin: Thomas Aquinas on the Validity of Moral Taxonomy." *The Thomist* 61 (1997): 279–99.

DiNoia, J.A., OP, and Romanus Cessario, OP, eds. *Veritatis Splendor and the Renewal of Moral Theology.* Chicago: Midwest Theological Forum, 1999.

Dougherty, M.V. *Moral Dilemmas in Medieval Thought: From Gratian to Aquinas.* Cambridge: Cambridge University Press, 2011.

Dreher, Rod. *The Benedict Option: A Strategy for Christians in a Post-Christian Nation.* New York: Sentinel, 2017.

Dublanchy, E. "Coopération." In the *Dictionnaire de théologie catholique*, 1762–70. Paris: Letouzey et Ane, 1936.

Eberstadt, Mary. *It's Dangerous to Believe: Religious Freedom and Its Enemies*. New York: Harper Collins, 2016.

———. *Adam and Eve after the Pill: Paradoxes of the Sexual Revolution*. San Francisco: Ignatius Press, 2012.

Eijk, W. J., L. M. Hendriks, J. A. Raymakers, and John I. Fleming, eds. *Manual of Catholic Medical Ethics: Responsible Healthcare from a Catholic Perspective*. Translated by M. Regina van den Berg and Janthony Raymakers. Ballarat: Connor Court Publishing, 2014.

Esolen, Anthony. *Out of the Ashes: Rebuilding American Culture*. Washington, DC: Regnery Publishing, 2017.

Fabro, Ronald. *Cooperation in Evil: A consideration of the Traditional Doctrine from the Point of View of the Contemporary Discussion about the Moral Act*. Rome: Pontifical Gregorian University, 1989.

Farrell, Walter, OP, and Dominic Hughes, OP. *Swift Victory: Essays on the Gifts of the Holy Spirit*. Providence, RI: Cluny Media, 2021.

Feingold, Lawrence. *The Natural Desire to See God in St. Thomas Aquinas and His Interpreters*. Naples, FL: Sapientia Press, 2010.

Feser, Edward. "In Defense of the Perverted Faculty Argument." In *Neo-Scholastic Essays*, 378–415. South Bend, IN: St. Augustine Press, 2015.

Feser, Edward, and Joseph M. Bessette. *By Man Shall His Blood Be Shed: A Catholic Defense of Capital Punishment*. San Francisco: Ignatius Press, 2017.

Finnis, John. "Restricting legalized abortion is not intrinsically evil." In *Cooperation, Complicity & Conscience: Problems in healthcare, science, law and public policy*, edited by Helen Watt, 209–45. London: The Linacre Centre, 2005.

———. "'A vote decisive for ... a *more* restrictive law'." In *Cooperation, Complicity & Conscience: Problems in healthcare, science, law and public policy*, edited by Helen Watt, 269–95. London: The Linacre Centre, 2005.

———. *Moral Absolutes: Tradition, Revision, and Truth*. Washington, DC: The Catholic University of America Press, 1991.

Finnis, John, Germain Grisez, and Joseph Boyle. "'Direct' and 'Indirect': A Reply to Critics of Our Action Theory." *The Thomist* 65 (2001): 1–44.

———. *Nuclear Deterrence, Morality and Realism*. Oxford: Oxford University Press, 1987.

Fisher, Anthony. *Catholic Bioethics for a New Millennium*. Cambridge: Cambridge University Press, 2011.

———. "HIV and condoms within marriage." *Communio* 36 (2009): 329–59.

———. "Co-operation in Evil" *Catholic Medical Quarterly* 44 (1994): 15–22.

Flannery, Kevin L., SJ. *Cooperation with Evil: Thomistic Tools of Analysis*. Washington, DC: The Catholic University of America Press, 2019.

———. "Voting, Intrinsic Evil, and Commensuration." *The American Journal of Jurisprudence* 60 (2015): 181–97.

———. "Voting Conscience: A Review of *Law's Virtues*." *First Things* (June/July 2015): 54–55.

————. *Action and Character according to Aristotle: The Logic of the Moral Life.* Washington, DC: The Catholic University of America Press, 2013.

————. "Two Factors in the Analysis of Cooperation in Evil." *The National Catholic Bioethics Quarterly* 13 (2013): 663–75.

————. "Aquinas and the NNLT on the Object of the Human Act." *The National Catholic Bioethics Quarterly* 13 (2013): 79–104.

————. *Christian and Moral Action.* Arlington, VA: The Institute for the Psychological Sciences Press, 2012.

————. "Counseling the Lesser Evil." *The Thomist* 75 (2011): 245–89.

————. "Vital Conflicts and the Catholic Magisterial Tradition." *The National Catholic Bioethics Quarterly* 11 (2011): 691–704.

————. "Review: *The Teleological Grammar of the Moral Act.*" *The Thomist* 78 (2008): 322–25.

————. "The Field of Moral Action According to St. Thomas Aquinas." *The Thomist* 69 (2005): 1–30.

————. *Acts Amid Precepts: The Aristotelian Structure of Thomas Aquinas's Moral Theory.* Washington, DC: The Catholic University of America Press, 2001.

————. "What is Included in a Means to an End?" *Gregorianum* 74 (1993): 499–513.

Flannery, Kevin L., SJ, and Thomas V. Berg. "*Amoris Laetitia*, Pastoral Discernment and Thomas Aquinas." *Nova et Vetera*, English edition, 16 (2018): 81–111.

Foran, John E. "Ectopic Pregnancy: Current Treatment Options déjà vu Humanae Vitae." *Linacre Quarterly* 66 (February 1999): 21–28.

Ford, John C., SJ, and Gerald Kelly, SJ. *Contemporary Moral Theology: Volume 1.* Westminster, MD: The Newman Press, 1964.

Ford, John C., SJ, and Germain Grisez. "Contraception and the Infallibility of the Ordinary Magisterium." *Theological Studies* 39 (1978): 258–312.

Furton, Edward J. "Ethics without Metaphysics: A Review of the Lysaught Analysis." *The National Catholic Bioethics Quarterly* 11 (2011): 53–62.

————, ed. *Urged on by Christ: Catholic Health Care in Tension with Contemporary Culture.* Philadelphia: The National Catholic Bioethics Center, 2007.

Gallagher, John A. *Time Past, Time Future: An Historical Study of Catholic Moral Theology.* Mahwah, NJ: Paulist Press, 1990.

Gallagher, Maggie. "(How) Does Marriage Protect Child Well-Being?" In *The Meaning of Marriage: Family, State, Market and Morals*, edited by Robert P. George and Jean Bethke Elshtain, 197–212. Dallas: Spence Publishing Company, 2006.

Gallagher, Raphael, CSsR. "Interpreting Thomas Aquinas: Aspects of the Redemptorist and Jesuit Schools in the Twentieth Century." In *The Ethics of Aquinas*, edited by Stephen J. Pope, 374–84. Washington, DC: Georgetown University Press, 2002.

————. "The Fate of the Moral Manual Since Saint Alphonsus." In *History and Conscience: Studies in Honor of Sean O'Riordan, CSsR*, edited by Raphael Gallagher, CSsR, and Brendan McConvery, CSsR, 212–39. Dublin: Gill and MacMillan, 1989.

————. "The systematization of Alphonsus' Moral Theology through the Manuals." *Studia Moralia* 25 (1987): 247–77.

————. "The Manual System of Moral Theology." *Irish Theological Quarterly* 51 (1985): 1–16.

Gardeil, Ambroise, OP. *The True Christian Life: Thomistic Reflections on Divinization, Prudence, Religion, and Prayer*. Translated by Matthew K. Minerd. Washington, DC: The Catholic University of America Press, 2022.

———. *The Gifts of the Holy Spirit in the Dominican Saints*. Tacoma: Cluny Media, 2017.

Garrigou-Lagrange, Reginald, OP. *The Theological Virtues*, vol. 1, *On Faith*. Translated by Thomas a Kempis Reilly, OP. St. Louis: B. Herder Book Co., 1965.

———. *Beatitude: A Commentary on St. Thomas' Theological Summa, ia iiae, qq. 1–54*. London: B. Herder Book Co., 1956.

———. *The Mother of the Saviour and Our Interior Life*. Translated by Bernard J. Kelly, CSSp. Dublin: Standard House, 1949.

———. *Christian Perfection and Contemplation*. London: B. Herder Book Co., 1937.

———. "Du caractère métaphysique de la théologie morale de saint Thomas, en particulier dans les rapports de la prudence et de la conscience." *Revue Thomiste* 30 (1925): 341–55.

George, Robert P. *Conscience and Its Enemies: Confronting the Dogmas of Liberal Secularism*. Wilmington, DE: Intercollegiate Studies Institute, 2016.

George, Robert P., and Christopher Tollefsen. *Embryo: A Defense of Human Life*. Princeton, NJ: Witherspoon Institute, 2011.

George, Robert P., and Jean Bethke Elshtain, eds. *The Meaning of Marriage: Family, State, Market and Morals*. Dallas: Spence Publishing Company, 2006.

Giertych, Wojciech, OP. "Free Will, Addiction, and Moral Culpability." In *Addiction and Compulsive Behaviors*, edited by Edward J. Furton, 113–24. Philadelphia: The National Catholic Bioethics Center, 2000.

Gilbert, Maurice, SJ. *Pontifical Biblical Institute: A Century of History (1909–2009)*. Rome: Gregorian and Biblical Press, 2014.

Gilby, Thomas, OP. *Justice*. Volume 37 of the Blackfriars *Summa Theologiae*. New York: McGraw-Hill Book Company, 1975.

———. *Prudence*. Volume 36 of the Blackfriars *Summa Theologiae*. New York: McGraw-Hill Book Company, 1974.

———. *Principles of Morality*. Volume 18 of the Blackfriars *Summa Theologiae*. New York: McGraw-Hill Book Company, 1966.

———. *Between Community and Society*. London: Longmans, Green and Co., 1953.

Girgis, Sherif, Ryan T. Anderson, and Robert P. George. *What is Marriage?: Man and Woman: A Defense*. New York: Encounter Books, 2012.

Gondreau, Paul. *The Passions of Christ's Soul in the Theology of Thomas Aquinas*. Providence, RI: Cluny Media, 2018.

———. "The 'Inseparable Connection' between Procreation and Unitive Love (*Humanae Vitae*, §12) and Thomistic Hylemorphic Anthropology." *Nova et Vetera*, English edition, 6 (2008): 731–64.

———. "The Passions and the Moral Life: Appreciating the Originality of Aquinas." *The Thomist* 71 (2007): 419–50.

Gormally, Luke, David Albert Jones, and Roger Teichmann, eds. *The Moral Philosophy of Elizabeth Anscombe*. Exeter: Imprint Academic, 2016.

Gorsuch, Neil M. *The Future of Assisted Suicide and Euthanasia*. Princeton, NJ: Princeton University Press, 2009.

Grabowski, John S. *Sex and Virtue: An Introduction to Sexual Ethics*. Washington, DC: The Catholic University of America Press, 2003.

Greene, Graham. *Monsignor Quixote*. New York: Simon & Schuster, 1982.

Gregory, Brad S. *The Unintended Reformation: How a Religious Revolution Secularized Society*. London: The Belknap Press of Harvard University Press, 2012.

Gregory the Great. *Pastoral Care*. Translated and annotated by Henry Davis, SJ. Westminster, MD: The Newman Press, 1950.

Grisez, Germain. *The Way of the Lord Jesus: Difficult Moral Questions*, vol. 3. Quincy, IL: Franciscan Press, 1997.

———. *The Way of the Lord Jesus: Living a Christian Life*, vol. 2. Quincy, IL: Franciscan Press, 1993.

———. *The Way of the Lord Jesus: Christian Moral Principles*, vol. 1. Chicago: Franciscan Herald Press, 1983.

Guilbeau, Aquinas, OP. "Was the Polish Pope a French Personalist?: An Indication from Evangelium Vitae." *Nova et Vetera*, English edition, 13 (2015): 1229–44.

Guilbeau, Aquinas, OP, and Romanus Cessario, OP. "Review: *Perfecting Human Actions: St. Thomas Aquinas on Human Participation in Eternal Law*. By John Rziha. Washington, DC: The Catholic University of America Press, 2009." *Nova et Vetera*, English edition, 10 (2012): 877–79.

Gury, Joanne P., SJ. *Casus Conscientiae*, edited by Joannis B. Ferreres. Barcelona: Typ. Eugenii Subirana, 1908.

———. *Compendium Theologiae Moralis*. Regensborg: Georgii Josephi Manz, 1868.

Haggerty, Donald F. *Jacques Maritain and the Notion of Connaturality: The Valid Role of Nonconceptual Moral Knowledge in the Existential Order*. Rome: Pontificia Universitas Lateranensis Academia Alphonsiana, 1995.

Hannigan, E. T., SJ. "Is it Ever Lawful to Advise the Lesser of Two Evils?" *Gregorianum* 30 (1949): 104–29.

Häring, Bernard. *Free and Faithful: My Life in the Catholic Church: An Autobiography*. Liguori, MO: Liguori/Triumph, 1998.

———. "Reciprocity of Conscience: A Key Concept in Moral Theology." In *History and Conscience: Studies in Honor of Sean O'Riordan, CSsR*, edited by Raphael Gallagher, CSsR, and Brendan McConvery, CSsR, 60–84. Dublin: Gill and MacMillan, 1989.

———. *Free and Faithful in Christ: Moral Theology for Priests and Laity*. 3 vols. Middlegreen: St. Paul Publications, 1978–81.

———. *The Law of Christ*. Translated by Edwin G. Kaiser. Westminster, MD: Newman Press, 1961.

Harrison, Jacob. "Karol Wojtyla, Sex Reassignment Surgery, and the Body-Soul Union." *The National Catholic Bioethics Quarterly* 17 (2017): 291–302.

Harte, Colin. "Problems of principle in voting for unjust legislation." In *Cooperation, Complicity & Conscience: Problems in healthcare, science, law and public policy*, edited by Helen Watt, 179–208. London: The Linacre Centre, 2005.

———. "The opening up of a discussion: a response to John Finnis." In *Cooperation, Complicity & Conscience: Problems in healthcare, science, law and public policy*, edited by Helen Watt, 246–68. London: The Linacre Centre, 2005.

Hause, Jeffrey. "Aquinas on Aristotelian justice: defender, destroyer, subverter, or surveyor?" In *Aquinas and the Nicomachean Ethics*, edited by Tobias Hoffmann, Jörn Müller, and Matthias Perkams, 146–64. Cambridge: Cambridge University Press, 2013.

Heck, Theodore H. *The Curriculum of the Major Seminary in Relation to Contemporary Conditions*. Washington, DC: National Catholic Welfare Conference, 1935.

Hendershott, Anne. *The Politics of Abortion*. New York: Encounter Books, 2006.

Henke, Donald Edward. *Artificially Assisted Hydration and Nutrition From: Karen Quinlan to Nancy Cruzan to the Present: An Historical Analysis of the Decision to Provide or Withhold/Withdraw Sustenance from PVS Patients in Catholic Moral Theology and Medical Practice in the United States*. Rome: Pontifical Lateran University Academia Alphonsiana, 2004.

Hilliard, Marie T. "Contraceptive Mandates and Immoral Cooperation." In *Catholic Health Care Ethics: A Manual for Practitioners*, 2nd ed., edited by Edward J. Furton with Peter J. Cataldo and Albert S. Moraczewski, OP, 275–81. Philadelphia: The National Catholic Bioethics Center, 2009.

Hittinger, Russell. "Introduction to Modern Catholicism." In *The Teachings of Modern Roman Catholicism: On Law, Politics, and Human Nature*, edited by John Witte Jr. and Frank S. Alexander, 1–38. New York: Columbia University Press, 2007.

Hochschild, Joshua P. *The Semantics of Analogy: Rereading Cajetan's De Nominum Analogia*. Notre Dame, IN: University of Notre Dame, 2010.

Hollenbach, David, SJ. "Nuclear Weapons and Nuclear War: The Shape of the Catholic Debate." *Theological Studies* 43 (1982): 577–605.

Hoose, Bernard. *Proportionalism: The American Debate and Its European Roots*. Washington DC: Georgetown University Press, 1987.

Horgan, John, ed. *Humanae Vitae and the Bishops: The Encyclical and the Statements of the National Hierarchies*. Shannon: Irish University Press, 1972.

Hütter, Reinhard, and Matthew Levering, eds. *Ressourcement Thomism: Sacred Doctrine, the Sacraments, and the Moral Life: Essays in Honor of Romanus Cessario, OP*. Washington, DC: The Catholic University of America Press, 2010.

Janz, Denis R. *Luther and Late Medieval Thomism: A Study in Theological Anthropology*. Waterloo, ON: Wilfrid Laurier University Press, 2009.

Jarrett, Bede, OP. *S. Antonino and Medieval Economics*. London: The Manresa Press, 1914.

Jensen, Steven J. "Causal Constraints on Intention: A Critique of Tollefsen on the Phoenix Case." *The National Catholic Bioethics Quarterly* 14 (2014): 273–93.

———, ed. *The Ethics of Organ Transplantation*. Washington, DC: The Catholic University of America Press, 2011.

———. *Good and Evil Actions: A Journey through St. Thomas Aquinas*. Washington, DC: The Catholic University of America Press, 2010.

———. "Do Circumstances Give Species?" *The Thomist* 70 (2006): 1–26.

———. "A Long Discussion Regarding Steven A. Long's Interpretation of the Moral Species." *The Thomist* 67 (2003): 623–43.

———. "A Defense of Physicalism." *The Thomist* 61 (1997): 377–404.

John of St. Thomas. *The Gifts of the Holy Spirit.* Translated by Dominic Hughes, OP. New York: Sheed & Ward, 1951.

Johnson, James Turner. "Holy War." *Nova et Vetera*, English edition, 10 (2012): 1099–1113.

Johnstone, Brian V., CSsR. "Bernhard Häring: An Appreciation." *Studia Moralia* 36 (1998): 587–95.

———. "The Meaning of Proportionate Reason." *The Thomist* 49 (1985): 223–47.

Jone, Heribert. *Commentarium in Codem iuris canonici.* Paderborn: F. Schoningh, 1950.

Jone, Heribert, OFM, Cap., and Urban Adelman, OFM Cap. *Moral Theology.* Westminster, MD: The Newman Bookshop, 1951.

Jones, Frederick M., CSsR. *Alphonsus de Liguori: The Saint of Bourbon Naples 1696–1787.* Dublin: Gill and MacMillan, 1992.

Jonsen, Albert R., and Stephen Toulmin. *The Abuse of Casuistry: A History of Moral Reasoning.* Berkley and Los Angeles: University of California Press, 1988.

Jordan, Mark D. *The Invention of Sodomy in Christian Theology.* Chicago: The University of Chicago Press, 1998.

Journet, Charles. *L'Église du Verbe incarné.* 3 vols. Paris: Desclée de Brouwer, 1943, 1951, 1969.

Kaczor, Christopher. *The Ethics of Abortion: Women's Rights, Human Life, and the Question of Justice*, 3rd ed. New York: Routledge, 2022.

———. *Proportionalism and the National Law Tradition.* Washington, DC: The Catholic University of America Press, 2002.

———. "Double Effect Reasoning from Jean Pierre Gury to Peter Knauer." *Theological Studies* 59 (1998): 297–316.

———. "Exceptionless Norms in Aristotle?: Thomas Aquinas and Twentieth-Century Interpreters of the *Nicomachean Ethics*." *The Thomist* 61 (1997): 33–62.

Kaveny, Cathleen. *Law's Virtues: Fostering Autonomy and Solidarity in American Society.* Washington, DC: Georgetown University Press, 2012.

———. "Appropriation of Evil: Cooperation's Mirror Image" *Theological Studies* 61 (2000): 280–313.

Kaveny, Cathleen, and Kevin L. Flannery, SJ. "Response and Rejoinder: On Voting, Intrinsic Evil, and Ranking of Political Issues." *The American Journal of Jurisprudence* 61 (2016): 259–73.

Keenan, James F., SJ. "Receiving *Amoris Laetitia*." *Theological Studies* 78 (2017): 193–212.

———. "Raising Expectations on Sin." *Theological Studies* 77 (2016): 165–80.

———. "Redeeming Conscience." *Theological Studies* 76 (2015): 129–47.

———. "Bernard Häring's Influence on American Catholic Moral Theology." *Journal of Moral Theology* 1 (2012): 23–42.

———. *A History of Catholic Moral Theology in the Twentieth Century: From Confessing Sins to Liberating Consciences.* New York: Continuum International Publishing Group, 2010.

———. "The Open Debate: Moral Theology and the Lives of Gay and Lesbian Persons." *Theological Studies* 64 (2003): 127–50.

————. "Not an Excessive Claim, Nor a Divisive One, But a Traditional One: A Response to Lawrence Welch on Immediate Material Cooperation." *Linacre Quarterly* 67 (2000): 83–88.

————. "Institutional Cooperation and the Ethical and Religious Directives." *Linacre Quarterly* 64 (1997): 53–76.

————. *Goodness and Rightness in Thomas Aquinas's Summa Theologiae.* Washington, DC: Georgetown University Press, 1992.

————. "Prophylactics, Toleration and Cooperation: Contemporary Problems and Traditional Principles." *International Philosophical Quarterly* 29 (1989): 205–20.

Keenan, James F., SJ, and Thomas A. Shannon, eds. *The Context of Casuistry.* Washington, DC: Georgetown University Press, 1995.

Kelly, Gerald, SJ. *Medico-Moral Problems.* St. Louis: The Catholic Hospital Association of the United States and Canada, 1958.

————. "The Morality of Mutilations: Towards a Revision of the Treatise." *Theological Studies* 17 (1956): 322–44.

Keown, John. *Euthanasia, Ethics and Public Policy: An Argument Against Legalisation,* 2nd ed. Cambridge: Cambridge University Press, 2018.

Kerr, Fergus. *After Aquinas: Versions of Thomism.* Oxford: Blackwell Publishing Company, 2002.

Koch, Antony. *A Handbook of Moral Theology,* vol. 5, Adopted and edited by Arthur Preuss. New York: Vail-Ballou Press, 1924.

Kopfensteiner, Thomas. "The Meaning and Role of Duress in the Cooperation in Wrongdoing." *Linacre Quarterly* 70 (2003): 150–58.

Kostko, Giovanni. *Beatitudine e vita cristiana nella Summa Theologiae di S. Tommaso d'Aquino.* Bologna: Edizioni Studio Domenicano, 2005.

————. *Doni Dello Spirito Santo E Vita Morale: San Tommaso Nella Somma Teologica.* Roma: Coletti A San Pietro, 1997.

Koterski, Joseph W., SJ. "Just War and the Common Good." *Nova et Vetera,* English edition, 10 (2012): 1031–48.

Kupczak, Jaroslaw, OP. *Gift and Communion: John Paul II's Theology of the Body.* Translated by Agata Rottkamp, Justyna Pawlak, and Orest Pawlak. Washington, DC: The Catholic University of America Press, 2014.

————. *Destined for Liberty: The Human Person in the Philosophy of Karol Wojtyla/John Paul II.* Washington, DC: The Catholic University of America, 2000.

La Soujeole, Benoît-Dominique de. *Introduction au mystère de l'Église.* Toulouse: Parole et Silence, 2006.

Labourdette, Michel, OP. *La Charité: Grand cours de théologie morale/ 10.* Paris: Parole et Silence, 2016.

————. *La Prudence: Grand cours de théologie morale/ 11.* Paris: Parole et Silence, 2016.

————. *Cours de théologie morale: Tome 2, Morale spéciale.* Paris: Parole et Silence, 2012.

————. *Cours de théologie morale: Tome 1, Morale fondamentale.* Paris: Parole et Silence, 2010.

————. "Théologie morale." *Revue Thomiste* 61 (1961): 257–76.

———. "Théologie morale." *Revue Thomiste* 50 (1950): 192–230.

Lamb, Matthew L., and Matthew Levering, eds. *Vatican II: Renewal within Tradition.* Oxford: Oxford University Press, 2008.

Lamont, John R. T. "Conscience, Freedom, Rights: Idols of the Enlightenment Religion." *The Thomist* 73 (2009): 169–239.

Langan, John P., SJ, ed. *Catholic Universities in the Church and Society: A Dialogue on Ex Corde Ecclesiae.* Washington, DC: Georgetown University Press, 1993.

———. "The American Hierarchy and Nuclear Weapons." *Theological Studies* 43 (1982): 447–67.

Lasnoski, Kent. "Alphonsus Liguori's Moral Theology of Marriage: Refreshing Realism, Continued Relevance." *Nova et Vetera*, English edition, 9 (2011): 1003–28.

Latkovic, Mark S. "The Morality of Tube Feeding PVS Patients: A Critique of the View of Kevin O'Rourke, OP." *The National Catholic Bioethics Quarterly* 5 (2005): 503–13.

Lee, Patrick and Robert P. George. *Conjugal Union: What Marriage Is and Why It Matters.* Cambridge: Cambridge University Press, 2014.

Lehmkuhl, Augustino. *Theologia Moralis.* Freiburg: Herder, 1890.

Levering, Matthew. *The Abuse of Conscience: A Century of Catholic Moral Theology.* Grand Rapids: Eerdmans, 2021.

———. *Paul in the Summa Theologiae.* Washington, DC: The Catholic University of America Press, 2014.

———. *The Betrayal of Charity: The Sins that Sabotage Divine Love.* Waco, TX: Baylor University Press, 2011.

Liguori, Alphonsus. *Theologia Moralis.* Gaudè. Rome: Ex Typographia Vaticana, 1905.

———. *Opere Ascetiche.* 4 vols. Torino: Marietti, 1867–1873.

Lombardo, Nicholas E. *The Logic of Desire.* Washington, DC: The Catholic University of America Press, 2011.

Long, Steven A. *The Teleological Grammar of the Moral Act.* 2nd ed. Naples, FL: Sapientia Press, 2015.

———. "The Gifts of the Holy Spirit and Their Indispensability for the Christian Moral Life: Grace as Motus." *Nova et Vetera*, English edition, 11 (2013): 357–73.

———. *Analogia Entis: On the Analogy of Being, Metaphysics, and the Act of Faith.* Notre Dame, IN: University of Notre Dame Press, 2011.

———. "Engaging Thomist Interlocutors." *Nova et Vetera*, English edition, 9 (2011): 267–95.

———. *Natura Pura: A Rediscovery of Nature in the Doctrine of Grace.* New York: Fordham University Press, 2010.

———. "Natural Law, the Moral Object, and Humanae Vitae." In *Ressourcement Thomism: Sacred Doctrine, the Sacraments, and the Moral Life,* edited by Reinhard Hütter and Matthew Levering, 285–31. Washington, DC: The Catholic University of America Press, 2010.

———. "Veritatis Splendor §78 and the Teleological Grammar of the Moral Act." *Nova et Vetera*, English edition, 6 (2008): 139–56.

———. "Regarding the Nature of the Moral Object and Intention: A Response to Steven Jensen." *Nova et Vetera*, English edition, 3 (2005): 101–8.

———. "A Brief Disquisition Regarding the Nature of the Object of the Moral Act According to St. Thomas Aquinas." *The Thomist* 67 (2003): 45–71.

Lord, Robert H., John E. Sexton, and Edward T. Harrington. *History of the Archdiocese of Boston*. New York: Sheed & Ward 1944.

Lottin, Odon. *Morale Fondamentale*. Paris: Desclée & Co., 1954.

———. *Principes de Morale*. Tome I–II. Paris: Desclée de Brouwer, 1947.

Luño, Angel Rodríguez. "Evangelium Vitae 73: The Catholic Lawmaker and the Problem of a Seriously Unjust Law." *L'Osservatore Romano*, English edition. September 18, 2002.

———. "Can Epikeia Be Used in the Pastoral Care of the Divorced and Remarried Faithful?" *L'Osservatore Romano*, English edition. February 9, 2000.

Lysaught, M. Therese. "Moral Analysis of a Procedure at Phoenix Hospital." *Origins* 40, no. 33 (January 2011): 537–49.

MacIntyre, Alasdair C. *After Virtue: A Study in Moral Theory*. Notre Dame, IN: University of Notre Dame Press, 1981.

Mahar, Christopher. *Providing or Withdrawing Artificial Nutrition and Hydration to Patients Diagnosed as Being in the Vegetative State: A Fundamental Investigation into the Underlying Moral-Theological Presuppositions in the Current North American Catholic Ethical Debate*. Doctoral dissertation, The Catholic University of Leuven, 2016.

Maher, Daniel P., ed. *The Bishop and the Future of Catholic Health Care: Challenges and Opportunities*. Boston: Pope John XXIII Medical-Moral Research and Education Center, 1997.

Mahoney, Edward P. "The Accomplishment of Jean Capreolus, OP." *The Thomist* 68 (2004): 601–32.

Mahoney, John. *The Making of Moral Theology: A Study of the Roman Catholic Tradition*. New York: Oxford University Press, 1990.

Mandonnet, P., OP. *Le Decret D'Innocent XI Contre Le Probabilisme. Extrait de la Revue Thomiste*. Paris: Bureaux de la Revue Thomiste, 1903.

Mangan, Joseph T. "A Historical Analysis of the Principle of Double Effect." *Theological Studies* 10 (1949): 41–61.

Mansini, Guy, OSB. "A Contemporary Understanding of St. Thomas on Sacerdotal Character." *The Thomist* 71 (2007): 171–98.

———. "Sacerdotal Character at the Second Vatican Council." *The Thomist* 67 (2003): 539–77.

———. "Episcopal *Munera* and the Character of Episcopal Orders." *The Thomist* 66 (2002): 369–94.

Marie-Eugene, O.C.D. *I Want to See God: A Practical Synthesis of Carmelite Spirituality*. Translated by Sister M. Verda Clare, CSC. Westminster, MD: Christian Classics, Inc. 1978.

Maritain, Jacques. *The Range of Reason*. New York: Charles Scribner's Sons, 1952.

Martens, Kurt, ed. *Justice and Mercy Have Met*. Washington, DC: The Catholic University of America Press, 2017.

Martino, Joseph P. *A Fighting Chance: The Moral Use of Nuclear Weapons*. San Francisco: Ignatius Press, 1988.

Masching, Frances Marie, OSF. "Response to 'The Principles of Cooperation and their Application to the Present State of Health Care Evaluation'." In *The Splendor of Truth and Health Care*, edited by Russell E. Smith, 232–37. Braintree, MA: The Pope John Center, 1995.

Mattson, Daniel C. *Why I Don't Call Myself Gay: How I Reclaimed My Sexual Reality and Found Peace*. San Francisco: Ignatius Press, 2017.

May, William E. *Catholic Bioethics and the Gift of Human Life*. 3rd ed. Huntington, IN: Our Sunday Visitor, 2013.

———. *Theology of the Body in Context: Genesis and Growth*. Boston: Pauline Books & Media, 2010.

———. *An Introduction to Moral Theology*. Huntington, IN: Our Sunday Visitor Publishing Division, 1994.

———. "The Management of Ectopic Pregnancies: A Moral Analysis." In *The Fetal Tissue Issue: Medical and Ethical Aspects*, edited by Peter J. Cataldo and Albert S. Moraczewski, OP, 121–47. Braintree, MA: The Pope John Center, 1994.

———. *Moral Absolutes: Catholic Tradition, Current Trends, and the Truth*. Milwaukee: Marquette University Press, 1989.

May, William E., and E. Christian Brugger. "John Paul II's Moral Theology on Trial: A Reply to Charles E. Curran." *The Thomist* 69 (2005): 279–312.

McAreavey, John. *The Canon Law of Marriage and the Family*. Dublin: Four Courts Press, 1997.

McCall, Brian M. *The Church and the Usurers: Unprofitable Lending for the Modern Economy*. Washington, DC: The Catholic University of America Press, 2013.

McCool, Gerald A. *Nineteenth Century Scholasticism: The Search for a Unitary Method*. New York: Fordham University Press, 1999.

———. *The Neo-Thomists*. Milwaukee: Marquette University Press, 1994.

McCormick, Richard A., SJ. "Moral Theology 1940–1989: An Overview." *Theological Studies* 50 (1989): 3–24.

———. *Notes on Moral Theology: 1965 through 1980*. Lanham, MD: University Press of America, 1981.

McCoy, John A. *A Still Quiet Conscience: The Archbishop Who Challenged a Pope, a President, and a Church*. Maryknoll, NY: Orbis Books, 2015.

McGuire, Ashley. *Sex Scandal: The Drive to Abolish Male and Female*. Washington, DC: Regnery Publishing, 2017.

McHugh, John A., OP. *The Mother of Jesus in the New Testament*. London: Darton, Longman & Todd, 1975.

McHugh, John A., OP, and Charles J. Callan, OP. *Moral Theology: A Complete Course*. New York: Joseph F. Wagner, Inc., 1929.

McInerny, Ralph. *Praeambula Fidei: Thomism and the God of the Philosophers*. Washington, DC: The Catholic University of America Press, 2006.

———. *Ethica Thomistica: The Moral Philosophy of Thomas Aquinas*, Revised Edition. Washington, DC: The Catholic University of America Press, 1997.

—. *Aquinas and Analogy*. Washington, DC: The Catholic University of America Press, 1996.

—. *Aquinas on Human Action. A Theory of Practice*. Washington, DC: The Catholic University of America Press, 1992.

McKeever, Paul E. "Seventy-Five Years of Moral Theology in America." In *The Historical Development of Fundamental Moral Theology in the United States*, edited by Charles E. Curran and Richard A. McCormick, SJ, 5–21. Mahwah, NJ: Paulist Press, 1999.

Melina, Livio. *Sharing in Christ's Virtues: For the Renewal of Moral Theology in Light of Veritatis Splendor*. Translated by William E. May. Washington, DC: The Catholic University of America Press, 2001.

Mellema, Gregory. *Complicity and Moral Accountability*. Notre Dame, IN: University of Notre Dame Press, 2016.

Merkelbach, Benoît-Henri, OP. *Summa Theologiae Moralis*. Bruges: Desclée de Brouwer, 1956.

—. *Mariologia*. Paris: Desclée de Brouwer, 1939.

—. "Quelle place assigner au traité de la conscience?" *Revue des Sciences Philosophiques et Théologiques* 12 (1923): 170–83.

Miller, Richard B. *Casuistry and Modern Ethics: A Poetics of Practical Reasoning*. Chicago: The University of Chicago Press, 1996.

Miner, Robert. *Thomas Aquinas on the Passions: A Study of Summa Theologiae, 1a2ae 22–48*. Cambridge: Cambridge University Press, 2009.

Moreno, Antonio, OP. "The Nature of St. Thomas' Knowledge 'Per Connaturalitatem'." *Angelicum* 47 (1970): 44–62.

Morlino, Robert C. *The Principle of the Lesser of Evils in Today's Conflict Situations: New Challenges to Moral Theology from a Pluralistic Society*. Rome: Pontifical Gregorian University, 1990.

Morse, Jennifer Roback. "Why Unilateral Divorce Has No Place in a Free Society." In *The Meaning of Marriage Family, State, Market, and Morals*, edited by Robert P. George and Jean Bethke Elshtain, 74–99. Dallas: Spence Publishing Company, 2006.

Mullady, Brian, OP. "The Virtue of Prudence and the Primacy of Conscience." *Angelicum* 92 (2015): 425–45.

Müller, Sigrid. "The Ethics of John Capreolus and the 'Nominales'." *Verbum: Analecta Neolatina* 6 (2004): 301–14.

Myers, John J. "A Voter's Guide: Pro-choice candidates and church teaching." *Wall Street Journal*. September 17, 2004.

Napier, Stephen. "The Missing Premise in the HIV-Condom Debate." *The Linacre Quarterly* 78 (2011): 401–14.

Nault, Dom Jean-Charles. *The Noonday Devil: Acedia, the Unnamed Evil of Our Times*. San Francisco: Ignatius Press, 2015.

Navarrete, Urbano Cardinal, SJ. "Transsexualism and the Canonical Order." *The National Catholic Bioethics Quarterly* 14 (2014): 105–18.

NCBC Ethicists. "Cooperating with Non-Catholic Partners." In *Catholic Health Care Ethics: A Manual for Practitioners*, 2nd ed., edited by Edward J. Furton with Peter J. Cataldo and Albert S. Moraczewski, OP, 265–70. Philadelphia: The National Catholic Bioethics Center, 2009.

Noldin, H., SJ, and A. Schmitt, SJ. *Summa Theologiae Moralis*, 3 vols., 31st ed., edited by G. Heinzel, SJ. Innsbruck: Feliciani Rauch, 1957.

Nugent, Robert., ed. *A Challenge to Love: Gay and Lesbian Catholics in the Church*. New York: The Crossroad Publishing Company, 1983.

O'Connor, Edwin D., C.S.C. *The Gifts of the Holy Spirit*. Volume 24 of the Blackfriars *Summa*. New York: McGraw-Hill Book Company, 1974.

Odozor, Paulinus Ikechukwu. *Moral Theology in an Age of Renewal: A Study of the Catholic Tradition Since Vatican II*. Notre Dame, IN: University of Notre Dame Press, 2003.

O'Malley, John F. "Sale of Contraceptives." *The Homiletic and Pastoral Review* 40 (1939): 282–90.

O'Meara, Thomas, OP. "Interpreting Thomas Aquinas: Aspects of the Dominican School of Moral Theology in the Twentieth Century." In *The Ethics of Aquinas*, edited by Stephen J. Pope, 355–73. Washington, DC: Georgetown University Press, 2002.

O'Rourke, Kevin D., OP. "The Catholic Tradition on Forgoing Life Support." *The National Catholic Bioethics Quarterly* 5 (2005): 537–53.

Osborne, Thomas M., Jr. *Human Action in Thomas Aquinas, John Duns Scotus, and William of Ockham*. Washington, DC: The Catholic University of America Press, 2014.

Parkinson, Joseph. *Material Cooperation and Catholic Institutions*. Doctoral dissertation, College of Theology, University of Notre Dame Australia, 2001.

Pastor, Ludwig, Freiherr Von. *The History of the Popes: From the Close of the Middle Ages*. Translated by Ernest Graf, OSB, vol. 32. St. Louis: B. Herder Book, Co., 1957.

Pègues, Thomas-M. OP. "Du Rôle de Capréolus dans la Défense de Saint Thomas." *Revue thomiste* 7 (1899): 507–29.

———. "La Biographie de Jean Capréolus." *Revue thomiste* 7 (1899): 317–34.

Peschke, Karl H. *Christian Ethics: Moral Theology in Light of Vatican II*. Alcester: C. Goodliffe Neale Ltd., 1975.

Petri, Thomas, OP. *Aquinas and the Theology of the Body: The Thomistic Foundations of John Paul II's Anthropology*. Washington, DC: The Catholic University of America Press, 2016.

Petri, Thomas, OP, and Michael A. Wahl. "Live Action and Planned Parenthood: A New Test Case for Lying." *Nova et Vetera*, English edition, 10 (2012): 437–62.

Pieper, Josef. *The Four Cardinal Virtues*. New York: Harcourt, Brace & World, Inc. 1965.

Pinckaers, Servais, OP. *The Spirituality of Martyrdom: to the Limits of Love*. Translated by Patrick M. Clark and Annie Hounsokou. Washington, DC: The Catholic University of America Press, 2016.

———. *Passions & Virtue*. Translated by Benedict M. Guevin, OSB. Washington, DC: The Catholic University of America Press, 2015.

———. *The Pinckaers Reader: Renewing Thomistic Moral Theology*. Edited by John Berkman and Craig Steven Titus. Translated by Sr. Mary Thomas Noble, OP, Craig

Steven Titus, Michael Sherwin, OP, and Hugh Connolly. Washington, DC: The Catholic University of America Press, 2005.

——. *Morality: The Catholic View*. Translated by Michael Sherwin, OP. South Bend, IN: St. Augustine's Press, 2001.

——. *Les Actes Humains*. Ia-Iiae, Questions 6–17, *Somme Théologique*, Notes et Appendices. Paris : Les Éditions du Cerf, 1997.

——. *The Sources of Christian Ethics*. Translated by Sr. Mary Thomas Noble, OP. Washington, DC: The Catholic University of America Press, 1995.

——. "The Use of Scripture and the Renewal of Moral Theology: The *Catechism* and *Veritatis Splendor*." *The Thomist* 59 (1995): 1–19.

——. *Les Actes Humains*. Ia-Iiae, Questions 18–21, *Somme Théologique*, Notes et Appendices. Paris: Descleée & Cie, 1966.

——. *Le renouveau de la morale*. Tournai: Casterman, 1964.

——. "Virtue Is Not a Habit." Translated by Bernard Gilligan. *Cross Currents* (1962): 65–81.

Pink, Thomas. "The Interpretation of *Dignitatis Humanae*: A Reply to Martin Rhonheimer." *Nova et Vetera*, English edition, 11 (2013): 77–121.

Ponnuru, Ramesh. *The Party of Death: The Democrats, the Media, the Courts, and the Disregard for Human Life*. Washington, DC: Regnery Publishing Inc., 2006.

Pope, Stephen J. "The Magisterium's Arguments against 'Same-Sex Marriage': An Ethical Analysis and Critique." *Theological Studies* 65 (2004): 530–65.

Porter, Jean. *Justice as a Virtue: A Thomistic Perspective*. Grand Rapids, MI: Eerdmans, 2016.

——. "Right Reason and the Love of God: The Parameters of Aquinas' Moral Theology." In *The Theology of Thomas Aquinas*, edited by Rik Van Nieuwenhove and Joseph Wawrykow, 167–91. Notre Dame, IN: University of Notre Dame Press, 2005.

——. *The Recovery of Virtue: The Relevance of Aquinas for Christian Ethics*. Louisville, KY: Westminster/John Knox Press, 1990.

Prümmer, Dominicus M., OP. *Handbook of Moral Theology*. Translated by Gerald W. Shelton. Cork: The Mercier Press, 1956.

——. *Manuale Theologiae Moralis: Secundum Principia S. Thomae Aquinatis*. Fribourg: Herder & Co., 1923.

Pruss, Alexander R. "Cooperation with past evil and use of cell-lines derived from aborted fetuses." In *Cooperation, Complicity & Conscience: Problems in healthcare, science, law and public policy*, edited by Helen Watt, 89–104. London: The Linacre Centre, 2005.

Quinn, Bernetta M. *Give Me Souls: A Life of Raphael Cardinal Merry del Val*. Westminster, MD: Newman Press, 1958.

Ramirez, Santiago, OP. "The Authority of St. Thomas Aquinas." *The Thomist* 15 (1952): 1–109.

Ramsey, Paul. *War and the Christian Conscience: How Shall Modern War Be Conducted Justly?* Durham, NC: Seeman Printery, 1961.

Reichberg, Gregory M. "Discontinuity in Catholic Just War Teaching? From Aquinas to the Contemporary Popes." *Nova et Vetera*, English edition, 10 (2012): 1073–97.

———. "Aquinas on Battlefield Courage." *The Thomist* 74 (2010): 337–68.

———. "The Intellectual Virtues (Ia IIae, qq. 57–58)." In *The Ethics of Aquinas*, edited by Stephen J. Pope, 131–50. Washington, DC: Georgetown University Press, 2002.

Reynolds, Norbert, OP. "Very Reverend John A. McHugh, OP, Very Reverend Charles J. Callan, OP, Masters of Sacred Theology." *Dominicana* 16, no. 2 (1931): 148–49.

Rhonheimer, Martin. "*Dignitatis Humanae*—Not a Mere Question of Church Policy: A Response to Thomas Pink." *Nova et Vetera*, English edition, 12 (2014): 445–70.

———. "Benedict XVI's 'Hermeneutic of Reform' and Religious Freedom." *Nova et Vetera*, English edition, 9 (2011): 1029–54.

———. *Ethics of Procreation and the Defense of Human Life: Contraception, Artificial Fertilization, and Abortion.* Edited by William F. Murphy, Jr. Washington, DC: The Catholic University of America, 2010.

———. *Vital Conflicts in Medical Ethics: A Virtue Approach to Craniotomy and Tubal Pregnancies.* Edited by William F. Murphy, Jr. Washington, DC: The Catholic University of America Press, 2009.

———. *The Perspective of the Acting Person: Essays in the Renewal of Thomistic Moral Philosophy.* Washington, DC: The Catholic University of America Press, 2008.

———. "The Truth about Condoms." *The Tablet.* July 10, 2004.

———. *Natural Law and Practical Reason. A Thomist View of Moral Autonomy.* Translated by Gerald Malsbary. New York: Fordham University Press, 2000.

———. "Intentional Actions and the Meaning of Object: A reply to Richard McCormick." *The Thomist* 59 (1995): 279–311.

Rice, Patricia. "Burke Would Refuse Communion to Kerry." *St. Louis Post-Dispatch*, January 30, 2004.

Riley, Lawrence Joseph. *The History, Nature and Use of Epikeia in Moral Theology.* Washington, DC: The Catholic University of America Press, 1948.

Robinson, John Martin. *Cardinal Consalvi: 1757–1824.* New York: St. Martin's Press, 1987.

Rodgers, Ann, and Mike Aquilina. *Something More Pastoral: The Mission of Bishop, Archbishop and Cardinal Donald Wuerl.* Pittsburgh: The Lambert Press, 2015.

Roy, Roger, CSsR. "La coopération selon Saint Alphonse de Liguori." *Studia Moralia* 6 (1968): 377–435.

Rubio, Julie Hanlon. "Cooperation with Evil Reconsidered: The Moral Duty of Resistance." *Theological Studies* 78 (2017): 96–120.

Rziha, John. *Perfecting Human Actions: St. Thomas Aquinas on Human Participation in Eternal Law.* Washington, DC: The Catholic University of America Press, 2009.

Sabetti, Aloysius, SJ. "Father Aloysius Sabetti: A Fellow Professor's Reminiscences." *Woodstock Letters* 29 (1900): 208–33.

Sanchez, Thomas, SJ. *Opus Morale in Praecepta Decalogi.* Paris: Michaelem Sonnium, 1615.

Schall, James V. *The Life of the Mind: On the Joys and Travails of Thinking.* Wilmington, DE: Intercollegiate Studies Institute, 2008.

Schantz, Harvey L. *Politics in the Era of Divided Government: The Election of 1996 and its Aftermath.* New York: Routledge, 2001.

Schumacher, Michele M. "Gender Ideology and the 'Artistic' Fabrication of Human Sex: Nature as Norm or the Remaking of the Human?" *The Thomist* 80 (2016): 363–423.

Seifert, Josef. "The Problem of the Moral Significance of Human Fertility and Birth Control Methods: Philosophical Arguments against Contraception." In *"Humanee Vitae": 20 Anni Dopo. Atti del II Congresso Internationale di Teologia Morale,* 661–72. Milan: Edizioni Ares, 1989.

Senior, John. *The Death of Christian Culture.* Norfolk, VA: IHS Press, 2008.

———. *The Restoration of Christian Culture.* Norfolk, VA: IHS Press, 2008.

Sertillanges, A. G., OP. *The Intellectual Life: Its Spirit, Conditions, Methods.* Translated by Mary Ryan. Washington, DC: The Catholic University of America Press, 1998.

Sgreccia, Elio. *Personalist Bioethics: Foundations and Applications.* Translated by John A. Di Camillo and Michael J. Miller. Philadelphia: The National Catholic Bioethics Center, 2012.

Shaw, Russell. "Contraception, Infallibility and the Ordinary Magisterium." In *Why Humane Vitae Was Right: A Reader,* edited by Janet E. Smith, 343–61. San Francisco: Ignatius Press, 1993.

Shea, C. Michael. "*Ressourcement* in the Age of Migne: The Jesuit Theologians of the *Collegio Romano* and the Shape of Modern Catholic Thought." *Nova et Vetera,* English edition, 15 (2017): 579–613.

Sherwin, Michael S., OP. "The Return to Virtue: Challenges and Opportunities." In *Dominicans and the Challenge of Thomism,* edited by Michał Paluch and Piotr Lichacz, 183–202. Warsaw : Instytut Tomistyczny, 2012.

———. *By Knowledge and by Love: Charity and Knowledge in the Moral Theology of St. Thomas Aquinas.* Washington, DC: The Catholic University of America Press, 2011.

———. "Eulogie pour le P. Servais Pinckaers, OP." *Nova et Vetera,* English edition, 84 (2009): 133–36.

———. "Infused Virtue and the Effects of Acquired Vice: A Test Case for the Thomistic Theory of Infused Cardinal Virtues." *The Thomist* 73 (2009): 29–52.

Sherwin, Michael S., OP, and Craig Steven Titus, eds. *Renouveler toutes choses en Christ : Vers un renouveau thomiste de la théologie morale : Hommage à Servis Pinckaers, OP.* Fribourg: Academic Press Fribourg, 2009.

Sirilla, Michael G. *The Ideal Bishop: Aquinas' Commentaries on the Pastoral Epistles.* Washington, DC: The Catholic University of America Press, 2017.

Slater, Thomas, SJ. *A Manual of Moral Theology for English Speaking Countries.* New York, Benziger Brothers, 1925.

———. *A Short History of Moral Theology.* New York, Benziger Brothers, 1909.

Smith, Janet E. "Fig Leaves and Falsehoods." *First Things* June/July 2011: 45–49.

———, ed. *Why Humanae Vitae Was Right: A Reader.* San Francisco: Ignatius Press, 1993.

————. *Humanae Vitae: A Generation Later.* Washington, DC: The Catholic University of America Press, 1991.

Smith, Russell E. "Ethical Quandary: Forming Hospital Partnerships." In *The Gospel of Life and the Vision of Health Care*, edited by Russell E. Smith, 109–23. Braintree, MA: The Pope John Center, 1996.

————. "The Principles of Cooperation and their Application to the Present State of Health Care Evolution." In *The Splendor of Truth and Health Care*, edited by Russell E. Smith, 217–31. Braintree, MA: The Pope John Center, 1995.

————. "The Principles of Cooperation in Catholic Thought." In *The Fetal Tissue Issue: Medical and Ethical Aspects*, edited by Peter J. Cataldo and Albert S. Moraczewski, OP, 81–92. Braintree, MA: The Pope John Center, 1994.

————. *Catholic Conscience: Foundation and Formation: Proceedings of The Tenth Bishops' Workshop, Dallas, Texas.* Braintree, MA: The Pope John Center, 1991.

————. *The Theology of Sin and Its Distinctions in the United States from 1960–1985.* Rome: Pontifical Lateran University Academy Alphonsiana, 1987.

Smith, Wesley J. *Culture of Death: The Assault on Medical Ethics in America.* San Francisco: Encounter Books, 2000.

Smith, William B. *Modern Moral Problems: Trustworthy Answers to Your Tough Questions.* Edited by Donald Haggerty. San Francisco: Ignatius Press, 2012.

————. "Questions Answered: Management of Ectopic Pregnancy." *Homiletic and Pastoral Review* 99, no. 10 (July 1999): 66–68.

Snell, R. J. *Acedia and Its Discontents: Metaphysical Boredom in an Empire of Desire.* Kettering, OH: Angelico Press, 2015.

Spaemann, Robert. "Ist die Ausstellung des Beratungsscheins eine »Formelle Mitwirkung« bei der Abtreibung?" In *Grenzen: Zur Ethischen Dimension des Handelns*, 401–406. Stuggart: Klett-Cotta, 2001.

Spencer, Mark K. "The Category of *habitus*: Accidents, Artifacts, and Human Nature." *The Thomist* 79 (2015): 113–54.

Spicq, Ceslaus. *Théologie morale du Nouveau Testament.* Paris: Librairie Lecoffre, 1965.

Sullivan, Denis F. "The Doctrine of Double Effect and the Domains of Moral Responsibility." *The Thomist* 64 (2000): 423–48.

Sulmasy, Daniel P., OFM. "Catholic Participation in Needle- and Syringe- Exchange Programs for Injection-Drug Users: An Ethical Analysis." *Theological Studies* 73 (2012): 422–41.

Taylor, Charles. *A Secular Age.* London: The Belknap Press of Harvard University Press, 2007.

Tettamanzi, Dionigi. *Nuova Bioetica Cristiana.* Segrete, Italy: Piemme, 2000.

Thomas Aquinas, Saint. *De Malo.* Translated by Jean Oesterle. Notre Dame, IN: University of Notre Dame Press, 1995.

Titus, Craig Steven. "Servais Pinckaers and the Renewal of Catholic Moral Theology." *Journal of Moral Theology* 1 (2012): 43–68.

————. *Resilience and the Virtue of Fortitude: Aquinas in Dialogue with the Psychological Sciences.* Washington, DC: The Catholic University of America Press, 2006.

————. *The Development of Virtue and "Connaturality" in Thomas Aquinas' Works*. STL thesis, University of Fribourg, 1990.

Tollefsen, Christopher. "Response to Robert Koons and Matthew O'Brien's 'Objects of Intention: a Hylomorphic Critique of the New Natural Law Theory.'" *American Catholic Philosophical Quarterly* 87 (2013): 751–78.

Tonti-Filippini, Nicholas. "Sex Reassignment and Catholic Schools." *The National Catholic Bioethics Quarterly* 12 (2012): 85–97.

Tremblay, Réal. *Cristo e la morale in alcuni documenti del Magistero*. Rome: Edizioni Dehoniane, 1996.

Ugorji, Lucius I. *The Principle of Double Effect: A Critical Appraisal of its Traditional Understanding and its Modern Reinterpretation*. Frankfurt: Peter Lang, 1993.

Uhlmann, Michael M., ed. *Last Rights? Assisted Suicide and Euthanasia Debated*. Grand Rapids, MI: Eerdmans, 1998.

Van Steenberghen, Fernand. "In Memoriam. Don Odon Lottin, OSB." *Revue Philosophique de Louvain* 63 (1965): 181–214.

Vereecke, Louis, CSsR. *Da Guglielmo d'Ockham a sant'Alfonso de Liguori: Saggi di storia della teologia morale moderna 1300–1787*. Milan: Edizioni Paoline, 1990.

————. "La Conscience selon Saint Alphonse de Liguori." *Studia Moralia* 21 (1983): 259–73.

————. "Moral Theology, History of (700 to Vatican Council I)." In *New Catholic Encyclopedia*, 9, 1119–22. New York: McGraw-Hill, 1967.

Vileo, Stephen L. *A Theological Analysis of Scandal in the Summa Theologiae of St. Thomas Aquinas*. Rome: Pontifical Lateran University Academia Alphonsiana, 1993.

Watt, Helen. "Complicity and How to Avoid It: Review: *The Servant and the Ladder*: Cooperation with Evil in the Twenty-First Century." *Faith* 49 (2016): 37–40.

————. "Cooperation and Immoral Laws: Preventing without Prescribing Harm." *The National Catholic Bioethics Quarterly* 12 (2012): 241–48.

————, ed. *Cooperation, Complicity & Conscience: Problems in healthcare, science, law and public policy*. London: The Linacre Centre, 2005.

Weigel, George. *Witness to Hope: The Biography of Pope John Paul II*. New York: Harper Collins, 2004.

————. *Tranquillitas Ordinis: The Present Failure and Future Promise of American Catholic Thought on War and Peace*. New York: Oxford University Press, 1987.

Welch, Lawrence J. "Direct Sterilization: An Intrinsically Evil Act—A Rejoinder to Fr. Keenan." *Linacre Quarterly* 68 (2001): 124–30.

————. "An Excessive Claim: Sterilization and Immediate Material Cooperation." *Linacre Quarterly* 66 (1999): 4–25.

Westberg, Daniel. "Good and Evil in Human Acts (Ia IIae, qq. 18–21)." In *The Ethics of Aquinas*, ed. Stephen J. Pope, 90–102. Washington, DC: Georgetown University Press, 2002.

————. "Did Aquinas Change His Mind about the Will?" *The Thomist* 58 (1994): 41–60.

White, Thomas Joseph, OP, ed. *The Analogy of Being: Invention of the Antichrist or Wisdom of God?* Grand Rapids, MI: Eerdmans, 2010.

Wicks, Jared, SJ, ed. *Cajetan Responds: A Reader in Reformation Controversy.* Translated by Jared Wicks, SJ. Washington, DC: The Catholic University of America Press, 1978.

Wildes, Kevin Wm., SJ, and Alan C. Mitchell., eds. *Choosing Life: A Dialogue on Evangelium Vitae.* Washington, DC: Georgetown University Press, 1997.

Williams, Watkin W. *The Moral Theology of the Sacrament of Penance.* Milwaukee: The Morehouse Publishing Co., 1919.

Woestman, William H., OMI. *Ecclesiastical Sanctions and the Penal Process: A Commentary on the Code of Canon Law.* Ottawa: St. Paul University, 2003.

Wojtyla, Karol. *Love and Responsibility.* San Francisco: Ignatius Press, 1993.

Woodward, P. A., ed. *The Doctrine of Double Effect: Philosophers Debate a Controversial Moral Principle.* Notre Dame: The University of Notre Dame Press, 2001.

Zimmerman, Anthony. "Duress and Contraceptive Sterilization: A Reply to Prof. Thomas Kopfensteiner." *Linacre Quarterly* 70 (2003): 210–17.

———. "Contraceptive Sterilization in Catholic Hospitals is Intrinsically Evil." *Linacre Quarterly* 68 (2001): 262–73.

Index

abortion, 95–96, 99; abortion counseling in Germany, 159–60; abortion-inducing drugs, 196; casuist authors on, 198–202; as a canonical crime, 131; in *Evangelium vitae*, 129–30; federal funding of, 238–39; fetal cells and vaccines, 69n63; instruments, manufacture of, 26; instruments used in, 65, 76, 102, 181–82, 199, 201; instruments used solely for, 188; as issue in political elections, 229; legal exceptions, 161–62

acedia, 222

Adelman, Urban, 80. *See also* Jone-Adelman *Moral Theology* manual

Aertnys, Joseph, 104

After Virtue: A Study in Moral Theory (MacIntyre), 117

alcohol, sale of, 70, 72, 83

Alexander VII, Pope, 40, 47

Alphonsus Liguori, St. (*See* Liguori, Alphonsus, St.)

Analogia Entis (Long), 142

Anscombe, Elizabeth, 117

Antoninus of Florence, St., 239

Aquinas, Thomas, *See* Thomas Aquinas, St.

Aristotle, 117, 162

Ashley, Benedict M., 74, 85, 95n187, 237–38

attendance at invalid weddings, 247

Aureolus, Peter, 28–29

Ballerini, Antonio, 56, 57

Barrett, Timothy, 57

beatitude, 73, 118–19, 123, 126

Benedict XVI, Pope, 157–58, 244. *See also* Ratzinger, Joseph Cardinal

Bouscaren, Timothy, 104

Busenbaum, Hermann, 47, 56, 71

Cajetan, Thomas de Vio Cardinal, 11, 33–38, 270–71

Callan, Charles J., 85, 107. *See also* McHugh-Callan *Moral Theology*

Called to Compassion and Responsibility, 155

Capreolus, Jean, 27–33, 270

casuistry: and abortion, 182; Bernhard Häring, 100; commandments vs. virtues, 218; conflicting opinions/unresolved questions, 101–10; and contraceptive mandates, 204n86; on cooperation with abortion, 198–202; and Dominican authors, 3n5; and enemies of the voluntary, 193; formal vs. material categories, 9–10, 170–71; fortitude, virtue of, not treated, 108; Lottin's critique of, 116; origins of, 41–42; nineteenth- and twentieth-century overview, 53–55; Pinkaers's critique of, 114–23; and private property, 163; and probabilism, 164; and proportionate reasoning, 85; and proximity, 180–82; on prudence, 31; restitution, emphasis on, 51; on scandal, 17–19; on tax-paying, 240; Thomas Slater, 59–68; use of implicitly formal cooperation, 171; use of ready-made categories, 14, 175; and the virtues, 240

Cataldo, Peter, 88n156, 196n61, 204n86

Catechism of the Catholic Church: on canonical penalties, 131; on cooperation with abortion, 131; on death penalty, 228n7; on euthanasia, 135; Fisher on, 166; on homosexuality, 250; on justice, 19–20;